THE LAW OF REGULATORY ENFO[R]
AND SANCTIONS

A Practical Guide

THE LAW OF REGULATORY ENFORCEMENT AND SANCTIONS

A Practical Guide

JULIE NORRIS
Barrister and Senior Associate, Kingsley Napley LLP

JEREMY PHILLIPS
Barrister, Francis Taylor Building, Inner Temple

OXFORD
UNIVERSITY PRESS

OXFORD

UNIVERSITY PRESS

Great Clarendon Street, Oxford OX2 6DP

Oxford University Press is a department of the University of Oxford.
It furthers the University's objective of excellence in research, scholarship,
and education by publishing worldwide in

Oxford New York

Auckland Cape Town Dar es Salaam Hong Kong Karachi
Kuala Lumpur Madrid Melbourne Mexico City Nairobi
New Delhi Shanghai Taipei Toronto

With offices in

Argentina Austria Brazil Chile Czech Republic France Greece
Guatemala Hungary Italy Japan Poland Portugal Singapore
South Korea Switzerland Thailand Turkey Ukraine Vietnam

Oxford is a registered trade mark of Oxford University Press
in the UK and in certain other countries

Published in the United States
by Oxford University Press Inc., New York

British Library Cataloguing-in-Publication Data
Data available

Library of Congress Cataloging in Publication Data
Data available

Typeset by Glyph International, Bangalore, India
Printed in Great Britain
on acid-free paper by
Ashford Colour Press Ltd, Gosport, Hampshire

ISBN 978-0-19-959320-0

1 3 5 7 9 10 8 6 4 2

CONTRIBUTORS

The following have contributed to the writing of this work:

KINGSLEY NAPLEY LLP

BEN KEMP
Senior Associate

MELINKA BERRIDGE
Senior Associate

CLAIRE HEGARTY
Solicitor

MARY PAGE
Solicitor

FRANCIS TAYLOR BUILDING

REBECCA CLUTTEN
Barrister, of Inner Temple

ANNABEL GRAHAM PAUL
Barrister, of Middle Temple

RICHARD HONEY
Barrister, of Inner Temple

JUAN LOPEZ
Barrister, of Lincolns Inn

CAIN ORMONDROYD
Barrister, of Lincolns Inn

SARAH SACKMAN
Barrister, of Inner Temple

NED WESTAWAY
Barrister, of Lincolns Inn

MARK WESTMORELAND SMITH
Barrister, of Lincolns Inn

11 KBW

TOM CROSS
Barrister, of Lincolns Inn

6 PUMP COURT

JAMES NEILL
Barrister, of Inner Temple

FOREWORD

Enforcement and sanctions are an important part of any regulatory system. They provide a deterrent and can act as a catalyst to ensure that regulations are effective in practice. However, to help encourage compliance in a fair and positive way, enforcement and sanctioning decisions need to follow a consistent and flexible approach across the country. The Better Regulation Executive leads for the government on reforming the regulatory enforcement and sanctions regime in the UK. This reform drive led to the introduction in 2008 of a new legislative and institutional framework, embodied in primary legislation and statutory guidelines and schemes, for improving the flexibility, consistency and appropriateness of regulatory enforcement and sanctions.

This book provides an authoritative compendium of current law and practice in this important regulatory area. Drawing on diverse sources, the book reviews the policy and legislative developments that have shaped the UK regulatory enforcement landscape in recent years, and presents a comprehensive analysis of the most significant piece of primary legislation in this area to date—the Regulatory Enforcement and Sanctions Act 2008—which is aimed at embedding a consistent and flexible approach to regulatory enforcement and sanctions among regulators. The authors' explanation of the different elements of the legislation will be valuable to readers whatever their levels of familiarity with, and understanding of, the issues.

The civil sanctions regime created by the Act, designed to introduce flexibility and proportionality into the way regulators deal with instances of regulatory non-compliance, forms the heart of the book. The authors comprehensively review the processes for obtaining and using the civil sanctioning powers, and give useful insights into the procedural and operational safeguards aimed at achieving consistency in the use of the sanctions, and preventing misuse by regulators. This will be as valuable for regulators using or seeking to use the sanctions, as for lawyers and businesses interested in the way the sanctions are used.

The reform of the UK regulatory landscape is an ongoing process. The focus of this reform will increasingly be on encouraging regulators to intervene only when it is really necessary and to consider all the alternatives to regulation and the way it is enforced. Enforcement and sanctions still have their place in the regulatory system, but they will need to be deployed consistently, flexibly and appropriately. This book sets out clearly and comprehensively the legislative and institutional framework that underpins this new approach.

I'm sure that regulators and regulated alike will find this book a valuable resource.

Philip Rycroft
Chief Executive, Better Regulation Executive

PREFACE

'The Regulatory Enforcement and Sanctions Act 2008'—not perhaps, a title to 'stiffen the sinews' or 'summon up the blood' and yet, as we know, many of the great statutes started life inauspiciously named: the Offences against the Person Act 1861, the Health and Safety at Work etc. Act 1974, or even (of lesser note certainly, but some significance nonetheless) the Local Government (Miscellaneous Provisions) Act 1982. The key, however, lay in the long title: '*An Act to make provision for the establishment of the Local Better Regulation Office; for the co-ordination of regulatory enforcement by local authorities; for the creation of civil sanctions in relation to regulatory offences; for the reduction and removal of regulatory burdens; and for connected purposes*'. Here then was legislation with a bold ambition, which sought to have an impact over time upon vast swathes of regulation in the British Isles. Certainly the new arrival can boast a lengthy period of gestation (over two decades) and an impressive pedigree: Hampton, Macrory, Rogers and Anderson. Each played an important part in the statute we see today. Whether the considerable amount of analysis and scholarship invested will ensure the Act's long-term survival will depend more, we feel, upon the ebbs and flows of political philosophy and fashion, than the qualities of the legislation itself, which are impressive.

Embarking upon the project we soon found, as those in DEFRA tasked with delivery of the Part 3 sanctions to their client agencies must similarly have experienced, that our enthusiasm was on occasion tempered by the sheer graft required to convert an exciting idea into a practical framework: the Hampton Implementation Reviews, the secondary legislation, the codes and guidance; each had to be considered before the process of awarding the new civil sanctions to the environmental regulators could properly begin. At the same time we were acutely conscious that others in distant offices were pursuing a parallel course in order to be able to deliver the first practical implementation of the Act—and all against a backdrop of seismic political and economic upheavals. The fact that the writing of this book straddled two (rather different) government administrations has not made our task any easier; yet whilst the new coalition government has yet to signal its endorsement of RESA (and is already reviewing the role of the Local Better Regulation Office), the Law Commission has taken up the mantle of Labour's 'Better Regulation Agenda', championing the use of civil sanctions for criminal offences in the regulatory context.[1]

In this book we have endeavoured to provide practitioners, enforcement officers and those working in the affected industries with a guide that both acknowledges the political and judicial heritage of RESA (as the Act came affectionately to be known within the editorial team), whilst at the same time offering a practical guide to its implementation.

We await with keen interest the practical implementation of the provisions of the Act to come and the outcome of the various cases that can clearly be anticipated in the swells far out to sea.

---

[1] See the Law Commission's Consultation Paper no. 195: *Criminal liability in regulatory contexts*. Published August 2010.

The book is divided into four parts: Chapter 1 is a necessarily brief historical analysis of the key steps along the long (and not infrequently winding) political road to RESA; Chapter 2 deals with the establishment of the important Local Better Regulation Office and its likely impact on the coordination of local authority enforcement; Chapter 3 addresses the creation of the primary authority scheme (taking over where the 'home' and 'lead' authorities leave off); whilst Chapters 4–8 cover in some detail the core aspects of the new civil sanctions regime, launched for the very first time in respect of the environmental regulators, more or less as we went to press.

Inevitably space has not permitted the inclusion of all of the materials that we would have liked. However, we have come to recognize that this may actually be for the best as there are a significant number of resources touched upon in our text. Had they been included, readers would have found themselves burdened with a far larger (and certainly more expensive) legal tome. As it is, using the links given, all can be accessed quickly and without additional cost on the web.

As we have described, we began (and indeed concluded) our writing with great enthusiasm. We now await the practical delivery of the new regime in a similar vein. We sincerely hope that we have communicated some of this spirit in our book and that it proves to be of value in helping others address this exciting new regime.

Julie Norris	Jeremy Phillips
Kingsley Napley	Francis Taylor Building
Knights Quarter	Inner Temple
London EC1M 4AJ	London EC4Y 7BY
	November 2010

ACKNOWLEDGMENTS

The authors were assisted by a number of experienced lawyers, all of whom made valuable contributions to the text; at Kingsley Napley LLP: Ben Kemp, Melinka Berridge, Claire Hegarty and Mary Page; from chambers at Francis Taylor Building: Annabel Graham Paul, Cain Ormondroyd, Richard Honey, Sarah Sackman, Mark Westmoreland Smith, Juan Lopez, Rebecca Clutten and Ned Westaway as well as Tom Cross (11 KBW) and James Neill (6 Pump Court). Elsewhere, many others assisted us with specialist aspects of the text, including David Stott and Anne Brosnan (Environment Agency), Dave Humphries (SIA), Darryl Dixon (Gangmasters Licensing Authority), Mike Hardy (Northumberland Sea Fisheries Committee), the legal department (English Heritage), Trudy Feaster-Gee (Competition Commission), Iwan Hughes (Countryside Council for Wales), staff at the Food Standards Agency, Linda McGinley (Forestry Commission), Neil McArthur (Gambling Commission), Dawn Woodward and James Whitman (DEFRA), Paul Horswill and Julie Lunt (Natural England), Philip Hogg (Ofcom), Jennifer Dinmore (Office of the Rail Regulator), Chris Bonney-James (Pensions Regulator), Martin Stringfellow (Office for National Statistics), Olu Fasan and Alan Pitt (BRE Better Regulation Executive). There were doubtless others along the way whose names we have inadvertently failed to mention. We extend our sincere thanks to them all. Whilst these individuals and organizations have generously provided us with their assistance, that should not be taken to suggest that they have endorsed any of the views expressed herein, which are entirely our own and for which we accept full responsibility.

On a personal note, Julie would like to thank Kie and Jon for their help; without which this work would not have been possible. Both authors would like also to pay tribute to the professional and enthusiastic support of the staff at Oxford University Press, most notably Roxanne Selby, Faye Judges, Fiona Stables and Julian Roskams, as well as Manojkumar Lakshmanan of Glyph International. Finally, thanks are due to Stephen Parkinson, Head of criminal and regulatory law at Kingsley Napley, for the original suggestion for the work.

CONTENTS

PART III: APPEAL AND JUDICIAL REVIEW

8. Appeal and Judicial Review

TABLE OF CASES

TABLE OF LEGISLATION

INTERNATIONAL CONVENTIONS

LIST OF ABBREVIATIONS

1974 Act	Health and Safety at Work etc. Act 1974
2009 (Enforcement Action) Order	The Coordination of Regulatory Enforcement (Enforcement Action) Order 2009
2009 (Procedure for References to LBRO) Order	The Coordination of Regulatory Enforcement (Procedure for References to LBRO) Order 2009
2010 Order	Environmental Civil Sanctions England Order 2010
BERR	Department of Business Enterprise and Regulatory Reform
The Bill	Regulatory Enforcement and Sanctions Bill
BIS	Department for Business, Innovation and Skills
BRTF	Better Regulation Task Force
The Code	Statutory Code of Practice for Regulators
Code of Practice	Code of Practice on Consultation
CCW	Countryside Council for Wales
DA	Ministerial Committee for Domestic Affairs
DEFRA	Department for Environment, Food and Rural Affairs
EA	Environment Agency
ECA	European Communities Act 1972
EHO	Environmental Health Officer
English Heritage	Historic Buildings and Monuments Commission for England
EU	European Union
FLA	Football Licensing Authority
FMP	Fixed Monetary Penalty
FSA	Financial Services Authority
GLA	Gangmasters Licensing Authority
HFEA	Human Fertilisation and Embryology Authority
HIR	Hampton Implementation Reviews
HSC	Health and Safety Commission
HSE	Health and Safety Executive
HTA	Human Tissue Authority
IA	Impact assessment
IA Toolkit	Impact Assessment Toolkit
IFCA	Inshore Fisheries and Conservation Authorities
LACORS	Local Authorities Coordinators of Regulatory Services
LBRO	Local Better Regulation Office
LRRA	Legislative and Regulatory Reform Act
MCAA	Marine and Coastal Access Act 2009
OECD	Organisation for Economic Cooperation and Development
Ofcom	Office of Communications
OFT	Office of Fair Trading
ORR	Office of Rail Regulation
PRA	Panel for Regulatory Accountability
RESA	Regulatory Enforcement and Sanctions Act 2008
RIA	Regulatory Impact Assessment
RIPA	Regulation of Investigatory Powers Act 2000

RPC	Regulatory Policy Committee
RRAC	Risk and Regulation Advisory Council
RRC	Reducing Regulation sub-Committee
SFCs	Sea Fisheries Committees
SIA	Security Industry Authority
TCEA	Tribunals, Courts and Enforcement Act 2007
TSA	Tenant Services Authority
TSO	Trading Standards Officers
VMP	Variable Monetary Penalties

1

AN HISTORIC PERSPECTIVE OF REGULATION AND ENFORCEMENT

A. Introduction

Regulatory reform has been a focus for political attention and policy development in the UK **1.01** for nearly two decades.[1] In more recent times, successive Labour governments have pursued the so-called 'Better Regulation' agenda with vigour, commissioning a series of reviews and initiatives, not to mention three pieces of primary legislation,[2] in an effort to improve regulatory effectiveness, whilst reducing the negative economic impact associated with regulatory burden.

The Regulatory Enforcement and Sanctions Act 2008 (RESA), as the third of the significant **1.02** pieces of primary legislation introduced in this area since 1997 might, with a little retrospective gloss, be depicted as a logical conclusion to this political journey. The reality, of course, is that the road has neither been so clearly marked, nor the route so coherent, as such superficial analysis might suggest. Moreover, as can be seen in the review below, there is actually no conclusion. Looking ahead in light of the new Conservative-led coalition government that took office in May 2010, the road continues, with regulatory reform once more very high on the political agenda. What is clear is that RESA was, and remains, an important output from a period of sustained policy development and one that appears destined to make a significant impact upon the way in which we regulate and are regulated. That being the case, it may be helpful to consider in a little more detail the historical context from which RESA emerged.

---

[1] In 1992 the then Prime Minister, John Major, established as part of the Cabinet Office, a central 'Deregulation Task Force' to coordinate eight separate Business Task Forces.

[2] The Regulatory Reform Act 2001, the Legislative and Regulatory Reform Act 2006 and the Regulatory Enforcement and Sanctions Act 2008.

1.03 Whilst focusing upon the UK perspective, it is relevant to consider also, in overview, developments at a European Union (EU) level. Immediately, however, one is troubled by an apparent terminological difficulty, as well as an obvious question.

The terminological difficulty—what do we mean by 'regulation'?

1.04 The apparent difficulty is a basic one and resides in the immediate problem of defining what we actually mean by 'regulation' and 'regulatory reform'. Considered broadly, the concept of 'regulation' may be difficult to distinguish from the body of the general law. It is remarkable that, of the numerous government-authored and -commissioned papers and reports that have been produced on this subject since the arrival of the Labour administration in 1997, relatively little attention appears to have been given to defining what actually is meant in this context by 'regulation'. In general parlance, it is often seen as being synonymous with unnecessary and resource-draining administrative requirements, or 'red tape'. We propose to define 'regulation' more neutrally, as referring to the intervention by government and other regulatory bodies in economic sectors and markets, such as to require individuals and other legal entities to act in a way in which they would not otherwise naturally behave.[3]

The question

1.05 The question is whether, given the potential breadth of this definition, recent policy and legislative developments actually mark any substantial departure or difference of approach from what has gone before? What does appear to be the case is that the 'theory of regulation', and indeed, for that matter, the subject of regulatory law as a legitimate and free-standing sphere of practice, have become much more clearly defined and established as a direct consequence of policy initiatives that have transformed the regulatory landscape since 1997.

B. The UK perspective

The Conservative administrations of the 1980s and '90s

1.06 Regulation, of course, is not new. It can readily be dated back to the Victorian era and the Industrial Revolution. The approach to regulation in those days was relatively crude and one-dimensional, in the sense that its objective was to protect employees and the public against the potentially unprincipled ambition of unfettered capitalists. It was also accordingly, by its nature, negative and reactive; informed by a perceived need to stem the worst excesses of rampant capitalism.

1.07 In more recent times, the second part of the twentieth century was marked by attempts to make regulation more efficient through modified and more systematic regulatory structures. By the 1980s, the emphasis was very clearly on the perceived need to 'deburden' business and, more widely, the economy, of what was perceived to be the excessive burden of a growing mountain of regulation, the origins of which included the ever-growing volume of

---

[3] Professor Anthony Ogus, in his 2008 Street Lecture, proposed a similar definition, as follows: 'I take [Regulation] to refer to obligations imposed by public law designed to induce individuals and firms to outcomes which they would not voluntarily reach. Regulation is largely enforced by public officials and compliance is aided by the threat or imposition of some sanction. As such, regulation covers a vast array of state controls over industrial and commercial activities.'(2008 *Street Lecture,* as revised for publication in (2009) 2 *Public Law*).

regulation emanating from the European Union. This 'regulatory backlash' became characterized on both sides of the Atlantic as the so-called 'deregulation movement' and was driven respectively by the Conservative and Republican administrations' agendas of the era. In the UK, the objective of reducing regulatory burden was conferred on the Enterprise and Deregulation Unit, which in 1987 became part of the Department for Trade and Industry (as it was then called).

Under the Conservative governments of Margaret Thatcher the cutting of so-called 'red tape' was accompanied by an extensive programme of deregulation and privatization of previously state-owned industries, including the telecommunications, transportation and energy sectors. Whilst the overall policy emphasis remained on deregulation,[4] privatization also brought with it new regulatory challenges. The privatization of previously state-controlled monopolies created artificial markets necessitating sophisticated regulation of price and product quality. **1.08**

There are perhaps three other trends, as Professor Ogus[5] notes, which are noteworthy as having their origins in this era. First, the 'deregulation initiative' was pursued by the Conservative governments of 1979–97 against a backdrop of increasingly sophisticated and complex regulated markets and sectors, rendering traditional hierarchical models of top-down imposed regulatory controls increasingly difficult to achieve effectively, without market cooperation. **1.09**

At the same time (and on one level converse to the policy direction of the 'deregulation initiative') there was a growing recognition of the importance of establishing greater regulatory control of the professional sectors. Some of these sectors had traditionally been run by professional bodies as self-regulating 'gentlemen's clubs'; a model which now seemed to demonstrate inadequate transparency and independence and was consequently no longer deemed acceptable.[6] **1.10**

Finally, as previously noted, the European Union continued to generate an ever-increasing volume of regulation. This gave rise to the challenge of integrating European provisions within a UK regulatory framework—whilst, conversely, not impeding the free-trade liberalism underpinning the concept of the European Single Market. **1.11**

Even this relatively superficial analysis of key trends illustrates that, whatever the attractive simplicity of the 'deregulation initiative', the UK's approach to regulation in the 1980s and 1990s was far from straightforward and was influenced by potentially conflicting developments, both within the UK and further afield. These trends and developments coincided in 1997 with a new political impetus to consider afresh our approach to regulation. **1.12**

---

[4] Guidelines, for example, published in 1986 by the Enterprise and Deregulation Unit called for an assessment by government departments of the objectives of proposed regulations, their positive and negative impacts on business, the regulatory alternatives and their impact costs. Each government department was also required to establish an internal 'Deregulation Unit', accountable to a minister, as a part of the monitoring and review of proposed regulatory reforms, under the 'deregulation initiative'.

[5] Ibid.

[6] Witness for example the establishment in 1983 of the United Kingdom Central Council for Nursing, Midwifery and Health Visiting; as well as the reconstitution of the General Medical Council in 1979, and the latter's subsequent new 'direction', in the 1990s, with a view to better engagement with the public and the introduction of more transparent standards for medical professionals.

The new agenda

1.13 With the arrival of Tony Blair's New Labour government in 1997, 'deregulation' became 'better regulation', with the implicit policy contention that 'good regulation' was a benefit to society. This point was subsequently made explicit in the introductions to some of the many papers and reports published and commissioned by the government in the period 1997–2010, in pursuance of the 'better regulation' agenda. So, for example, by 2005, the newly established Better Regulation Executive boldly stated that 'the Government makes no apologies for targeted regulation to improve standards and protect rights'.[7]

1.14 What follows is an overview of some of the key milestones in the period following 1997; a period remarkable not least for the sheer volume of regulatory policy which it produced.

The Better Regulation Task Force and the 'Principles of Good Regulation'

1.15 One of the first acts of the new administration in 1997 was the establishment of the Better Regulation Task Force (BRTF), under the auspices of the Cabinet Office. This was the successor to a creation of the previous government, the Deregulation Task Force, established as an independent think-tank to advise the government on the quality of its regulation. One of its very first initiatives was the publication of what it called its 'Principles of Good Regulation'. These principles became the effective touchstone for effective regulation, according to the better regulation agenda, and were subsequently given statutory recognition by the Legislative and Regulatory Reform Act 2006.[8]

1.16 Another early initiative of the new administration was to introduce, in August 2000, guidance on the conduct of regulatory impact assessments. This was a direct response to the first recommendation in the Better Regulation Task Force's first report, *Alternatives to State Regulation*, which had been published in July 2000.[9]

1.17 In this significant early paper, *Alternatives to State Regulation,* the BRTF sought to test the proposition that 'anything less than direct Government regulation is … less effective than state regulation'.[10] It produced three recommendations for government:

(i) that the government review its analysis, suggesting that alternatives to state regulation can provide a more effective solution and appropriate protection according to the level of risk, in relation to different activities and sectors; and that the government should publish an assessment of its final proposals for its quality mark scheme against the Principles of Good Regulation;

(ii) that the government review and publish its arrangements for the provision of redress in the public sector; in particular focusing on the transparency of procedures in the public sector for the handling of complaints and compensation; and

---

[7] See Introduction to *Formal Government Response; Regulation–Less is More. Reducing Burdens, Improving Outcomes–a Better Regulation Task Force Report*, published by the Better Regulation Executive, 2005. A copy is available via the Cabinet Office online archive: <http://archive.cabinetoffice.gov.uk>.

[8] Section 21 requires that persons exercising relevant regulatory functions must have regard to these principles. The principles, in short, require that regulatory activities are carried out in a way that is transparent, accountable, proportionate and consistent, as well as being targeted at cases in which action is needed.

[9] See *Better Policymaking: a Guide to Regulatory Impact Assessment*, published by the Cabinet Office in August 2000 and *Better Policymaking: a Guide to Regulatory Impact Assessment*, published in January 2003.

[10] *Alternatives to State Regulation*, page 5, published by the Better Regulation Task Force.

(iii) that the government should develop and publish guidance for policy makers on the alternatives to state regulation.

1.18 Building on these ideas in its report, *Imaginative Thinking for Better Regulation* (2003), the BRTF set out nine recommendations aimed at achieving cultural change within government in its attitude to regulation. The report considered alternatives to prescriptive state regulation, or what it described as 'classic regulation'.

1.19 The BRTF went on to publish a total of around fifty official papers and reports in the period to 2005, before being succeeded in 2006 by the establishment of the Better Regulation Commission.

1.20 One of the most important papers produced by the BRTF over this period was *Regulation—Less is More, Reducing Burdens, Improving Outcomes*.[11] Published in March 2005, this report set out to present, 'radical but practical options for cutting the administrative costs of regulation to business' and, as such, might be seen to mark, if not a complete sea change, then a distinctive shift towards the policy of reducing regulation; a policy which gained further momentum following the publication of the important and influential Hampton Review[12] of the same year. Key recommendations of the BRTF's March 2005 paper included:

(i) Taking steps to reduce the overall administrative burden, including:
    (a) adopting what was known as the 'standard costs model' and using it to provide a systematic measurement of the administrative burden in the UK;
    (b) setting a target for the reduction of the administrative burden; and
    (c) putting in place an organizational structure to facilitate measurement and target achievement in relation to the administrative burden;
(ii) pursuing the policy of 'one in, one out' in relation to new regulation, to promote the removal, consolidation and rationalization of existing regulation and to promote regulatory simplification; and
(iii) developing methodology for assessing the total cumulative costs of regulatory proposals.

1.21 The government's response, produced by the Better Regulation Executive,[13] accepted all eight of the BRTF's specific recommendations. The formal government response stated that:

> [t]he Government is committed to the full implementation of the BRTF recommendations. The Government agrees with the BRTF conclusion that this will help release energy, promote innovation and improve productivity and value for money.[14]

The Hampton Review

1.22 2005 was a significant year in the development of regulatory policy. In March of that year, an important and influential report was published by Sir Philip Hampton. Entitled, *Reducing Administrative Burdens: Effective Inspection and Enforcement*, Sir Philip's report considered

---

[11] A copy is available on the BIS website: <http://www.bis.gov.uk>.
[12] Philip Hampton, *Reducing Administrative Burdens: Effective Inspection and Enforcement* (March 2005).
[13] The Better Regulation Executive was established in September 1997 within the Cabinet Office as the operative body which in effect succeeded the Regulatory Impact Unit as responsible for the implementation of regulatory reform.
[14] Introduction to *Formal Government Response; Regulation–Less is More. Reducing Burdens, Improving Outcomes–a Better Regulation Task Force Report*, published by the Better Regulation Executive in 2005.

proposals to reduce unnecessary administration for business. It focused on the importance of risk assessment in order to reduce regulatory inspections by up to one-third and reduce the number of forms issued by regulators by almost 25 per cent. The Hampton report put forward a total of thirty-five detailed recommendations,[15] as well as a number of principles, which would influence directly government policy in the period 2005–10. Sir Philip's principal recommendations included the following:

(i) risk assessment should be used comprehensively by every regulator;

(ii) regulators should use the resources released through full implementation of risk-based assessment to provide improved advice;

(iii) regulators should reduce the number of duplicated data requests and reduce the over-all burden of forms;

(iv) over the longer term regulators should look to improve cooperation and data sharing to reduce the need for businesses to submit the same data more than once;

(v) every regulatory impact assessment should include, in addition to implementation on regulatory costs, an assessment of the practicality of enforcement;

(vi) the penalty regime should be based on managing the risk of reoffending, and the impact of the offence, with a sliding scale of penalties that are quicker and easier to apply for most breaches with tougher penalties for rogue businesses which persistently break the rules;

(vii) early warning before enforcement action should allow companies to correct problems before going to court, and therefore cut the administrative burden;

(viii) regulators should be structured around simple, thematic areas, in order to create fewer interfaces for businesses, to improve risk assessment and to reduce the amount of conflicting advice and information that businesses receive;

(ix) thirty-one national regulatory bodies should be consolidated into seven, with individual regulators covering the entire scope of environment, health and safety, food standards, consumer and trading standards, animal health, agricultural inspections, and rural and countryside issues;

(x) a new consumer and trading standards agency, incorporating the work of four existing regulators, should help coordinate local authority services to improve the use of risk-based inspection and consistency for businesses whilst maintaining national standards for consumers;

(xi) all regulators should ensure they have a performance management framework and systems in place to deliver fully risk-based inspection, improved advice services and to monitor the impact of these changes on those they regulate;

(xii) entrenching reform by requiring all new policies and regulations to consider enforcement, using existing structures wherever possible;

(xiii) the accountability of regulators for implementing the approach recommended in the Hampton Report should be increased through, for example, suggesting enhanced Parliamentary scrutiny; and

(xiv) in place of the existing Regulatory Impact Unit, a new Better Regulation Executive, led by a senior business person, should be created in the Cabinet.[16]

---

[15] Philip Hampton, *Reducing Administrative Burdens: Effective Inspection and Enforcement*; for the full list of specific recommendations, see Annex D, p. 115 of Sir Philip's report, which can be found at <http://www.berr.gov.uk/files/file22988.pdf>.

[16] Ibid., Executive Summary, pp 9–10.

The Hampton Principles

Sir Philip also proposed a number of principles, to become known as the *Hampton* **1.23**
Principles:

(i) regulators, and the regulatory system as a whole, should use comprehensive risk assessments to concentrate resources on the areas that need them most;

(ii) regulators should be accountable for the efficiency and effectiveness of their activities, while remaining independent in the decisions they take;

(iii) all regulations should be written so that they are easily understood, easily implemented and easily enforced, and all interested parties should be consulted when they are being drafted;

(iv) no inspection should take place without a reason;

(v) businesses should not have to give unnecessary information, nor give the same piece of information twice;

(vi) the few businesses that persistently break regulations should be identified quickly and face proportionate and meaningful sanctions;

(vii) regulators should provide authoritative, accessible advice easily and cheaply;

(viii) when new policies are being developed, explicit consideration should be given to how they can be enforced using existing systems and data to minimize the administrative burden imposed;

(ix) regulators should be of the right size and scope, and new regulators should not be created where an existing one can do the work; and

(x) regulators should recognize that the key element of their activity will be to allow, or even to encourage, economic progress and only to intervene where there is a clear case for protection.

Identifying risk assessment as a key tool in better regulation, the Hampton Review focused **1.24**
policy attention on a risk-based approach to regulatory reform.

In response to the Hampton Review, the government published a paper entitled *Implementing* **1.25**
Hampton: from Enforcement to Compliance.[17] An immediate impact of Hampton was the
creation of the Better Regulation Executive, whose remit was to oversee the reduction of
regulatory burdens on business and hold government departments and regulators to account.
Established under the auspices of the Cabinet Office in 2006, it was subsequently merged
with the Department for Trade and Industry to form the Department of Business Enterprise
and Regulatory Reform (BERR), later to become the Department for Business Innovation
and Skills (BIS).

The government accepted Sir Philip's recommendations and principles in full. The Hampton **1.26**
Review not only led to the establishment of the Better Regulation Executive, from 2006, but
to the introduction of the Legislative and Regulatory Reform Act (the LRRA), which received
Royal Assent in November of the same year. The LRRA for the first time placed a statutory
obligation on regulators to have regard to the 'Principles of Good Regulation'.[18]

---

[17] Published in November 2006. A copy is available at <http://webarchive.nationalarchives.gov.uk>.
[18] The Legislative and Regulatory Reform Act 2006, s. 21; see also para. 1.15 above.

The Regulators' Compliance Code

1.27 The LRRA also provided the statutory footing for the subsequent incorporation, in December 2007, of the Hampton Principles in the form of the *Regulators' Compliance Code*. Coming into force on 6 April 2008, the stated aim of the Compliance Code was to 'embed a risk-based, proportionate and targeted approach to regulatory inspection and enforcement amongst the regulators it applies to'. Initially applicable to national regulators and local authorities in England, the scope of the Code was subsequently extended to apply to local authorities in the devolved administrations in respect of reserved matters, as well as to a growing list of other regulators,[19] in relation to the exercise of their regulatory functions. Regulators to whom the Code applies must have regard to the Code when determining general policy or principles about the exercise of relevant regulatory functions and when exercising specified regulatory functions.[20]

1.28 The government implemented the Hampton recommendation to merge and thereby reduce the total number of regulators, as well as introducing an implementation review (the 'Hampton Implementation Review') designed to measure the extent of regulators' compliance with the Hampton principles. The government additionally introduced a standardized and simplified approach to regulatory cost impact assessment, for use across government departments.

The Macrory Review

1.29 The Macrory Review was commissioned by the government in direct response to, and implementation of, the Hampton Report. Where the Hampton Report established the principles that would dictate the course of regulatory reform for the remainder of the New Labour era, the Macrory Report looked specifically at the question of regulatory enforcement. Published in November 2006, Professor Richard Macrory's final report, entitled *Regulatory Justice: Making Sanctions Effective*, sought to develop specific principles that would apply in the use of regulatory sanctions. The idea was to provide for an 'enforcement toolkit' fit for the post-Hampton era. As Professor Macrory suggested in his Report, his aim was to identify 'a set of fit for purpose sanctioning tools that can be used effectively, fairly and proportionately by regulators and those enforcing regulations in situations of regulatory non-compliance'.[21]

1.30 The enforcement landscape which provided the context for the Macrory Report saw more than 3.6 million enforcement actions, at least 2.8 million regulatory inspections, at least 400,000 warning letters, 3,400 formal cautions, 145,000 statutory notices and at least 25,000 prosecutions each year in the UK, all undertaken by regulators falling within the scope of the Report. Professor Macrory observed that the burden of this raft of regulatory action was not targeted according to any assessment of actual risk and, moreover, small and legitimate businesses tended to experience a greater weight of regulation as opposed to larger companies, or for that matter, those actually engaged in rogue trading activity. Professor Macrory proposed a risk-based approach to regulatory enforcement, such that 'repeat offenders as well as those

---

[19] For example, the Code now applies to public sector regulators as well as some private sector bodies enforcing regulations on behalf of the state.

[20] See further para. 4.35 for more about the Regulators' Compliance Code.

[21] Richard Macrory, *Regulatory Justice: Making Sanctions Effective*, p. 6, para. E.1.

that have an intentional disregard for the law should, under a risk-based system, face tough sanctions'.[22]

Recommendations

Professor Macrory recommended that the government should consider: **1.31**

   (i) examining the way in which it formulates criminal offences relating to regulatory non-compliance;

  (ii) ensuring that regulators have regard to 'Six Penalty Principles' and seven 'characteristics' when enforcing regulations;

 (iii) making sentencing in the criminal courts, in relation to regulatory offences, more effective;

 (iv) introducing schemes of fixed and variable administrative penalties, available to those regulators who are Hampton compliant, with an appeal to an independent tribunal rather than the criminal court;

  (v) strengthening the system of statutory notices;

 (vi) introducing pilot schemes involving restorative justice techniques; and

(vii) introducing alternative sentencing options in the criminal courts for cases relating to regulatory non-compliance.

Sir Philip Hampton had found in his review that current regulatory penalty regimes were both cumbersome and ineffective. Professor Macrory developed the regulatory principles espoused by Sir Philip, in proposing an enforcement framework which offered greater flexibility to regulators and the judiciary whilst, at the same time, more effectively meeting the objectives and principles identified by Hampton: improving regulatory compliance and enhancing transparency and fairness.   **1.32**

A key finding of the Macrory Report was that regulators were at the time too heavily reliant on criminal prosecution for the purposes of regulatory enforcement. Professor Macrory proposed that, in many situations, a more flexible and risk-based approach could provide a more proportionate and effective route to regulatory enforcement.[23]   **1.33**

The Six Penalty Principles

According to the 'Six Penalty Principles' proposed by Professor Macrory, a regulatory sanction should: **1.34**

   (i) aim to change the behaviour of the offender;

  (ii) aim to eliminate any financial gain or benefit from non-compliance;

 (iii) be responsive and consider what is appropriate for the particular offender and regulatory issue, which can include punishment and the public stigma that should be associated with a criminal conviction;

 (iv) be proportionate to the nature of the offence and the harm caused;

  (v) aim to restore the harm caused by regulatory non-compliance, where appropriate; and

 (vi) aim to deter future non-compliance.[24]

---

[22] Ibid., p. 6, para. E.3.
[23] Ibid., p. 7, para. E.9.
[24] Ibid., pp 29–31, para. 2.11.

Seven characteristics

1.35 To some extent, it might be observed that Professor Macrory's Six Principles involved, albeit in a regulatory context, the transfer and recognition of principles already underpinning the criminal justice system. Professor Macrory also set out, however, seven 'characteristics', which he considered regulators should exhibit. These characteristics comprised:

(i) *publishing* an enforcement policy;

(ii) *measuring* outcomes, not just outputs;

(iii) *justifying* their choice of enforcement actions year on year to stakeholders, ministers and Parliament;

(iv) *following up* enforcement actions where appropriate;

(v) *undertaking* enforcement in a transparent manner;

(vi) *being transparent* in the way in which they apply and determine administrative penalties; and

(vii) *avoiding perverse incentives* that might influence the choice of sanction response.[25]

1.36 Professor Macrory made a number of proposals with a view to enhancing the effectiveness of the criminal justice system in relation to the prosecution of regulatory offences. These recommendations included the proposed introduction of general sentencing guidelines for regulatory non-compliance cases, and hearing prosecutions in certain regulatory fields in designated magistrates' courts (in England and Wales). Equally, Professor Macrory proposed the introduction of alternative sanctions, to be applied by the criminal courts in relation to regulatory offences, including 'profit orders' (requiring the repayment by offenders of the profits of regulatory non-compliance), 'corporate rehabilitation orders' and 'publicity orders', where a business has been convicted of a regulatory offence.

Regulatory enforcement

1.37 Perhaps most important, however, at least from the perspective of subsequent policy direction, were Professor Macrory's proposals for the development of regulatory enforcement routes, other than through the criminal courts. First, Professor Macrory proposed the introduction of monetary 'administrative penalties', which would be made available to regulators who had been demonstrated to comply with the Hampton and Macrory principles. Second, Professor Macrory proposed the improvement of the system of statutory notices, the use of which would be widened, following a 'risk-based' approach, as part of the new 'regulatory toolkit'. Third, Professor Macrory proposed the introduction of enforceable undertakings, again to be used by Hampton and Macrory-compliant regulators as an alternative to criminal prosecution. He recommended that appeals against the imposition of administrative penalties, as well as possibly against statutory notices, should be routed through a regulatory tribunal, rather than through the criminal courts. In short, the professor proposed a more varied and flexible range of enforcement machinery, which would be made available to responsible regulators who had demonstrated their commitment to the Hampton and Macrory principles. These comprised Professor Macrory's Six Penalty Principles, together with Hampton's ten principles of inspection and enforcement.[26]

---

[25] Ibid., pp 32–33, para. 2.12.

[26] Professor Macrory made it clear, equally, that he regarded his proposals as linking directly with the Better Regulation Task Force's Five Principles of Good Regulation, which underpinned the wider 'Better Regulation' agenda. The Macrory Report proposed that these changes should be facilitated and coordinated by the Better

2007–10: A new impetus for change

The reviews conducted by Sir Philip Hampton and Professor Macrory were the bedrock for **1.38** a new wave of reforming energy, coinciding with the succession of Gordon Brown as Prime Minister in 2007. The final years of the New Labour government were indeed marked, not only by further policy initiative in this field (most notably in the form of the government-commissioned reviews produced by Peter Rogers (March 2007) and by Sarah Anderson (January 2009)), but also by government restructuring, which saw regulatory reform for the first time placed within a specific departmental and ministerial brief. Of even greater tangible importance was the enactment of the Regulatory Enforcement and Sanctions Act 2008 (RESA). Although introduced in direct response to Hampton and Macrory, RESA can more properly be seen to be the product of policy development in this area since the launch of the Better Regulation agenda—and the Principles of Good Regulation—in 1997.

The Rogers Review

Published in March 2007, the Rogers Review[27] took up the themes developed by Hampton **1.39** and Macrory, and aimed to set out national enforcement priorities for local regulatory services in England. The Rogers Review was commissioned specifically by the government as part of its implementation of the recommendations put forward by Sir Philip Hampton. The terms of reference for the Rogers Review were threefold:

(i)   to define the policy areas (and their enforcement mechanisms) that come under the remit of local authority regulatory services;
(ii) to collect and collate the evidence on the relative priority of these policy areas for central government, local citizens and business; and
(iii) to make recommendations on around five policy areas that are central government priorities for local authorities, based on their level of risk, political priority and the perceptions of citizens and business.

The Rogers Review recommended six national regulatory priority areas, as follows: **1.40**

(i)   air quality, including the regulation of pollution from factories and homes;
(ii) alcohol, entertainment and late night refreshment licensing and its enforcement;
(iii) hygiene in relation to businesses selling, distributing and manufacturing food and the safety and fitness of food on the premises;
(iv) improving health in the workplace;
(v)   fair trading (trade description, trade-marking, misdescription, doorstep selling); and
(vi) animal and public health, animal movements and identification.[28]

Taking an evidence-based approach, based upon the identification of risk associated **1.41** with each of these priority areas and positive outcomes that might be achieved through their prioritization by local authorities, the Rogers Review made seven particular recommendations:

(i)   government should specify these enforcement priorities to local authorities;

Regulation Executive, as the body within government responsible for delivering the government's reform agenda.

[27] Peter Rogers, *National enforcement priorities for local authority regulatory services* (March 2007).
[28] Ibid., p. 12.

(ii) the soon-to-be incorporated Local Better Regulation Office (LBRO) should develop and disseminate best practice that would assist local authorities to focus upon these priorities;

(iii) government departments should work with the LBRO when they draw up advice on minimum levels of enforcement and reporting requirements for policy areas that are not priorities but which implement European Union legislation;

(iv) the LBRO should refresh the enforcement priorities set out in the Rogers Review on a regular basis (at least every three years), and recommend them to government;

(v) government should consider the impact on local authority regulatory services of any new enforcement demands and ensure that such demands are fully funded;

(vi) government should ensure that the proposed establishment of 200 national indicators setting out its priority outcomes for local authorities appropriately reflects the national enforcement priorities proposed by the Rogers Review; and

(vii) government should not use part funding or 'seed monies' to introduce new priorities 'by the back door', outside of the central prioritization focus.

1.42 The review proposed and emphasized the importance throughout of a risk-based approach, with a view to ensuring the most effective targeting of regulatory resources.

The institutionalization of regulatory reform

1.43 The accession to the premiership of Gordon Brown in 2007 was accompanied by the creation of a new Department for Business, Enterprise and Regulatory Reform (BERR), replacing the previous Department of Trade and Industry. From the perspective of regulatory reform, the new arrangement was significant, in that the Better Regulation Executive, the operative body for the implementation of government policy in this area, was moved from the Cabinet Office to become part of the remit of BERR. Responsibility for the government's policy agenda in relation to regulatory reform was in effect (and for the first time) brought within the remit of a specific department and a specific ministerial portfolio.[29] Whilst the move on the one hand afforded regulatory reform specific ministerial status within a dedicated department, it also had the potential in the longer term to dilute, to an extent, its cross-department relevance and consequently its central position at the heart of government.

1.44 On one view, the regulatory reform policy agenda was from that point on explicitly aligned with the interests of business, rather than being seen as a set of principles and philosophy to guide and underpin government policy direction more widely. Where the Better Regulation Task Force had begun, in its early days, by asking some quite philosophical questions about the role of government, the new organizational structure did perhaps reflect the shift in emphasis, since 2005, to the narrower remit of reducing regulatory burdens. Typically, it was the voice of business that could be heard most loudly in this particular debate and there was therefore a perceived and actual logic in bringing the Better Regulation Executive under the auspices of the newly formed Department for Business Enterprise and Regulatory Reform.

1.45 The Better Regulation Commission—which had taken over from the Better Regulation Task Force in 2006 as the think-tank and policy advisory unit responsible for advising government in this area—continued as a non-departmental public body, independent of

---

[29] Initially within the remit of the first Minister of State for Business and Regulatory Reform at BERR, the Rt Hon Lord Drayson, serving between June 2007 and January 2008.

government, but under the oversight of BERR. The Better Regulation Commission continued until its replacement by the newly formed Risk and Regulation Advisory Council (RRAC), in 2008.

Established with the remit of improving understanding of public risk, the RRAC published **1.46** its principal report in May 2009, *Response with Responsibility: Policy-Making for Public Risk in the Twenty-First Century*.[30] The recommendations of the RRAC, set out in that report, were recognized by the government in its response of December 2009. The government also established a Regulatory Policy Committee at the end of 2009, tasked with providing external scrutiny, in an advisory capacity, as to whether the government had been effective in minimizing costs of regulatory intervention and maximizing the benefits of such intervention. The programme of the RRAC itself was completed by the end of 2009.

Interestingly, one of the recommendations of the RRAC was that the newly formed **1.47** Regulatory Policy Committee should 'embrace issues across society, not simply in the narrow realm of business'. The government responded as follows:

> [t]he new Regulatory Policy Committee (RPC) will advise on whether the Government is doing all it can to accurately assess the costs and benefits of regulation and on whether regulators are appropriately risk-based in their work. The creation of the Committee is an important innovation in regulatory management that will improve the way regulation is made and implemented.[31]

The initial focus of the Regulatory Policy Committee would be 'a scrutiny of the govern- **1.48** ment's cost-benefit analysis'. In particular, the Committee would oversee implementation of the government's impact assessment template, designed specifically to require policy makers to assess the cost to business or the third sector of regulatory intervention.[32] The government's regulatory priority and focus clearly remained to address the needs of business.

Department for Business, Innovation and Skills (BIS)

In June 2009, BERR merged with the Department of Innovation, Universities and Skills to **1.49** form the Department for Business, Innovation and Skills (BIS). BIS assumed responsibility for the policy area of 'Better Regulation', and in particular for the Better Regulation Executive.

---

[30] The RRAC report concluded by making the following recommendations:

   (i) that the government should take on the analysis, thinking, approach and tools which the RRAC proposed in improving policy-making;
   (ii) that the Regulatory Policy Committee should embrace issues across society, not simply in the narrow realm of business;
   (iii) that the government, as part of its commitment to create the optimal risk and regulatory government framework, should without delay establish an independent Public Risk Commission.

[31] *The Government Response to the Risk and Regulation Advisory Council (RRAC) Report, 'Response with Responsibility: Policy Making for Public Risk in the Twenty-First Century'* (December 2009).

[32] A new system of impact assessments was introduced by the government and made fully operational in November 2007, under the auspices of the Better Regulation Executive. The Better Regulation Executive produced guidance, a 'tool-kit' and standard templates to assist policy makers in the preparation of impact assessments. Impact assessments required to be applied to all government interventions, including those emanating from EU legislation. It was intended that this would achieve a greater level of transparency as to the purpose of the proposed intervention, how and to what extent intervention would impact, as well as providing a cost/benefit analysis in terms of the proposed and actual impact of the measures introduced. All new regulatory proposals likely to impose a major new burden on business required also to obtain clearance from the Panel for Regulatory Accountability, chaired by the prime minister.

Designed to bring 'all of the levers of the economy together in one place', its policy remit includes, in addition to better regulation, business law, business sectors, consumer issues, economics and statistics, employment matters, enterprise and business support, Europe, trade and export control, further and higher education, regional economic development and science. If there had been concerns as to the narrowing of the better regulation policy agenda following the creation of BERR, the focus on business, and deregulation for the benefit of business, were clearly central to the remit of this new super-department.

The Anderson Review

1.50 The interests of business were the focus for the review conducted by Sarah Anderson CBE. Commissioned by the government and published in January 2009, her report, *The Good Guidance Guide*,[33] was designed to recommend ways in which the government could give more effective regulatory guidance to business. This was a response to evidence suggesting that businesses in the UK were spending at least £1.4 bn obtaining external advice about how to follow government regulations. The Anderson Report made recommendations including the following:

(i)   increasing certainty over outcome, by providing access for small and medium-sized businesses to a tailored, insured advice helpline and taking responsibility for the quality of its guidance;

(ii) making guidance more accessible, by expanding the contents of business open advice days and reviewing the brand of its single guidance website;

(iii) making guidance clearer, by introducing quick start guides and moving to ensure that all guidance complies with the code of practice on guidance;

(iv) achieving consistent guidance across government; and

(v)   introducing culture change and increasing communication of improvements.[34]

1.51 The government's response, published on 5 March 2009, set out specific commitments to the following:

(i)   a telephone advice service, which would provide tailored, insured advice to help business comply with employment and health and safety law;

(ii) removing the disclaimers that create uncertainty when relying on government guidance;

(iii) giving inspectors greater discretion about the prosecution of businesses that reasonably believe they are following guidance; and

(iv) setting out when it will update the most frequently used guidance to comply with the 'code of practice on guidance'. [35]

1.52 As the first decade of the twenty-first century—and the 'Better Regulation' era—drew to a close, the emphasis on lightening the load for business was clear. Whilst a natural evolution of its philosophical beginnings, the subsequent manifestation of the initiative perhaps reflected in equal measure the turbulent economic climate and the state of increasing political fragility in which the government found itself. The imperative finally seemed to be one of

---

[33] *The Good Guidance Guide: taking the uncertainty out of regulation* (The Anderson Review), p. 7.
[34] Ibid.
[35] BERR, *Government Response to the Anderson Review* (March 2009).

direct pragmatism rather than philosophical analysis; more about telephone helplines than the development of more ephemeral principles.

It is perhaps, therefore, a little ironic that what could turn out to be the most important **1.53** and tangible legacy of the 'better regulation' era emerged during this period. Born of the principles established by Hampton and introduced in direct implementation of Macrory, RESA was, by any measure, radical in both vision and implementation.

The Regulatory Enforcement and Sanctions Act 2008

Receiving Royal Assent on 21 July 2008, and coming into force between October 2008 **1.54** and April 2009, RESA was conceived by the government as part of its commitment to implement Professor Macrory's recommendation that regulatory enforcement should be established on a more flexible, proportionate and risk-based footing. RESA comprises four distinct, but related parts.

First, RESA provides the Local Better Regulation Office (LBRO) with a statutory footing, **1.55** with statutory functions and powers designed to improve regulation at local authority level. The LBRO is to exercise the function of promoting best practice in this respect and, fundamentally, to ensure compliance by local authorities with the Principles of Good Regulation.[36]

Second, and again with reference to regulatory enforcement by local authorities, RESA **1.56** establishes a primary authority scheme, the aim of which is to achieve improved consistency of advice and enforcement across different local authority areas.

Undoubtedly most radical, however, are the provisions contained within Part 3, which pro- **1.57** vide for the conferral of new powers of civil sanction upon approved regulators. Derived directly from Macrory, the policy intention is to allow regulatory bodies to administer a more proportionate and flexible response to regulatory non-compliance, as an alternative to criminal prosecution.

Finally, Part 4 of RESA places a statutory duty on specified regulators to review their **1.58** functions, not to impose unnecessary burdens and to remove burdens that are found to be unnecessary. Again, the legislation is arguably bold in imposing specific statutory duties on regulators, building on and strengthening the existing obligation to have regard to the *Regulators' Compliance Code*, which had come into force in April 2008.

The Tribunals, Courts and Enforcement Act 2007

The Tribunals, Courts and Enforcement Act 2007 (the 2007 Act) provided an important **1.59** structural component in the government's implementation of the Macrory vision. Introducing a new consolidated tribunal system, the 2007 Act enabled the creation of a dedicated General Regulatory Chamber of the new First-tier Tribunal, designed to hear appeals against administrative sanctions imposed under Part 3 of RESA. Intended to meet Professor Macrory's call for an 'effective and quick appeal route', it is envisaged that the new tribunal

---

[36] On 11 August 2010, the government announced a review of LBRO 'to examine how successful LBRO has been in achieving its objectives of creating the conditions for regulatory reform at the local level, and delivering consistency for business, primarily through the Primary Authority Scheme'.

framework will deliver a quicker, more proportionate and flexible route for appeals under RESA, as contrasted with the court and in particular, the criminal justice system.[37]

1.60 Before considering RESA in further detail, it will be informative to consider the EU perspective, then concluding our contextual analysis by casting an eye to the future. First, though, a word about the regulatory reform programme recently instigated by the Organisation for Economic Cooperation and Development.

The OECD initiative—a wider viewpoint

1.61 The Organisation for Economic Cooperation and Development (OECD) has put in place a regulatory reform programme aimed at helping governments improve regulatory quality— helping governments to reform 'regulations that raise unnecessary obstacles to competition, innovation and growth, while ensuring that regulations efficiently serve important social objectives'.

1.62 In 2008–10, the OECD, in partnership with the European Commission, put in place its 'EU 15' project, to assess 'capacities for effective regulatory management across the EU, through individual reviews of 15 member states'. According to the OECD review of the UK in 2010,[38] 'the vigour, breadth and ambition of the United Kingdom's better regulation policies are impressive'. Overall, progress in relation to better regulation in the UK received a glowing endorsement. In relation specifically to compliance and enforcement, the OECD Report had this to say:

> [t]he changes proposed by Hampton were innovative and have been a source of inspiration to other countries. Change was particularly necessary in the United Kingdom, given its complex and overlapping structures for enforcement. Consistent change across all regulatory agencies and local authorities will take time. The recent BRE/NAO reviews of progress note this issue in relation to the five non-economic regulators. The [range] of initiatives which has been put in place, including statutory requirements and [the Compliance Code], as well as 'softer' approaches, such as the Hampton Implementation Network Group to exchange views seems appropriate to the challenge. The new regulatory sanctions regime is another positive development. The new regime will give regulatory agencies new, more flexible simple administrative sanction powers as an alternative to criminal prosecution. It is too early to assess its effectiveness in practice.

1.63 The OECD did make a number of recommendations, in light of its review of the UK Better Regulation agenda. Amongst these, interestingly, it suggested that the UK government should seek to, 'ensure that significant new better regulation policies and developments do not succeed each other too rapidly, by bearing in mind the perspective of external stakeholders and their need to keep up'. There also appeared to be an implicit recognition that, to a significant extent, better regulation in the UK had had its focus in the business community. The OECD suggested that the UK government should:

> aim to reinforce and develop initiatives that reach out to the non-business community. The project on burdens for frontline public sector workers and on the third sector (voluntary and community sector) is a valuable starting point. Citizen and community focused initiatives are

---

[37] Ibid.
[38] A copy is available on the Organisation for Economic Cooperation and Development website: <http://www.oecd.org>.

also evident across other parts of government and at the local level, and could be given greater support.

C. The European perspective

The importance of addressing the European Union (EU) position was identified relatively early in the Better Regulation era. A paper produced by the Better Regulation Task Force in December 2004, *Make it Simple–Make it Better,* took as its starting point a recognition that around half of all significant legislation in the UK emanated from Europe. It focused on proposals to simplify European legislation in three specific areas: data protection, food labelling and integrated pollution prevention and control. **1.64**

This followed the publication by the European Commission of its *Better Regulation Action Plan* in 2002 and a subsequent inter-institutional agreement on better law-making between the European Parliament and Council in December 2003. There followed an EU programme on legislative 'simplification', which was defined as follows: **1.65**

> simplification is to be understood in a wide sense, covering modification of legislation to apply more efficient or proportional legal instruments, but also simplification of the substance of our policies while preserving their essential elements.[39]

The recommendations proposed by the Better Regulation Task Force included the following: **1.66**

(i) that the EU Council and Parliament should meet their commitment under the inter-institutional agreement to adopt 'ad hoc structures' to expedite simplification proposals, by mid 2005;

(ii) for each new legislative proposal, the document that sets out the rationale for deciding on what legal instrument is appropriate, the impact assessment for the Commission's explanatory memorandum, should include consideration of how a favoured instrument can be amended in future;

(iii) any proposal for new legislation should include an holistic review of all relevant legislation applying to the activities to be regulated, and an explanation of how the new proposal will fit with the existing regulatory regime;

(iv) enforcement authorities should be consulted at an early stage on the practicalities of implementation;

(v) legislation should aim to reduce unnecessary administrative burdens by streamlining or eliminating the need to apply for multiple permits, authorizations, or make multiple notifications. In particular, to be consistent with the Single Market they should allow single commercial bodies with operations in different member states to make single applications/notifications;

(vi) when there are procedures aimed at supporting implementation by the issue of guidance or reference documents, the process must be transparent and conducted according to clear plans and timetables; and

(vii) the ability of small firms to comply with the legislation should be considered in particular, with specific emphasis on the importance of communication in this respect.

---

[39] First report published by the European Commission on the action programme on '*updating and simplifying the community acquis*'. A copy is available on the European Commission website: <http://ec.europa.eu>.

1.67 Even prior to this, the Mandelkern Report (2001)[40] had provided the basis for the development of Better Regulation policy at an EU level. It identified the need for high-level and cross-governmental political support and appropriate resources if the potentially daunting challenge of simplifying the way in which the EU went about regulation was to be tackled. The Report identified seven key areas for action:

(i) consideration of policy implementation options: EU and national policy makers should always consider the full range of possible options for solving public policy issues and choose those that are most appropriate for the circumstances;

(ii) impact assessment: regulatory impact assessment (RIA) was identified as an effective tool in evidence-based policy making and it was proposed that this should be an integral part of the policy-making process at EU and national levels;

(iii) consultation: effective consultation was identified as important as a means to ensure that regulation is effective;

(iv) simplification: 'a constant need' was identified to update and simplify existing regulations. Interestingly, the Report stated as follows in this regard:

> … simplification does not mean deregulation. It is aimed at preserving the existence of rules while making them more effective, less burdensome and easier to understand and to comply with;

(v) access to regulation: the Report emphasized the importance of enabling those who were affected by regulation to access and understand it. The Report suggested that the coherence and clarity of regulations should be enhanced through consolidation;

(vi) structures: the Report highlighted that better regulation required appropriate supporting structures responsible for implementing the new regime; and

(vii) implementation: the Report emphasized the importance of considering fully the consequences of implementation, with member states giving a higher priority to the implementation of European regulation.[41]

1.68 The Mandelkern Report provided the foundation for the subsequent design and implementation of the EU's own Better Regulation policy. In 2006, the European Commission produced a guide entitled, *Better Regulation—simply explained*,[42] designed in part to explain the steps that the European Commission was taking to reduce 'red tape'. It endorsed the importance of regulatory impact analysis, effective communication with stakeholders, reduction in paperwork, regulatory simplification and in identifying alternatives to regulation.

1.69 The EU agenda at the time may be seen to draw directly on initiatives being pursued by member states, not least by the UK, but also, and relatedly, as a response and self-justification in the face of a long-standing perception of EU 'over-regulation'. In direct rebuttal of the contention that European regulation was the source of 'red tape', Mandelkern asserted that European-level regulation has in fact reduced the regulatory burden. This upon the basis that:

> one common rule to apply in all member states is much simpler and more efficient than a complex web of varying rules on the same subject matter at national and regional level.

---

[40] *Mandelkern Group on Better Regulation: Final Report* (13 November 2001). A copy is available on the European Commission website: <http://ec.europa.eu>.
[41] Ibid., Executive Summary, p. i.
[42] A copy of which is available on the European Commission website: <http://ec.europa.eu>.

European legislation has been effective in removing harmful barriers that distort competition and create conflict between different national systems.

At the heart of this particular debate was a deep-rooted and polarized argument about the **1.70** relative merits of EU governance; a debate that goes beyond the scope of the Better Regulation agenda.

Whatever its policy motivation, the EU Better Regulation policy initiative saw the introduc- **1.71** tion of annual reports on better law-making, as well as, to date, three strategic reviews on the subject of better regulation, published in November 2006, January 2008 and January 2009. The EU has operated regulatory impact assessments,[43] measuring the impact of new legislative and policy proposals in terms of economic, social and environmental impacts, since their introduction in 2002.

In 2005, the EU Commission put forward proposals for the standardization of methodology **1.72** across the member states for the measurement of administrative costs, drawing on the model applied in several other member states, and has proposed a target for the reduction of administrative burdens by 25 per cent by 2012.[44] The Commission has additionally, amongst other initiatives, introduced its rolling simplification programme, as well as a programme of codification of existing legislation, with the result that it claims to have reduced the volume of EU regulation by 10 per cent since 2005.

At an EU level, the drive towards better regulation, and in particular towards a reduction of **1.73** administrative burdens and regulatory simplification, stands in contrast to the previous emphasis on the precautionary principle in its approach to regulation.[45] Some commentators have anticipated a swing back at EU level to a more precautionary approach.[46]

At a philosophical level, the Better Regulation initiative promoted by the UK and equally **1.74** favoured by, for example, Sweden, has not attracted unanimous endorsement. France has for example adopted the precautionary principle within its Constitution and there has been a traditional scepticism amongst French policy makers about the Better Regulation experiment. Equally, if the acid test of the Better Regulation agenda is the extent to which regulation has actually been reduced, again some commentators have found little if any evidence to support this conclusion, either at UK or EU level.[47]

To some extent, then, the debate at EU level is more acute, not least because of the conver- **1.75** gence of different interests and philosophical traditions, as well as the fact that the EU has not traditionally been associated with regulatory reduction. In practice, the Better Regulation

---

[43] See further in relation to the European Commission's Impact Assessment system, including reports of its Impact Assessment Board for 2007–09: <http://ec.europa.eu/governance/impact/key_docs/key_docs_en.htm>.

[44] *Action Programme for reducing administrative burdens*, launched January 2007.

[45] The approach to regulation such that regulatory intervention is justified and necessary where there is the possibility of risk or harm, in the absence of such regulation, even where the scientific evidence of the risk is inconclusive. It is therefore to be contrasted with a risk-based approach. Regulation is seen as a precautionary measure to protect the public pending scientific proof that the perceived risk is in fact negligible or non-existent. In February 2000 the European Commission had issued a Communication on the precautionary principle, effectively positioning the principle as one of the principles informing the EU policy agenda.

[46] See for example paper by Rangnar Lofstedt, *The Plateau-ing of the European better regulation agenda; an analysis of activities carried out by the Barroso Commission* (30 September 2006).

[47] See, for example, Lofstedt (2006).

debate went against the grain of a legislative tradition informed by a precautionary approach to public protection.

1.76 The conceptual attraction of the Better Regulation agenda, at least in principle, is however hard to dismiss, and the EU has undoubtedly taken significant steps to advocate the principles that underpin it. The Lisbon Strategy, originally conceived at the Lisbon Summit in March 2000 and simplified and relaunched in 2005, saw the agreement by member states of 'integrated guidelines', including specific agreed objectives designed to achieve a cohesive approach to better regulation across the member states. Guideline 14 of the integrated guidelines states as follows:

> [t]o create a more competitive business environment and encourage private initiative through better regulation, member states should:
> (1) reduce the administrative burden that bears upon enterprises, particularly on SMEs and start-ups;
> (2) improve the quality of existing and new regulations, while preserving their objectives, through systematic and rigorous assessment of their economic, social (including health) and environmental impacts, while considering and making progress in measurement of the administrative burden associated with regulation, as well as the impact on competitiveness, including in relation to enforcement; and
> (3) encourage enterprises in developing their corporate social responsibility.[48]

1.77 The overall objective, in European terms, is to 'help Europe's enterprises to prosper and to bring the full benefits of the internal market to consumers'. Looking forward, this may be reflected in the European Commission's 'Communication on Smart Regulation', due to be published in late 2010.[49]

D. Looking to the future

1.78 It is, as the OECD states in its review, too early to assess fully the impact of RESA. There is no doubt, however, that it is radical in its vision and, potentially, ground breaking in its implementation and significance in the course of the Better Regulation policy agenda. That agenda, in the UK at least, has in the meantime once more changed tack, with the accession, in May 2010, of a new Conservative-led coalition administration. The new government has already announced 'an action plan to bring an end to the excessive regulation that is stifling business growth'. On the face of it, the creation of a new cabinet 'star chamber' to spearhead the government's drive to reduce regulation brings the focus of regulatory reform back within the Cabinet. The government has stated that its Reducing Regulation sub-Committee[50] will

---

[48] See <http://ec.europa.eu/enterprise/policies/better-regulation/other-initiatives/lisbon-strategy/index_en.htm>.

[49] Following the Commission's recent 'Consultation on Smart Regulation', in which it proposed a number of steps designed to improve existing legislation (including cutting red tape for business) and to develop its regulatory impact assessment system. 'Smart regulation', according to the consultation document, 'is not about more or less legislation—it is about delivering results in the least burdensome way'. (See <http://ec.europa.eu/governance/better_regulation/smart_regulation/docs/smart_regulation_consultation_en.pdf>.)

[50] The remit of the new sub-committee, which replaces the Panel for Regulatory Accountability (see fn. 32 above) and reports to the Economic Affairs Committee within the Cabinet Office, is to 'consider issues relating to reducing regulation'. It is envisaged that the sub-Committee 'will be crucial to setting a new tone around regulation, creating and maintaining momentum of the Better Regulation agenda'. The government has also proposed some new principles of regulation under the new regime, as follows: (1) The government will regulate

'enforce a new approach to new laws and regulations, ensuring that their costs are being properly addressed across the entire British economy'. Further, the government has announced 'an immediate review of all regulation in the pipeline implementation of which has been inherited from the last Government'. Additionally, a new 'challenge group' is tasked with coming up with 'innovative approaches to achieving social and environmental goals in a non-regulatory way'. The government also states that it favours a 'new approach that will control and reduce the burden of regulation'. It is to be a 'one in, one out approach, designed to change the culture of Government' and to 'make sure that new regulatory burdens on business are only brought in when reductions can be made to existing regulations'. [51]

The focus of these very early initiatives in the lifetime of the new administration is clearly again the business sector. Whether they will represent a substantive change in policy will remain to be seen. In the meantime, it appears that the agenda of regulatory reform is here to stay. The Regulatory Enforcement and Sanctions Act 2008 can properly be regarded as one of the most important moments in the journey to date. **1.79**

---

to achieve its policy objectives only. (2) There will be a general presumption that regulation should not apply to small and medium sized enterprises unless a robust and compelling case has been made for including SMEs within the scope of the regulation. (3) Exceptions to these principles must be explicitly cleared through the Reducing Regulation sub-Committee.

[51] See generally the BIS website: <http://www.bis.gov.uk/bre>.

THE COORDINATION OF LOCAL
AUTHORITY ENFORCEMENT

2

ENFORCEMENT BY LOCAL AUTHORITIES: THE LOCAL BETTER REGULATION OFFICE

A. Introduction

The provisions of Part 2 of RESA have heralded a new era in the way that local authorities **2.01** carry out their regulatory functions. In this chapter, we look at how the Local Better Regulation Office, through its general and specific statutory functions, is able to coordinate local authority enforcement at a national level, through the provisions of advice and support and the setting of enforcement priorities. Setting these reforms in their proper context, Part B looks at the pre-RESA regime, whilst Parts C and D address the establishment and remit of the body respectively. Finally, in Part G, consideration is given to the far-reaching statutory obligation placed on certain regulators by virtue of Part 4 of RESA, not to impose unnecessary burdens.

B. Local authority enforcement before the LBRO

Introduction

2.02 There are 375 local authorities in England and Wales with a wide range of responsibilities for regulatory enforcement. County authorities are responsible, *inter alia*, for trading standards, which includes product standards, food standards, weights and measures and consumer protection. Smaller district authorities are in charge of environmental health, licensing, highways control, building control and planning. Unitary authorities have the functions of both county and district councils.

2.03 Prior to RESA, the way in which local authorities would carry out their enforcement functions in these areas was not entirely uncoordinated. Innumerable codes of conduct, guidelines and advice documents existed (and continue to exist) at differing levels of importance, designed to bring about a consistency of approach across local authorities.[1] Government agencies such as the Food Standards Agency, the Health and Safety Executive and the Environment Agency produced both general and specific guidance for local authorities on how to carry out their regulatory functions as well as how to deal with specific enforcement issues. Similarly, central government departments gave directions to, and oversaw, local authority performance.[2]

2.04 In some areas, there was considerable muscle behind the coordination of enforcement at a local level. The Food Standards Agency, for example, has had wide powers of oversight over local authority regulation under the Food Standards Act 1999. Similarly, s. 18 of the Health and Safety at Work Act etc. 1974 imposes a duty on local authorities to comply with such guidance as the Health and Safety Executive may generate; if an authority fails to properly perform its enforcement functions, the Secretary of State can make an order declaring the local authority to be in default.

2.05 The 'home' and 'lead' authority arrangements, albeit voluntary, also resulted in a degree of coordination in regulatory enforcement for businesses that traded across council boundaries.[3]

Enforcement Concordat

2.06 An important step in the general coordination of local enforcement was the 1998 Cabinet Office *Enforcement Concordat*, to which most local authorities signed up.[4] This single-page document set out principles of good enforcement, such as consistency and openness, which local authorities were obliged to follow. The Concordat was, however, a voluntary non-statutory code. Were a local authority to ignore their own published commitments, it might have been possible for the Local Government Ombudsmen to make a finding of maladministration against them, but there was no clear procedure for central coordination. The Ombudsman in England and Wales[5] existed primarily to respond to public concerns.

---

[1] Circular 10/97 on enforcing planning control is a good example of influential guidance produced by the (then) Department of the Environment.

[2] See Philip Hampton, *Reducing Administrative Burdens: Effective Inspection and Enforcement*, para. C.39.

[3] See further para. 3.07.

[4] A copy is available on the Northern Ireland, Department of Enterprise, Trade and Investment website: <http://www.detini.gov.uk>.

[5] Wales is today serviced by the Public Services Ombudsman for Wales.

Hampton Review

Against this background, as explained in the preceding chapter, in his 2005 report, *Reducing* **2.07**
Administrative Burdens: Effective Inspection and Enforcement,[6] Sir Philip Hampton identified
an uneven patchwork in the way that local authorities carried out their regulatory tasks.
Whilst finding 'some excellent, innovative practice', the executive summary concluded that
'the system as a whole is uncoordinated and good practice is not uniform'.[7] At a local level,
Hampton's two principal concerns were inefficiency (or lack of risk assessment) and
inconsistency.

Inefficiency was illustrated by the practice of local trading standards officers in 2002–03. In **2.08**
that year, 35,000 inspections were made of 60 per cent of high-risk premises across Great
Britain; however 72,000 inspections, a far greater number, were made to low-risk premises.[8]
In another example of the same year,[9] trading standards officers inspected 10 per cent of all
traders' weights (18,600 inspections) and identified inaccuracies in 6 per cent of all cases, yet
they also inspected 22 per cent of all alcohol measures (370,000 inspections) even though
only 2 per cent were found to be inaccurate. Hampton concluded that 'unnecessary inspections are carried out, but also that necessary inspections may not be carried out'.

The Review also identified a wide variation in local enforcement standards across the **2.09**
country. Within Greater London in 2003 for example, the ratio of *inspectable* premises to
trading standards officers was 381:1 in Sutton, which could be contrasted with 3,487:1
in Lambeth.[10] In terms of health and safety enforcement, a 2003 report identified a 'huge
variation between local authorities in levels of inspection, investigations in enforcement
notices and in the numbers of health and safety inspectors'.[11]

The review recommended setting out clear principles of effective regulation and 'for the first **2.10**
time, coordinating local authority regulatory functions and holding them more effectively to
account'.[12]

Legislative and Regulatory Reform Act 2006

The recommendations of the Hampton Review, championing the coordination of local **2.11**
authority enforcement, were taken some way by the Legislative and Regulatory Reform Act
2006 (LRRA). Under the LRRA, local authorities exercising any of the hundreds of regulatory
functions specified in Part 3 to the Schedule of the Legislative and Regulatory Reform
(Regulatory Functions) Order 2007 (the 2007 Order) are required to have regard to the statutory Principles of Good Regulation, as provided by s. 21(2). These principles are as follows:

   (i) regulatory activities should be carried out in a way that is transparent, accountable,
        proportionate and consistent; and
  (ii) regulatory activities should be targeted only at cases in which action is needed.

---

[6] See fn. 2 above.
[7] Ibid., p. 1.
[8] Ibid., para. 11.
[9] Ibid., p. 29, para. 2.27.
[10] Ibid., para. 21. See also paras 4.100–4.103.
[11] *Safety Lottery. How the level of enforcement of health and safety depends on where you work* (Unison and
Centre for Corporate Accountability, 2003) cited Hampton, *Reducing Administrative Burdens: Effective
Inspection and Enforcement*, para. 4.98.
[12] Hampton, *Reducing Administrative Burdens: Effective Inspection and Enforcement*, para. 26.

2.12 This general duty to have regard to the Principles of Good Regulation applies both at policy and operational levels.

Regulators' Compliance Code

2.13 Section 22(1) of LRRA provides that the minister may produce a more specific code of practice. This came into force on 6 April 2008 in the form of the *Regulators' Compliance Code*.[13] Local authorities are required to have regard to this Code in determining any general policy or principles by reference to which they exercise functions set out in the 2007 Order. For more about the applicability of the Code, see further para. 3.5

2.14 The specific obligations under the Code were drawn up by reference to the Hampton Review under the following headings:

> (i) regulators should recognize that a key element of their activity will be to allow, or even encourage, economic progress and only to intervene when there is a clear case for protection;
>
> (ii) regulators, and the regulatory system as a whole, should use comprehensive risk assessment to concentrate resources in the areas that need them most;
>
> (iii) regulators should provide authoritative, accessible advice easily and cheaply;
>
> (iv) no inspection should take place without a reason;
>
> (v) businesses should not have to give unnecessary information or give the same piece of information twice;
>
> (vi) the few businesses that persistently break regulations should be identified quickly and face proportionate and meaningful sanctions; and
>
> (vii) regulators should be accountable for the efficiency and effectiveness of their activities, while remaining independent in the decisions they take.

2.15 When developing their own policies, setting standards or giving guidance, these arrangements require local authorities to take into account the considerations under these headings, unless they properly conclude that they are not relevant, or are outweighed by other considerations.

2.16 In practice, the application of the Code ought to have led to fewer inspections and a reduction in the amount of enforcement action being taken, with the exception perhaps of that taken against persistent rule breakers.[14] It was soon recognized, however, that these reforms were incomplete, and in particular that they lacked central direction in being able to ensure that the aims of the Hampton Review were met.

---

[13] A copy can be found on the Department for Business, Innovation and Skills website: <http://www.bis.gov.uk>.

[14] The LRRA 2006 applies to local authorities in England, as well as to local authorities in the devolved administrations but, in the case of the latter, only in respect of reserved matters (see s. 24(3)). The Compliance Code originally applied only to local authorities in England, but was subsequently extended to apply to local authorities in the devolved administrations subject to the described restriction.

C. The establishment of the LBRO

Introduction

Hampton identified the delivery of regulatory objectives by local authorities as being one of the primary problems with the existing regulatory regime. The sheer scale of local authority regulatory services[15] created a multitude of problems, including difficulties arising from a lack of coordination between central bodies and local regulators; a lack of effective priority setting from the centre; cross-boundary problems; inconsistent application of national standards and variations in levels of activity. Philip Hampton noted in particular that these problems increased uncertainty and administrative burdens for business. Uncoordinated action on the ground meant businesses receiving unnecessary inspections, or even conflicting advice.[16] **2.17**

Overview of functions

Part I of RESA was intended to go further in addressing these concerns, creating a framework for the centralized control of regulatory enforcement and a greater coordination of enforcement, in which the Local Better Regulation Office (LBRO) is placed firmly in the centre. **2.18**

Under this Part, the LBRO is given a statutory footing and assigned general and specific functions, designed to ensure that local authorities exercise their regulatory functions effectively and achieve the twin aims of the centralization, and the coordination, of local authority regulatory enforcement. **2.19**

First, through the provision of guidance to local authorities on the exercise of their relevant functions,[17] and the provision of advice to central government,[18] the LBRO has the general function of promoting adherence to the Principles of Good Regulation amongst local authorities, facilitating greater coordination between local authorities and central government. **2.20**

Second, the LBRO is given the specific function of the setting of national enforcement priorities for regulatory activity at a local level.[19] This amounts 'to an extensive rationalisation of regulatory activities with a clear hierarchy extending up from local to national government, taking in national regulators'.[20] **2.21**

Finally, the LBRO is tasked with working together with national regulators, including the Environment Agency, the Food Standards Agency, and the Health and Safety Executive, through memoranda of understanding, to achieve its statutory objective.[21] **2.22**

Through the exercise of these functions, businesses can expect financial benefits to accrue; in particular, the issuing of guidance to local authorities by the LBRO will result in increased **2.23**

---

[15] Advice and inspection is provided by no less than 203 trading standards offices and 408 environmental health offices in England, Scotland and Wales, all of which are responsible to the local authority they belong to but implement and enforce regulation from ten different central government bodies: Philip Hampton, *Reducing Administrative Burdens: Effective Inspection and Enforcement*, para. 4.9.

[16] See paras 4.86 and 4.87.

[17] RESA, s. 6.

[18] Ibid., s. 9.

[19] Ibid., s. 11.

[20] *Regulatory Enforcement and Sanctions Bill Research Paper* 08/46, 16 May 2008, p. 30.

[21] RESA, s. 5.

clarity about the regulations that apply to them, helping them work together to keep the burdens of regulation on compliant businesses to a minimum.[22]

2.24 Local authorities, in turn, have their own responsibilities under Part I. These include the need to have regard to any guidance given to them by the LBRO, comply with that guidance when directed to do so by the LBRO, and to have regard to any list of enforcement priorities published by the LBRO.

2.25 Whilst the LBRO may in certain circumstances direct local authorities to have regard to any guidance it issues under this Part, RESA provides certain safeguards to ensure that the LBRO exercises this power sparingly and only when absolutely necessary, for example where a local authority has consistently disregarded a particular piece of LBRO guidance.

2.26 The functions of the LBRO are looked at in detail in parts E–H of this chapter.

The nature of the body

2.27 Even before RESA received Royal Assent in July 2008, the LBRO was established in shadow form,[23] as part of a package of measures introduced to implement the Hampton recommendations.

2.28 RESA dissolved the previous LBRO company,[24] formally establishing in its place a statutory corporation with a range of statutory duties and powers in support of achieving its objectives.

2.29 The Secretary of State is required to review the LBRO's discharge of its functions as soon as practicable after 1 October 2011.[25] The LBRO will continue in existence for as long as it is needed and is considered to be performing a useful role.

Constitution

2.30 Schedule 1 of RESA makes detailed provision about the membership of the LBRO. The LBRO has an independent board, made up of a chair and board members[26] appointed by the Secretary of State,[27] who set the strategic direction for the organization and act as its top-level ambassadors. The LBRO is headed by a senior management team under a chief executive.[28]

2.31 The government's expectation was that the constitution of the board would reflect a 'range of experiences from local government and national regulation, business and consumer groups'.[29] Despite recognizing that the board could not function 'without a lot of input from

---

[22] See BERR, *Regulatory Enforcement and Sanctions Act 2008: Guidance to the Act*, p. 6. A copy is available at <http://www.berr.gov.uk>.

[23] As a government-owned company in May 2007, at the time of the beginning of the consultation on the draft Regulatory Enforcement and Sanctions Bill.

[24] RESA, ss 1 and 2, Schs 1 and 2.

[25] Three years after s. 17 of Part I came into force, that being 1 October 2008, by virtue of the Regulatory Enforcement and Sanctions Act 2008 (Commencement No. 1) Order 2008, SI 2371/2008. See Chapter 1, fn. 36.

[26] There are to be at least five and no more than ten ordinary members of the board, plus the chief executive and such other employees of LBRO as may be appointed by the chair after consulting the chief executive. See RESA, Sch. 1, paras 3(1) and 4(1).

[27] After consultation with the Welsh ministers.

[28] See the LBRO website for details of current board members: <http://www.lbro.org.uk>.

[29] BERR, *Consultation on the Draft Regulatory Enforcement and Sanctions Bill* (May 2007), p. 32.

the sector',[30] the provisions of RESA were never amended to incorporate a requirement as to the experience or expertise of board members.[31]

Review

Section 17 provides for a review by the Secretary of State of the LBRO's discharge of **2.32** functions. The review will answer two particular questions:

(i) generally, whether the LBRO is discharging its functions effectively and efficiently; and
(ii) specifically, in relation to the provision of guidance, support and advice to local authorities (RESA, ss 6–11), the extent to which the s. 5 objective for local authorities has been attained. [32]

In conducting the review, the Secretary of State must consult the Welsh ministers and any **2.33** other persons considered appropriate.[33] The results of the review must be published and laid before Parliament and the National Assembly for Wales[34] to enable the legislature to consider its response.

According to RESA, this review will take place 'as soon as practicable' after 1 October 2011.[35] **2.34** The Minister for Business and Enterprise announced a review of the LBRO in July 2010. The background to the review was said to be the Coalition government's commitment to 'reduce the number and cost of quangos' as well as to examine the purpose of and continued need for the functions performed by the LBRO and to consider the options for future delivery.

Dissolution

The LBRO was only ever intended to be a temporary body with the singular purpose **2.35** of improving the culture and efficiency of local government regulation. In light of this, the expectation is that once its objectives are achieved (or now, perhaps sooner), the LBRO will be dissolved.[36]

The Secretary of State will provide for the dissolution of the LBRO by order, and detailed **2.36** arrangements for this, including the transfer of its property, rights, liabilities and tax arrangements are provided in RESA.[37]

Before any order of dissolution is made, the Secretary of State must consult the Welsh min- **2.37** isters and other such persons as appear to the Secretary of State to be 'substantially affected' by the dissolution of the LBRO. Although not expressly stated, this is likely to include the LBRO itself.

---

[30] Hansard, HL Deb., cols GC5–11 (21 January 2008).
[31] An amendment specifying that at least 25 per cent of the board members should have direct experience of local government was withdrawn: Hansard, HL Deb., cols GC5–11 (21 January 2008).
[32] RESA, s. 17(3).
[33] Ibid., s. 17(4).
[34] Ibid, s. 17(5) and (6).
[35] Ibid., s. 17(2). See footnote 25.
[36] See BERR, *Regulatory Enforcement and Sanctions Act 2008: Guidance to the Act,* p. 9, published July 2008. A copy is available on the Department for Business Innovation and Skills (BIS) website: <http://www.bis.gov.uk>. See also *Regulatory Enforcement and Sanctions Act 2008: Explanatory Notes,* at p. 55. A copy can be found on the Office of Public Sector Information website <http://www.opsi.gov.uk>.
[37] RESA, ss 18 and 19 and Sch. 2.

2.38 An order may also provide for the transfer of functions of the LBRO to 'another person'. This provision would allow certain parts of the LBRO's work to be continued under another guise.[38]

D. Remit of the LBRO

Introduction

2.39 The general functions of the LBRO, provided for in ss 6–10, and the specific functions relating to enforcement priorities in s. 11, are only applicable to local authorities in England and Wales, in so far as they exercise certain *relevant functions*. This means for example that the LBRO will be able to issue guidance to which local authorities in both England and Wales must have regard.

2.40 In respect of the devolved administrations of Scotland and Northern Ireland, the LBRO only works with local authorities where Part 2 of RESA applies, and a primary authority partnership is in place.[39] Primary authority partnerships are considered in detail in Chapter 3.

2.41 Considered below is the extent of the applicability of the LBROs functions in England and Wales, by reference to the terms *local authority* and *relevant function*.

Local authority

2.42 In England and Wales, the LBRO works across the whole range of its functions with all local authorities. Local authorities are defined in RESA and include, in addition to the councils one would expect, fire and rescue authorities, port health authorities and authorities established under s. 10 of the Local Government Act 1985 (waste disposal authorities for Greater London and metropolitan counties).[40]

2.43 The definition of a local authority in England and Wales is considered further in para. 3.19.

Relevant function

2.44 The LBRO works with local authorities in England and Wales to the extent that they are exercising a relevant function.

2.45 Schedule 3 of RESA provides the list of enactments[41] to which a relevant function must relate. By virtue of s. 4(3), a relevant function also includes all regulatory functions exercisable by local authorities conferred by secondary legislation made under s. 2(2) of the European Communities Act 1972, in relation to food hygiene, food standards and animal feed.

2.46 The determination of whether a European enactment relates to any of the specified purposes will be made by order by the Secretary of State[42] (with the consent of the Welsh ministers

---

[38] Ibid., s. 18(2), (c) and (d).
[39] See further Chapter 3 for more about where the primary authority scheme applies.
[40] RESA, s. 3.
[41] Some 184 individual Acts of Parliament are set out in the Schedule, which is reproduced at Appendix 1.
[42] RESA, s. 4(7).

where the determination relates to local authorities in Wales and the European enactment relates to a Welsh ministerial matter).[43]

A function under any of these enactments is *relevant* if it: **2.47**

  (i) imposes requirements, restrictions or conditions in relation to any activity;
 (ii) sets standards or gives guidance in relation to any activity; or
(iii) relates to the securing of compliance with, or the enforcement of, requirements, restrictions, conditions, standards or guidance which under or by virtue of any relevant enactment relate to any activity.[44]

'Activities' include providing goods and services and employing or offering employment **2.48** to any person.[45] A function cannot include the function of conducting criminal or civil proceedings.[46]

The LBRO's scope in relation to local authority regulation is to be kept under review and **2.49** the relevant enactments may be amended by order made by the Secretary of State.[47] Such an order may make different provisions for different purposes (for example, to extend the LBRO's scope to include further regulatory functions), and may make different provision in relation to local authorities in England and Wales respectively. Where an amendment relates to local authorities in Wales in respect of a Welsh ministerial matter, the consent of the Welsh ministers is required.[48] At the time of going to press, no orders amending the scope of local authorities' relevant functions have been made.

Primary authorities

The LBRO's functions also apply to primary authorities created under Part 2 of RESA, **2.50** wherever they are based in the UK.

A primary authority is a local authority registered by the LBRO as having responsibility for **2.51** a particular business or organization that operates across council boundaries. The registration may relate to a single function of the local authority, for example health and safety, or it may relate to multiple functions, for example health and safety and trading standards.

The scheme is designed to ensure that key trading laws are applied consistently across the **2.52** UK, and local inspection and enforcement activity is better coordinated.[49] The LBRO has important functions in relation to the nomination and registration of these partnerships, as well as overseeing enforcement action taken by local authorities within such arrangements. The primary authority partnership scheme is considered in detail in Chapter 3.

---

[43] Ibid., s. 4(8).
[44] Ibid., s. 4(1).
[45] Ibid., s. 4(9)(b). See further para. 3.24 for more about the definition of 'activity'.
[46] Ibid., s. 4(9)(a).
[47] Ibid., s. 4(4).
[48] Ibid., s. 4(6).
[49] So, for example, before local regulators can take enforcement action against a partner authority, they must first obtain the consent of the primary authority. That consent may only be refused where the proposed enforcement action is inconsistent with advice or guidance previously issued by the primary authority. This is discussed in detail in paras 3.91–3.131.

E. General functions of the LBRO

Introduction

2.53 The LBRO has three general functions provided for in ss 6–10 of RESA, through which it aims to support improvement in local authority regulatory services:

    (i) providing guidance to local authorities in respect of regulatory services, and where necessary, ensuring that local authorities comply with this guidance;[50]

    (ii) providing advice to government on enforcement and regulatory issues associated with local authorities;[51] and

    (iii) providing financial support and assistance to local authorities in the exercise of their relevant functions.[52]

2.54 In addition, the LBRO also has a broad range of ancillary powers. These are considered in para. 2.92.

Objective relating to general functions

2.55 In exercising its general functions, the LBRO must act in accordance with its statutory objective,[53] which is to secure that local authorities exercise their functions 'effectively', 'in a way that does not give rise to unnecessary burdens', and in a way which conforms to the Principles of Good Regulation,[54] as provided for in s. 5(2). The principles are that:

    (i) regulatory activities should be carried out in a way which is transparent, accountable, proportionate and consistent; and

    (ii) regulatory activities should be targeted only at cases in which action is needed.

2.56 The Principles of Good Regulation provide that regulatory activities should be carried out in a way that is:

    (i) proportionate: enforcement action should reflect the level of risk to the public and the penalty should relate to the seriousness of the offence;

    (ii) accountable: activities should be open to public scrutiny, with clear and accessible policies, and fair and efficient complaints procedures;

    (iii) consistent: advice to business should be reliable and robust and applicable in different parts of the country. Services should operate in similar ways in similar circumstances;

    (iv) transparent: businesses should be able to understand what is expected from them by local regulators and what they can anticipate in return; and

    (v) targeted: resources should be focused on high-risk enterprises, reflecting local needs and national priorities.

In adopting such an approach, RESA was, as explained in the previous chapter, merely implementing the principles first laid down by Hampton and then given substance by Macrory.

---

[50] RESA, s. 6.
[51] Ibid., ss 9–10.
[52] Ibid., s. 8.
[53] Ibid., s. 5.
[54] See Legislative and Regulatory Reform Act 2006, s. 21; BERR, *Regulatory Enforcement and Sanctions Act 2008: Guidance to the Act*, p. 10.

Guidance to local authorities

Introduction

One of the LBRO's key functions is the provision of statutory guidance to local authorities **2.57** on how they should go about exercising their relevant functions.[55] Through the issuing of guidance to local authorities, the LBRO is working towards the Hampton vision of a more centrally controlled system of national regulation, where local authorities regulate in a more consistent way.

The government consider that this guidance will also have 'an important role in supporting **2.58** improvement in local authority regulatory services, and its role here will serve as a basis for gathering and disseminating information on good practice'.[56]

The LBRO must conduct a consultation before issuing any guidance[57] and publish any **2.59** guidance given.[58] Local authorities are obliged to 'have regard to' any guidance issued to them by the LBRO under s. 6,[59] and may be directed to comply with it in certain circumstances.[60]

Guidance to whom?

The LBRO has the flexibility to provide guidance where it is needed the most. Guidance **2.60** issued under s. 6 may be given to one or more local authorities and may relate to one or more relevant functions.

Where the LBRO gathers evidence from businesses, regulators or others about a particular **2.61** practice, it may consider that one or more local authorities might benefit from specific support on that point, and provide targeted guidance accordingly.[61]

For example, the LBRO could in future give specific guidance 'to a single local authority **2.62** about how often it should be carrying out inspections of premises of a certain type, or more specific guidance relevant to all authorities on how to enforce specific pieces of legislation, or in respect of areas of regulation'.[62]

As the LBRO may not necessarily want, or need, all local authorities to have regard to all of **2.63** its guidance (for example, in instances where practice is already strong in one particular area), it can give guidance to an individual authority or to a selection of authorities.[63] Such guidance may additionally be directed to a particular relevant function or a group of functions,[64] and may relate to the exercise of that or those relevant functions in a particular case.[65]

---

[55] RESA, s. 6.
[56] BERR, *Regulatory Enforcement and Sanctions Act 2008: Guidance to the Act*, p. 13.
[57] RESA, s. 6(4).
[58] Ibid., s. 6(5).
[59] Ibid., s. 6(3).
[60] Ibid., s. 7(1)(a).
[61] BERR, *Regulatory Enforcement and Sanctions Act 2008: Guidance to the Act*, p. 13.
[62] *Explanatory Notes to the Regulatory Enforcement and Sanctions Act 2008*, p. 7, para. 28.
[63] RESA, s. 6(2)(a).
[64] Ibid., s. 6(2)(b).
[65] Ibid., s. 6(2)(c).

Nature of the advice

2.64   The LBRO may issue guidance only where this will promote its objective relating to its general functions, namely in a way that does not give rise to unnecessary burdens, and in a way that conforms to the Principles of Good Regulation.[66]

2.65   Whilst the guidance issued under this section is intended to be detailed, and will set out specific guidelines affecting local authorities and particular enforcement actions, it will not provide a technical interpretation of legislation; this remains the responsibility of the relevant national regulator or policy department. For example, the Food Standards Agency continues to have responsibility for the Food Law Codes of Practice and associated guidance. The LBRO works with these national regulators, however, to ensure a 'joined-up' approach to issuing guidance to local authorities.[67]

Consultation

2.66   Before giving guidance in relation to any relevant function, the LBRO must consult with:

(i)   the persons whose activities are regulated by the exercise of the function (i.e. businesses), or organizations that represent them (for example the Confederation of British Industry, the British Retail Consortium, the Federation of Small Businesses and the British Chambers of Commerce);

(ii)   the local authorities that the LBRO considers appropriate, or their representatives (such as Local Government Association and the Local Authorities Co-ordinators of Regulatory Services); and

(iii)   such other persons as the LBRO considers appropriate.[68]

2.67   According to the BERR *Regulatory Enforcement and Sanctions Act 2008: Guidance to the Act*, those consulted are generally likely to include:

(i)   national regulators, such as the Food Standards Agency, Office of Fair Trading, Health and Safety Executive, Environment Agency, Gambling Commission or relevant policy department;

(ii)   representative bodies for regulatory professionals, such as the Trading Standards Institute, and the Chartered Institute of Environmental Health; and

(iii)   bodies that speak on behalf of consumers, such as the National Consumer Council.[69]

2.68   Recent consultation includes *Taking Stock, Moving Forward—Shaping a Strategy for Better Local Regulation 2010–2013*.[70]

2.69   See further paras 4.106 onwards for more about the nature and scope of consultations.

---

[66]   BERR, *Regulatory Enforcement and Sanctions Act 2008: Guidance to the Act*, p. 13.
[67]   Ibid., p. 14. The LBRO is required to enter into memoranda of understanding with certain national regulators which provide clarity as to how joined up working will be achieved: RESA, s. 12. See further para. 2.119.
[68]   RESA, s. 6(4)(c).
[69]   BERR, *Regulatory Enforcement and Sanctions Act 2008: Guidance to the Act*, p. 13.
[70]   Published on 4 January 2010 and closed 26 February 2010.

Publication

The LBRO must publish any guidance it gives in such manner as it considers appropriate.[71] **2.70**
The provision of further guidance may vary or revoke any previous guidance given.[72]
Publication is likely to be through a combination of direct communication with local
authorities and publication on the LBRO's website.[73]

At the time of going to press such guidance published[74] by the LBRO comprises: **2.71**

(i) The New Local Performance Network
Published on 30 May 2008 this is described by the LBRO as 'a guide to the implications of the new framework for local authority regulatory services, giving background
on Local Area Agreements, Comprehensive Area Assessments, and the central indicator set'. The briefing is in two sections: section 1 sets out the new local performance
framework and section 2 provides detail of the new national indicators for local authority regulatory services and the implications for setting service priorities.

(ii) Applying the Regulators' Compliance Code
Also published on 30 May 2008 this is described by the LBRO as 'a guide to what local
authority regulatory services need to do to comply with the Code'. The guidance:

… introduces the Regulators' Compliance Code, which comes into force in April
2008, and compares it with the current Enforcement Concordat.
… [It] looks at what else regulatory services need to do to comply with the new
statutory requirements of the Code. It should be read alongside the statutory code of
practice published by the Department for Business, Enterprise and Regulatory Reform
(BERR) and guidance from the Local Authorities Coordinators of Regulatory Services
(LACORS).

The Regulators' Compliance Code introduced new statutory requirements for all
English local authorities, including fire and rescue services.[75] It does not replace the
Enforcement Concordat.

(iii) Primary Authority Guidance
Published on 6 April 2009 this comprises the LBRO's statutory guidance to local
authorities shaping the future operation of the scheme. This Guidance is considered in
detail in para. 3.39.

(iv) Better Local Regulation: Supporting Businesses Towards Recovery
'Getting full value from regulatory services by maximizing their contribution to local
economic prosperity' is the central theme of this advice and guidance, published on
30 June 2009. It is described by the LBRO as 'advocat[ing] greater innovation and
collaboration, and is intended for local authority leaders, elected members, chief

---

[71] RESA, s. 6(5).
[72] Ibid., s. 6(6).
[73] BERR, *Regulatory Enforcement and Sanctions Act 2008: Guidance to the Act*, p 13, para. 9.
[74] Copies of each document may be found on the LBRO website at <http://www.lbro.org.uk/publications-guidance.html>.
[75] Whilst the Code originally applied only to English local authorities, its application was subsequently
extended to: (1) specified regulatory functions of local authorities in Scotland, Northern Ireland and Wales; (2)
specific business-facing functions of public sector regulators in England; and (3) functions of other relevant
national regulators currently omitted from the coverage of the Code.

executives and service directors in England and Wales. It proposes practical ways in which councils can harness the potential of their regulatory services.' The guidance explains that:

> It is set out in two sections and illustrated by good practice examples from local authorities. Section 1 introduces the principles of better regulation and approaches to support service improvements geared to both prosperity and protection. Section 2 proposes ways for local authorities to harness the potential of regulatory services alongside other business-facing services during difficult economic circumstances.
>
> This guide should help local authorities and regulatory services to support businesses towards recovery and future growth.

Directing compliance with guidance

2.72   It was recognized by the Bill team that there may be circumstances in which the requirement for local authorities to 'have regard' to any LBRO guidance issued under this section may not always be sufficient to secure compliance with the Principles of Good Regulation. In circumstances where a local authority chooses persistently to ignore advice, the LBRO would effectively be rendered impotent if it had no residual power to rein in the authority. The government considered that whilst, in the majority of cases, the duty to have regard to the guidance would be sufficient, a stronger power to ensure compliance with certain guidance, in certain circumstances, was necessary.

2.73   In circumstances where it considers it 'appropriate to do so', and with the approval of the Secretary of State, the LBRO may direct one or more local authorities to comply with any guidance given, which relates to the exercise of a relevant function.[76] Further, the LBRO may also give a direction requiring a local authority to comply with guidance given by another regulator.[77]

2.74   The power of the LBRO, a non-department public body (and thus unelected) to direct a local authority to conduct its enforcement functions in a particular way is contentious and seemingly without precedent,[78] Viscount Eccles noting at the Bill's third reading that the '[l]aw is often enforced ... but guidance, in this way, never before'.[79]

2.75   The government considers that the power to direct compliance should be 'a reserve measure', a backstop power which would be used infrequently. The LBRO might choose to use the power 'where, for example, a local authority persistently acts with disregard for a particular piece of guidance and the consequences of this disregard are detrimental to businesses or the public'.[80]

2.76   The exercise of the LBRO's power to direct compliance with its own guidance is constrained by the following requirements:

(i)   in all cases, the Secretary of State, or the Welsh Ministers (as applicable), must consent to the LBRO giving the direction to comply;[81]

---

[76]   RESA, s. 7(1)(a).
[77]   Ibid., s. 7(1)(b).
[78]   See Hansard, HL Deb., col. 300 (19 March 2008), where Lord Bach argued that the closest precedent was the power of the Food Standards Agency, under the Food Safety Act 1990, to direct a local authority to comply with a code of practice.
[79]   Hansard, HL Deb., col. 12 (28 April 2008).
[80]   BERR, *Regulatory Enforcement and Sanctions Act 2008: Guidance to the Act*, p. 15.
[81]   RESA, s. 7(2) and (3).

(ii) where the advice is issued to two or more local authorities, the consent referred to in (i) above must be given by order;

(iii) prior to directing compliance, the LBRO must have consulted with the local authorities in England or Wales to whom the direction is to be given, any relevant regulator or policy department, as well as any other bodies that LBRO considers appropriate.[82] For example, where the guidance in question had been issued by the Food Standards Agency (FSA) in relation to a food safety matter, the LBRO must consult with the FSA; and

(iv) the LBRO must publish the direction in an appropriate manner.[83]

2.77 The provision requiring that the LBRO directions to two or more authorities must be made by order subject to the negative resolution procedure[84] was inserted at a late stage in the Bill's progress through Parliament, the House of Lords Delegated Powers and Regulatory Reform Select Committee having pointed out the legislative character of mandatory guidance to local authorities.[85]

2.78 Section 20(2) provides that a statutory instrument made by the Secretary of State under this part will be made by the negative resolution procedure, either in the UK Parliament in Westminster, or in the National Assembly for Wales, where appropriate.

2.79 A direction given by the LBRO to a local authority to comply with guidance previously issued, may be revoked or varied by a further direction.[86]

2.80 The LBRO is also able to give directions to local authorities in relation to enforcement action referred to it under the primary authority scheme: this is considered in Chapter 3.

Advice to ministers

2.81 In considering the burden of regulation on businesses, Hampton concluded that there was a lack of coordination between government departments and local authorities at a national level.[87] The government intended that this issue be addressed through the award of the power to the LBRO to provide practical advice to ministers, and through the setting of national enforcement priorities. The former is considered below, the latter in para. 2.93.

Nature of the advice

2.82 Section 9 provides that the LBRO *may* at any time give advice or make proposals to a minister of the Crown about:

(i) the way in which any one or more local authorities in England and Wales exercises any of their relevant functions;

(ii) the effectiveness of legislation (or proposed legislation) relating to the exercise by local authorities in England and Wales of their relevant functions;

---

[82] RESA, s. 7(5) and (6). This too was a late addition to the Bill and followed government-tabled amendments at the third reading.

[83] Ibid., s. 7(7).

[84] Ibid., ss 7(4) and 20(2).

[85] Second Report of Session 2007–08, HL Paper 21, printed 5 December and published 6 December 2007.

[86] RESA, s. 7(8).

[87] Para. 4.86.

(iii) whether any other regulatory functions could appropriately be exercised by local authorities in England and Wales; and

(iv) any other matter relating to the exercise by local authorities in England or Wales of their relevant functions.[88]

2.83 Additionally, where a minister of the Crown or the Welsh ministers request such advice or proposals, the LBRO is obliged to provide such advice or make such proposals.[89]

2.84 In giving advice, the LBRO will have regard to any guidance given to it by the Secretary of State and will comply with any directions they might give.[90] The LBRO's function of giving advice to ministers provides government with a valuable source of evidence-based expertise on local authority regulatory services, while at the same time providing businesses and local authority regulators with a high-profile voice to highlight issues arising from the way regulation is enforced by local authorities. The LBRO may also assist government in relation to the ways in which a policy under development might be better tailored to reflect effective ways of working, as well as the resource implications of particular forms of regulation. Issues concerning how such policies might be better targeted, or aligned with other types of work, may be covered, as may cases where the existing framework set by central government and national regulators makes it difficult for local authorities to pursue an effective, or risk-based, overall strategy.[91]

Advice to Welsh ministers

2.85 The provisions for providing advice are repeated in relation to the Welsh ministers and local authorities' exercise of their relevant functions and Welsh ministerial matters.[92]

Financial support and assistance

Introduction

2.86 Section 8 allows the LBRO to provide financial support to local authorities in relation to the exercise of their relevant functions, and to any other persons for the purpose of assisting local authorities in the exercise of their relevant functions.

2.87 The Hampton Report[93] recognized that much good practice existed within local authority regulators, and that innovative approaches to service delivery were being developed by single authorities and groups of authorities. It is expected that the LBRO will use this function to support and promote this innovation and best practice.[94]

2.88 This provision enables the LBRO to use a proportion of its budget to support projects or activities that will help to promote its statutory objective and decrease the regulatory burden on business, especially where that burden is related to the actions, approach or policies of local authority regulatory services.[95]

---

[88] RESA, s. 9(1).
[89] Ibid., s. 9(2).
[90] See BERR, *Regulatory Enforcement and Sanctions Act 2008: Guidance to the Act*, p. 18.
[91] Ibid., pp 17–18.
[92] RESA, s. 10.
[93] Philip Hampton, *Reducing Administrative Burdens: Effective Inspection and Enforcement*.
[94] *Regulatory Enforcement and Sanctions Act 2008: Explanatory Notes*, para. 35.
[95] See BERR, *Regulatory Enforcement and Sanctions Act 2008: Guidance to the Act*, p. 17.

Support and assistance to whom?

The LBRO may provide financial support and assistance to: **2.89**

    (i) a local authority in England and Wales in relation to its exercise of its relevant functions; and

    (ii) any other person for the purposes of assisting local authorities in England and Wales in the exercise of their relevant functions.[96]

'Other persons' might include professional associations, business representatives, consumer **2.90** groups, or charities.

The following examples of recent LBRO-funded projects demonstrate the potential for **2.91** awards under this section:

    (i) the *Cutting Red Tape* category of the *Beacons* scheme, a competition that highlights the achievements of local authorities delivering excellent front-line services in order to encourage learning and development;[97] and

    (ii) the *Retail Enforcement Pilot*, which encourages councils to find ways of reducing the regulatory burdens on law-abiding businesses, with resulting spin-off benefits for consumers and workers.[98]

Ancillary powers

The LBRO has been afforded broad ancillary powers to do anything that it thinks necessary **2.92** or expedient for the purpose of, or in connection with, the exercise of any of its functions.[99] In particular the LBRO may:

    (i) enter into agreements;
    (ii) acquire or dispose of property;
    (iii) borrow money; and
    (iv) invest money.[100]

F. Enforcement priorities

Introduction

Central to a coordinated approach to local authority enforcement is the LBRO's function of **2.93** preparing and publishing a list of enforcement priorities, specifying the matters to which local authorities in England and Wales must have regard when allocating resources to their relevant functions.[101] In essence, this requires the LBRO to review and revise the list of enforcement priorities for local authorities, originally published in the Rogers Review of 2007.[102]

---

[96] RESA, s. 8.
[97] Details are available on the LBRO website: <http://www.lbro.org.uk>.
[98] Ibid.
[99] RESA, s. 14(1).
[100] Ibid., s. 14(2).
[101] Ibid., s. 11(1).
[102] Peter Rogers, *National enforcement priorities for local authority regulatory services* (March 2007). A copy is available on the archived Cabinet Office website: <http://archive.cabinetoffice.gov.uk/rogersreview/>.

Rogers Review

2.94   The original list of six national enforcement priorities was prepared by Peter Rogers after comprehensive research, leading to the publication of his report in 2007.[103] The Rogers Review produced five main national enforcement priorities, as described in the preceding chapter.[104]

Enforcement priority lists

2.95   Under RESA there are two separate enforcement priority lists, one for England[105] and one for Wales.[106] This reflects the partially devolved scheme of RESA.

2.96   The LBRO has the responsibility to manage these lists and, at the time of writing, is in the process of preparing fresh lists in accordance with its duty under RESA. For England, the intention is to have a list ready to put before ministers in the Coalition government in early 2011. Early indications are that the emphasis will change 'to focus on outcomes and risk',[107] although this is not radically different to the approach taken by the Rogers Review.

2.97   Whether in practice there is a significant difference between the two lists will depend on the outcomes of the consultation processes. At the time of writing, the LBRO has completed work on the Welsh list and is commencing work on the English list, subject to the review of the LBRO itself (see para. 2.34 above).[108]

When must local authorities have regard to the list?

2.98   A local authority must have regard to the list of enforcement priorities when allocating resources to its relevant functions. Relevant functions are defined in s. 4 of RESA, as to which see para. 2.44.

2.99   Whilst local authorities are required to 'have regard' to the appropriate list, this does not act as an absolute fetter on their resources allocation policies, especially where deviation from the list can be justified due to differences in local circumstances. The government advice on the status of the list is that the requirement to have regard to it will not prevent 'councils giving due weight to their own local priorities. In addition, local authorities will still have to meet with minimum levels of enforcement or any reporting requirements set by relevant domestic or European legislation.'[109] Where there are no convincing local reasons, local authorities should give priority to the national list.

---

[103]   The Rogers Review evaluated over sixty policy areas enforced by local authority trading standards and environmental health services. See further Chapter 1, para. 1.39.

[104]   Para. 1.41.

[105]   RESA, s. 11(1)(a).

[106]   Ibid., s. 11(1)(b).

[107]   See LBRO press release *National priorities to focus on outcomes* (30 March 2010).

[108]   In December 2009 the Welsh Assembly government and LBRO published a consultation paper on the first national enforcement priorities for Wales. A copy is available on the Welsh Assembly Government website: <http://wales.gov.uk/>.

[109]   BERR, *Regulatory Enforcement and Sanctions Act 2008: Guidance to the Act*, p. 19.

Consent of the Secretary of State

The consent of the Secretary of State is required before the enforcement priority list for **2.100** England is published.[110] For the Welsh list, the consent of the Welsh ministers is required, and the Secretary of State must also be consulted.[111] The form of the consent procedure is not prescribed by RESA; all that is known is that the Secretary of State, or the Welsh ministers, will have regard to representations received pursuant to the consultation process, which must be published pursuant to s. 11(3) of RESA.

Consultation

Before publishing an enforcement priority list the LBRO must consult such persons as it **2.101** considers appropriate.[112] This is likely to include the Secretary of State, as well as local authorities and some of the larger national regulators. The requirement to publish details of any representations made as a result of any consultation ought to enhance the openness and consistency of the process.[113]

Review

There is a duty on the LBRO to review the enforcement priority lists from time to time.[114] **2.102** Such review should primarily be carried out on the LBRO's own initiative, although there is a procedure for the Secretary of State (or Welsh ministers) to trigger a review by making a request.[115]

Whether the review is wholesale or partial before the LBRO publishes a revised list, the **2.103** consultation and consent procedures in subss. (2)–(6) of s 11 continue to apply.[116]

The Rogers Review recommended that these national enforcement priorities should be **2.104** updated at least every three years to fit with the *Comprehensive Spending Review* and local authority planning cycles.[117]

G. Duty not to impose burdens

Introduction

Part 4 of RESA places a general duty on regulators exercising any regulatory function to **2.105** keep 'that function under review and secure that in exercising the function the person does not' impose burdens that are unnecessary, or maintain burdens that have become unnecessary.[118]

---

[110] RESA, s. 11(5).
[111] Ibid., s. 11(6).
[112] Ibid., s. 11(3).
[113] Ibid., s. 11(4).
[114] Ibid., s. 11(7).
[115] Ibid., s. 11(7)(b) and (c).
[116] Ibid., s. 11(8).
[117] Rogers, *National Enforcement Priorities for Local Authority Regulatory Services*, para. 5.70.
[118] RESA, s. 72(1).

To whom does the duty apply?

2.106   The duties not to impose or maintain unnecessary burdens apply to those regulators listed in s. 73(2) (referred to in this chapter as 'Part 4 regulators') and, by virtue of s. 13, to the LBRO itself.

Part 4 regulators

2.107   The duties imposed under s. 72 apply to those functions[119] carried out by the regulators listed in s. 73(2), namely functions exercised by:

    (i) the Gas and Electricity Markets Authority;
    (ii) the Office of Fair Trading;
    (iii) the Office of Rail Regulation;
    (iv) the Postal Services Commission; and
    (v) the Water Services Regulation Authority.[120]

2.108   A government minister may by order specify further regulatory functions (and regulators) to which the duty will apply,[121] although at the time of writing, no such orders had been made. Before making such an order, the minister must consult with the regulatory authority whose functions are concerned and any other appropriate person.[122] Such persons would be likely to include the LBRO and the regulated parties.[123] Where the existing *Regulators Compliance Code* is seen to be sufficient, that will also be a factor against extending the s. 72 duty.[124]

The LBRO

2.109   The duties not to impose or maintain unnecessary burdens apply to the LBRO by virtue of s. 13. The LBRO is additionally required under s. 13(3) to ensure that it exercises its functions in a way which is transparent, accountable, proportionate and consistent[125] and that it targets its activities only at cases where action is needed. This is a repetition of the duty imposed on the LBRO by s. 5 (statutory objective in relation to general functions), making it clear that it applies in relation to each of the LBRO's functions.[126]

Extent of the duty

2.110   The duty to remove unnecessary burdens placed on the LBRO and Part 4 regulators, does not require the removal of an unnecessary burden 'where [their] removal would, having regard to all the circumstances, be impractical or disproportionate'.[127] This caveat would apply for example where the costs of lifting the burden would outweigh the benefits.

---

[119] Other than functions exercised under competition law, non-reserved functions in Scotland, transferred matters in Northern Ireland or functions that relate to Welsh ministerial matters.

[120] S. 6 of the Communications Act 2003 places a similar duty on Ofcom.

[121] RESA, s. 73(1)(b).

[122] Ibid., s. 73(6).

[123] BERR, *Regulatory Enforcement and Sanctions Act 2008: Guidance to the Act*, pp 52–3.

[124] Ibid., p. 53; the *Regulators' Compliance Code* provides that '[r]egulators should keep under review their regulatory activities and interventions with a view to considering the extent to which it would be appropriate to remove or reduce the regulatory burdens they impose'.

[125] The Better Regulation Commission's Principles of Good Regulation.

[126] See para. 2.55 for more about the statutory objective.

[127] RESA, ss 13(2) and 72(2).

The reasons for the failure to remove an unnecessary burden in such circumstances must be set out in the annual statement.[128]

2.111

'Unnecessary'

What is an 'unnecessary burden' will be for the person exercising the regulatory function to decide, taking all the circumstances into account. Whilst RESA provides no further definition or list of relevant criteria, the BERR *Regulatory Enforcement and Sanctions Act 2008: Guidance to the Act* suggests that a burden may be unnecessary if the regulator considers that the way it exercises its regulatory function:

2.112

(i) is disproportionate to the regulator's policy objective; that it goes further than is necessary to achieve that objective;

(ii) is targeted at situations where action is not required to achieve that objective; or

(iii) is imposed in circumstances where it is possible achieve the desired outcome in a less burdensome way.[129]

A burden imposed directly by an Act, regulations or order cannot (for the purposes of this legislation at least) be said to be unnecessary.

2.113

Examples of burdens that might well be considered to be unnecessary may include:

2.114

(i) the requirement on a business to use a particular technology to reduce emissions (for example) where cheaper alternative equipment would achieve the same result;

(ii) unnecessary forms, or the needless duplication of paperwork, where (for example) multiple exemptions could be registered in one submission; and

(iii) poorly targeted inspections, where (for example) those with newer equipment or machinery require fewer inspection visits than those with older equipment or machinery.[130]

Review of burdens

Part 4 regulators[131] must also keep the regulatory function under review[132] and 'from time to time' publish statements setting out what the regulator has done, or intends to do, pursuant to the review of the regulatory function.[133] These requirements do not apply to the LBRO.

2.115

Statement of burdens

The first statement should be published as soon as practicable after the review and apply to the twelve months following publication.[134] Subsequently, the review will be a 'rolling process' and statements are required to be published annually.[135] The government does not anticipate that subsequent reviews be as in-depth as the initial one, but states that 'they will need to be sufficient to explore whether any changing circumstances could have led to the

2.116

---

[128] Ibid., s. 72(3)(c).
[129] BERR, *Regulatory Enforcement and Sanctions Act 2008: Guidance to the Act*, p. 49.
[130] Adapted from the BERR, *Regulatory Enforcement and Sanctions Act 2008: Guidance to the Act*, pp. 49–50.
[131] Those listed in s. 73 and any order made pursuant to s. 73(1)(b).
[132] RESA, s. 72(1).
[133] Ibid., s. 72(3).
[134] Ibid., s. 72(4).
[135] Ibid., s. 72(5).

creation of unnecessary burdens or whether more could be done to reduce burdens which remain'.[136]

Status of the statement

2.117 Whilst the Part 4 regulator must 'have regard' to its issued statement,[137] RESA itself provides no direct sanction for failure to have such regard; enforcement decisions taken contrary to the statement may be open to challenge by judicial review however.

2.118 Where such a review or statement produced is inadequate, subsequent action or inaction arising from such a position may also be judicially reviewable on the grounds of procedural impropriety (although it is easy to envisage circumstances where it would be difficult to isolate the specific action or inaction upon which such a claim might be founded).

H. Memoranda of understanding

2.119 The LBRO must enter into statutory memoranda of understanding with certain specified national regulators, setting out how they will work together in the exercise of their respective functions.[138] By virtue of s. 12(2), this applies to the following regulators:

  (i)   the Environment Agency;
  (ii) the Food Standards Agency;
  (iii) the Gambling Commission;
  (iv) the Health and Safety Executive; and
  (v)   the Office of Fair Trading.

2.120 These five regulators were included in particular as their spheres of operation were considered to overlap with those of the LBRO.[139]

At the time of writing, memoranda of understanding have been agreed and signed with the Health and Safety Executive, the Office of Fair Trading, the Financial Services Authority, the Environment Agency, the Gambling Commission and the National Measurement Office. The expectation is that the memoranda will include or facilitate agreements for mutual consultation and other issues arising from their overlapping regulatory duties[140] and the corporate plan published by the LBRO indicates an intention to 'build an excellent organisation, focusing on: stakeholder engagement—understanding the needs and interests of our stakeholders, maximising opportunities to work collaboratively with both regulatory partners and those affected by regulation, including business representatives'.[141]

2.121 The LBRO may also enter into formal or informal agreements with other regulators.[142] The *Coalition for Better Regulation,* coordinated by the LBRO, includes the listed five national regulators amongst others, and is such an example.

---

[136] BERR, *Regulatory Enforcement and Sanctions Act 2008: Guidance to the Act,* p. 54.
[137] RESA, s. 72(7).
[138] Ibid., s. 12.
[139] BERR, *Regulatory Enforcement and Sanctions Act 2008: Explanatory Notes,* para. 42.
[140] BERR, *Regulatory Enforcement and Sanctions Act 2008: Guidance to the Act,* p. 18.
[141] A copy of the corporate plan is available on the LBRO website.
[142] RESA, s. 14. See para. 2.119 above.

I. Guidance or directions by the Secretary of State

The Secretary of State may give guidance or directions to the LBRO as to the exercise of any of its functions.[143]

2.122

Restrictions on directions

The principal restriction on the use of directions by the LBRO under s. 7 in relation to the exercise of its functions in relation to two or more local authorities in England and Wales is that such directions may not be made without an order[144] made by the Secretary of State.[145] In cases involving Welsh ministerial matter, consent must be given by Welsh ministers.[146] Subject to such an order, s. 7 empowers the LBRO to direct local authorities to comply with its own (or another national body's) guidance.

2.123

By s. 15(6), the Secretary of State may not issue a direction to the LBRO on the exercise of its functions in relation to 'two or more local authorities' without an appropriate order.[147]

2.124

Consultation

Before giving either guidance or directions, there is a duty on the Secretary of State to consult the LBRO and other affected persons.[148] Guidance issued by the Secretary of State is published and a copy must be laid before Parliament.[149]

2.125

Variation and revocation

Guidance and directions can only be changed or revoked by the giving of further guidance or directions.[150]

2.126

Status of guidance

In the event such guidance is given, the LBRO is obliged to have regard to it and to comply with any direction so given.[151]

2.127

Guidance or directions by Welsh ministers

Section 16 sets out equivalent and identical powers for Welsh ministers as set out above in relation to England, the only difference being that the copy of the guidance or directions must be laid before the National Assembly for Wales.[152]

2.128

---

[143] Ibid., s. 15(1).
[144] See para. 2.76 (ii) above.
[145] RESA, s. 7(4).
[146] Ibid., s. 7(3).
[147] Ibid., s. 15(7).
[148] Ibid., s. 15(2).
[149] Ibid., s. 15(3)(b).
[150] Ibid., s. 15(5).
[151] Ibid., s. 15(4).
[152] Ibid., s. 16(3)(b).

3

ENFORCEMENT BY PRIMARY AUTHORITIES

A. Introduction

By far the most radical of the reforms in RESA, in respect of local authority regulatory **3.01** enforcement at least, are found in Part 2, and concern the creation and operation of primary authority partnerships. This chapter provides a step-by-step guide on how local authorities should go about entering into such arrangements, as well as a detailed analysis of their statutory obligations once in a partnership. The final part of this chapter is concerned with the Local Better Regulation Office's role in respect of primary authority partnerships, with particular focus on its important dispute resolution function.

B. Overview of the primary authority partnership scheme

Introduction

Part 2 of RESA introduced a revolutionary new scheme designed to coordinate regulatory **3.02** enforcement across local authority boundaries, with the twin aims of improving the way local regulators work with businesses, charities and other organizations (referred to throughout this text as businesses) and easing the regulatory burdens placed on businesses. Historically, local authorities have had the responsibility of enforcing regulations in areas such as health and safety and food and product safety, only against those businesses trading within their boundaries. This has often led to a wide variation in inspection and enforcement standards and to disproportionate burdens being placed on certain authorities due to the concentration of particular businesses within their locality.[1]

3.03 Through the creation of new legal partnerships known as primary authorities, local authorities will be able to advise and assist businesses in all matters concerned with regulation, where those businesses trade across council boundaries.

3.04 Where primary authority agreements are in place, primary authorities will act as a single, authoritative source of advice in the areas of environmental health, licensing and trading standards legislation, which will apply regardless of where a business's factories or stores are based or where their products are sold.[2]

3.05 The primary authority scheme has its origins in Sir Philip Hampton's report:

[t]rading standards and environmental health laws are designed to provide a broadly similar level of protection to all citizens of the country. The review believes that action needs to be taken to make services more consistent across the country.[3]

3.06 Hampton was convinced that the best way to ensure consistency of service provision by local authorities was through the creation of a central partnership between local authorities, government departments and national regulators. Although his vision was not fully realized, the important underlying concept of the coordination of regulatory enforcement was carried through, with the establishment of these new legal partnerships.[4]

The home authority principle

3.07 The precursor to the primary authority scheme was the 'home' authority principle,[5] an informal agreement between local authorities that had cross-boundary issues relating to either trading standards or food, allowing the home authority to liaise between businesses and other local authorities on matters of regulatory responsibilities.

3.08 Whilst the primary authority scheme is intended to develop the home and lead[6] authority schemes, they will continue to operate if businesses wish to maintain those relationships. This is likely to be the case, particularly in Scotland and Northern Ireland where the primary authority scheme does not extend to the devolved functions of regulatory enforcement.

---

[1] For example, many multiples are based in the City of London or the City of Westminster, and so these authorities have a disproportionately high home authority burden. Philip Hampton, *Reducing Administrative Burdens: Effective Inspection and Enforcement*, p. 74, para. 4.105.

[2] Partnerships can specify which areas of environmental health, licensing and trading standards legislation they wish their partnersip to cover.

[3] Hampton, *Reducing Administrative Burdens: Effective Inspection and Enforcement*, p. 75, para. 4.106.

[4] Hampton recommended the establishment of the National Regulatory Forum which could act as a partnership arrangement between government departments, national regulators, and local authorities.

[5] The home authority would be the local authority with the company's head office or main production centre in its area.

[6] The lead authority scheme covers health and safety legislation and is led by the Health and Safety Executive.

Key elements of the primary authority scheme

The primary authority scheme was launched by the Local Better Regulation Office (LBRO) **3.09**
on 6 April 2009.[7] The operation of the scheme is the statutory responsibility of the LBRO,
which has the function of formally nominating and registering the partnerships, as well as
resolving disputes between enforcing authorities, businesses and primary authorities.

According to the Local Better Regulation Office, by 2011 it is expected that hundreds **3.10**
of companies will be in such a partnership. At the time of the introduction of the scheme,
the government estimated that businesses could save £48 m a year through its operation.
Although take up was initially slow,[8] the LBRO is moving ever closer to achieving its target
of having 200 schemes in operation by 2011; at the time of publication of this work, over
125 partnerships were in existence, spread over dozens of local authorities. A full and updated
list of partnerships can be found on the LBRO website.[9]

Primary authority partnerships may either be forged at the request of a particular business or **3.11**
they may be proposed by a local authority and a business jointly, for example as a natural
progression from an existing home authority relationship. Where a business cannot find a
partner, it can ask the LBRO to help them find a suitable authority to work with.

The partnerships can cover the full range of regulatory services or just specific functions, such **3.12**
as product labelling or licensing. It may be that the LBRO nominates one local authority as
the primary authority in respect of one relevant function for the business in question (for
example, trading standard matters) and a different authority in respect of another relevant
functions (for example, environmental health matters).[10]

The scheme attempts to strike a balance, allowing businesses to grow and prosper, without **3.13**
compromising consumer protection, and in doing so benefits businesses, local authorities
and consumers alike. For businesses, the scheme will eliminate the possibility of their receiving contradictory or inconsistent enforcement actions from local authorities, whilst reducing regulatory burdens through the reduction of unwarranted enforcement actions and
(where an inspection plan is in place) through the reduction in unnecessary checks and
tests.[11] For local authorities, because the question of resourcing the partnership is left up to
the businesses and local authority concerned, the primary authority may provide for the
recovery of the costs of the service. As the BERR *Regulatory Enforcement and Sanctions Act
2008: Explanatory Notes* explain, for local authorities, the ultimate benefits will be an increase
in their operational efficiency and effectiveness.[12]

---

[7] The Regulatory Enforcement and Sanctions Act 2008 (Commencement No. 1) Order 2008,
SI 2371/2008.
[8] Three partnerships were established when the scheme was launched in April 2008: B&Q (Eastleigh);
Moto (Central Bedfordshire); and Iceland (Flintshire). In July 2008, two new partnerships were launched:
Boots (Nottinghamshire); and the Trading Standards Institute (Essex).
[9] <www.lbro.org.uk>.
[10] BERR, *Regulatory Enforcement and Sanctions Act 2008: Explanatory Notes*, para. 69.
[11] BERR, *Regulatory Enforcement and Sanctions Act 2008: Guidance to the Act*, p. 20.
[12] At p. 20.

C. Who can enter into a partnership?

Introduction

3.14 The primary authority scheme is open to any business operating across council boundaries where they are regulated by two or more local authorities in respect of the relevant function.

3.15 Section 25(1) provides that the LBRO may nominate a *local authority* to be the primary authority for the exercise of the *relevant function* in relation to the *regulated person*. The nomination of the primary authority is one of the Local Better Regulation Office's most important functions.

3.16 Businesses that might want to enter into a partnership include:[13]

    (i) a multi-site retailer with branches in a number of local authority areas;
    (ii) a food manufacturer whose goods are distributed for sale across a number of local authority areas;
    (iii) an internet retailer who sells goods or services over a wide area;
    (iv) a tour operator whose customers may be located in any area;
    (v) an importer whose products are distributed nationally;
    (vi) a chain of gyms with outlets in a number of local authority areas;
    (vii) a charitable care home provider with premises in several local authority areas;
    (viii) a national chain of petrol filling stations; or
    (ix) a restaurant company that offers franchises across several local authority areas but retains central control of particular relevant functions.

3.17 This part deals with the provisions in Part 2 concerning those bodies that may enter into a partnership, and in respect of which regulatory functions, by reference to the terms, *local authority, regulated person* and *relevant function*.[14]

Local authority

3.18 Any local authority in England, Wales, Scotland or Northern Ireland may be nominated as a primary authority,[15] although what constitutes such an entity differs depending on whether the authority is based in England, Wales, Scotland or Northern Ireland.

3.19 According to s. 23(2), in England and Wales, a local authority is any one of the following bodies:

In England:[16]
    (i) a county or district council in England;
    (ii) a London borough council;
    (iii) the Common Council of the City of London;
    (iv) the Sub-Treasurer of the Inner Temple and the Under-Treasurer of the Middle Temple;

---

[13] LBRO, *Primary Authority Guidance*, p. 6, para. 2.
[14] RESA, s. 25(1).
[15] Ibid., ss 23(1) and 25(1).
[16] Ibid., s. 3(1).

(v) the Council of the Isles of Scilly;

(vi) a fire and rescue authority in England (not being an authority referred to in paras (a)–(e));

(vii) a port health authority in England (not being an authority referred to in paras (a)–(e)); and

(viii) an authority established under s. 10 of the Local Government Act1985 (c. 51) (waste disposal authorities for Greater London and metropolitan counties).

In Wales:[17]

(i) a county or county borough council in Wales;

(ii) a fire and rescue authority in Wales (not being a county or county borough council);

(iii) a port health authority in Wales (not being a county or county borough council).

For the purposes of Part 2, references to a local authority in Scotland are to a council constituted under s. 2 of the Local Government etc. (Scotland) Act 1994 (c. 39).[18]   **3.20**

References to a local authority in Northern Ireland are to a district council constituted under s. 1 of the Local Government Act (Northern Ireland) 1972 (c. 9). [19]   **3.21**

Regulated person

The term 'regulated person' is defined in s. 22(2) as any person that carries on an *activity* in the area of two or more local authorities. A regulated person is eligible to form a primary authority partnership where the (two or more) local authorities have the same *relevant function* in relation to the activity that they (the regulated person) are carrying on.[20]   **3.22**

The council nominated as the primary authority need not be the council closest to the company HQ or even the existing lead or home authority.   **3.23**

Activity

No definition of what constitutes an 'activity' is provided in RESA. According to the BERR *Regulatory Enforcement and Sanctions Act 2008: Guidance to the Act*,[21] the types of activity that are envisaged include those carried out directly, such as the activities of retailers with outlets across the country, as well as those performed by single site businesses which indirectly makes them subject to regulatory enforcement by a number of local authorities. This will include activities such as internet-based sales, or manufacture where products are sold on by others. An example of an eligible business would be a retailer that sells a product in two different local authorities and is subject to regulatory enforcement by trading standards in both those authorities.[22]   **3.24**

---

[17] Ibid., s. 3(2).

[18] Ibid., s. 23(3).

[19] Ibid., s. 23(4).

[20] Ibid., s. 22(1)(b).

[21] At p. 19.

[22] BERR, *Regulatory Enforcement and Sanctions Act 2008: Explanatory Notes*, p. 13, para. 61.

Relevant function

Overview

3.25 A local authority may only enter into a partnership in respect of those relevant functions for which it has regulatory responsibility. The term 'relevant function' is defined in s. 24 and the orders made under RESA, and broadly covers matters that are commonly referred to as trading standards, environmental health and licensing legislation. The applicability of Part 2 varies depending on where the authority is based.

3.26 The LBRO has allocated the relevant regulatory enforcement enactments applicable to all local authorities in the UK into eighteen separate categories of relevant function. These categories range from agriculture to health and safety and pollution control, and include all the relevant functions within the scope of the primary authority. The full list of categories appears in the LBRO, *Primary Authority Guidance*.[23] Whilst businesses may enter into different partnerships with different primary authorities in respect of different categories of relevant function,[24] the LBRO recommends that wherever possible, partnerships should cover one or more of the complete categories of relevant function.[25]

3.27 Whether or not a local authority has a relevant function in relation to the regulated person (eligible business) depends upon the geographical location of that authority, as the scheme operates differently in different parts of the UK.[26]

3.28 In England and Wales, the primary authority scheme is available for *all* relevant functions exercised by local authorities. The scope of Part 2 is limited in respect of the devolved administrations of Scotland and Northern Ireland.[27]

England and Wales

3.29 For local authorities in England and Wales, ss 24 and 4 read together, provide that a relevant function is either:

(i) a function under a relevant enactment of imposing requirements, restrictions or conditions, or setting standards or giving guidance, in relation to any activity;[28] or

(ii) a function that relates to the securing of compliance with, or the enforcement of, requirements, restrictions, conditions, standards or guidance which under or by virtue of a relevant enactment relate to an activity.[29]

3.30 The relevant enactments are set out in full at Sch. 3 and broadly include legislation relating to consumer protection, the environment, health and safety and trading standards. Schedule 3 is reproduced in full at Appendix 1.

---

[23] A copy is available on the LBRO website.

[24] For example, retailer 'A' may enter into a partnership with district council 'B' for health and safety, with county council 'C' for product safety and food standards, and with fire authority 'D' for petroleum and explosives licensing: LBRO, *Primary Authority Guidance*, p. 7, para. 6.

[25] LBRO, *Primary Authority Guidance*, p. 6, para. 5.

[26] RESA, s. 24.

[27] Section 24(6) provides that 'transferred matter' and 'Northern Ireland' have the same meanings as in the Northern Ireland Act 1998 (c. 47).

[28] RESA, s. 4(1)(a).

[29] RESA, s. 4(1)(b).

Scotland

In relation to local authorities in Scotland, a relevant function is defined as a regulatory func- **3.31** tion exercised by that authority and specified by an order made by the Secretary of State.[30] Schedule 1 of the Co-ordination of Regulatory Enforcement (Regulatory Functions in Scotland and Northern Ireland) Order 2009[31] (the 2009 Order) lists those functions that are specified in relation to a local authority in Scotland.

Relevant functions that have been devolved to the Scottish government, such as food stan- **3.32** dards and food hygiene, are outside the scope of the primary authority.[32] The 2009 Order is reproduced in full at Appendix 3.

Northern Ireland

Schedule 2 of the 2009 Order lists those functions that are specified in relation to a local **3.33** authority in Northern Ireland. These are principally in the product safety category.

D. Establishing a primary authority partnership

Introduction

The LBRO may register a primary authority partnership where the local authority and the **3.34** business have agreed in writing to establish such a partnership[33] or, alternatively, where a business or organization has not been able to reach an agreement with a local authority and the business requests the LBRO to nominate a local authority to be its primary authority.[34] In both cases, the LBRO must be satisfied that the authority is suitable for nomination.[35]

Where a business wishes to enter into a partnership but has not yet found a willing and suit- **3.35** able local authority, it can request the LBRO to nominate a primary authority. The LBRO will consult with any local authority it considers might be suitable, as well as the regulated person.[36] Where a potential primary authority is identified by the LBRO, the authority will then need to work with the business to develop an agreement.

Where an authority and a business have agreed that the local authority will be the primary **3.36** authority, all that is needed for the LBRO to register a primary authority partnership is a completed and signed legal agreement (known as a primary authority agreement) between the business and the local authority. The parties will then need to request the LBRO to nominate the local authority as the primary authority, using the template on the website.[37] The LBRO will then assess the local authority's suitability for nomination and, where they are deemed to be suitable, enter them onto the register[38] and notify both parties accordingly.

---

[30] RESA, s. 24(1)(b).
[31] SI 669/2009. In force 6 April 2009.
[32] LBRO, *Primary Authority Guidance*, p. 7, para. 10.
[33] RESA, s. 26(1)(a).
[34] Ibid., s. 26(1)(b).
[35] Ibid., s. 26(1).
[36] Ibid., s. 26(3). Section 26(4) requires that the LBRO must pay particular regard to any representations made by the proposed primary authority regarding the resources available to it.
[37] <www.lbro.org.uk>.
[38] RESA, s. 26(6).

3.37 Where necessary, fledgling partnerships will be assigned an account manager by the LBRO, to advise and guide the partners through the process of setting up and running the partnership.

Guidance for contracting partners

3.38 In addition to the RESA *Explanatory Notes* and the BERR *Guidance to the Act* (as to which see para. 4.47), parties entering into primary authority schemes should have regard to the following four further sources of guidance in respect of the setting up and operation of the partnerships:

    (i) LBRO *Primary Authority Guidance*, published March 2009;
    (ii) LBRO *Primary Authority Mini-Guides*, published June 2010:
        a. *Advice*
        b. *Inspection Plans*
        c. *Resourcing Partnerships*;
    (iii) Westminster City Council *Primary Authority in Practice: Insight for Local Authorities*, published May 2010; and
    (iv) *LBRO References to LBRO for Determinations Policy and Procedure*, published January 2010.

LBRO Primary Authority Guidance

3.39 In March 2009, the LBRO issued *Primary Authority Guidance* about the operation of Part 2, aimed at local authorities and businesses entering into primary authority partnerships. This guidance is to be read in conjunction with RESA and any orders made under it. By virtue of s. 33, local authorities are obliged to have regard to this guidance before acting. See paras 2.70–2.71 for more about the LBRO's functions in relation to the publication of guidance.

LBRO Primary Authority Mini-Guides

3.40 These guides are available on the LBRO website and are supplementary to the statutory guidance published pursuant to s. 33. The guides on advising businesses and producing inspection plans are intended for primary authority officers, while the guide on establishing effective resourcing arrangements for partnerships is aimed at local authorities. They provide practical advice based on the experiences of the scheme to date; there is no requirement on local authorities to follow the guidance in these papers.

Westminster City Council, Primary Authority in Practice: Insight for Local Authorities

3.41 This publication, *Primary Authority in Practice: Insight for Local Authorities*, is intended to provide an insight into the experiences of Westminster City Council in the setting up of a primary authority with the aim of assisting other local authorities wishing to do the same. It provides particularly helpful advice as to costing considerations and actions taken to ease the transition from the voluntary home and lead authority schemes into the new approach. There is no requirement on local authorities to have regard to this guide when setting up a primary authority.

LBRO References to LBRO for Determinations Policy and Procedure

3.42 In January 2010, the LBRO published guidance on their website as to the LBRO determination procedure for references from primary authorities, enforcing authorities and businesses.

The document 'indicates the conduct that LBRO will expect of parties to the determination process'.[39] Particularly detailed guidance is provided about the factors that the LBRO will take into account when making decisions about consent and determination applications.

The guidance has no legal force and should be read alongside RESA and the orders made under it. A copy appears at Appendix 4.   **3.43**

The primary authority agreement

The first step in the process of applying for a partnership will involve the partners reaching agreement on those matters which will be covered in the primary authority agreement. This is a formal, legally binding agreement between the parties. The LBRO, in their *Sample agenda for the first meeting of a potential primary authority partnership*,[40] suggest that these early negotiations include a number of key considerations, covering matters such as which categories of legislation should be covered and how the partnership should be resourced. The *LBRO: Primary Authority Guidance*[41] requires that the decisions reached on these matters are reflected in the primary authority agreement, which should additionally include the following: **3.44**

  (i) the name of the legal entity or entities covered by the agreement;
  (ii) the category or categories of relevant function covered;
 (iii) the geographical scope of the partnership—this should coincide with all the areas of the UK where the relevant function is within scope;
 (iv) the limitations of liability;
  (v) details of the resource requirements of the partnership and how these will be provided, including the basis for any charges that will be made;
 (vi) a statement about the status of information provided to and by the local authority and the LBRO in respect of the Freedom of Information Act 2000, or the Freedom of Information (Scotland) Act 2002;
 (vii) arrangements for handling notifications of proposed enforcement action;
(viii) arrangements for reviewing the agreement; and
 (ix) arrangements for terminating the agreement.

Partnerships are encouraged to use the template agreement, which can be found on the LBRO website, although it is recognized that this will need to be adapted to suit the particular partnership.   **3.45**

The terms of the agreement can be amended at a later stage; the LBRO recommend using the *Primary Authority Change Agreement* template for this purpose, which can also be found on their website.   **3.46**

Assessment of suitability

The Local Better Regulation Office must assess the suitability of any proposed partnership before it may nominate a local authority as a primary authority.[42] This stands whether the   **3.47**

---

[39] Para. 1.9.
[40] Available on the LBRO website: <www.lbro.org.uk>.
[41] Pursuant to RESA, s. 33.
[42] RESA, s. 26.

partnership is one reached by mutual agreement, or where the primary authority has been nominated by the LBRO.

3.48 In determining whether, in principle, the partnership is a suitable one, the LBRO will have regard to the statutory guidance provided in RESA, supplemented by the guidance in the BERR *Regulatory Enforcement and Sanctions Act 2008: Guidance to the Act.*

3.49 Section 26(2) of RESA suggests as a starting point that the local authority in whose area the regulated person principally carries out the activity in relation to which the relevant function is exercised, and the local authority in whose area the regulated person administers the carrying out of that activity, may be suitable candidates for primary authority status.

3.50 The BERR *Regulatory Enforcement and Sanctions Act 2008: Guidance to the Act*[43] anticipates that the LBRO will additionally take into account the location of the business and where it carries out its activities, the resources and capacity of the local authority, and any relevant specialism of the local authority.

3.51 Turning to the detail of the proposed arrangements, when assessing suitability, the LBRO must assess the agreement against the following criteria:[44]

    (i) the adequacy of the proposed arrangements for resourcing the partnership;

    (ii) the relevant expertise of the local authority;

    (iii) any proposed arrangements for preparing relevant local authority staff for the primary authority role; and

    (iv) the commitment of both parties to making the proposed arrangements operate effectively.

Where LBRO makes a nomination

3.52 Where the LBRO is asked by a business to nominate a local authority as the primary authority, and prior to making any assessment of their suitability, the LBRO must consult with the local authority and the regulated person. Such nominations may be made without the consent of the local authority concerned, such is the importance placed upon all authorities having access to the scheme. Where that is the case, the LBRO must pay particular regard to any representations made by the local authority in respect of the resources that are available to it.[45]

Resourcing the partnership

Introduction

3.53 The resourcing of the partnership is a crucial decision that should be made at the outset of the negotiations between partners. According to the LBRO, the funding of primary authorities is a crucial feature in their effective operation:

> [e]ffective primary authorities, providing reliable advice to business and supporting regulators nationwide, need to have expertise and appropriate resources. Many local authorities see the importance of helping local companies comply with the law, and may offer some Primary

---

[43] At p. 19.
[44] LBRO *Primary Authority Guidance*, p. 11, para. 29.
[45] RESA, s. 26(3) and (4).

Authority services at a reduced rate or for free. However, the law allows local authorities that provide Primary Authority services to recover their costs from the business.[46]

The LBRO report that the experience of local authorities in established partnerships is that businesses are willing to pay for the benefits of the scheme where they are satisfied that the proposed charges are 'transparent and reasonable, and justified by the expected benefits'.[47] **3.54**

The LBRO has issued guidance on fee charges in the form of the LBRO mini-guide, *Primary Authority: Resourcing Partnerships;* the following should be read in conjunction with the advice in that publication. **3.55**

Partnerships need first to consider what resources they will need to fund their functions and, second, how they will meet those costs, whether by cost recovery or otherwise; this part looks at both considerations in turn. **3.56**

Assessing the resource requirements

It will be for the partners to decide how to resource their primary authority responsibilities and these discussions should take place at the very outset of the negotiations. The resources required will vary widely between partnerships, but as the LBRO *Primary Authority Guidance* cautions, both parties will need to have a clear understanding of the needs of the business for regulatory advice, the expectations of the business, and the scope of the service being offered by the local authority, in order that there is a shared understanding of how the partnership will be resourced. **3.57**

The LBRO *Primary Authority Guidance* suggests that particular regard should be paid to the necessary resources needed to deliver the requirements of local authorities in respect of the provision of advice and guidance about how they should exercise their relevant functions in relation to the business; the setting of inspection plans; and advising on and responding to proposed enforcement actions.[48] Partners should also '... consider the amount of staff resource and the level of expertise needed, both in terms of knowledge of the relevant function and understanding of this business and its practices'.[49] **3.58**

Because the scheme is new, partnerships may wish to undertake a comprehensive review of their arrangements for resourcing once they have experience of the scheme, revising the agreement if necessary. **3.59**

Applying cost recovery

Once the partnership has made an assessment of its resource requirements, the local authority and the business will need to agree how the costs will be met. Should it wish to do so, a primary authority will be able to charge fees to a partner business or organization to recover costs 'reasonably incurred' in acting as the primary authority for the business or organization.[50] If local authorities do impose a charge, then this is capped at a maximum of full cost recovery.[51] **3.60**

---

[46] See the LBRO website: <www.lbro.org.uk>.
[47] LBRO *Primary Authority: Resourcing Partnerships*, p. 3.
[48] P. 8, para. 18.
[49] LBRO *Primary Authority Guidance*, p. 9, para. 19.
[50] RESA, s. 31.
[51] See *Resourcing your Partnership* at <http://www.lbro.org.uk>.

3.61 The approach taken by local authorities to the funding of primary authority services should be consistent with the council's overall approach to supporting local businesses. According to the LBRO *Primary Authority Guidance*, the local authority should consider the following when considering the extent to which businesses should be charged:

    (i) the local authority's policy in respect of supporting local economic prosperity;

    (ii) the existing resources provided to this business (both by the regulatory service and by other services of the local authority);

    (iii) any responsibility to provide free advice and guidance to the business under the Regulators' Compliance Code;[52]

    (iv) the requirement of the Regulators' Compliance Code, where applicable, that where advice and guidance go beyond basic advice and guidance, any charges should be reasonable; and

    (v) when advice and guidance have been developed for use with more than one business, an individual business should pay no more than a reasonable proportion of the costs.

3.62 Some local authorities already participating in the scheme have adopted a model whereby a limited and specified level of support is funded by the local authority, with any further additional support being charged to the business.

3.63 The LBRO *Primary Authority: Resourcing Partnerships* mini-guide suggests that consideration should also be given to matters such as the cost recovery rate (which must be calculated in accordance with the *HM Treasury Guidance: Managing Public Money*[53]) and whether charges will be made on the basis of an hourly rate or a monthly charge.[54]

3.64 Where services are already provided under a lead or home authority arrangement, these can be transitioned into primary authority and in many cases local authorities will only seek to recover any additional costs incurred.

Register of partnerships

3.65 The LBRO must maintain a list of partnerships on their website, providing access to information about local authority enforcement to all its stakeholders. [55]

Ending a partnership

By LBRO revocation

3.66 As well as having the power to create primary authorities, the LBRO has the power to dissolve them. Section 26(5) provides that the LBRO may at any time revoke a nomination under this part if, having consulted the authority and the regulated person, it considers that either the authority is no longer suitable for nomination, or it is appropriate to do so for any other reason, for example where the partnership is simply failing.

3.67 If the LBRO is considering such a revocation, they must have particular regard to any representations made by the local authority as to the resources made available to it.[56]

---

[52] See para. 4.35 for more about the Regulator's Compliance Code.
[53] Annex 2. Available on HM Treasury website: <www.hm-treasury.gov.uk>.
[54] At p. 6.
[55] See RESA, s. 26(6).
[56] RESA, s. 26(4).

This provision might be used to end a primary authority partnership where the business or **3.68** organization no longer require the primary authority, or where a change of primary authority is required for whatever reason. This may happen where a business is relocating or where a change of ownership means that the decision-making base of the business moves. However, it could also be used where a partnership is no longer effective due to irreconcilable differences between the parties.[57]

By agreement

There are no specific provisions in RESA permitting a primary authority to be changed **3.69** to another local authority, or for a primary authority to seek to terminate their status altogether. According to the LBRO *Primary Authority Guidance*, this is something that can be provided for in the primary authority agreement; indeed the standard LBRO terms and conditions contain such provisions. When a notification is received by either party wishing to terminate the partnership, the LBRO should consider whether to consult with the parties before revoking its nomination of the partnership.[58] Given the comments by the LBRO, that this was a 'purely administrative process and that LBRO would readily issue revocation notices if this was requested',[59] it is likely that such requests will readily be acceded to.

In either case, where the LBRO decides to revoke a nomination, both parties will be notified **3.70** and the register amended.

E. Functions of primary authorities

Overview

Once registered with the LBRO, a primary authority partnership has a number of key **3.71** statutory functions, as provided for in ss 27–30 of RESA.[60] These are:

  (i) providing advice and guidance to business: s. 27(1)(a);
 (ii) providing advice and guidance to local authorities: s. 27(1)(b);
(iii) checking the consistency of enforcement action taken by local authorities: ss. 28 and 29; and
 (iv) making inspection plans: s. 30.

The Department for Business Innovation and Skills (BIS) expects that in order to make the **3.72** partnership successful, the partner business will be expected to work closely with the primary authority and other local authorities to ensure that they comply with the regulations that apply to them.[61]

---

[57] See BERR, *Regulatory Enforcement and Sanctions Act 2008: Guidance to the Act*, p. 26.
[58] P. 11, para. 30.
[59] See the *Primary Authority in Practice: Insight for Local Authorities*, p. 11.
[60] RESA, s. 25(2).
[61] BERR, *Regulatory Enforcement and Sanctions Act 2008: Guidance to the Act,* p. 21, para. 22.

Advice and guidance

3.73   The main function of a primary authority is the provision of advice; in entering a primary authority partnership, the local authority accepts responsibility for being the principal source for local authority regulatory advice and guidance to businesses.

3.74   According to s. 27, advice and guidance must be given by the primary authority to:

   (i)   the regulated person[62] in relation to the relevant function[63] (advice to businesses); and

   (ii) other local authorities with the relevant function as to how they should exercise it in relation to the regulated person (advice to local authorities).

3.75   There are no further provisions in RESA as to the nature, content or form of this advice and guidance, nor as to the frequency with which it must be given.[64]

Primary authority advice to businesses

3.76   Businesses in a partnership will be able to seek bespoke, tailored advice about the routes to compliance, from a primary authority that has a sound understanding of the legislation and the partner business. The advice will assist the business in choosing a route to compliance that will be acceptable to all regulators[65] and protect them should the advice be challenged by another local authority.[66]

3.77   Primary authority advice to businesses can cover any aspect of compliance in the categories of relevant function defined in the primary authority agreement, ranging from help in identifying or interpreting legal requirements, to assurance that their compliance systems are accepted. The advice and guidance may supplement any inspection plan made under s. 30.[67]

Agreement as to the provision of advice

3.78   Section 27(2) provides that the primary authority *may* make arrangements with the regulated person as to how it will discharge this function. As the RESA *Explanatory Notes to the Act* suggest, this might include 'entering into an agreement or memorandum of understanding which sets out the rights and obligations of each party'.[68]

The nature of the advice

3.79   Primary authority advice to businesses can cover any matter relating to compliance in legislative areas covered by the partnership, dealing with matters as diverse as food labelling, and the prevention of personal injury at work.[69]

---

[62] See paras 3.22–3.23.

[63] See paras 3.25–3.33.

[64] See para. 2.70 and LBRO, *Primary Authority Guidance* and the *Primary Authority Advice: Providing Assurance* publications.

[65] LBRO, *Primary Authority Advice: Providing Assurance,* p. 3.

[66] Ibid., p. 2.

[67] See paras 3.135–3.160 for more about inspection plans.

[68] P. 23, para. 72.

[69] For practical examples of the types of advice that the LBRO can issue see: LBRO, *Primary Authority Advice: Providing Assurance*, p. 4.

According to the LBRO, the primary authority will need to consider and agree with the business key aspects of the advice to be provided.[70] Importantly, and in order to protect the primary authority and the businesses, the agreement needs to make clear how the status of the advice will be attributed, differentiating between advice that is 'primary authority advice' and that which is not. The LBRO *Primary Authority Guidance* gives more general guidance about the nature of the advice.[71]

Status of the advice

Prior to April 2009, a business seeking to rely on the advice of a local authority (under the lead or home authority scheme) would have had no protection against challenges to their approach brought by another local authority. In the future, where a business has acted upon the advice given by the primary authority, it will be able to rely on that advice if challenged by another local authority. **3.80**

A local authority wishing subsequently to take enforcement action against a regulated person (a business) can be refused permission to so act by the primary authority, provided such direction is given within five working days beginning with the day after that on which the primary authority was notified of the proposed action,[72] if the proposed enforcement action is inconsistent with any advice and guidance previously given by the primary authority.[73] **3.81**

The LBRO recognizes that the primary authority is not able to give a definitive interpretation of the law, only giving an 'informed and professional view' of it.[74] **3.82**

Publication of advice

Unsurprisingly, given the potential for commercially sensitive data to be involved, there is no statutory requirement that the primary authority need publish the advice that they give to businesses, although they would need to be able to produce this advice in relation to a request from enforcing authorities. The LBRO website has a facility to enable partnerships to provide additional information to local authorities through a secure area, where both parties agree to that course of action. **3.83**

Updating of advice

The primary authority agreement should include a provision reflecting the partners' agreement about the maximum interval at which the advice will be reviewed and updated. According to the LBRO publication, *Primary Authority Advice, Providing Assurance,* '… a review of the advice should take into account any feedback received from enforcing authorities and should be seen as an opportunity to improve systems and procedures'.[75] **3.84**

---

[70] LBRO, *Primary Authority Guidance*, p. 12, para. 34.
[71] P. 13, para. 37.
[72] Or such longer period beginning with that day as the LBRO may direct.
[73] RESA, s. 28(2).
[74] LBRO, *Primary Authority Advice: Providing Assurance*, p. 2.
[75] P. 6.

Funding the advice

3.85   The resources required to fund the provision of this advice will, according to Hampton, simply be redirected from the cessation of unnecessary inspections (through the provision of inspection plans).[76]

3.86   Where a primary authority wishes to recover the costs of the provision of some or all of this advice, they may do so having reached agreement with the partner business.[77] See further paras 3.53–3.64 for more about resourcing a primary authority partnership.

Primary authority advice to local authorities

3.87   The provision of advice and guidance to local authorities is aimed at improving the consistency of enforcement.[78]

3.88   The advice may be given to one or more local authorities where they have responsibility for the relevant functions covered by the partnership, and must relate to the exercise of those functions in relation to the business. The LBRO anticipates, however, that unlike advice to businesses, this advice will normally be issued to all local authorities, rather than being targeted to any specific authority.[79]

Nature of the advice

3.89   The LBRO *Primary Authority Guidance* provides suggestions as to the general nature of the advice, and specifically provides that it:

  (i)   should relate to a specific issue where the primary authority is actively addressing compliance on a national level with the business;
  (ii) should be time limited where it relates to improvement activity of the business;
  (iii) should not relate to the frequency or conduct of inspections, or the risk assessment of the business (which may be dealt with in an inspection plan);
  (iv) may relate to the precautions that the business is taking to achieve compliance, but should not relate to the local exercise of due diligence in following the nationally agreed precautions; and
  (v)   may be used as a basis for directing against enforcement action if the primary authority subsequently receives a notification of proposed enforcement action that would be inconsistent with the advice.[80]

Publication of advice

3.90   The LBRO *Primary Authority Guidance* suggests that as a matter of good practice, primary authority advice to local authorities should be communicated through the LBRO's secure website, although there is no statutory requirement to do so.

---

[76] Philip Hampton, *Reducing Administrative Burdens: Effective Inspection and Enforcement*, p. 11, para. 12.
[77] RESA, s. 31.
[78] LBRO *Primary Authority Guidance*, p. 18, para. 55.
[79] Ibid., para. 53.
[80] P. 18, para. 54.

Oversight of enforcement action

The oversight and supervision of enforcement action taken by local authorities against busi- **3.91**
nesses is the second key aspect of the primary authorities' role. According to s. 28(1): '… a
local authority other than the primary authority ("the enforcing authority") must notify the
primary authority before taking any enforcement action against the regulated person pursuant to the relevant function'.

Where a business has a primary authority relationship in respect of any of its relevant func- **3.92**
tions, any other local authority must notify the primary authority of proposed enforcement
action against the business concerned. The primary authority may then consent to the proposed action or, in certain circumstances, direct the enforcing authority not to proceed.

This function is designed to improve the consistency of enforcement action taken against **3.93**
those businesses that trade across local authority boundaries through the facilitation of effective discussions between local authorities, regulators and businesses.

Definition of 'enforcement action'

'Enforcement action' includes prosecutions, stop notices and simple cautions, and is defined **3.94**
in RESA and the order[81] made under it.[82]

Section 28(5) provides that enforcement action is: **3.95**

  (i) any action related to securing compliance with any restriction, requirement or condition in the event of breach (or putative breach) of a restriction, requirement or
condition;

 (ii) any action taken with a view to, or in connection with, the imposition of any sanction
(criminal or otherwise) in respect of an act or omission; and

(iii) any action taken with a view to or in connection with the pursuit of any remedy
conferred by an enactment in respect of an act or omission.

The Co-ordination of Regulatory Enforcement (Enforcement Action) Order 2009[83] (the **3.96**
2009 (Enforcement Action) Order) has supplemented this wide definition through the
provision of detailed guidance specifying the types of action that are to be considered as
'enforcement action' for these purposes.

Action taken under the following enactments is specifically excluded from the definition of **3.97**
'enforcement action' by the 2009 (Enforcement Action) Order, and thus the prior notification requirements: the Regulatory Reform (Fire Safety) Order 2005, the Licensing Act 2003,
and the Gambling Act 2005.[84] The 2009 (Enforcement Action) Order is reproduced in full
at Appendix 5.

Investigatory activities into suspected non-compliance are not considered to fall within **3.98**
the meaning of enforcement action and as such, do not require formal notification to the
primary authority. The LBRO *Primary Authority Guidance* provides a list of examples of such
activities.

---

[81] The Co-ordination of Regulatory Enforcement (Enforcement Action) Order 2009, SI 665/2009.
[82] Pursuant to RESA, s. 28(6).
[83] SI 665/2009.
[84] The Co-ordination of Regulatory Enforcement ((Enforcement Action)) Order 2009, art. 2, para. 2.

3.99 The LBRO maintain that, despite the absence of a statutory obligation on local authorities to notify the primary authority of investigatory activities, 'authorities will clearly benefit from a dialogue with the primary authority in relation to certain of these activities'. [85]

Notification and determination procedure

Overview

3.100 The procedure for the formal notification of proposed enforcement action by the local authority, and determination by the primary authority, is provided for in ss 28–29 of RESA and the 2009 (Enforcement Action) order, and summarized in Figure 3.1.[86]

3.101 Other than in certain limited circumstances,[87] once the local authority has formally notified the primary authority of its intention to act, they must wait for five working days before they may continue to so do.[88] At the end of that period (the relevant period), the local authority may continue with the proposed action where the primary authority have either consented to the proposed action or have not responded at all, so long as they inform the regulated person of their intention to act.[89] A primary authority may only refuse to give consent where the proposed enforcement action is inconsistent with some previously issued advice or guidance, in which case they must notify the local authority of that fact.[90]

3.102 The LBRO plays an important role in respect of determinations and may, by consent, consider referrals from enforcing authorities, regulated persons (businesses) and primary authorities, as to whether the proposed enforcement action should proceed.[91] Such determinations are based upon an expanded version of the criteria that the primary authority must apply as provided for in Sch. 4 to RESA.[92] The procedure by which determinations by the LBRO are made is considered in full in the final part of this chapter.

Before considering enforcement action

3.103 Early communication is encouraged between enforcing authorities and primary authorities in order to help to achieve and promote a consistent approach to enforcement for businesses. It is for this reason that enforcing authorities are required to establish a dialogue with the primary authority from the moment that non-compliance is identified, and enforcement contemplated.

3.104 The LBRO *Primary Authority Guidance* makes clear that the full benefits of primary authority can best be realised if the primary authority and the enforcing authority 'engage at an early stage over any proposed enforcement action rather than using statutory notification as the beginning of that process'.[93]

---

[85] LBRO, *Primary Authority Guidance*, p. 21, para. 62.
[86] Reproduced from the BERR, *Regulatory Enforcement and Sanctions Act 2008: Guidance to the Act*, p. 22.
[87] Provided for in RESA, s. 29(1) and (3) and the Coordination of Regulatory Enforcement (Enforcement Action) Order 2009. See further para. 3.129.
[88] RESA, s. 28(4).
[89] Ibid., s. 28(3).
[90] Ibid., s. 28(2).
[91] Ibid., s. 28(7) and Sch. 4.
[92] Pursuant to s. 28(7).
[93] P. 20, para. 57.

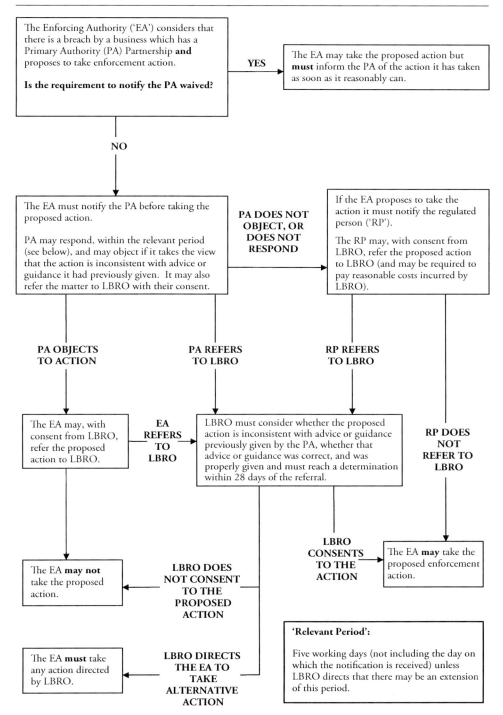

The Enforcing Authority ('EA') considers that there is a breach by a business which has a Primary Authority (PA) Partnership **and** proposes to take enforcement action.

Is the requirement to notify the PA waived?

YES

The EA may take the proposed action but **must** inform the PA of the action it has taken as soon as it reasonably can.

NO

The EA must notify the PA before taking the proposed action.

PA may respond, within the relevant period (see below), and may object if it takes the view that the action is inconsistent with advice or guidance it had previously given. It may also refer the matter to LBRO with their consent.

PA DOES NOT OBJECT, OR DOES NOT RESPOND

If the EA proposes to take the action it must notify the regulated person ('RP').

The RP may, with consent from LBRO, refer the proposed action to LBRO (and may be required to pay reasonable costs incurred by LBRO).

PA OBJECTS TO ACTION

PA REFERS TO LBRO

RP REFERS TO LBRO

The EA may, with consent from LBRO, refer the proposed action to LBRO.

EA REFERS TO LBRO

LBRO must consider whether the proposed action is inconsistent with advice or guidance previously given by the PA, whether that advice or guidance was correct, and was properly given and must reach a determination within 28 days of the referral.

RP DOES NOT REFER TO LBRO

LBRO CONSENTS TO THE ACTION

The EA **may** take the proposed enforcement action.

The EA **may not** take the proposed action.

LBRO DOES NOT CONSENT TO THE PROPOSED ACTION

'Relevant Period':

Five working days (not including the day on which the notification is received) unless LBRO directs that there may be an extension of this period.

The EA **must** take any action directed by LBRO.

LBRO DIRECTS THE EA TO TAKE ALTERNATIVE ACTION

Figure 3.1 Summary of agreement provisions for enforcement

3.105   The Guidance suggests that even where an enforcing authority is not considering taking enforcement action, it should still discuss any possible non-compliance with the primary authority in the following circumstances:[94]

    (i)   where the matter is likely to be a local example of wider non-compliance, for example a price promotion that is misleading, a labelling problem with a product that is widely sold or an unguarded machine that is known to be in use at other branches of the business;

    (ii) where the enforcing authority has identified a contravention that requires an amendment to a national system or process, for example where pest control procedures used by the business are not proving effective; or

    (iii) where the problem cannot be addressed purely through local action, for example where the local premises required input from its head office, such as structural changes to the premises that will incur costs.

Notification

3.106   Once a decision has been taken by the local authority that enforcement action is necessary, they are required to notify the primary authority prior to taking any such action.[95] Notification is only required where action is proposed against the business; it is not required when action is proposed against an individual employee.

3.107   Notification of proposed enforcement action by the enforcing authority should be made via the LBRO's secure website, by a person with authorization to initiate the enforcement action proposed, or by a person who has been specifically authorized to make that notification.[96]

3.108   Notification should include the following details which are provided for in the template for notification:[97]

    (i)   full details of the contravention, including, where appropriate, the address of the relevant premises;

    (ii) full details of any affected products or services;

    (iii) details of the proposed enforcement action: and

    (iv) the reason for proposing the enforcement action.

3.109   Enforcement authorities will need to consider carefully whether the proposed action is proportionate (whether a less restrictive method would meet the enforcement outcomes) and ensure that it is consistent with any advice or guidance previously given by the primary authority, either in general terms or specifically.

Determination

3.110   Once notified of any proposed enforcement action, the primary authority will consider whether it can go ahead, based on its conformity or otherwise with any advice and guidance previously issued.

---

[94] P. 20, para. 59.
[95] RESA, s. 28(1).
[96] The Co-ordination of Regulatory Enforcement (Procedure for References to LBRO) Order 2009, art. 2; LBRO, *Primary Authority Guidance*, p. 22, para. 70. See Appendix 6.
[97] A copy of which can be found on the secure LBRO website.

Section 28(2) provides that: 3.111

> If the primary authority determines within the relevant period that the proposed enforcement action is inconsistent with advice or guidance previously given by the primary authority (generally or specifically), it may within that period direct the enforcing authority not to take the enforcement action.

The enforcing authority must not take any enforcement action during the period set aside   3.112
for that determination to be made, unless the action is required urgently, as provided for in
art. 3 of the 2009 (Enforcement Action) Order.[98]

Definition of 'relevant period'

'Relevant period' is defined in s. 28(9) as being either the period of five working days[99] begin- 3.113
ning with the day after that on which the primary authority has notified of any proposed
enforcement, or such longer period beginning with that day, as the LBRO may direct.

The primary authority should use the five working days to review its previous advice and   3.114
guidance and to discuss the matter with relevant parties, which may include the enforcing
authority, the business, the LBRO and any relevant national regulator.[100]

The primary authority's response should be made to the person making the original notifica-   3.115
tion within the relevant period and should be copied to the LBRO.

The statutory timescale is very short and the primary authority will need to have 'robust   3.116
internal arrangements in place for handling notifications of proposed enforcement action
within the statutory timescale'.[101] The LBRO *Primary Authority Guidance* provides some
direction to primary authorities in developing these arrangements, urging that consideration
should be given to matters such as the identity of the appropriate person to receive notifications at different levels of enforcement action and 'the availability and form of information
that will be needed to support any decision to direct any enforcing authority not to take the
proposed enforcement action'.[102]

Determination outcomes

Once notified of proposed enforcement action, the primary authority may either: 3.117

 (i) direct against the enforcement action because the enforcement action is inconsistent
     with advice or guidance previously given by the primary authority (either specifically
     or generally): s. 28(2);
 (ii) confirm that it will not be directing against the proposed action (where there has been
      no advice previously given or where the advice previously given is consistent with the
      enforcement action proposed); or
(iii) decide not to make a determination under s. 28(2) and instead to apply to the LBRO
      for consent to refer the matter to the LBRO for determination: s. 28(7) and Sch. 4,
      para. 3(1).

---

[98] This exception to the notification requirements is considered further at para. 3.129.
[99] Working day is defined in s. 28(10). See also, the LBRO, *Primary Authority Guide to the meaning of
'working day'*, a copy of which can be found on the LBRO website: <www.lbro.org.uk>.
[100] LBRO, *Primary Authority Guidance*, p. 23, para. 77.
[101] Ibid., para. 76.
[102] P. 23, para. 76.

3.118 Whichever route is taken by the primary authority, it is reminded that 'active and early responses should be provided by the primary authority to all notifications of proposed enforcement action'.[103]

Primary authority directs against the proposed action

3.119 In responding to a notification, the primary authority is only entitled to consider whether the proposed enforcement action is inconsistent with any primary authority advice given to the business or local authority. Where no relevant advice has previously been given by the primary authority, it is not able to direct against the proposed enforcement action.

3.120 Where the primary authority directs the enforcing authority not to take the proposed action, the response should include: details of the advice previously given with which the proposed enforcement action would be inconsistent; details of how and when the advice was previously given; and the rationale for why the proposed enforcement action would be inconsistent with the advice previously given.[104]

3.121 Where the decision is disputed and the enforcing authority still feels that the proposed enforcement action is appropriate, it may apply to the LBRO for consent to refer the matter to the LBRO for determination.[105] The procedure for references to the LBRO is considered in paras. 3.172–3.217 below.

3.122 If the enforcing authority does not refer the matter to the LBRO, or the LBRO does not consent to a referral, then the enforcing authority cannot take the proposed enforcement action.[106]

Primary authority does not object/does not respond

3.123 If the enforcing authority is not directed not to proceed with the enforcement action, and continues to propose to take the enforcement action, it must inform the regulated person.[107] Thus where the moratorium period has elapsed resulting in either a positive response or no response at all from the primary authority *and* enforcement action is still proposed, the enforcing authority must notify the non-compliant business that it proposes to proceed.

3.124 The LBRO *Primary Authority Guidance* requires that this notification be made in writing by letter or by email, and addressed to the principal primary authority contact within the business whose details are held by the primary authority. This notification should be copied to the primary authority.[108]

3.125 The notification should contain information as to the details of the contravention and the proposed enforcement action, and must confirm that the primary authority does not object to the proposed enforcement action.[109] A template notification is available on the LBRO website.[110]

---

[103] LBRO, *Primary Authority Guidance,* p. 23, para. 79.
[104] Ibid., p. 24, para. 80.
[105] RESA, s. 28(7) and Sch. 4, paras 1 and 2.
[106] Ibid., s. 28(4).
[107] Ibid., s. 28(3).
[108] P. 24, para. 84.
[109] LBRO, *Primary Authority Guidance,* p. 24, para. 85.
[110] <www.lbro.org.uk>.

Once the moratorium period has elapsed, an enforcing authority can proceed with impunity; RESA does not allow a primary authority to revoke or revise its response to a notification after this period. **3.126**

A business against which the proposed enforcement action is directed may, if it considers that the proposed action is inconsistent with primary authority advice, apply to the LBRO for consent to refer the matter to the LBRO for determination.[111] This must be done within ten working days, starting on and including the day after it received the notification of the proposed enforcement action.[112] In those circumstances the enforcing authority cannot proceed with the proposed action until the ten-day period has expired. **3.127**

Referral to the LBRO by the primary authority

Where the primary authority is required to consider a notification under s. 28(1), it may instead, with the consent of the LBRO, refer the action to the LBRO for determination.[113] The LBRO is thus able to support the primary authority by making determinations in less straightforward notifications, perhaps where there is uncertainty about whether the advice was properly given or indeed correct in the first place. The procedure for referrals to the LBRO is considered below in paras. 3.172–3.217. **3.128**

Exceptions to the notification and response requirements

The requirement on an enforcement authority to notify the primary authority of proposed enforcement action is subject to any exceptions provided for by order.[114] The 2009 (Enforcement Action) Order provides that the notification and determination provisions under s. 28(1)–(4) shall not apply in the following circumstances: **3.129**

  (i) where the enforcement action is required urgently, or in the opinion of the enforcing authority is required urgently, to avoid a significant risk of harm to human health or the environment (including the health of animals or plants) or the financial interests of consumers;

 (ii) where the enforcement action is the service of a notice referred to in art. 2(1)(d) (an abatement notice under s. 80 of the Environmental Protection Act 1990); or

(iii) where the application of s. 28(1)–(4) of RESA would be, or in the opinion of the enforcing authority would be, wholly disproportionate.[115]

In making this determination, the BERR *Regulatory Enforcement and Sanctions Act 2008: Guidance to the Act,* suggests that relevant factors are likely to include: whether the delay might inhibit effective evidence-gathering or investigation of a breach, or whether it would be impractical to seek the views of the primary authority (for example, dealing with a faulty alarm in the early hours of the morning).[116] **3.130**

---

[111] RESA, s. 28(7) and Sch. 4, para. 2.
[112] The Co-ordination of Regulatory Enforcement (Procedure for References to LBRO) Order 2009, art. 4.
[113] RESA, s. 28(7) and Sch. 4, para. 3.
[114] RESA, s. 29(1) and (3).
[115] The Co-ordination of Regulatory Enforcement (Procedure for References to LBRO) Order 2009, art. 3.
[116] P. 25, para. 27.

3.131 Where an enforcement authority takes enforcement action under an exemption to the statutory notification and determination procedure, the authority must inform the primary authority of the enforcement action it has taken as soon as it reasonably can.[117]

Inspection plans

Overview

3.132 An inspection plan makes recommendations to local authorities about the frequency, nature and circumstances of the proactive checks on the partner business and requiring feedback on those checks.[118] They are intended to support local authorities in targeting their local inspection resources in relation to the business and are key to the operation of the primary authority scheme. According to s. 30(2): '[a]n "inspection plan" is a plan containing recommendations as to how a local authority with the function of inspection should exercise it in relation to the regulated person'.

3.133 Inspection plans may be prepared by a primary authority in respect of the regulated person with whom they have a relationship, where a relevant function includes the function of inspection.[119] Plans will be prepared in consultation with the partner business and must be approved by the LBRO before they become operational, requiring local authorities to have regard to them.[120]

3.134 Inspection plans involve the carrying out of a risk assessment of each regulated person and may include recommendations about how local authorities should carry out inspections of particular businesses or organizations, thereby assisting them in determining the appropriate frequencies for their proactive interventions through their local risk assessment processes.

3.135 The key advantage of an inspection plan, so far as a business trading across council boundaries is concerned, is that the problems associated with having its premises viewed in isolation by local authority regulators are effectively cured, thereby relieving the burden of multiple inspections and removing the possibility of inconsistent enforcement. For enforcing authorities, inspection plans are a useful tool in helping them to better regulate businesses locally.

Prior to making the inspection plan

3.136 Before making the inspection plan, the primary authority must consult the regulated person.[121] The LBRO recommends that this consultation happens at an early stage so that businesses can have input into its development.[122] For more about the manner and form of consultations, see Chapter 4, paras 4.106–4.125.

3.137 Where a business has more than one partnership, the primary authority that is considering making the inspection plan should consult with the other primary authorities to ensure that their plans are compatible.[123]

---

[117] RESA, s. 29(2).
[118] LBRO, *Primary Authority Inspection Plans: A Tool For Change*, p. 2.
[119] RESA, s. 30(1).
[120] Ibid., s. 30(7).
[121] Ibid., s. 30(4).
[122] LBRO, *Primary Authority Guidance*, p. 17, para. 44.
[123] Ibid., para. 47.

At this stage, the primary authority should also consider 'any relevant recommendations and guidance relating to inspections which are published by any person (other than a local authority) pursuant to a regulatory function'.[124] For example, where a national regulator plays a significant role in relation to inspection of the business in respect of the relevant function, it too should be consulted and offered the opportunity to be engaged in the development of the plan. **3.138**

Requirements of the inspection plan

In common with many of the enabling provisions in RESA, little guidance is provided to primary authorities as to what ought to be contained in an inspection plan, leaving it to the precise terms of the order issued under s. 30(1) to stipulate the detailed provisions. They are intended to be a flexible tool, capable of serving a number of different purposes.[125] The LBRO has issued guidance about the use of inspection plans, aimed at officers within primary authority partnerships, *Primary Authority Inspection Plans: A Tool for Change*, which should be considered alongside the material below. **3.139**

The LBRO suggests that local authorities 'work with their partner businesses to understand its needs in relation to local regulation of its premises', and in doing so, seek to design a plan which meets the joint objectives in the following areas: informing risk assessment; improving targeting and reducing duplication of effort; improving focus and effectiveness; and ensuring effective communications.[126] **3.140**

Primary authorities drawing up an inspection plan must have regard to any relevant guidance regarding the frequency of inspections and be 'conscious of the need for flexibility in dealing with emergencies and unique local circumstances'.[127] **3.141**

There is only one statutory requirement as to the content of the plan, provided for in s. 30(3): **3.142**

> An inspection plan may in particular set out—
> (a) the frequency at which, or circumstances in which, inspections should be carried out;
> (b) what an inspection should consist of.

The LBRO has issued guidance about the contents of inspection plans in the form of the LBRO *Primary Authority Guidance*. According to the LBRO, the following matters should be included within the inspection plan: **3.143**

(i) an expiry date, which may be revised with agreement with LBRO;
(ii) provision for review by the primary authority at appropriate intervals or in response to information received from enforcing authorities; and
(iii) definition of the scope of the relevant functions covered and the geographical applicability of the plan.[128]

---

[124] RESA, s. 30(5).
[125] LBRO, *Primary Authority Inspection Plans: A Tool For Change*, p. 6.
[126] Ibid.
[127] According to the BERR, *Regulatory Enforcement and Sanctions Act 2008: Guidance to the Act*, p. 21, para. 23.
[128] P. 15, para. 43.

3.144 The guidance also lists a number of other matters that may be included in the plan, for example information to assist local authorities in developing their risk-based and intelligence-led programmes of proactive interventions, including its inspections, sampling and test purchasing as well as recommendations as to areas where local inspection activities might best be focused.[129]

3.145 The guidance goes on to say that inspection plans should take into account guidance published by relevant national regulators, government departments and others; in particular, the plan should take into account the risk assessment methodologies of relevant national regulators.[130]

3.146 There is one prohibition cited in the guidance, that inspection plans 'should not address reactive interventions in response to a specific complaint or intelligence, or responses to specific local issues'.[131]

LBRO consent

3.147 All draft inspection plans must be submitted to the LBRO for its consent, which must be forthcoming before the plan becomes operational.[132] Examples of existing inspection plans to which the LBRO has given consent are available on the LBRO website.[133]

3.148 The LBRO will assess the proposed inspection plan and, if it finds that it has been prepared in accordance with the LBRO *Primary Authority Guidance,* and in accordance with the Principles of Good Regulation,[134] it will consent to the inspection plan. If, on the other hand, the LBRO is not satisfied that the proposed inspection plan has been prepared in accordance with the guidance, it will work with the partners to address any issues.[135]

Publishing the plan

3.149 Where a primary authority has made an inspection plan that has been approved by the LBRO, it must bring the plan to the notice of the other local authorities with the function of inspection.[136] This requirement ensures that firms operating in more than one local authority face a consistent and risk-based approach to enforcement.

3.150 The LBRO will publish the plan on behalf of the primary authority through the secure LBRO website where it will be available to local authorities, relevant national regulators and government departments. According the BERR *Regulatory Enforcement and Sanctions Act 2008: Guidance to the Act,* '[i]t is envisaged that storing the plans on a secure LBRO Primary Authority database will meet this requirement'.[137]

---

[129] P. 16, para. 43.
[130] P. 16, para. 45.
[131] P. 16, para. 43.
[132] RESA, s. 30(6).
[133] <www.lbro.org.uk>.
[134] Namely that regulatory activities are carried out in a way which is transparent, accountable, proportionate, consistent and targeted only at cases in which action is needed: RESA, s. 5(2).
[135] LBRO, *Primary Authority Guidance,* p. 17, para. 48.
[136] RESA, s. 30(6).
[137] P. 21, para. 23.

Status of the plan

In order for a local authority to meet its statutory duty in relation to inspection plans, once **3.151** a plan has been published, a local authority must have regard to the plan when conducting its risk assessment of the business and its programmed activity at the business.[138] Section 30(7) states as follows: '[a] local authority (including the primary authority) exercising the function of inspection in relation to the regulated person must have regard to a plan to which consent has been given under subsection (6)'.

'Must have regard to'

The local authority is not required to follow the inspection plan in all cases and it **3.152** may deviate from an element of it where it considers it appropriate to do so due to local circumstances.[139] In those circumstances, s. 30(8) requires that the local authority must notify the primary authority of its intention to do so, giving its reasons. The LBRO *Primary Authority Guidance* suggests that this be done via the LBRO's secure website.

Notification of any proposed deviation should normally be in advance unless this is imprac- **3.153** tical due to unforeseen circumstances. Where retrospective notification takes place, the local authority should notify the primary authority at the earliest practicable opportunity,[140] giving reasons for the deviation.[141]

A primary authority is not required to respond to notification of deviations from inspection **3.154** plans made by other local authorities, although it may choose to do so.

Review and update of the inspection plan

The inspection plan should be reviewed in light of changes to a business's procedures or **3.155** information received from enforcing authorities, and agreement should be reached between partners as to the appropriate interval for this review.[142] The LBRO *Primary Authority Guidance* suggests that 'any notifications should be considered by the primary authority as part of its periodic review of the inspection plan'.[143]

Other matters which the partners may agree to monitor at any review include whether **3.156** hoped-for feedback is being received from enforcing authorities and whether the feedback is proving helpful in driving improvements and changes in the level of local inspections of the business's premises.[144]

A primary authority may from time to time revise a plan made by it and where this happens **3.157** s 30(3)–(9) continues to apply.[145] This means, for example, that the primary authority must consult the regulated person and must take into account any relevant recommendations

---

[138] LBRO, *Primary Authority Guidance*, p. 17, para. 49.
[139] Ibid., p. 18, para. 50.
[140] P. 18, para. 51.
[141] RESA, s. 30(9).
[142] LBRO, *Primary Authority Inspection Plans: A Tool For Change*, p. 10.
[143] P. 18, para. 52.
[144] LBRO, *Primary Authority Inspection Plans: A Tool For Change*, p. 10.
[145] RESA, s. 30(10).

relating to inspections which are published by any person pursuant to a regulatory function.[146] The revised inspection plan must also be approved by the LBRO.[147]

F. The role of the Local Better Regulation Office

3.158   As well as the general functions in Part 1 of RESA,[148] the LBRO has three key functions in relation to the administration of the primary authority scheme:

(i)   nominating primary authorities and maintaining a register of partnerships;[149]
(ii) giving guidance to local authorities about the operation of Part 2;[150] and
(iii) resolving disputes between primary authorities, enforcement authorities and businesses.[151]

3.159   In addition to these specific functions, the LBRO 'may do anything it considers appropriate for the purpose of supporting the primary authority in the exercise of the authority's functions under this Part', including issuing grants to the authority.[152]

3.160   The nomination and registration of partnerships is considered above, in paras 3.34–3.70. The following parts of this chapter look at the remaining two functions of the LBRO— issuing guidance about the operation of Part 2, and resolving disputes between contracting parties.

Issuing guidance

Overview

3.161   The provision in s. 33 allowing the LBRO to issue guidance to local authorities about the operation of Part 2 is separate and supplementary to its general functions of issuing advice under ss 6 and 7.[153]

3.162   Guidance issued under this section must comply with the provisions of s. 33, including the provisions requiring consultation[154] and publication of the guidance.[155]

3.163   In March 2009, the LBRO issued *Primary Authority Guidance* about the operation of Part 2, aimed at local authorities and businesses entering into primary authority partnerships. This guidance is to be read in conjunction with RESA and any orders made under it. The LBRO is not obliged to issue such guidance, but may do so in accordance with s. 33(1).

Consultation

3.164   The undertaking of a consultation is particularly important, as the guidance will have an impact on the way in which regulation is handled by local authorities. Before giving

---

[146]   RESA, s. 30(4) and (5).
[147]   Ibid., s. 30(6).
[148]   As to which see Chapter 2, Part E.
[149]   RESA, ss 25(1), 26(5) and 26(6).
[150]   Ibid., s. 33.
[151]   Ibid., s. 28(7) and Sch. 4.
[152]   Ibid., s. 32(1) and (2).
[153]   The general functions of the LBRO are discussed in Chapter 2, Part E.
[154]   RESA, s. 33(4).
[155]   Ibid., s. 33(6).

guidance under this section, the LBRO must consult such persons as it considers appropriate.[156] This requirement is sufficiently flexible to enable the LBRO to consult those affected by the guidance and ensures that they act transparently.

Stakeholders that are likely to be consulted include businesses, local authorities, national **3.165** regulators and representative bodies for regulatory professionals. The LBRO consulted a wide range of bodies[157] between December 2008 and February 2009, before finalizing its guidance. In light of the responses received, the LBRO was able to adapt the draft guidance, for example by amending the categorization of relevant offences, expanding upon the guidance provided about the status of primary authority advice, and providing practical examples to illustrate the applicability of the scheme.[158]

Content of guidance

The guidance is directed to the primary authority and the enforcing authority and is intended **3.166** to assist them in the operation of their respective statutory functions. Section 33(2) provides that the guidance *may* include advice in respect of:

(i) any arrangements made by a primary authority in relation to its function of providing advice and guidance to businesses;[159]
(ii) the notification of inspection plans to local authorities;[160] and
(iii) the primary authority's power to charge fees.[161]

Any guidance issued in respect of the charging of fees by the local authority is subject to the **3.167** caveat that it may not be issued without the consent of the Secretary of State and requires prior consultation with the Welsh ministers.[162]

Status of guidance

By virtue of s. 33(3), a local authority must 'have regard' to any guidance issued under this **3.168** Part. This represents a watered-down version of the original clause in the Regulatory Enforcement and Sanctions Bill 2008, which permitted the LBRO to *direct* compliance with certain guidance. The empowerment of an unelected non-departmental public body to be able to direct a locally elected council to comply with its guidance raised important questions as to the legitimacy of councils. The resulting requirement, to 'have regard' to the guidance is flexible enough to ensure that local authorities give due weight to the guidance whilst allowing for local variation and departure from it where there are good reasons to do so.

If any guidance issued puts a local authority under a duty to act in a way that contradicts **3.169** other requirements placed upon it by law, it will not be obliged to follow it.

---

[156] Ibid., s. 33(4). Chapter 4 looks at the consultation process in more detail.
[157] All UK local authorities, fire and rescue authorities, government departments, national regulators, professional bodies and business and consumer organizations.
[158] See LBRO, *Response to Consultation on the Draft Primary Authority Guidance* (March 2009), a copy of which is available on the LBRO website: <www.lbro.org.uk>.
[159] RESA, s. 27(2).
[160] Ibid., s. 30(6).
[161] Ibid., s. 31.
[162] Ibid., s. 33(5).

Revocation of guidance

3.170 The LBRO may at any time vary or revoke any guidance given under this Part and substitute it for further guidance as long as it complies with the terms of s. 33.[163]

Publication

3.171 The LBRO must publish (in such manner as it considers appropriate) any guidance given by it under this section.[164] This may mean publication on the LBRO website or direct publication, only to those local authorities affected by the guidance.

Resolving disputes

Introduction

3.172 Where there is a dispute between the parties about the proposed enforcement action, the LBRO is able to receive referrals and make determinations about whether or not the proposed action should go ahead, acting as arbitrator between the parties. It is not anticipated that such applications will be commonplace: the LBRO suggests that this will be an exceptional procedure. Where a dispute does arise, however, this procedure is intended to be quick and cheap and used to prevent parties having to go to court.[165]

3.173 The power of the LBRO to refuse to consent to proposed enforcement action (albeit on limited grounds) is contentious; decisions taken by the LBRO (an unelected body) are arguably undemocratic in nature and constitute a centralization of power. For businesses, however, the power provides the certainty that they need to be able to operate effectively within the regulatory framework. The government considered that non-binding decisions were unlikely to be effective, as the LBRO's involvement may simply delay a case until it is brought to court, rather than actually resolving an issue, and businesses would be more likely to decide that the cost of a possible court case is too great. They may therefore 'simply concede to an Enforcing Authority even where its advice conflicts with previously given advice from their primary authority'.[166]

3.174 RESA allows all three parties involved in the proposed enforcement action, the business, the primary authority and the enforcing authority, to apply for consent to refer proposed enforcement action to the LBRO for determination. The referral and determination procedure is provided for in Sch. 4 and in the Co-ordination of Regulatory Enforcement (Procedure for References to LBRO) Order 2009 (the 2009 (Procedure for References to LBRO) Order), which came into force on 6 April 2009.[167] The 2009 (Procedure for References to LBRO) Order is reproduced in full at Appendix 6.

3.175 The BERR *Regulatory Enforcement and Sanctions Act 2008: Guidance to the Act* underlines the importance of the LBRO's role in the enforcement process.[168]

---

[163] Ibid., s. 33(7).
[164] Ibid., s. 33(6).
[165] BERR, *Consultation on the Draft Regulatory Enforcement and Sanctions Bill* (May 2007), p. 26, para. 3.28.
[166] Ibid., p. 26, para. 3.30.
[167] Made pursuant to para. 6(2) of Sch. 4, which provides that '[t]he Secretary of State may by Order make further provision as to the procedure to be followed for the purposes of this Schedule, by the primary authority, the enforcing authority, the regulated person and LBRO'.
[168] P. 25, para. 29.

Determination by the LBRO is a two-stage process. A local authority or business must first **3.176** apply to the LBRO for consent to make a referral. If the LBRO gives consent, the application will enter the LBRO determination process. The LBRO will manage the referral, consent and determination process in line with its *References to LBRO for Determinations Policy and Procedure* document.[169] Any decision made by the LBRO is binding on the parties.

The LBRO encourages, and indeed expects, continued communication between the parties **3.177** at all stages of the process, right up until a determination is made.[170] In this way, questions may be resolved between the parties without the need for a determination by the LBRO, and where this happens, the LBRO must be notified of the agreement reached as soon as practicable.[171] The LBRO account manager will work with the parties to facilitate any such negotiations.

Stage 1: obtaining consent to refer

Before the LBRO can consider a referral from any party, it must firstly consent to **3.178** receiving the referral.[172] Upon receipt of an application for consent, the LBRO will notify the other parties in writing (electronically) of that fact.[173]

Which parties may apply for consent?

According to the terms of Sch. 4, the following parties may apply to the LBRO for consent **3.179** to refer a determination to them:

(i)   an enforcing authority that has been directed by the primary authority not to take the proposed enforcement action;[174]

(ii) a regulated person that has been informed by the enforcing authority that it proposes to take enforcement action (in circumstances where the primary authority has not directed that the enforcement action should not be taken);[175] and

(iii) a primary authority that has been notified of the proposed enforcement action, but has not directed the enforcing authority not to take the proposed action.[176]

The LBRO expects that the majority of referrals for consent will be from either the regulated **3.180** person (where the enforcement action has not been blocked) or the enforcing authority (where its action has been blocked).[177]

In cases where the primary authority makes an application for consent to refer, it will be **3.181** because it was unable to reach a definitive decision itself on whether the proposed enforcement action should go ahead. In relation to these applications, the LBRO expects that:

> … a primary authority would only make a reference in default of this decision in exceptional circumstances, and that it would be able to provide good reasons why it was not appropriate

---

[169] See para. 3.38 for more about this guidance. This is reproduced in Appendix 4.
[170] LBRO, *References to LBRO for Determinations Policy and Procedure*, p. 4, para. 3.1.
[171] Ibid., para. 3.3.
[172] RESA, Sch. 4, paras 1(1), 2(1) and 3(1).
[173] LBRO, *References to LBRO for Determinations Policy and Procedure*, p. 9, para. 6.1.
[174] Para. 1(1).
[175] Para. 2(1).
[176] Para. 3(1).
[177] LBRO, *References to LBRO for Determinations Policy and Procedure*, p. 5, para. 4.4.

for it to make the decision. These reasons will be relevant to whether or not LBRO grants consent to the application from a primary authority.[178]

3.182 Where more than one party makes a concurrent application in relation to the same enforcement action, the LBRO will consider all applications received but will 'not usually grant consent to more than one'.[179] The approach that the LBRO will take in relation to related applications is set out at para. 5.5 of the LBRO *References to LBRO for Determinations Policy and Procedure* (Appendix 4).

Manner of application

3.183 All applications for consent to a reference and any representations made to the LBRO must be made in writing to the address provided in the 2009 Order (<www.lbro.org.uk>) or such other address (whether electronic or otherwise) as may from time to time be published by the LBRO on its website.[180] On receipt of an application for consent to a reference, the LBRO must give notice of it to the other parties.[181]

Time limits

3.184 Articles 4–7 of the 2009 (Procedure for References to LBRO) Order make provision for the time limits relevant to applications for consent. All applications must be made as soon as reasonably practicable and specifically:

(i)   in respect of an enforcing authority, within the period of ten working days beginning with the day after that on which the enforcing authority received a direction from the primary authority under s. 28(2) that the proposed enforcement action must not be taken;[182]

(ii) in respect of a regulated person, within the period of ten working days beginning with the day after that on which the regulated person is informed by the enforcing authority under s. 28(3) of the enforcement action proposed to be taken;[183]

(iii) in respect of the primary authority, within the period of five working days beginning with the day after that on which the primary authority is notified under s. 28(1) that the enforcing authority proposed to take enforcement action against a regulated person.[184]

3.185 The cut-off point for the receipt of applications to refer is 5 pm; any application received after this time will be deemed to have been received on the next working day.[185]

3.186 In exceptional circumstances, the LBRO may allow an application for consent to a reference to be made after the time limits set out in arts 4, 5 and 6 above.[186] Parties seeking to apply to

---

[178] Ibid., para. 4.5.

[179] Ibid., p. 6, para. 5.3.

[180] The Co-ordination of Regulatory Enforcement (Procedure for References to LBRO) Order 2009, art. 2.

[181] Ibid., art. 8.

[182] Ibid., art. 4.

[183] Ibid., art. 5.

[184] Ibid., art. 6.

[185] LBRO, *References to LBRO for Determinations Policy and Procedure*, p. 6, para. 4.8.

[186] The Co-ordination of Regulatory Enforcement (Procedure for References to LBRO) Order 2009, art. 7.

extend the usual time period for applications are advised to contact the LBRO before the expiry of the time period, as the 'LBRO will not usually consider applications for extensions of time after the initial period has expired'.[187]

Content of application

Article 3 of the 2009 Order sets out in detail the specific information that must be included within the application to LBRO for consent to make a reference. The information requirements vary slightly depending on the source of the application; the specific information requirements for each type of applicant are set out in art. 3(2) of the 2009 (Procedure for References to LBRO) Order, which is reproduced in full at Appendix 6. **3.187**

As a minimum, however, all applications must contain the applicant's name and business address, the name and contact details of an individual within the applicant's organization who has responsibility for the application and reference; the names and business address of the other parties; and a description of the proposed enforcement action.[188] **3.188**

As to the form of the application, the LBRO requires that wherever possible, any application is made using the template on its website. In order to avoid unnecessary delay in the determinations process, applicants should look carefully at the guidance provided in the LBRO *References to LBRO for Determinations Policy and Procedure* document, as to the form of the application.[189] **3.189**

Representations

The LBRO expect to have a dialogue with all parties during the consent and determination procedure. The LBRO expects the applicant to submit all relevant information with the application for consent, and does not expect applicants to submit further information for the determination procedure should consent be forthcoming.[190] **3.190**

Before or after giving consent to a reference, the LBRO may request that the other parties (not the applicant) submit any written representations in relation to the reference;[191] this may include 'other persons who are not parties but have an interest in the case or useful information to contribute'.[192] These representations must be made within the time limit set down by the LBRO,[193] and is likely to be within five to ten working days of a request for information.[194] Representations by the other parties must include the information that they would have to have given had they been the applicant (the specific information requirements **3.191**

---

[187] LBRO, *References to LBRO for Determinations Policy and Procedure*, p. 4, para. 4.11.
[188] The Co-ordination of Regulatory Enforcement (Procedure for References to LBRO) Order 2009, art. 3(1).
[189] See in particular, paras 4.13–4.17.
[190] LBRO, *References to LBRO for Determinations Policy and Procedure*, p. 13, para. 8.1.
[191] The Co-ordination of Regulatory Enforcement (Procedure for References to LBRO) Order 2009, art. 9(1), made pursuant to RESA, Sch. 4, para. 8.
[192] LBRO, *References to LBRO for Determinations Policy and Procedure*, p. 4, para. 2.2.
[193] The Co-ordination of Regulatory Enforcement (Procedure for References to LBRO) Order 2009, art. 9(2).
[194] LBRO, *References to LBRO for Determinations Policy and Procedure*, p. 10, para. 6.3.

of art. 3(2)), [195] and may include any other information that the LBRO reasonably believes appropriate to be included.[196]

3.192 Whilst any information disclosed during the course of a reference from any party does not have to be treated by the LBRO as confidential,[197]it may not be used for any unconnected purpose without the consent of the LBRO, the applicant and the other parties.[198] The LBRO would generally expect to disclose the full content of the application for consent to refer and any other information received to all parties.

Decision on application for consent to a reference

3.193 Decisions on consent and full determinations of the reference will be made by the Consents and Determinations Committee (the Committee), which will normally consist of three members of the LBRO's board.[199] A report will be prepared on each application for consideration by the Committee and may include a recommendation as to whether consent should be granted. Where such a recommendation is made, the Committee is not bound to follow it and 'will exercise its own judgment based on the information before it'.[200] For guidance as to the information that may be contained in the report, see the LBRO *References to LBRO for Determinations Policy and Procedure*.[201]

3.194 The LBRO considers that consent will typically be refused where:

    (i)   an application is incomplete or has otherwise been improperly made;

    (ii) the subject of an application is not an appropriate question for the LBRO to determine;

    (iii) consent has already been given to another party relating to the same question;

    (iv) consent has already been given to another applicant making a related application;

    (v) the LBRO is not satisfied that the applicant has provided sufficient and appropriate reasons for making the application;

    (vi) when the Committee considers the report, the LBRO has not received the information it has requested from any party; and

    (vii) the application is frivolous or vexatious.[202]

3.195 There is no specific time limit within which the decision on consent must be made. The 2009 (Procedure for References to LBRO) Order provides only that the LBRO must decide whether to consent to a reference 'as soon as reasonably practicable after receiving an application … '.[203] Once it has made its decision, the LBRO must inform the applicant and all other parties in writing of that decision as soon as reasonably practicable.[204]

---

[195] The Co-ordination of Regulatory Enforcement (Procedure for References to LBRO) Order 2009, art. 9(3).

[196] LBRO, *References to LBRO for Determinations Policy and Procedure*, p. 11, para. 6.6.

[197] The Co-ordination of Regulatory Enforcement (Procedure for References to LBRO) Order 2009, art. 12(1).

[198] Ibid., art. 12(2).

[199] LBRO, *References to LBRO for Determinations Policy and Procedure*, p. 4, para. 2.5.

[200] Ibid., p. 12, para. 7.4.

[201] P. 12, para. 7.1. Appendix 4.

[202] LBRO, *References to LBRO for Determinations Policy and Procedure*, p. 12, para. 7.6.

[203] The Co-ordination of Regulatory Enforcement (Procedure for References to LBRO) Order 2009, art. 10(1).

[204] Ibid., art. 10(2).

If the LBRO refuses consent to a reference, it must give a written statement of reasons for that decision at the same time that it informs the applicant and the other parties of the decision.[205] The decision on consent is final and 'will not be reconsidered by the LBRO'.[206] **3.196**

Stage 2: determination of a reference

Once the LBRO has consented to receiving a reference from a party, the question raised will automatically be referred to the LBRO which must then determine the reference in accordance with the provisions of Sch. 4. The reference is deemed to be made on the day after the date on which notice of consent is given to the parties.[207] **3.197**

Consultation

Prior to the making of any determination under Sch. 4, the LBRO 'must consult any relevant regulator, where appropriate, and may consult such other persons as it thinks fit'.[208] **3.198**

A relevant regulator is a person (other than a local authority) with regulatory functions that relate to the matter to which the determination relates.[209] **3.199**

The determination

In the first instance, a report[210] will be prepared for presentation to the Committee which may request any further information required or, in rare cases, request that parties appear before it to make oral representations or submissions. A party that refuses to attend may 'prejudice the determination process to the detriment of that party'.[211] **3.200**

In all cases, the Committee will decide whether: **3.201**

  (i) the proposed enforcement action is inconsistent with advice or guidance previously given by the primary authority;[212]

 (ii) the advice or guidance given by the primary authority was correct;[213] and

(iii) the advice or guidance was properly given by the primary authority.[214]

Determination outcomes

The determination of a reference can result in one of two possible outcomes: **3.202**

  (i) where the LBRO is satisfied as to the matters in (i)–(iii) above, it *must* confirm the direction given by the primary authority to the enforcing authority (where the reference is from an enforcing authority) or 'direct the enforcement authority not to take the proposed enforcement action' (where the reference is from another party);[215]

---

[205] Ibid., art. 10(3).
[206] LBRO, *References to LBRO for Determinations Policy and Procedure*, p. 13, para. 7.10.
[207] Ibid., para. 7.9.
[208] RESA, Sch. 4, para. 5(1).
[209] Ibid., para. 5(2).
[210] See LBRO, *References to LBRO for Determinations Policy and Procedure*, p. 13, para. 8.3 for more about the contents of the report.
[211] Ibid., p. 14, paras 8.5–8.8.
[212] RESA, Sch. 4, paras 1(3)(a), 2(3)(a), 3(3)(a).
[213] Ibid., Sch. 4, paras 1(3)(b), 2(3)(b), 3(3)(b).
[214] Ibid., Sch. 4, paras 1(3)(c), 2(3)(c), 3(3)(c).
[215] Ibid., Sch. 4, paras 1(2)(a), 2(2)(a), 3(2(a).

(ii) in any other case, the LBRO must revoke the direction given by the primary authority (where the reference is from an enforcing authority), or consent to the action, in which case the enforcement action will go ahead (where the reference is from another party).[216]

3.203 In reaching a view on whether the advice or guidance was correct, the LBRO will consider in particular:

(i) whether the advice or guidance was legally correct, in that the advice or guidance was in accordance with the correct interpretation of any relevant legislative provisions; and

(ii) whether, with regard to other matters, the advice or guidance was within the range of advice or guidance that could reasonably have been given by the primary authority.[217]

3.204 In considering whether the advice or guidance was properly given by the primary authority, the LBRO will consider:

(i) the primary authority's status as primary authority for the regulated person;

(ii) the application of RESA to the enforcement activity; and

(iii) whether the advice or guidance was effectively communicated to the regulated person.[218]

When considering whether advice was properly given, the LBRO may also consider whether 'due regard has been given to its own Guidance for Primary Authorities' (i.e. LBRO *Primary Authority Guidance*).[219]In this context see BERR *Regulatory Enforcement and Sanctions Act 2008: Guidance to the Act.*[220]

3.205 Where the LBRO confirms the direction of the primary authority or directs an enforcing authority not to take the proposed enforcement action, it may direct the enforcing authority to take some other enforcement action instead.[221] The enforcing authority must comply with any direction made by the LBRO in this regard.[222] The LBRO will normally direct an enforcing authority to take some other enforcement action only where it is necessary in the public interest to do so.[223]

3.206 Notification of the determination must be communicated to the applicant and the other parties in writing 'as soon as reasonably practicable' after the determination has been made.[224]

3.207 There is no mechanism for a party to appeal the decision of the LBRO in relation to enforcement action. Such decisions are however subject to the usual constraints of administrative

---

[216] Ibid., Sch. 4, paras 1(2)(b), 2(2)(b), 3(2(b).
[217] LBRO, *References to LBRO for Determinations Policy and Procedure*, p. 16, para. 8.10.
[218] Ibid., para. 8.13.
[219] BERR, *Regulatory Enforcement and Sanctions Act 2008: Guidance to the Act*, p. 26, para. 29.
[220] P. 25, para. 29.
[221] RESA, Sch. 4, paras 1(4), 2(5), 3(5).
[222] Ibid., paras 1(5), 2(6), 3(6).
[223] LBRO, *References to LBRO for Determinations Policy and Procedure*, p. 16, para. 8.10.
[224] The Co-ordination of Regulatory Enforcement (Procedure for References to LBRO) Order 2009, art. 13.

law that apply to public bodies carrying out public functions, namely that their decisions are ultimately subject to judicial review.[225]

Time limits

3.208 The LBRO must determine any reference under Sch. 4 within the period of twenty-eight days beginning with the day on which the reference is made.[226] The LBRO must provide to the applicant and the other parties, a written statement of reasons as soon as reasonably practicable after the determination has been made, and in any event within twenty-eight days of this determination being made.[227]

Effect of the reference

3.209 Where the LBRO determines that the proposed enforcement action cannot go ahead and directs accordingly, the enforcing authority 'may not take the proposed enforcement action'.[228] Its decision is binding on all parties.

3.210 The enforcing authority is prohibited from taking the proposed enforcement action during the period in which the regulated person (business) may make an application for consent to make a referral under para. 2 of Sch. 4,[229] namely ten working days[230] 'beginning with the day after that on which the regulated person is informed by the enforcing authority … of the enforcement action proposed to be taken'.[231]

3.211 Once a reference has been made to the LBRO for determination, the enforcing authority may not take the proposed enforcement action until there has been a determination.[232]

Withdrawal of application for consent or of reference

3.212 The applicant may apply to the LBRO for consent to withdraw its application either before or after consent has been granted, by giving notice in writing to the LBRO.[233] No other party may apply to have the application withdrawn and the application cannot be withdrawn without the consent of the LBRO.

3.213 The LBRO shall not consent to the withdrawal in either case, without having first consulted the other parties.[234] The LBRO will normally only refuse to consent to a withdrawal where:

(i) multiple applications were received and the withdrawal of the reference may prejudice other applicants;

---

[225] Judicial review is considered in Chapter 8.
[226] RESA, Sch. 4, para. 6(1).
[227] The Co-ordination of Regulatory Enforcement (Procedure for References to LBRO) Order 2009, art. 14.
[228] RESA, Sch. 4, paras 2(4) and 3(4).
[229] Ibid., Sch. 4, para. 4(a).
[230] Defined in RESA, s. 28(10).
[231] The Co-ordination of Regulatory Enforcement (Procedure for References to LBRO) Order 2009, art. 5.
[232] RESA, Sch. 4, para. 4(b).
[233] The Co-ordination of Regulatory Enforcement (Procedure for References to LBRO) Order 2009, art. 11(1) and (3).
[234] Ibid., art. 11(2) and (4).

   (ii) the time period for another party to make an application has expired and withdrawal
         of the current application or reference may prejudice the interests of that other
         party; or
   (iii) determination of the reference would be in the public interest.[235]

Guidance and directions

3.214 The LBRO may issue guidance or give directions to any one or more local authorities about
any enforcement action referred to it under Sch. 4.[236] A local authority must have regard to
any guidance so issued and must comply with any such direction.[237] Where the LBRO issue
guidance or directions under this part, they must publish it in such a manner as it considers
appropriate.[238]

Costs

3.215 Provision is made in Sch. 4 for the LBRO to recover any costs incurred as a result of a
reference by the regulated person, so long as those costs as 'reasonably incurred'.[239]

3.216 The LBRO *References to LBRO for Determinations Policy and Procedure* provides that the
LBRO will usually require regulated persons who are applicants to pay for the costs of the
applications, unless it chooses in its own discretion not to do so.[240] The guidance lists a
number of factors which are likely to be relevant as to whether the regulated persons should
pay the costs and to the level of those costs:

   (i)   the outcome of the reference;
   (ii)   the conduct of all parties during the reference process;
   (iii) the complexity of the reference;
   (iv)   any public interest implications of the reference;
   (v)   any application made by the regulated person to withdraw the reference;
   (vi)   the circumstances of the regulated person; and
   (vii) whether multiple or related applications have been considered by LBRO.[241]

3.217 The regulated person should expect notification of whether it is required to pay costs and, if
so, the amount due, within 28 days of determination of the reference.[242]

---

[235] LBRO, *References to LBRO for Determinations Policy and Procedure*, p. 17, para. 10.3.
[236] RESA, Sch. 4, para. 7(1).
[237] Ibid., Sch. 4, para. 7(2).
[238] Ibid., Sch. 4, para. 7(3).
[239] Ibid., Sch. 4, para. 2(7).
[240] P. 18, para. 13.2.
[241] Ibid., para. 13.4.
[242] Ibid., para. 13.6.

PART II

THE CIVIL SANCTIONS

4

OBTAINING THE CIVIL SANCTIONS

A. Introduction

Civil sanctions have become an established part of the regulatory enforcement landscape,[1] although not all regulators presently have access to them. Part 3 of RESA provides a framework under which a wide range of regulators may seek the award of new administrative sanctions, known generally as 'civil sanctions'. The powers are available to sixty-two regulators identified by Hampton[2] and fifty-six identified by Macrory,[3] as well as more than 400 local authorities with regulatory responsibility and [add] up to tens of thousands of regulators'.[4]

4.01

This chapter looks at those regulatory authorities that have access to the civil sanctions provided for in Part 3, and in respect of which potential offences those sanctions may attach. There then follows, in Part G, a detailed guide for regulators seeking the award of the

4.02

---

[1] Per Lord Bach, Hansard, HL Deb., vol. 698, col. GC340 (30 January 2008).

[2] In his report, Philip Hampton, *Reducing Administrative Burdens: Effective Inspection and Enforcement*, published 16 March 2005. A copy can be found on the Department for Business Innovation and Skills (BIS) website: <http://www.bis.gov.uk>.

[3] In his report, Richard Macrory, *Regulatory Justice: Making Sanctions Effective* (November 2006). A copy can be found on the Department for Business Innovation and Skills (BIS) website: <http://www.bis.gov.uk>.

[4] Hansard, HL Deb., vol. 701, col. 26 (28 April 2008).

sanctions, with practical advice from carrying out the necessary consultation, through to the drafting of the terms of the required order.

B. Overview of the civil sanctions

Introduction

4.03   The powers under Part 3 are intended to provide a swift, effective and proportionate response to regulatory non-compliance.[5] They were implemented as a direct result of the recommendations made by Professor Richard Macrory in his report, *Regulatory Justice: Making Sanctions Effective*. The sanctions represent an attempt to rectify what Macrory called the 'compliance deficit', whereby regulators fail to take enforcement action where there has been regulatory non-compliance because there is no suitable sanction to deal with it in an appropriate and proportionate manner.[6]

4.04   The sanctions are designed to complement regulators' existing criminal sanction tools. Regulators acquiring access to them may use them without compromising their existing criminal sanction capability; they are intended to supplement, rather than replace, existing measures. Importantly for businesses, imposition of these sanctions will not constitute a conviction.

4.05   According to both Macrory[7] and the government,[8] it should be recognized that access to the criminal law will still play an important role in achieving regulatory compliance and there will still be cases in which exposure to criminal prosecution is the most appropriate method of dealing with regulatory non-compliance. This will be especially so in the case of serious, egregious offences, or in cases brought against those who habitually transgress the rules and regulations. It is also a stated expectation of the government that regulators will continue to use more informal methods of securing enforcement, such as the provision of advice, or the issuing of warning letters, where it remains appropriate and proportionate to do so.[9]

4.06   In attempting to deliver the Macrory vision through the introduction of these powers, the government has claimed that the overall cost benefit would be somewhere between £2.05 m and £59.75 m, made up of savings to the court system, operating costs for regulators, and businesses not needing to go to court.[10]

---

[5] See BERR, *Regulatory Enforcement and Sanctions Act 2008: Guidance to the Act*, p. 27, published July 2008. A copy is available on the BIS website: <http://www.bis.gov.uk>.

[6] Richard Macrory, *Regulatory Justice: Making Sanctions Effective*, at p. 34, para. 1.33. A detailed analysis of this report appears in paras 1.29–1.37.

[7] Ibid., p. 4.

[8] Hansard, HL Deb., vol. 696, col. 1282 (28 November 2007); Hansard, HL Deb., vol. 698, cols GC339 and GC341 (30 January 2008).

[9] BERR, *Regulatory Enforcement and Sanctions Act 2008: Guidance to the Act*, para. 31.

[10] BERR, *Consultation on the Draft Regulatory Enforcement and Sanctions Bill: Implementing the Hampton Vision*, p. 39, para. 5.9, published May 2007. A copy can be found at: <http://www.berr.gov.uk>.

The sanctions available

Part 3 of RESA provides that a minister of the Crown[11] may grant a regulator the power to **4.07** apply one or more of the four civil sanctions in the event of regulatory non-compliance through the commission or likely commission of certain criminal offences (known as 'relevant offences'[12]).

Section 36(1) states that a minister of the Crown[13] may by order, grant a regulator[14] any one **4.08** of the following sanctions:

(i) **Fixed monetary penalties** (s. 39)—under which the regulator will be able to impose a monetary penalty of a fixed amount. According to the *Guidance on creating new regulatory penalties and offences* published by BERR,[15] these are suitable for the more minor instances of non-compliance.

(ii) **Discretionary requirements** (s. 42)—which will enable the regulator to impose one or more of the following: a variable monetary penalty (VMP) the amount of which will be determined by the regulator (although these are capped for summary only offences); a requirement to take specified steps within a stated period to secure that an offence does not continue or happen again (a compliance notice); or a requirement to take specified steps within a stated period to secure that an offence does not happen again (a restoration notice). The BERR publication, *Guidance on creating new regulatory penalties and offences*, suggests that discretionary requirements are generally aimed at more complex cases of non-compliance.[16]

(iii) **Stop notices** (s. 46)—which will prevent a person from carrying out an activity until they have taken steps to come back into compliance. These are 'reserved for serious breaches, reflected in the high threshold before issue (there must be a "significant risk" of "serious harm" to human health, the environment or the financial interests of consumers)'.[17]

(iv) **Enforcement undertakings** (s. 50)—which will enable a person that the regulator reasonably suspects of having committed an offence to give an undertaking to the regulator to take one or more of the restorative actions set out in the undertaking.

The nature of the sanctions

The true nature of the sanctions available in Part 3 is debatable. According to the administra- **4.09** tion that introduced them,[18] the sanctions are categorically civil, both in name and in substance, even though the underlying offence will of course be of a criminal nature. This issue was one of the most contentious during the Bill's parliamentary progress. In response to a question from Lord Cope, Lord Bach (the introducing minister) explained that the sanctions

---

[11] Section 36(2) of RESA provides that where the provision relates to a Welsh ministerial matter, the Welsh ministers may make any such provision under s. 36(1) by way of a statutory instrument. Section 71(1) defines both ministers of the Crown and Welsh ministers as the 'relevant authority'.

[12] Relevant offence is defined in RESA, s. 38.

[13] Or Welsh minister, where the provision relates to a Welsh ministerial matter: RESA, s. 36(2).

[14] Defined in RESA, ss 37 and 62. See para. 4.58 for more on the definition of the term 'regulator'.

[15] At p. 4, para. 11, published 26 January 2009. Reproduced in full at Appendix 7.

[16] BERR, *Guidance on creating new regulatory penalties and offences*, p. 4, para. 11.

[17] Ibid.

[18] The Labour administration under Gordon Brown.

were not criminal as they were an 'alternative to criminal prosecution' and would be 'imposed administratively'.[19]

4.10 This approach appears to ignore a number of important factors, including the fact that two of the sanctions[20] require a regulator to be satisfied to the criminal standard of proof that the offence has been committed before they may be imposed,[21] and that RESA contains an express provision preventing concurrent criminal proceedings being undertaken for the same conduct.[22]

Article 6 European Convention on Human Rights (ECHR)

4.11 This debate will be of interest to regulators and businesses alike. Whilst the general procedural protections of Art. 6 of the ECHR[23] (as implemented by Human Rights Act 1998) apply to the regime, whatever its true nature,[24] the more specific procedural safeguards provided for in Art. 6(2) (the presumption of innocence)[25] and Art. 6(3) would only come into play were the offences to which the sanctions may be attached deemed to be criminal offences.

4.12 The guarantees enshrined in Art. 6(3) are as follows:

Everyone charged with a **criminal offence** has the following minimum rights:

(i) to be informed promptly, in a language which he understands and in detail, of the nature and cause of the accusation against him;

(ii) to have adequate time and facilities for the preparation of his defence;

(iii) to defend himself in person or through legal assistance of his own choosing or, if he has not sufficient means to pay for legal assistance, to be given it free when the interests of justice so require;

(iv) to examine or have examined witnesses against him and to obtain the attendance and examination of witnesses on his behalf under the same conditions as witnesses against him; and

(v) to have the free assistance of an interpreter if he cannot understand or speak the language used in court (emphasis added).

---

[19] Hansard, HL Deb., vol. 698, col. GC341 (30 January 2008).

[20] Fixed monetary penalties and discretionary requirements.

[21] See also in this regard the comments of Lord Lyell of Markyate during the Grand Committee stage in the House of Lords, in which he said, 'I suspect that this provision [the criminal standard of proof] has been put in by those drafting the bill partly because the Government realise that, although this is described as a civil system, it is not a civil system at all; it is a criminal system under a civil disguise': Hansard, HL Deb. 30, vol. 698, col. GC334 (January 2008).

[22] There is usually no bar to concurrent civil and criminal proceedings.

[23] Article 6 states that: '[i]n the determination of his civil rights and obligations or of any criminal charge against him, everyone is entitled to a fair and public hearing within a reasonable time by an independent and impartial tribunal established by law. Judgement shall be pronounced publicly by the press and public may be excluded.'

[24] As they are applicable '[i]n the determination of . . . civil rights and obligations' and in relation to 'any criminal charge': Art. 6(3) ECHR.

[25] Article 6(2) provides that: '[e]veryone charged with a criminal offence shall be presumed innocent until proved guilty according to law'.

The criteria relevant to the determination of whether a penalty is truly civil or criminal in **4.13** nature are well established in Strasbourg jurisprudence[26] and have been recognized and applied in the English courts.[27] In determining the true nature of a penalty, the courts will consider the following:

  (i) the domestic classification of the offence;
 (ii) the essential nature of the offence; and
(iii) the severity of the potential penalty.

Given that the part of RESA creating the penalties is entitled 'civil sanctions', it may seem at **4.14** first blush that there is little room for doubt about their classification in domestic law. This view appears to be fortified when allied to the fact that the imposition of the sanctions does not lead to a criminal record,[28] and that recovery of any unpaid monies is to be through the civil courts.

Tending against the domestic classification, however, are three factors: first, the sanctions **4.15** are to be applied to criminal offences created in other statutory regimes; second, two of the sanctions require the regulator to be sure beyond reasonable doubt (ie to the criminal standard of proof) before they may be imposed; and finally, in respect of fixed monetary penalties, discretionary requirements and stop notices,[29] there is express provision preventing criminal proceedings from being brought in respect of the same conduct for which the civil sanction has been imposed.[30] Given these additional features of the regime, even the domestic classification of these sanctions as 'civil' begins to look uncertain.

The European Court of Human Rights has held that the domestic classification of the pen- **4.16** alty is only the starting point, and that other factors 'carry more weight' in any determination as to whether an offence is administrative, regulatory, civil or criminal in nature.[31] This approach ensures that member states are not able to undermine the Convention's guarantees by simply reclassifying an offence as civil rather than criminal.

The court will examine a number of separate but related considerations in making this **4.17** particular determination, including the scope of the rules' applicability, whether the proceedings are instituted by a public body with statutory powers of enforcement,[32] and the function of the rule.[33]

The first consideration involves an analysis of the group at which the offence is aimed. An **4.18** offence targeting an individual group is less likely to be considered to be criminal in nature; offences that are generally binding in character are more likely to be classified as criminal.

---

[26] See *Engel v Netherlands (No 1)* (1976) 1 EHRR 647; *International Transport Roth GmbH v SSHD* [2003] QB 728 (CA); *Albert and Le Compte v Belgium* (1983) 5 EHRR 533.

[27] See, for example, *Han & Yau v Commissioners of Customs and Excise* [2001] EWCA Civ 1048.

[28] This issue is relevant, but unlikely to be decisive: *Benham v United Kingdom* (1996) 22 EHRR 293; *Campbell and Fell v United Kingdom* (1985) 7 EHRR 165.

[29] Enforcement undertakings are consensual in nature and may only be imposed where the business proposes an undertaking to the regulator, with which the regulator agrees.

[30] There is usually no bar to concurrent civil and criminal proceedings.

[31] *Benham v United Kingdom* (1996) 22 EHRR 293, para. 56.

[32] In respect of the Part 3 powers, they must be instituted by a body with statutory powers of enforcement: see the definition of 'regulator', 'relevant offence' and 'enforcement function' in paras 4.58–4.80 of this chapter.

[33] *Benham v United Kingdom* (1996) 22 EHRR 293, paras 47 and 56.

The RESA sanctions may be applied to both restricted groups[34] and more generally to the public at large,[35] raising the possibility that some offences may properly be classified as civil, whilst others would continue to have the hallmarks of a criminal offence.

4.19   In respect of the final consideration, the question that the courts have posed is, does the liability involve blameworthiness?[36] Offences that give rise to deterrent penalties will typically be defined as criminal in nature;[37] both fixed and variable monetary penalties are capable of falling into this category.

4.20   This is the criterion to which the most importance will be attached in any determination, and is often decisive.[38] Where the penalty is financial in nature, the determinative issue is the *potential* penalty that may be imposed, not the actual penalty issued.[39] Even where the financial penalty is relatively minor, this may suffice where the purpose is clearly punitive.[40] In *Han & Yau v Commissioners of Customs and Excise*,[41] the Court of Appeal ruled that the system of VAT civil penalties gave rise to 'criminal charges' within the meaning of Art. 6.[42] The unlimited nature of the fines that may be imposed in respect of some offences[43] may mean that they could properly to be classified as punitive and thus criminal in nature.

Consequences of a criminal classification

4.21   One only has to compare the procedure for the imposition of the civil sanctions with that applicable to criminal prosecution in England and Wales to see the additional procedural protections that are afforded to those prosecuted for criminal charges. Those suspected of a criminal offence can expect the following: the prosecution must be deemed to be in the public interest before a suspect can be charged;[44] the allegation must be clearly specified in the charge or summons; both the evidence and any unused material must be served; the case will be heard in front of an independent tribunal; evidence is tested by way of cross-examination; a verdict is given; and finally, sentence is passed publicly.

4.22   A determination that the regime under Part 3 may in fact give rise to criminal charges would have the following possible consequences in respect of its conformity with the ECHR:

(i)   At the very least, the regime could be said to offend against the twin guarantees permitting the accused the opportunity to defend himself in person and to examine witnesses

---

[34]   For example, the offence of an authorized officer of a local authority disclosing a trade secret obtained pursuant to entering premises under a warrant: s. 96 of the Building Act 1984 (c. 55).

[35]   For example, the offence of applying a false trade description to goods, under s. 1 of the Trade Descriptions Act 1968 (c. 29).

[36]   Per Simon Brown LJ in *International Transport Roth GmbH v Secretary of State for the Home Department* [2003] QB 728 (CA).

[37]   The leading case on the question of the true nature of administrative offences is *Ozturk v Germany* (1984) 6 EHRR 409.

[38]   *Brown v United Kingdom* (1998) 28 EHRR CD 233.

[39]   *Engel v Netherlands (No 1)* (1976) 1 EHRR 647, para. 85, where the court said that 'the final outcome of the appeal cannot diminish the importance of what was initially at stake'.

[40]   See for example: *Schmautzer v Austria* (1996) 21 EHRR 511; *Pfarrmeier v Austria* (1996) 22 EHRR 175; *Um-lauft v Austria* (1996) 22 EHRR 76; *Lauko v Slovakia* (1998) 33 EHRR 25.

[41]   [2001] EWCA Civ 1048.

[42]   The income tax system of civil penalties also gives rise to criminal charges: *Commissioners for her Majesty's Revenue and Customs and Tahir Iqbal Khawaja* [2008] EWHC 1687 (Ch).

[43]   Indictable only offences.

[44]   See *The Code for Crown Prosecutors*, latest edition February 2010. A copy can be found on the Crown Prosecution Service website : <http://www.cps.gov.uk>.

adverse to his case. Rather than the evidence being presented to an independent tribunal, it will be for an official within the regulatory authority to decide whether the offence has been committed, without the accused being given the opportunity to test any of the evidence brought against him. In respect of FMPs, discretionary requirements and stop notices, this decision is made without the business even having been notified of the allegation brought against it.

(ii) It is also arguable that the regime fails to protect the presumption of innocence guarantee.[45] The sending of a notice of intent could be equivalent to the imposition of a criminal charge,[46] after which there is no right to be heard by an independent tribunal, only to appeal, by which time the sanction will already have been imposed.

C. Territorial application

Introduction

The devolution of Scotland, Wales and Northern Ireland was a central part of the 1997 **4.23** Labour government's manifesto, aimed at modernizing the British constitution by enabling different policies to be pursued to reflect different needs in the constituent parts of the UK. The devolution legislation, the Scotland Act 1998, the Government of Wales Acts 1998 and 2006, and the Northern Ireland Act 1998, made provision for the establishment of these three devolved administrations and their new legislative powers.

Whilst the terms of RESA extend to all four devolution settlements (the three devolved **4.24** administrations and the UK Parliament in Westminster), each devolution settlement confers different powers upon the legislatures in question and, as such, the specific applicability of the provisions of Part 3 differ for each settlement. The powers of Part 3 apply as follows:

(i) in the Scottish context, to any function that is reserved to the UK government or Parliament under Sch. 5 to the Scotland Act 1998, or not transferred to the Scottish ministers under other legislation;

(ii) in the Welsh context, to any function exercisable by the Welsh ministers, or any matter[47] within the legislative competence of the National Assembly for Wales; and

(iii) in the Northern Ireland context, to any matter that is excepted or reserved to the UK Parliament, under Schs 2 and 3 to the Northern Ireland Act 1998.

With the assistance of the Scotland, Wales and Northern Ireland Offices (the Territorial **4.25** Offices), ministers seeking to award the powers to regulators should identify at an early stage whether the provisions of the order relate to reserved or devolved matters in each part of the UK, and ensure that the devolved administration in question shares their understanding of this.[48]

---

[45] ECHR, Art. 6(2).
[46] Article 6 applies from the moment an individual is 'charged'. The term charge has been defined as: '[t]he official notification given to an individual by the competent authority of an allegation that he has committed a criminal offence . . .' *Deweer v Belgium* (1980) 2 EHRR 439, para. 46.
[47] A matter is a statement of the scope of an aspect of legislative competence.
[48] Cabinet Office, *Guide to Making Legislation*, para. 15.11. This was last updated on 2 September 2009. A copy can be found on the Cabinet Office website: <http://www.cabinetoffice.gov.uk>. Whilst this guidance relates to Bills, it is suggested that the same approach be adopted in relation to subordinate legislation.

Definition of 'devolved'

4.26 The devolved administrations define the respective functions of the UK government and the devolved administrations in different ways. The term 'devolved' is used in this text to encompass the term 'transferred' and refers to those matters about which policy decisions can be taken by the devolved administrations. The term 'non-devolved' is used to encompass both the terms 'reserved' and 'excepted', and refers to matters that involve policy decisions affecting Scotland, Wales and Northern Ireland that are still taken by the UK Parliament at Westminster.

Wales

4.27 All parts of RESA, including the provisions in Part 3, apply to Wales in respect of both devolved and non-devolved matters. By virtue of s. 36, all the powers given to ministers of the Crown can also be used by Welsh ministers where the provision relates to a Welsh matter.

Scotland

4.28 Part 3 of RESA applies to Scotland only in respect of non-devolved matters (i.e. that have been reserved to the UK Parliament); for example, an order could be made awarding the civil sanctions to a regulator that was enforcing offences in Scotland relating to consumer protection or rail regulation as these are non-devolved matters.

4.29 Section 56 prohibits (save for consequential purposes) an order under Part 3 from making any provision that would be within the legislative competence of the Scottish Parliament, if it were contained in an Act of that Parliament. As the *Explanatory Notes*[49] to RESA explain, this would prevent, for example, such an order from being used to grant regulators the sanctions under this Part for offences that relate to matters that have been devolved to the Scottish regulators, such as environmental health.[50]

4.30 The Scotland Office[51] has published two helpful lists summarizing those matters that are non-devolved (Part 3 applies) and those that are devolved (Part 3 does not apply).[52]

Northern Ireland

4.31 The provision that limits applicability of Part 3 to the devolved administration of Scotland[53] is mirrored by the terms of the provision limiting its applicability to the Northern Ireland Assembly. Section 57 of RESA provides that: 'An order under this Part may not, except for consequential purposes, make any provision which would be within the legislative competence of the Northern Ireland Assembly if it were contained in an Act of that Assembly.'

4.32 Part 3 of RESA thus only applies to Northern Ireland in respect of non-devolved matters, i.e. matters that have either been excepted or reserved to the UK Parliament. Excepted matters are matters that Parliament retains indefinitely, whereas reserved matters are those matters

---

[49] See further para. 4.44 for more about the status of these notes.
[50] *Regulatory Enforcement and Sanctions Act 2008: Explanatory Notes*, at p. 28, para. 150. A copy can be found on the Office of Public Sector Information website <http://www.opsi.gov.uk>.
[51] The Scotland Office is part of the Ministry of Justice, within the UK government and has a number of functions in relation to devolution, including representing Scottish interests within the UK government.
[52] See: <http://www.scotlandoffice.gov.uk>.
[53] RESA, s. 56.

that may be transferred to the Northern Ireland Assembly at a future date. In either case, the provisions of Part 3 may be applied to these matters as they are not 'within the legislative competence of the Northern Ireland Assembly'.[54]

Consequential purposes

Sections 56 (Scotland) and 57 (Northern Ireland) limit the applicability of the terms of Part 3 to non-devolved matters, 'except for consequential purposes'. A 'consequential purpose' in this context is the result of the making of a 'consequential provision', as provided for in s. 55. **4.33**

D. Non-statutory sources

In addition to RESA and the statutory instruments created under it, there are a number of non-statutory guides, aimed variously at local authorities, national regulators, businesses, consumer groups, lawyers and members of the public. The detail and application of these sources will be considered alongside the relevant statutory provisions in this chapter; in this part their status is briefly considered. The sources are as follows: **4.34**

- (i) *Regulators' Compliance Code*, published December 2007;
- (ii) *Explanatory Notes to the Regulatory Enforcement and Sanctions Act 2008*;
- (iii) BERR, *Regulatory Enforcement and Sanctions Act 2008: Guidance to the Act*, published July 2008;
- (iv) BERR, *Guidance on creating new regulatory penalties and offences*, published 26 January 2009.

Regulators' Compliance Code

The Statutory Code of Practice for Regulators (the Code) was issued under s. 22(1) of the Legislative and Regulatory Reform Act 2006 and came into force on 6 April 2008.[55] The Code has its origins in the Hampton Report[56] and is intended to promote more effective inspection and enforcement by regulatory authorities, through requiring those regulators exercising specified regulatory functions to have regard to its principles. A full copy of the Code can be found on the Department for Business Innovation and Skills' website.[57] **4.35**

According to the terms of the Code itself, it is intended to help regulators foster 'a positive and proactive approach towards ensuring compliance, by helping and encouraging regulated entities to understand and meet regulatory requirements more easily, and [to respond] proportionately to regulatory breaches'.[58] **4.36**

What are the principles?

The Code requires regulators to have regard to principles based around nine separate but related areas of their work: economic progress, risk assessment, advice and guidance, **4.37**

---

[54] RESA, s. 57.

[55] By virtue of the Legislative and Regulatory Reform Code of Practice (Appointed Day) Order 2007, SI 3548/2007.

[56] See paras 1.22–1.26 for further detail about the Hampton Report.

[57] <http://www.bis.gov.uk>.

[58] BERR, *Statutory Code of Practice for Regulators*, p. 7, para. 1.3.

inspections and other visits, information requirements, compliance and enforcement actions and accountability.

To whom does it apply?

4.38 The Code only applies to those regulatory functions specified by order made under s. 24(2) of the Legislative and Regulatory Reform Act 2006. The Legislative and Regulatory Reform (Regulatory Functions) Order 2007[59] provides that the Code applies to:

   (i) all the regulatory functions exercisable by the statutory regulators listed in Part 1 (including the Financial Services Authority, the Health and Safety Commission and the Office of Fair Trading);

  (ii) the regulatory functions exercisable by ministers of the Crown listed in the various enactments in Part 2 (relating to regulatory areas such as agriculture, food standards and safety, and road transport);

 (iii) the regulatory functions exercisable by local authorities listed in the various enactments in Part 3 (relating to regulatory areas such as anti-social behaviour, consumer protection, licensing and public health and safety); and

 (iv) all regulatory functions exercisable by local authorities conferred by secondary legislation made under s. 2(2) of the European Communities Act 1972, in relation to food hygiene, food standards and animal feed.

4.39 A 'regulatory function' is defined as:[60]

   (i) a function under any enactment of imposing requirements, restrictions or conditions, or setting standards or giving guidance, in relation to any activity; or

  (ii) a function that relates to the securing of compliance with, or the enforcement of, requirements, restrictions, conditions, standards or guidance which under or by virtue of any enactment relate to any activity.

4.40 In accordance with s. 24(3) of the Legislative and Regulatory Reform Act 2006, the Code does not apply to:[61]

   (i) regulatory functions so far as exercisable in Scotland to the extent that the functions relate to matters that are not reserved matters;

  (ii) regulatory functions so far as exercisable in Northern Ireland to the extent that the functions relate to transferred matters; and

 (iii) regulatory functions exercisable only in or as regards Wales.

Which decisions does it apply to?

4.41 Regulators required to have regard to the Code's provisions must do so in two circumstances:

   (i) when determining any general policy or principles about the exercise of those specified functions;[62] or

---

[59] SI 3544/2007.
[60] Legislative and Regulatory Reform Act 2006, s. 32(2).
[61] For more about the devolved administrations see paras 4.23–4.33.
[62] Legislative and Regulatory Reform Act 2006, s. 22(2).

(ii) when exercising a specified regulatory function that is itself a function of setting standards or giving general guidance about other regulatory functions (whether their own functions or someone else's functions).[63]

The duties to have regard to the Code   **4.42**

> do not apply to the exercise by a regulator. . . of any specified regulatory function in individual cases. The duty on the regulator to 'have regard' to the Code is a positive obligation requiring them to take into account the Code's provisions and give them due weight in developing their policies or principles, in setting standards or giving advice. This means, for example, that while an inspector or investigator should operate in accordance with a regulator's general policy or guidance on inspections, investigations and enforcement activities, the Code does not apply directly to the work of that inspector or investigator in carrying out any of these activities in individual cases.[64]

Deviation from the terms of the Code is permissible in certain prescribed circumstances.   **4.43**
According to the terms of the Code itself:

> The regulator is not bound to follow a provision of the Code if they *properly* conclude that the provision is either not relevant or is outweighed by another relevant consideration. They should ensure that any decision to depart from any provision of the Code is properly reasoned and based on material evidence. Where there are no such relevant considerations, regulators should follow the Code.

Explanatory notes to the Regulatory Enforcement and Sanctions Act 2008

The explanatory notes to RESA were prepared by the Department for Business and Regulatory   **4.44**
Reform (BERR), the department with the responsibility for the introduction of the Bill[65]
(now known as the Department for Business, Innovation and Skills (BIS)).[66]

Since the first Public General Act of 1999, all new Public Acts which result from Bills intro-   **4.45**
duced into either House of Parliament by a government minister[67] must be accompanied by explanatory notes. Their purpose is to make the Act accessible to readers who are not legally qualified and who have no specialized knowledge of the matters dealt with; this will include explaining the legal and political implications of the legislation.

According to the introduction to the explanatory notes, they 'do not form part of the Act and   **4.46**
have not been endorsed by Parliament'.[68] Thus whilst the notes may be of some assistance in the interpretation of the provisions of the Act, they should not be seen as directory in any way. Where there is, or appears to be, a conflict between the notes and the Act, the terms of the Act should always prevail.

---

[63] Ibid., s. 22(3).
[64] BERR *Statutory Code of Practice for Regulators*, para. 2.4.
[65] A copy can be found on the Office of Public Sector Information website: <http://www.opsi.gov.uk>.
[66] In June 2009, the Department for Business, Enterprise and Regulatory Reform (BERR) merged with the Department for Innovation, Universities and Skills, creating the newly formed Department for Business, Innovation and Skills (BIS).
[67] With the exception of Appropriation, Consolidated Fund, Finance and Consolidation Acts.
[68] P. 1, para. 1.

BERR, *Regulatory Enforcement and Sanctions Act 2008: Guidance to the Act*

4.47 The Department for Business Enterprise and Regulatory Reform (BERR) published guidance to RESA in July 2008.[69] The guidance is intended to provide 'assistance in understanding the provisions contained in the Act' and to 'help illustrate how the provisions of the . . . Act should work'.[70]

4.48 As with the explanatory notes, this guidance is not directory in nature and adherence to its terms is not mandatory. Regulatory bodies seeking the award of the sanctions or looking for advice on how best to implement the powers, would do well to look at the suggestions made within the guidance as to how these decisions ought to be made although, again, they are not bound by its terms.

BERR, *Guidance on creating new regulatory penalties and offences*

4.49 In January 2009, the Department for Business Enterprise and Regulatory Reform published further guidance on the Act in the form of the *Guidance on creating new regulatory penalties and offences,*[71] a copy of which is reproduced in full at appendix 7.

4.50 The paper sets out guidelines relating to the drafting of any new legislation creating the civil sanctions. It contains both practical guidance on matters such as who to contact at BERR (now Department for Business Skills and Innovation (BIS)) when preparing the legislation, and guidance on important procedural considerations such as the setting up of appeal and enforcement processes.

4.51 Unlike the earlier, more general, guidance to the Act, the guidelines in this document 'represent agreed Government policy and following them will help [regulators] through the clearance process more smoothly'.[72] Regulatory authorities considering seeking the award of the civil sanctions should consider the terms of this guidance at the earliest possible stage of policy making. As the guidance points out, when DA[73] clearance is sought for any new proposals, any departure from the principles will have to be justified.[74]

E. Who can apply for the sanctions?

Introduction

4.52 Part 3 of RESA creates three groups of regulators who may apply for the award of the sanctions, and in respect of them all, requires that the civil sanctions may only be applied in respect of relevant offences—that is to say, offences for which they have an enforcement function.

4.53 The practical effect of the categorization of the regulators in this way is that some regulators (such as the Environment Agency or the Information Commissioner[75]) will automatically be

---

[69] A copy is available on the Department for Business Innovation and Skills (BIS) website: <http://www.bis.gov.uk>.

[70] BERR, *Regulatory Enforcement and Sanctions Act 2008: Guidance to the Act*, p. 5.

[71] A copy can be found on the Ministry of Justice website: <http://www.justice.gov.uk>.

[72] P. 1, para. 2.

[73] Domestic Affairs.

[74] P. 1, para. 2.

[75] These bodies are designated regulators under Sch. 5.

able to apply to the minister for access to the sanctions to attach to any offences in relation to which they have an enforcement function,[76] whilst other regulatory authorities, such as local authorities and ministers, may only apply for the sanctions in relation to offences created by enactments listed in the schedules to the Act[77] (or offences created under secondary legislation from such enactments).

4.54 This part looks in detail at which bodies have access to the civil sanctions by reference to the definitions of the terms, 'regulator', 'relevant offence' and 'enforcement function'.

The minister's powers to award the sanctions

4.55 The minister empowered to seek the award of the sanctions on behalf of the regulator must have responsibility for the particular policy area covered by the enforcement work of that authority, for example the Secretary of State for Work and Pensions would make any application on behalf of the Health and Safety Executive, and the Secretary of State for Environment, Food and Rural Affairs would make any application on behalf of the Environment Agency. Not all of the powers will be necessary in all cases and as such the minister is able to select particular options depending on the nature of the regulatory regime and the type of regulator seeking the award of the powers.

4.56 According to ss 39(1) (fixed monetary penalties), 42(1) (discretionary requirements), 46(1) (stop notices), and 50(1) (enforcement undertakings), permission to use the powers may only be conferred by a minister on a *regulator* and in respect of a *relevant offence*.

4.57 The circumstances in which the minister may award the sanctions are as follows (emphasis added):

(i) **fixed monetary penalties**: s. 39(1)

The provision which may be made under this section is provision to confer on a **regulator** the power by notice to impose a fixed monetary penalty on a person in relation to a **relevant offence**.

(ii) **discretionary requirements**: s. 42(1)

The provision which may be made under this section is provision to confer on a **regulator** the power by notice to impose one or more discretionary requirements on a person in relation to a **relevant offence**.

(iii) **stop notices**: s. 46

    (1) The provision which may be made under this section is provision conferring on a **regulator** the power to serve a stop notice on a person.

    (2) . . .

    (3) Provision under this section may only confer such a power in relation to a case falling within subsections (4) or (5).

    (4) A case falling within this subsection is a case where—

        (a) the person is carrying on the activity,

        (b) the regulator reasonably believes that the activity as carried on by that person is causing, or presents a significant risk of causing, serious harm to any of the matters referred to in subsection (6), **and**

---

[76] RESA, ss 38(1) and 71(1).
[77] Ibid., Schs 6 and 7.

    (c) the regulator reasonably believes that the activity as carried on by that person involves or is likely to involve the commission of a **relevant offence** by that person.

  (5) A case falling within this subsection is a case where the **regulator** reasonably believes that—

    (a) the person is likely to carry on the activity,

    (b) the activity as likely to be carried on by that person will cause, or will present a significant risk of causing, serious harm to any of the matters referred to in subsection (6), **and**

    (c) the activity as likely to be carried on by that person will involve or will be likely to involve the commission of a **relevant offence** by that person.

(iv) **enforcement undertakings**: s. 50(1)

The provision which may be made under this section is provision—

(a) to enable a regulator to accept an enforcement undertaking from a person in a case where the **regulator** has reasonable grounds to suspect that the person has committed a **relevant offence**, and

(b) for the acceptance of the undertaking to have the consequences in subsection (4).

Definition of 'regulator'

4.58 The three categories of regulator created by Part 3 are as follows:

(i) those listed in Sch. 5 (designated regulators);[78]

(ii) those that have an enforcement function in relation to offences listed in Sch. 6 (enactments specified for the purposes of orders under Part 3);[79] and

(iii) relevant enforcement authorities that have an enforcement function in relation to offences in secondary legislation made under enactments listed in Sch. 7 (enactments specified for the purposes of s. 62).

Designated regulators

4.59 The term 'regulator' is principally defined in s. 37 of RESA, in which the first two categories of regulator are provided for: designated regulators and those who have an enforcement function in relation to an enactment specified in Sch. 6. In respect of the former, s. 37(1) provides:

> In this Part, 'regulator' means—
> (a) a person specified in Schedule 5 (in this Part called a 'designated regulator') . . .

4.60 This group of regulators includes non-departmental public bodies, non-ministerial departments, principal national regulators and public corporations. Their regulatory reach covers areas such as public health and protection, finance and information and the built and natural environment. In total, there are nine different government departments with responsibility for these twenty-seven different regulatory authorities. Schedule 5 contains

---

[78] Ibid., s. 37(1)(a).
[79] Ibid., s. 37(1)(b).

the complete list of regulators designated for the purposes of s. 37 and is reproduced in full at Appendix 1.

4.61 There are a number of notable omissions from the list at Sch. 5, for example the Civil Aviation Authority, Ofgem, and Ofwat. The constitution of Sch. 5 was debated at some length in Parliament,[80] during which the government explained that these bodies were not included as they (the regulators) were 'confident that their current mix of civil and criminal powers [was] sufficient to carry out their regulatory duties'.[81] There is no power in RESA to amend Sch. 5.

Regulators with an enforcement function in relation to Schedule 6 offences

4.62 The second group of regulators that may apply for the sanctions are those bodies that have an enforcement function in relation to any of the 142 enactments specified in Sch. 6. Section 37 provides:

(1) In this Part, 'regulator' means—
    (a) . . .
    (b) a person, other than a designated regulator, who has an enforcement function in relation to an offence to which subsection (2) applies.
(2) This subsection applies to an offence contained, immediately before the day on which this Act is passed, in an enactment specified in Schedule 6.

4.63 Schedule 6 contains a list of specified enactments for the purposes of s. 37(2) and is reproduced in full at Appendix 1. This group of regulators will largely consist of local authorities and ministers with enforcement functions, for example in relation to regulatory matters concerning agriculture, animals, the environment, food safety, consumer protection, transport, and health and safety.

4.64 Specifically excluded under this section by virtue of s. 37(3) are the Crown Prosecution Service, a member of a police force in England and Wales, a procurator fiscal, a constable of a police force in Scotland, the Public Prosecution Service for Northern Ireland and a member of the Police Service of Northern Ireland. These bodies do not come within the definition of a regulator and are not able to avail themselves of the civil sanctions. As Lord Bach explained to the Grand Committee, this decision was taken because the '. . . powers in Part 3 are an alternative to criminal prosecution . . .' and are '. . . designed specifically for use by regulators'.[82]

Regulators with enforcement functions in relation to Schedule 7 offences

4.65 A third category of regulator is envisaged by s. 62, namely those bodies that enforce offences under certain secondary legislative enactments. The effect of s. 62 is to widen the definition of regulator provided for in s. 37 to include bodies that have an enforcement function in relation to any offence created by secondary legislation under one of the forty-five enactments listed in Sch. 7.[83] Regulatory authorities falling within this group are known

---

[80] Hansard, HL Deb., vol. 698, cols GC347–GC355 (30 January 2008).
[81] Ibid., col. GC353 (30 January 2008).
[82] Hansard, HL Deb., vol. 698, col. GC342 (January 2008).
[83] Sch. 7 is reproduced in full at Appendix 1.

as relevant enforcement authorities.[84] Such a body may be awarded the powers under Part 3 as *if they were a regulator* (as defined in s. 37). In this regard, s. 62 provides as follows:

(1) This section applies where, by virtue of a specified enactment—
  (a) a Minister of the Crown has, or Welsh Ministers have, power by statutory instrument to make provision creating a criminal offence, and
  (b) the power has been or is being exercised so as to create the offence.
(2) The power includes power to make, in relation to a relevant enforcement authority, any provision which could be made by an order under this Part if, for the purposes of this Part—
  (a) **the relevant enforcement authority were a regulator, and**
  (b) the offence were a relevant offence in relation to that regulator.
(3) . . .
(4) In subsection (1) 'specified enactment' means any enactment specified in Schedule 7.
(5) In subsection (2) 'relevant enforcement authority' means a person, other than a person referred to in section 37(3), who has an enforcement function in relation to the offence. (Emphasis added.)

F. To which offences can the sanctions be attached?

4.66 Regulators[85] may only seek access to the powers under Part 3 in respect of *relevant offences*; they cannot be attached to all criminal offences. There is no single definition of the term 'relevant offence' in the legislation; its meaning differs depending on which category of regulator it relates to.

4.67 Whilst a regulator is likely to seek the award of the sanctions in respect of particular offences, the minister will ultimately decide which relevant offences should be covered by any provisions that are conferred on that regulator.

Definition of 'relevant offence'

4.68 The term 'relevant offence' is defined in s. 38:

(1) In this Part, 'relevant offence', in relation to a designated regulator, means an offence —
  (a) in relation to which the designated regulator has an enforcement function, and
  (b) which is contained in an Act immediately before the day on which this Act is passed.
(2) In this Part 'relevant offence', in relation to a regulator other than a designated regulator, means an offence —
  (a) which is contained, immediately before the day on which this Act is passed, in an enactment specified in Schedule 6, and
  (b) in relation to which that regulator has an enforcement function.

Enforcement function

4.69 'Enforcement function' is defined in s. 71 as '. . . a function (whether or not statutory) of taking any action with a view to or in connection with the imposition of any sanction, criminal or otherwise'.

4.70 The definition of enforcement function includes any person who (emphasis added) 'is in any circumstances *capable* of exercising an enforcement function in relation to the offence'.[86]

---

[84] As defined in RESA, s. 62(5).
[85] See paras. 4.58–4.65 for the definition of a 'regulator'.
[86] RESA, s. 71(2).

This definition is broad enough to encompass regulatory authorities which, whilst they have the power to enforce regulatory non-compliance, in practice, arrange for that function to be undertaken by another body. For example, the Department for Environment, Food and Rural Affairs (DEFRA) undertakes regulatory enforcement action on behalf of the Gangmasters Licensing Authority.

Designated regulators

Designated regulators (those listed in Sch. 5) may seek the award of the civil sanctions if they are to be applied to a relevant offence. In relation to designated regulators, an offence is said to be a relevant offence if: **4.71**

(i) the criminal offence was in existence before 1 October 2008:[87] s. 38(1)(b); and
(ii) the regulator has an enforcement function[88] in relation to that offence: s. 38(1)(a).

In contradistinction to the other two classes of regulator envisaged by Part 3, for designated regulators there is no requirement that the offence in respect of which the sanctions are sought be listed in any of the Schedules to RESA.   **4.72**

Regulators with an enforcement function in relation to Schedule 6 offences

The second group of regulators envisaged by Part 3 are those bodies with an enforcement function in relation to any offence contained in any enactment listed in Sch. 6. These regulators may apply for the Part 3 sanctions if they are to be applied to a relevant offence. Section 38 provides that for these regulatory authorities, an offence is said to be a relevant offence if: **4.73**

(i)   it is contained in any of the enactments listed in Sch. 6:[89] s. 38(2)(a);
(ii) it was in existence on a day before 1 October 2008:[90] s. 38(2)(a); and
(iii) it is an offence in relation to which the regulator has an enforcement function:[91] s. 38(2)(b).

Regulators with enforcement functions in relation to Schedule 7 offences

Finally, in respect of the group of regulators known as relevant enforcement authorities, s. 62(2) provides that if the offence in respect of which the sanctions are to be applied is created by subordinate legislation under any of the forty-five Acts listed in Sch. 7, that offence is to be treated *as if it were* a relevant offence for the purposes of an application for an Order under Part 3. Section 62 provides as follows (emphasis added):   **4.74**

(1) This section applies where, by virtue of a specified enactment—
    (a) a Minister of the Crown has, or the Welsh Ministers have, power by statutory instrument to make provision creating a criminal offence, and
    (b) the power has been or is being exercised so as to create the offence.

---

[87] By virtue of The Regulatory Enforcement and Sanctions Act 2008 (Commencement No. 1) Order 2008, SI 2371/2008 (c. 104).
[88] RESA, s. 71. See para. 4.69 for more on the definition of 'enforcement function'.
[89] Which was in existence up to (but not including) 1 October 2008, by virtue of the Regulatory Enforcement and Sanctions Act 2008 (Commencement No. 1) Order 2008, SI 2371/2008 (c. 104).
[90] By virtue of the Regulatory Enforcement and Sanctions Act 2008 (Commencement No. 1) Order 2008, SI 2371/2008 (c. 104).
[91] RESA, s. 71. See para. 4.69 for more on the definition of 'enforcement function'.

(2) The power includes power to make, in relation to a relevant enforcement authority, any provision which could be made by an order under this Part if, for the purposes of this Part—
(a) the relevant enforcement authority were a regulator, and
(b) the offence were a relevant offence in relation to that regulator.

4.75 The enactments listed in Sch. 7 largely cover the same regulatory subject matter as covered by Schs 5 and 6, although s. 22 of the European Communities Act 1972 (ECA) is not listed as it was considered by the Bill team that the power in the ECA is sufficiently wide to allow for the creation of civil sanctions for criminal offences created under the ECA.[92]

4.76 During the debate of this issue in the House of Lords, Lord Bach noted that the government would 'expect any new civil sanctions created under the ECA to follow the principles of the Macrory review and the model set out in Part 3'.[93] For an example of the approach taken by a regulator seeking to apply the civil sanctions to offences made by regulations[94] under ECA (and thus outside the operation of RESA), see the Department for Business Innovation and Skills, *A consultation on the pilot operation of civil sanction powers for consumer law enforcers.*[95] This scheme is discussed in more detail in paras 6.190–6.191.

4.77 Section 62 provides that the regulator may only seek the award of the powers in respect of offences that the relevant authority[96] has already created (or that he is seeking to create) by way of secondary legislation under any of the Sch. 7 enactments.

4.78 Additionally, in order for any offence created under a Sch. 7 enactment to be deemed a relevant offence, it must have been in existence on a day before the day on which RESA came into force, namely 1 October 2008.[97]

'Which is contained in an Act immediately before the day on which this Act is passed'

4.79 The Part 3 sanctions may only be applied to criminal offences[98] existing at the time that Part 3 and Schs 5–7 of RESA came into force.[99] In respect of the first two categories of regulators (designated regulators and bodies that have an enforcement function in relation to any enactment listed in Sch. 6), ministers may only make orders under Part 3 conferring the powers in relation to offences in Acts of Parliament existing before 1 October 2008.[100] It is expected that any new offences created after that date will provide for the imposition of the civil sanctions should they be required.

---

[92] *Regulatory Enforcement and Sanctions Act 2008: Explanatory Notes*, para. 163. See also Hansard, HL Deb., vol. 698, col. GC350 (30 January 2008).

[93] Hansard, HL Deb., vol. 698, col. GC351 (30 January 2008).

[94] It is proposed that the pilot should cover the Consumer Protection from Unfair Trading Regulations 2008, SI 1277/2008 and the General Product Safety Regulations 2005, SI 1803/2005. These regulations are made under the European Communities Act 1972.

[95] Published March 2010. A copy can be found on the Department for Business Innovation and Skills (BIS) website: <http://www.bis.gov.uk>.

[96] RESA, s. 71(1): minister of the Crown or Welsh minister.

[97] The Regulatory Enforcement and Sanctions Act 2008 (Commencement No. 1) Order 2008, SI 2371/2008 (c. 104).

[98] Or pre-existing powers to make criminal offences: RESA, s. 62.

[99] 1 October 2008, by virtue of the Regulatory Enforcement and Sanctions Act 2008 (Commencement No. 1) Order 2008, SI 2371/2008 (c. 104).

[100] RESA, s. 38(1)(b) and (2)(a).

In respect of the third category of regulators, the provisions of Part 3 only apply to enact- **4.80**
ments containing the power to create criminal offences existing before 1 October 2008.[101]
Hence any power granted to a minister in the future to create new offences will need to make
its own provision for the inclusion of the civil sanctions were they required. As the *Explanatory
Notes to RESA* suggest,[102] this section (s. 62), '. . . would allow, for example, the Minister
when amending or consolidating criminal offences contained in secondary legislation made
under a listed enactment, to make provision for fixed monetary penalties', but not to create
a new criminal offence where there is presently no such power.

G. How are the civil sanctions obtained?

Introduction

The provisions in Part 3 are enabling powers and require implementation by statutory **4.81**
instrument,[103] hence although they came into force on 1 October 2008,[104] their effect will
not be felt immediately. There are a number of procedural hurdles that must be cleared
before the enabling legislation can be passed and the sanctions acquired; they do not accrue
to the regulator automatically.[105] The process for obtaining the civil sanctions is set out in the
flowchart at Figure 4.1.[106]

First, the minister will require evidence of the regulator's ability to comply with the Principles **4.82**
of Good Regulation to ensure that they will be 'Hampton-compliant'.[107] There must then be
cross-governmental approval, the matter may have to be considered by the Reducing
Regulation Sub-committee (formerly Panel for Regulatory Accountability (PRA), and there
must be an extensive consultation exercise. If, after that, there has been a significant change
in what had been proposed, a further consultation process will need to take place. Only then
can the matter reach Parliament[108] where it will need to be considered by both the House of
Commons and the House of Lords, by way of the affirmative resolution procedure.[109]

Whilst a regulator may in theory have access to the civil sanctions, the process for obtaining **4.83**
them is, therefore, far from straightforward. During the Bill's passage through Parliament,
these procedural hurdles were described as being so high as to be 'almost unscaleable'.[110]
There is no doubt that the process for obtaining the sanctions is protracted and regulators
are reporting that it is infuriatingly slow. Only now, some two years after RESA came into
force, are regulators beginning to be able to avail themselves of the powers. On 6 April
2010, the Environment Agency and Natural England were the first regulators to be

---

[101] Ibid., s. 62(1)(a) and (b).
[102] *Regulatory Enforcement and Sanctions Act 2008: Explanatory Notes*, para. 162.
[103] RESA, s. 36(3).
[104] By virtue of the Regulatory Enforcement and Sanctions Act 2008 (Commencement No. 1) Order 2008,
SI 2371/2008 (c.104).
[105] For more about the procedure for obtaining the sanctions see paras 4.84–4.130.
[106] Reproduced from BERR, *Regulatory Enforcement and Sanctions Act 2008: Guidance to the Act*, p. 29.
[107] RESA, s. 66.
[108] Or the Welsh Assembly in relation to orders made by Welsh ministers: RESA, s. 61(2).
[109] For more on the affirmative resolution procedure see para. 4.129.
[110] Hansard, HL Deb., vol. 696, col. 1258 (28 November 2007).

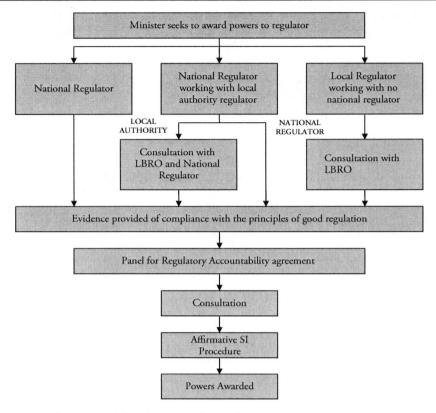

Figure 4.1 Process for obtaining the civil sanctions

awarded the civil sanctions, by virtue of the Environmental Civil Sanctions (England) Order 2010.[111]

First steps: obtaining the civil sanctions

4.84 A regulator seeking to obtain the civil sanctions should approach the relevant minister at the earliest possible stage of policy development as this will be likely to save time in the long run. Regulators will need to consider whether any other government departments have an interest and should be contacted, as well as contacting any stakeholders who may have an interest in the legislation.

4.85 The BERR *Guidance on creating new regulatory penalties and offences*[112] is an invaluable resource and should be consulted by regulators throughout the process and particularly at this early stage. As discussed in para. 4.51, adherence to this guidance would be well advised and any deviation from it will need to be justified.

---

[111] SI 1157/2010. For more about these regulators see Chapter 7.
[112] A copy can be found on the Ministry of Justice website: <http://www.justice.gov.uk>.

Compliance with the Principles of Good Regulation

The first formal step in the process for the relevant authority (minister of the Crown or Welsh minister[113]) is to satisfy themselves that, if the regulator is granted the powers, they will use them in accordance with the Principles of Good Regulation as enunciated by Hampton[114] and codified in s. 66 of RESA—that is to say, will they use the powers in a transparent, accountable, proportionate, consistent and targeted way? The assessment of whether a regulator is likely to comply with these principles was seen by Macrory as a key element in ensuring that the sanctions were to be effective.[115] **4.86**

Section 66 requires that: **4.87**

> The relevant authority may not make any provision under or by virtue of this Part conferring power on a regulator to impose a civil sanction in relation to an offence unless the authority is satisfied that the regulator will act in accordance with the principles referred to in section 5(2) in exercising that power.

The principles referred to in s. 5(2) are that: **4.88**

 (i) regulatory activities should be carried out in a way which is transparent, accountable, proportionate and consistent; and

 (ii) regulatory activities should be targeted only at cases in which action is needed.

This section does not require the minister to be satisfied that the regulator is *currently* complying with the Principles of Good Regulation, only that they will do so in the future application of the sanctions. A provision requiring the minister to be satisfied that there was current compliance with the principles was seen as being 'a step too far',[116] it being regarded as sufficient that s. 22 of the Legislative and Regulatory Reform Act 2006 already requires a regulator to have regard to the principles in the form of the *Regulators' Compliance Code.*[117] **4.89**

Ensuring that regulators will adhere to the Principles of Good Regulation is seen as a valuable safeguard, designed to ensure that the award of the sanctions is made only to those regulatory authorities who are able and willing to comply with the Hampton vision. **4.90**

How will the evidence for this be generated?

Whilst the provision is forward-looking, requiring the minister to consider whether the regulator *will* comply with the Principles of Good Regulation, it is expected that the minister will make this decision based upon evidence of previous compliance with those Principles. **4.91**

Where will the minister look to find evidence to satisfy himself that the Principles of Good Regulation are presently being met? The terms of RESA do not require the minister to have regard to any particular source when making the determination under s. 66. Turning to the **4.92**

---

[113] RESA, s. 71.

[114] In his report, *Reducing Administrative Burdens: Effective Inspection and Enforcement*, published 16 March 2005, at p. 43.

[115] Richard Macrory, *Regulatory Justice: Making Sanctions Effective*, at p. 52, para. 3.50. For more about the Principles of Good Regulation, see para 1.15.

[116] Per Lord Bach, Hansard, HL Deb., vol. 698, col. GC346 (30 January 2008).

[117] The Statutory Code of Practice for Regulators, published 17 December 2007. See in particular p. 8, para. 2.3. A copy can be found on the Department for Business Innovation and Skills website: <http://www.bis.gov.uk>. See para. 4.35 for more about the status of the Code.

BERR *Regulatory Enforcement and Sanctions Act 2008: Guidance to the Act* however, it is clear that the government envisages that this information will largely come from Hampton Implementation Reviews[118] (HIR), carried out by the Department of Business Innovation and Skills, of the work of regulators:

> Before making an order, the Minister must be satisfied that a regulator will use the powers in a way that is compliant with the principles of good regulation – transparent, accountable, proportionate, consistent and targeted only at cases where action is needed.[119]

4.93 According to the Department for Business Innovation and Skills, 'the Hampton Implementation Reviews assess how well regulators are following the Hampton Principles of Better Regulation and the characteristics of effective sanctions defined by the Macrory review'.[120] Where a regulator has not been through an HIR, they should follow the *Hampton Implementation Reviews: Guidance for Review Teams* (HIR Guidance)[121] and provide qualitative evidence based on this.[122]

4.94 The aim of the HIR guidance is to provide regulators and stakeholders with a clear understanding of how compliance with the Hampton Principles will be assessed during the review. The HIRs are divided into two parts: the first contains six separate sections on specific subject areas, namely the design of regulations, advice and guidance, data requests, inspections, sanctions and focus on outcomes. The second part of the review requires the reviewer to consider how far the regulator is 'living the Hampton vision'. This will include consideration of the six principles referred to above as well as the following: the extent to which the regulator uses or employs risk-based regulation, the extent to which the regulator can be said to be both transparent and accountable, and the extent to which the regulator encourages or permits economic progress.

4.95 Initially, HIRs were carried out on five major national regulators (Environment Agency, Financial Services Authority, Food Standards Agency, Health and Safety Executive and Office of Fair Trading) between August and December 2007. The review process was then rolled out to a further thirty-one national regulatory bodies in 2008–09, and those reports have now been published.[123]

4.96 The BERR *Regulatory Enforcement and Sanctions Act 2008: Guidance to the Act* makes some further suggestions as to possible sources of information that the relevant authority may look to in order to make the decision required of them under s. 66. For example, in respect of local authority regulators, the government may wish to look to the Local Better Regulation Office (LBRO) and in cases where there is co-regulation, the relevant authority may also seek information from the National Regulator.

---

[118] For more about HIR see para. 1.28.

[119] At p. 28, para. 33.

[120] Richard Macrory, *Regulatory Justice: Making Sanctions Effective.* A copy can be found on the Department for Business Innovation and Skills (BIS) website: <http://www.bis.gov.uk>.

[121] Published 1 March 2008. A copy can be found on the National Audit Office website: <http://www.nao.org.uk>.

[122] BERR, *Regulatory Enforcement and Sanctions Act 2008: Guidance to the Act,* p. 28, para. 33.

[123] The reports can be found on the Department for Business Innovation and Skills (BIS) website: <http://www.bis.gov.uk>.

'Unless the authority is satisfied'

Section 66 requires only that the relevant authority must be *satisfied* that the regulator will comply with the Principles of Good Regulation before he may proceed to confer the powers on them. No further guidance is provided as to the meaning of the term 'satisfied' either in RESA itself or in the BERR *Regulatory Enforcement and Sanctions Act 2008: Guidance to the Act.* Where a regulator has received a favourable HIR, this decision is unlikely to be contentious, past compliance being a strong indicator of likely future compliance. Where a regulator has not fared so well in the HIR, or has yet to have a review, the decision may be less straightforward. **4.97**

In the criminal courts, a decision requiring magistrates to be 'satisfied' of a particular fact has been taken to mean a decision based 'on solid grounds on which they could reasonably found a reliable opinion'.[124] Thus whilst the decision is necessarily a subjective one, it must be based on objectively observable criteria. **4.98**

Reducing Regulation sub-committee

Once the relevant authority is satisfied that the regulator within his responsibility is ready to use the additional powers, he must, where appropriate, seek the agreement of the Reducing Regulation sub-committee (RRC) (formerly the Panel for Regulatory Accountability (PRA)). **4.99**

The RRC is a Cabinet sub-committee set up by the Coalition government in the summer of 2010, with the stated terms of reference being '[t]o consider issues relating to reducing regulation'. The RRC is chaired by the Secretary of State for Business Innovation and Skills. **4.100**

Not all proposals will need clearance by the RRC, although at the time of writing, the precise operating principles of the new committee were unknown. As with approvals by the PRA, any such proposal must be accompanied by an impact assessment. **4.101**

The Cabinet Office website[125] may in due course be updated to provide detailed guidance on how a relevant authority should go about securing the agreement of the RRC; in the meantime, and if there is any doubt about whether policy clearance is required, the relevant committee secretary may be contacted, and they will be able to give advice based on the individual circumstances of the case. **4.102**

On a practical note, the relevant authority would be well advised to check at an early stage whether the proposal needs to be considered by the RRC, as it can take a long time to obtain collective agreement for a policy, and this will need to be factored in to the planning. **4.103**

Impact assessments

Impact assessments (IA) must follow strict guidelines as to their content, form and publication. When preparing an IA, ministers should have regard to the *Impact Assessment Guidance,*[126] which provides details on when and how an IA should be completed and **4.104**

---

[124] *R v Liverpool City Justices, ex p Grogan* [1991] COD 148.
[125] <http://www.cabinetoffice.gov.uk>.
[126] The Department for Business Innovation and Skills (BIS), *Impact Assessment Guidance*, published 1 April 2010. A copy can be found on the BIS website: <http://www.bis.gov.uk>.

published, as well as the *Impact Assessment Toolkit* (IA Toolkit),[127] which is a step-by-step guide on how to complete an IA.

4.105 According to the government, impact assessments are intended to be useful tools for policy makers, helping them to assess and present the likely costs and benefits and the associated risks of a proposal that might have an impact on the public, private or third sector. They should also help policy makers to fully think through the reasons for government intervention, to weigh up various options for achieving an objective and to understand the consequences of a proposed intervention.[128]

Duty to consult: initial consultation

4.106 Once the relevant authority is satisfied that the regulator is Hampton-compliant and the RRC has given the proposal policy clearance (in appropriate cases), a consultation must be conducted.[129]

4.107 As can be seen from Figure 4.1, the duty to consult arises at two discrete stages of the process and the approach taken at each stage will vary depending on the nature of the regulator seeking the award of the powers. The consultation process for orders made in relation to Scottish or Welsh offences also differs slightly.[130] For the purposes of this text, the consultation that takes place at this stage of the process shall be referred to as the initial consultation.

4.108 This initial consultation exercise will enable the relevant authority to gather valuable information on the likely impact of any new legislation, helping it to make informed decisions about the preliminary policy analysis and about the choice of powers that may be awarded. Consultations are a valuable tool in ensuring that all stakeholders have the opportunity to comment on any new proposals, helping the regulator in turn to remain accountable and thus retain legitimacy.

Who must be consulted?

4.109 Before any of the powers under Part 3 can be awarded, s. 60 requires that the relevant authority (a minister of the Crown or the Welsh ministers[131]) proposing to make an order under Part 3 *must* consult with:

 (i) the regulator to which the order relates: s. 60(1)(a);
 (ii) such organizations as appear to the relevant authority to be representative of persons substantially affected by the proposals: s. 60(1)(b); and
 (iii) such other persons as the relevant authority considers appropriate: s. 60(1)(c).

The regulator to which the order relates

4.110 Section 60(1)(a) requires that the relevant authority must consult the regulator to which the order relates; this will be either the relevant local authority, ministerial department or Sch. 5 regulator. Occasionally more than one body may have an enforcement function in

---

[127] A copy of this can be found on the Department for Business Innovation and Skills website: <http://www.bis.gov.uk>.
[128] Department for Business Innovation and Skills (BIS), *Impact Assessment Guidance*, para. 4, p. 2.
[129] RESA, s. 60(1).
[130] As to which see paras 4.116–4.120.
[131] RESA, s. 71.

relation to a relevant offence and, in those circumstances, all such bodies will need to be consulted.

Such organizations as appear to the relevant authority to be representative of persons substantially affected by the proposals

The minster is required by virtue of s. 60(1)(b) to consult such organizations as appear to be representative of persons substantially affected by the proposals. This provision ensures that the relevant authority consults all those bodies that may be affected by the legislation, in other words stakeholders or their representatives. It will be for the relevant authority to decide which bodies should be considered to be *representative* of those *substantially* affected by the legislation; neither of these terms is further defined in RESA. **4.111**

Such other persons as the relevant authority considers appropriate

Section 60(1)(c) permits the relevant authority to widen the scope of the consultation to those bodies that, whilst they may not be directly affected by the provisions, may neverthe-less have a view about them. **4.112**

The form of the consultation

Whilst RESA does not require a particular form of consultation to be undertaken, where it does take the form of a formal written public consultation, because the Department for Business, Innovation and Skills (BIS) have adopted the *Code of Practice on Consultation*[132] (the Code of Practice), it is expected that any such consultation will adhere to its terms. The Code of Practice sets out seven 'consultation criteria' to which ministers must adhere; stipu-lating matters such as when the consultation ought to take place, the duration of any such exercise and the manner of its conduct. **4.113**

Not all consultations undertaken by ministers under the terms of s. 60 will be in the form of a *formal* consultation however. The Code of Practice recognizes that **4.114**

> [a]t times, a formal, written, public consultation will not be the most effective or proportion-ate way of seeking input from interested parties, e.g. when engaging with stakeholders very early in policy development (preceding formal consultation) or when the scope of an exercise is very narrow and the level of interest highly specialised.[133]

The Code of Practice refers to two further guidance documents that ought to be used in conjunction with the Code:[134] *Consultation and Policy Appraisal—Compact Code of Good Practice,* which supports the *Compact on Government's Relations with the Voluntary and Community Sector*;[135] and the *Central-Local Government Concordat,* which establishes a framework of principles for how central and local government should work together to serve the public.[136] **4.115**

---

[132] The third version was published in July 2008. A copy can be found on the Department for Business Innovation and Skills website : <http://www.bis.gov.uk>.

[133] BIS, *Code of Practice on Consultation,* p. 5.

[134] Ibid.

[135] A copy can be found at: <http://www.thecompact.org.uk>.

[136] A copy can be found at: <http://www.communities.gov.uk>.

Scotland

4.116   The consultation provisions differ slightly in Scotland. In addition to complying with s. 60 (the general duty to consult), if a minister of the Crown proposes to make an order that affects the prosecution of any offence in Scotland, he is required to obtain the agreement of the Lord Advocate.[137]

4.117   Under s. 58(2), if a minister of the Crown proposes to make an order that affects the power of a regulator that is a local authority in Scotland then he will also be required to consult the Scottish ministers, as they will have an interest in the functions of local authorities in Scotland.

Wales

4.118   The powers contained within Part 3 given to a minister of the Crown can also be used by Welsh ministers in relation to matters that affect Wales and that are the responsibility of Welsh ministers. Section 59(1) provides that a minister of the Crown must consult with Welsh ministers before making an order under Part 3 that relates to an offence that applies in, or in relation to, Wales.

4.119   Section 59(2) requires that a minister of the Crown, after having consulted with Welsh ministers on the provisions of an order under Part 3, must also seek the agreement of the Welsh ministers, if the order relates to an offence that applies in, or in relation to, Wales and relates to the functions that are exercised by Welsh ministers.

4.120   Finally, it is a requirement of the consultation provisions that the Welsh ministers must consult the Secretary of State for the particular policy area, before making any order under Part 3.

Pre-RESA consultations

4.121   There is express provision in RESA allowing consultations that had already been carried out before the Act came into force on 1 October 2008[138] to be sufficient in certain circumstances to satisfy the provisions of s. 60(1). In such situations, s. 60(3) provides that so long as the consultation would satisfy the requirements of s. 60, those requirements 'may to that extent be taken to have been satisfied'. This section would also apply to a second consultation undertaken after the initial consultation, but before this part of the Act came into force.[139]

Second consultation

4.122   Once the initial consultation has been carried out, the relevant authority may determine that the proposals require amending in light of the responses received. If this is the case, and the proposals require substantial alteration, a further, second, consultation must take place. Section 60(2) provides:

> If, as a result of any consultation required by subsection (1), it appears to the relevant authority that it is appropriate substantially to change the whole or any part of the proposals, the

---

[137]   RESA, s. 58(1).

[138]   The Regulatory Enforcement and Sanctions Act 2008 (Commencement No. 1) Order 2008, SI 2371/2008 (c. 104).

[139]   1 October 2008, by virtue of the the Regulatory Enforcement and Sanctions Act 2008 (Commencement No. 1) Order 2008, SI 2371/2008 (c. 104).

relevant authority **must** undertake such further consultation with respect to the changes as it considers appropriate. (Emphasis added.)

What is deemed to be a *substantial* change will be a matter for the relevant authority to determine. RESA provides no further definition or list of relevant criteria that must be taken into account. The term 'substantial' may be taken to mean 'considerable'; a change that is of such character or importance as to merit consideration. **4.123**

As to the form that this second consultation should take, the *Code of Practice on Consultation* suggests that when further consultation is required, in most cases consultation on a more limited scale will be more appropriate than a formal exercise. The Code suggests that the relevant authority should 'weigh up the level of interest expressed by consultees in the initial exercise and the burden that running several consultation exercises will place on consultees and any potential delay in implementing the policy'.[140] **4.124**

In those cases where a formal consultation is not deemed appropriate or necessary, the relevant authority may choose instead to have a more targeted, informal consultation incorporating those bodies or groups that have expressed an interest. According to the *Code of Practice on Consultation,* 'in these cases, the Code need not be observed but may instead provide useful guidance'.[141] **4.125**

Drafting the order: contents

The order granting regulators the power to award the civil sanctions is likely to contain much of the detail about their operation as required by Part 3. Amongst other things, the order will need to contain provisions dealing with the following matters: **4.126**

- (i) the regulator(s) to whom the order applies;[142]
- (ii) the sanctions to which the regulator(s) will have access and to which offences they may be applied;
- (iii) non-compliance and enforcement;
- (iv) appeals;
- (v) the issuing of penalty guidance;
- (vi) the issuing of an enforcement policy;
- (vii) the procedure for imposing the sanctions; and
- (viii) in respect of fixed monetary penalties, the level of the penalty.

These criteria will be set down in the order and regulators will not be able to be vary them without a further order. The order will be subjected to the affirmative resolution procedure. **4.127**

The specific procedural provisions relating to each of the civil sanctions are looked at in detail in Chapter 5. **4.128**

---

[140] BIS, *Code of Practice on Consultation*, p. 7, para. 1.5.
[141] Ibid.
[142] The regulators with an enforcement function in relation to the offences to which the sanctions are to be attached.

Parliamentary procedure

4.129   Section 61 requires that any order made under Part 3 must be made by the affirmative resolution procedure.

4.130   The affirmative resolution procedure requires that the statutory instrument be laid in draft before both Houses of Parliament[143] or in the National Assembly of Wales[144] and will not take effect unless its terms are agreed. In this way, proper scrutiny of the order is ensured; a measure going some way to allaying the concerns of those members of the opposition claiming that too much detail of the new sanctions was to be left to be made by ministers in secondary legislation.[145]

---

[143] Where the statutory instrument is made by a minister of the Crown.
[144] Where the statutory instrument is made by the Welsh ministers.
[145] For a more detailed analysis of the constitutional concerns raised about the Regulatory Enforcement and Sanction Bill, see paras 5.02–5.06.

5

OPERATION OF THE CIVIL SANCTIONS

A. Introduction

In this chapter, the separate but related questions of how the sanctions will be issued to regu- **5.01** lators by ministers and how regulators will apply them to non-compliant businesses are considered. In many ways, the operation of each of the sanctions is unique, and for this reason they are considered separately in parts C–F, although some of the concepts affecting them do overlap.[1] In the final part of this chapter, consideration is given to the provisions that may be made in any order awarding the civil sanctions to regulators as to the recovery of costs.

---

[1] For example the standard of proof for the imposition of (some of) the sanctions and considerations relevant to appeals.

B. Overview of the operation of the civil sanctions

5.02 The civil sanctions created by Part 3 are intended to be applied administratively by regulators in their enforcement capacity, as opposed to being independent judicial decisions made after the hearing of evidence and argument. Officials within the regulatory body concerned will be able to determine which sanctions to apply and in what circumstances. Access to the courts will be restricted to appeals to the First-tier Tribunal[2] against unfavourable decisions made by regulators.

5.03 After the Regulatory Enforcement and Sanctions Bill (the Bill) was introduced in the House of Lords,[3] there was concern expressed in Parliament about the constitutionality of the provisions, both in relation to the extent of the use of executive powers to make orders in connection with legislation, the reduced level of parliamentary involvement, and the amount of detail that was left to be determined by statutory instrument. As Lord Lyell of Markyate commented, the Bill:

> … transfers enormous powers … away from the supervision of the independent courts and puts them into the hands of officials … creating a parallel system of justice … with its only safeguard being an ultimate right of appeal, if the subject can afford it.[4]

5.04 Prior to its second reading,[5] the Bill was the subject of inquiries by two committees in the House of Lords, the Delegated Powers and Regulatory Reform Committee and the Select Committee on the Constitution. In its first report of the 2007–08 session, the Constitution Committee expressed its concern over the constitutional questions raised:[6]

> An element of the core meaning of the rule of law is, in the words of A.V. Dicey: 'that no man is punishable or can be lawfully made to suffer in body or goods except for a distinct breach of the law established in the ordinary legal manner before the ordinary Courts in the land …'

5.05 It continued: 'Although many aspects of Dicey's account of the rule of law are now contested, this passage in our view continues to provide a powerful reminder of the importance of the role of ordinary courts.'

5.06 The other significant criticism of the regime concerns the increasingly prevalent over-reliance on secondary legislation, that too much detail about how the sanctions will be awarded and how they will be imposed is left to be determined by secondary legislation and regulators' guidance. Both the House of Lords Select Committee on the Constitution[7] and the Delegated Powers Committee[8] described the new scheme as requiring the use of statutory instruments on an 'unprecedented' scale.

---

[2] As established by s. 3 of the Tribunals, Courts and Enforcement Act 2007 (c. 15).

[3] On 8 November 2007.

[4] Hansard, HL Deb., vol. 698, col. GC327 (30 January 2008).

[5] On 28 November 2007.

[6] First Report of session 2007–08, HL Paper 16, printed 28 November 2007 and published 4 December 2007 at p. 5, para. 9. A copy can be found on the UK Parliament website: <http://www.publications.parliament.uk>.

[7] First Report of session 2007–08, HL Paper 16, printed 28 November 2007 and published 4 December 2007 at p. 5, para. 9.

[8] Second Report of session 2007–08, HL Paper 21, printed 5 December and published 6 December 2007 at p. 10, para. 34. A copy can be found on the UK Parliament website: <http://www.parliament.the-stationery-office.co.uk>.

C. Fixed monetary penalties

Introduction

Section 39(1) of RESA enables a minister to confer on a regulator the power to impose a fixed **5.07** monetary penalty (FMP) in respect of a relevant offence. An FMP is a requirement to pay to a regulator a penalty of a prescribed amount,[9] following an act of regulatory non-compliance. The prescribed amount will be limited to a statutory maximum and must not exceed the maximum fine available if the offence were to have been tried in a criminal court.[10] They are the simplest of the civil sanctions and are designed for low-level instances of non-compliance.

The government described FMPs in the following terms: **5.08**

> ... [As] fines for relatively low fixed amounts that are intended to be used in respect of low-level, minor instances of regulatory non-compliance. We see fixed penalty notices as enabling regulators, in suitable cases, to enforce less serious offences in a more proportionate way than a prosecution.[11]

FMPs are not an entirely new phenomenon in the UK. For example, **5.09**

> the Competition Act 1998 gives the Competition Commission powers to impose financial sanctions on businesses which infringe prohibitions on anti-competitive agreements and abuse of dominant position [and] the Financial Services Authority may, under the Financial Services and Markets Act 2000, impose monetary penalties. Local authority officers and others have powers under several enactments to issue penalty notices in respect of a range of criminal offences.[12]

Where there has been regulatory non-compliance, it is clear that businesses may benefit **5.10** significantly from the imposition of FMPs, as opposed to the alternative option of prosecution through the criminal courts. Most significant perhaps is the fact that the imposition of an FMP will not constitute a criminal offence.[13]

Perhaps as important for some businesses, however, is the fact that FMPs will represent considerable cost savings compared to those that businesses are exposed to in criminal litigation. **5.11** Businesses will not have to pay to go to court and regulators will not have the power to seek repayment of the costs of investigating the offence leading to the imposition of an FMP.[14]

The idea of imposing FMPs on non-compliant businesses has attracted a good deal of criticism, both during the Bill's passage through Parliament and beyond. Concerns were repeatedly expressed in Parliament that FMPs will be regarded rather like parking fines;[15] applied **5.12**

---

[9] RESA, s. 39(3).
[10] Ibid., s. 39(4).
[11] BERR, *Regulatory Enforcement and Sanctions Act 2008: Guidance to the Act,* at p. 31, para. 35.
[12] As the House of Lords Select Committee on the Constitution noted in its First Report of session 2007–08, HL Paper 16, printed 28 November 2007 and published 4 December 2007, at p. 5, para. 7.
[13] See BERR, *Regulatory Enforcement and Sanctions Act 2008: Guidance to the Act,* p. 31.
[14] Cf. discretionary requirements and stop notices: RESA, s. 53(1) and (2).
[15] See for example, Hansard, HL Deb., vol. 696, cols 1250–1 (28 November 2007).

to businesses in private rather than in public, with little or no opprobrium attached. Some members of the opposition were anxious that the imposition of financial penalties would have a more profound effect on small businesses as compared to their larger counterparts.[16] In treating the fines as just another business loss, any rehabilitative impact is likely to be limited, an outcome which would be contrary to an important aim of the civil sanctions, namely to secure a change in the behaviour of non-conforming businesses. A further concern is whether the costs that such businesses incur when paying monetary penalties may simply be passed on to the ultimate consumer.

Determining the level of the fixed monetary penalty

5.13   The amount of the FMP must be specified in the order made by the minister; the regulator will not be able to exercise discretion in determining the amount of the FMP in any individual case. Thus once the regulator has been awarded access to FMPs by way of the enabling statutory instrument, they will generally have no discretion as to the level of the fine that may be imposed in any particular case, only as to whether or not to apply it.

5.14   There is, however, some flexibility about the level of the FMP that may be imposed by the minister.[17] The BERR Guidance suggests by way of an example that a sole trader may be given a £50 penalty, whereas a company might receive a £100 penalty.

Upper limit

5.15   The upper limit of an FMP is capped for summary only offences and offences that are triable either way. Section 39(4) provides that when setting the level of the FMP in the order, if the relevant offence is triable summarily (or is an either-way matter) and is punishable by a fine, the minister must not set an upper limit that exceeds the maximum amount of the fine applicable to that offence. This cap does not apply to indictable only offences.

Power to impose

5.16   Before an FMP may be imposed against a business or regulated individual, the regulator must make a decision as to their liability. In order to do this, the regulator must be satisfied to the criminal standard (i.e. beyond reasonable doubt) that the person has committed the relevant offence.[18] Guilt is therefore a jurisdictional fact that needs to be established before the notice setting out the regulator's intention to impose the sanction may be served.

5.17   The decision as to liability is taken by the regulator after they have undertaken whatever investigation they consider appropriate in order to satisfy themselves that the offence has been committed to the requisite standard of proof. The position relating to FMPs may be contrasted with that for enforcement undertakings, where the determination as to liability is to the somewhat lower standard of proof, *reasonable suspicion* of the commission of a relevant offence, whilst the service of a stop notice requires the regulator to be satisfied that he 'reasonably believes' that the pre-requisites for the imposition of the order exist: that serious harm is or will be caused, and that a relevant offence is or will be committed.[19]

---

[16]   Ibid., vol. 476, cols 341–2 (21 May 2008).
[17]   See BERR, *Regulatory Enforcement and Sanctions Act 2008: Guidance to the Act,* p. 31, para. 36.
[18]   RESA, s. 39(2).
[19]   See para. 5.164 for more on 'reasonable suspicion', and para. 5.126 for more on 'reasonable belief'.

Strikingly, in respect of each of the sanctions, other than enforcement undertakings, RESA **5.18** anticipates that the decision as to liability takes the form of an ex parte decision made without notice. The decision may be made before the business or individual concerned is even aware that that they may be liable for the imposition of a sanction and without providing them with an opportunity to make representations about their putative liability.

'Beyond reasonable doubt'

The criminal standard of proof, beyond reasonable doubt, is a familiar concept to those **5.19** practising in the criminal courts of the UK. Deciding something beyond reasonable doubt does not require the decision maker to be certain of the accused's guilt,[20] rather they must satisfy themselves beyond all reasonable doubt.[21]

The nature of the decision

What will perhaps be less familiar to practitioners is the process by which the standard of **5.20** proof is to be applied to the evidence available to the regulator. According to the procedural requirements laid down by RESA, there need be no independent tribunal to assess whether the standard of proof has been satisfied on the evidence before the regulatory authority. According to these provisions, the regulatory authority alone[22] decides if the offence has been committed, needing only to satisfy itself, and no one else, of that fact. The regulatory authority thus 'becomes the policeman, judge and jury' in relation to the imposition of the civil sanction.[23]

Given the importance of the decision taken at this early stage and the absence of statutory **5.21** prescription, regulators ought to give careful consideration as to the identity of this decision maker, as well as to the form that the decision will take. Since the business or individual concerned would not have the opportunity to be present and make representations in their defence, there is limited value in regulators providing for an assessment of the evidence by an independent tribunal at this stage. In those circumstances, and given the approach suggested below (an independent panel to make the final determination as to whether to impose the sanction), at this stage it will be sensible to ensure that the decision is taken by an independent officer of sufficient seniority and experience to conduct this important exercise in a fair and balanced manner.

To minimize the possibility of personalities coming into play (where, for example, there has **5.22** been a prolonged history of dealings and perhaps conflict between an enforcement officer and a local business), it would certainly be prudent for the decision maker to be independent of the investigator. Field officers therefore should be excluded, as should anyone involved in the latter stage of the process as to whether a final notice should be issued. FMPs may well come to be issued by lower levels of staff after appropriate training.[24] The member of staff responsible for making the decision about whether to issue the FMP and the process to be followed must be clearly identified in the enforcement policy. For more about the enforcement policy that must be prepared and published, see Chapter 6.

---

[20] *Miller v Minister of Pensions* [1947] 2 All ER 372; *R v Bracewell* (1979) 68 Cr App R 44, CA.
[21] This is sometimes expressed as 'a' or 'any' reasonable doubt; see *Woolmington v DPP* [1935] AC 462, HL.
[22] Or more specifically, an official within the regulatory authority.
[23] Hansard, HL Deb., vol. 696, col. 1250 (28 November 2007).
[24] Macrory, *Regulatory Justice: Making Sanctions Effective*, p. 50, para. 3.43.

Gathering evidence: covert surveillance

5.23 In order for regulators to arrive at the 'beyond reasonable doubt' level of satisfaction, investigations will necessarily need to be carried out, some of which may have to be covert. In those circumstances, a question arises as to whether the Regulation of Investigatory Powers Act 2000 (RIPA) applies, given that authorisation to carry out directed (or covert) surveillance[25] can only be given in such cases where it is required in order to prevent or detect 'crime'.[26]

5.24 What is the position to be with these sanctions; they are said to be civil in nature but are to be imposed in respect of what would otherwise be criminal offences. Will the regulator (or local authority) be governed by the terms of RIPA? In *C v Police and the Secretary of State for the Home Department*,[27] decided in 2006, the Investigatory Powers Tribunal decided that where public authority employers investigate misfeasance committed by their employees, such surveillance is not susceptible to the provisions of RIPA. It follows that covert surveillance by regulators for the purposes of specific investigations against businesses may not engage the provisions of RIPA. The position is far from clear though, as Viscount Colville of Culross, a member of the Office of Surveillance Commissioners, made clear during the Bill's second reading in the House of Lords:

> The Government will have to make up their mind about [the applicability of RIPA to the civil sanctions]. Either they must persuade the Home Office to extend the grounds on which covert surveillance can be used, in order to carry out the necessary investigations to implement the civil sanctions, or they will leave a large area of doubt.[28]

Imposing an FMP where there is a primary authority contract

5.25 If a local authority regulator has entered into a primary authority contract with another local authority, it will require the permission of that authority before it can issue an FMP.[29] Once it has informed the primary authority of its intention to issue the sanction, it must then wait five days before it may act,[30] unless:

(i) the enforcement action is required urgently, or in the opinion of the enforcing authority is required urgently to avoid a significant risk of harm to human health or the environment (including the health of animals or plants) or the financial interests of consumers; or

(ii) such a stay of the enforcement action would be, or in the opinion of the enforcing authority would be, wholly disproportionate.[31]

5.26 Chapter 3 provides a full discussion of the issues arising where there is a primary authority contract in existence.

---

[25] The term 'directed surveillance' is defined in s. 26 of RIPA.

[26] RIPA, s. 28(3)(b).

[27] 14 November 2006; No. IPT/03/32/H.

[28] Hansard, HL Deb., vol. 696, col. 1253 (28 November 2007).

[29] RESA, s. 28(1)–(5).

[30] Ibid., s. 28(9)(a).

[31] The Co-ordination of Regulatory Enforcement (Enforcement Action) Order 2009, SI 665/2009, para. 3. See Appendix 5.

Procedure for issuing FMPs

Introduction

Once a regulator, which has been awarded access to FMPs by way of an order under this Part, has determined that an offence has been committed by a business or individual and wants to proceed to impose an FMP, it must follow the procedural steps set out in the order for its imposition. **5.27**

The procedure for applying an FMP against a business or individual is governed by s. 40 of RESA, which provides that certain results must be secured when an order awarding the power to impose an FMP is made. These are as follows: **5.28**

- (i) service of a notice of intent by the regulator: s. 40(2)(a);
- (ii) provision for the business to discharge its liability through payment of a prescribed sum (a discharge payment): s. 40(2)(b);
- (iii) provision for the business to make written representations and objections to the regulator about the imposition of the penalty: s. 40(2)(c)(i);
- (iv) provision requiring the regulator to decide whether to impose the FMP after the period for making representations has elapsed: s. 40(2)(c)(ii);
- (v) provision permitting the regulator to decide not to impose the FMP because the business has a defence to the offence or for any other reason that the minister may provide for in the order: s. 40(4)(a)–(b);
- (vi) service of a final notice by the regulator: s. 40(2)(d); and
- (vii) provision permitting the business to appeal the imposition of the FMP: s. 40(2)(e).

It is expected that the procedural requirements of s. 40 will be replicated in the order awarding the sanctions to the regulator. These requirements are looked at in detail below. **5.29**

Notably, this process does not provide a mechanism whereby a business or individual may elect to be prosecuted rather than accepting an FMP; the decision to apply the sanction rather than, say, pursue a criminal prosecution or issue a warning, is one for the regulator alone.[32] **5.30**

Figure 5.1 sets out the process which must be followed when a regulator is seeking to impose an FMP, and which may be followed should there be an appeal, or if enforcement action becomes necessary.[33] **5.31**

Notice of intent

An order awarding regulators the power to impose FMPs must contain a provision requiring the regulator to serve a notice of intent.[34] **5.32**

A notice of intent gives the business notification that the regulator proposes to impose the penalty against it, including details of the penalty and the grounds for action. By the time the notice of intent has been issued, the regulator will have already made a positive determination as to the liability of the business or individual concerned and is simply notifying them of their intention to impose the sanction. The order awarding the power to a regulator to impose FMPs must also prohibit the issuing of a notice of intent to impose an **5.33**

---

[32] For more about the compatibility of the provisions with the European Convention on Human Rights, see paras 4.09-4.22.
[33] Reproduced from the BERR, *Regulatory Enforcement and Sanctions Act 2008: Guidance to the Act*, p. 32.
[34] RESA, s. 40(2)(a).

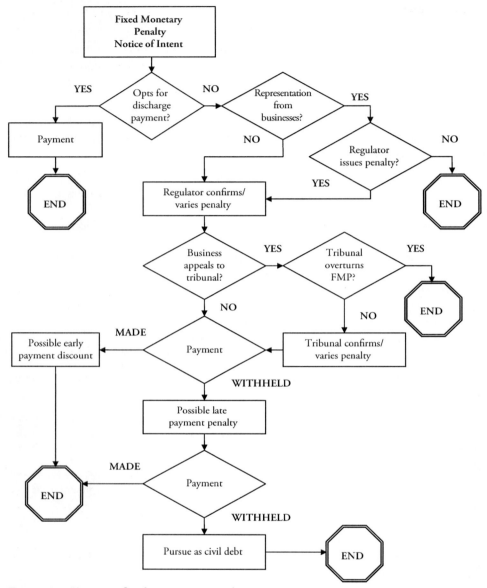

Figure 5.1 Issuing a fixed monetary penalty

FMP where a discretionary requirement or stop notice has already been imposed in respect of the same act or omission.[35]

5.34 The notice must afford the business the opportunity of either discharging its liability or making representations against the imposition of the FMP, which importantly includes the ability of the business to advance any applicable defences, and obliges the regulator to

---

[35] RESA, s. 51(1)(a) and (2)(a).

consider the same. Whether the business chooses to discharge its liability or make representations, it has twenty-eight days from the day on which it receives the notice of intent to act.[36]

According to s. 40(3) of RESA, the notice of intent must include certain minimum information, including, but not limited to, the following: **5.35**

  (i) the grounds for proposing to impose the FMP: s. 40(3)(a);
  (ii) the effect of paying a discharge payment: s. 40(3)(b);
 (iii) the right to make representations and objections against the proposed penalty: s. 40(3)(c);
 (iv) the circumstances in which the regulator is not allowed to impose the FMP: s. 40(3)(d);
  (v) the period of time within which liability for the FMP may be discharged, which may not exceed twenty-eight days beginning with the day on which the notice of intent was received: s. 40(3)(e); and
 (vi) the period of time within which the business may make representations and objections, which may not exceed twenty-eight days beginning with the day on which the notice of intent was received: s. 40(3)(f).

Apart from these requirements, no particular form is required for the notice and no further provision is made in RESA about the manner of service. **5.36**

Given that this may very well be the first occasion that the business in question will have been made aware that they have been adjudged to have committed an offence, and that they are expected to advance any representations against the sanction or defences to the charge, it is vital that the regulator serve as much information about the offence as possible. It is of central importance to any fair legal system that the accused be provided with sufficient detail about their (alleged) transgression to enable them to properly challenge the charge. As will be discussed in para. 6.40, regulators ought to consider providing early disclosure of the evidence upon which they rely in order that the business is able to know clearly the case against it.[37] **5.37**

Discharge payment

The order must also meet the results stipulated in s. 40(2)(b), relating to discharge payment: '[T]he notice of intent also offers the person the opportunity to discharge the person's liability for the FMP by payment of a prescribed sum (which must be less than or equal to the amount of the penalty).' **5.38**

Once the notice of intent has been issued, the business may decide to discharge its liability for the FMP by payment of a prescribed sum known as a discharge payment. The sum of the discharge payment must be less than, or equal to, the amount of the penalty. In practice, the order is likely to stipulate that the discharge payment consist of a percentage figure of the full penalty owing; the Environmental Civil Sanctions (England) Order 2010, for example, specifies an amount of 50 per cent of the penalty.[38] This is comparable to other **5.39**

---

[36] Or any other shorter period which the minister may provide for in the order.

[37] As Lord Diplock in *O'Reilly v Mackman* [1983] 2 AC 237, stated: 'the requirement that a person who is charged with having done something which, if proved to the satisfaction of a statutory tribunal, has consequences that will, or may, affect him adversely, should be given a fair opportunity of hearing what is alleged against him … is so fundamental to any civilised legal system that it is to be presumed that Parliament intended a failure to observe it should render null and void any decision reached in breach of this requirement' (at 276B-C).

[38] SI 1157/2010.

criminal offences for which this type of penalty already exists. Such an incentive for reduced payment is also likely significantly to increase the payment of penalties without the need for further action.

5.40   Discharge payments are likely to be used when a business accepts liability for the commission of a relevant offence. In those circumstances, rather than waiting for the period for representations and objections to expire, it may instead choose to pay the discharge payment, meaning that liability for the sanction is removed and the proceedings are stopped at that stage. This early admission of liability has advantages for the regulator and the business. For the regulator there are savings in terms of the costs of enforcement. For the business, as well as saving costs, it can avoid the reputational risk of having been made the subject of a more formal civil sanction. Businesses should nevertheless be alert to the fact that regulators are required to publish details of cases that end in a discharge payment.[39]

Representations and objections

5.41   Section 40(2)(c) provides that in circumstances where a business decides not to discharge its liability by making a discharge payment, it may alternatively make representations and/or objections to the regulator in relation to the proposed imposition of the FMP.

5.42   Any representations or objections must be submitted to the regulator within twenty-eight days of receipt of the notice of intent or such shorter period as the minister may provide for in the order.[40] It is envisaged by RESA that any representations will be made in writing.

5.43   The provision allowing a business to make representations before an FMP is imposed against it was also a late addition to RESA; the government originally maintained that the notice of intent stage was not necessary at all in relation to FMPs.[41] Eventually, due to growing concerns over whether the imposition of this sanction without the hearing of representations met the minimum requirements of procedural fairness and the common law principle of natural justice, this section was included.

The regulator's decision

5.44   By virtue of s. 40(2)(c)(ii), any order made under Part 3 must include a provision securing the following result: '[T]he regulator must at the end of the period for making representations and objections decide whether to impose the fixed monetary penalty.'

5.45   The decision about whether or not to impose the FMP must take place no sooner than twenty-eight days after the date of receipt of the notice of intent by the business. During this twenty-eight-day period, a business may also raise any defences to the proposed sanction. Section 40(4)(a) requires that the notice of intent must include a provision stipulating that the regulator, when considering any representations or objections, must also consider whether or not to impose the FMP were it to be satisfied that the business 'would not, by reason of any defence, be liable to be convicted of the relevant offence'.

5.46   A minister may, by virtue of s. 40(4)(b), include in the order further provisions granting the regulator the power to not impose an FMP in situations other than where there is an existing

---

[39] RESA, s. 65(2)(b). For more about publication of enforcement action, see para. 6.63.
[40] Ibid., s. 40(3)(f).
[41] Hansard, HL Deb., vol. 698, col. 366 (30 January 2008).

statutory defence available to the business by, for example, 'creating new defences to the offence'.[42]

Having received representations from the business or individual concerned, the regulator **5.47** needs to decide whether the sanction should be imposed taking all relevant considerations into account. It is not a requirement of RESA that this decision needs to be made by any particular individual, or in any specific manner. This leaves open the option for the inclusion of a provision in the order permitting this important decision to be made after the hearing of live evidence and oral representations, rather than being conducted as a purely paper-based exercise. Indeed, where resources allow, such a measure would be highly desirable in terms of compliance with the principles of procedural fairness, particularly where a business denies the allegation in the first place.[43]

Final notice

At the end of the period for making representations and objections, and if the decision has **5.48** been taken to impose the FMP, the regulator must issue a notice imposing the penalty, known as the 'final notice', which must set out certain specified information. Section 40(2)(d) provides that where the regulator decides to impose the FMP, the notice imposing it ('the final notice') must comply with subs. (5), which sets out the minimum requirements for the information that must be contained, namely:

  (i) the grounds for imposing the penalty: s. 40(5)(a);
 (ii) how payment may be made: s. 40(5)(b);
(iii) the period within which payment must be made: s. 40(5)(c);
(iv) whether there are any early payment discounts or late payment penalties: s. 40(5)(d);
 (v) the rights of appeal: s. 40(5)(e); and
(vi) the consequences of failing to pay the penalty: s. 40(5)(f).

Service of the final notice is a formality, which not only sets out important information about **5.49** enforcement but triggers the start of the time limit for any appeal.

Appeal

The business or individual against whom an FMP has been imposed may appeal against the **5.50** decision to impose it.[44]

It is not a requirement of RESA that appeals against the imposition of an FMP need to be **5.51** provided for 'as of right'; the order must instead provide for the grounds under which an appeal can be brought. Section 40(6) sets out the *minimum grounds* for appeal that must be included in the order, which are that the decision was:

  (i) based on an error of fact;
 (ii) wrong in law; or
(iii) unreasonable.

In conferring the powers to impose FMPs, a minister may make provision in the order for **5.52** appeals on other grounds. Given that there is no requirement placed on regulators to provide

---

[42] *Regulatory Enforcement and Sanctions Act 2008: Explanatory Notes*, p. 22, para. 116.
[43] Further consideration of these matters can be found in Chapter 8.
[44] RESA, s. 40(2)(e).

for determinations of liability to be made by independent tribunals after the consideration of evidence and argument, access to the courts through an appeal is of fundamental importance in ensuring that minimum guarantees of procedural fairness are afforded to businesses. Regulators seeking the award of these powers would be wise to open up the permissible grounds of appeal so as to reduce the likelihood of challenge to the provisions on the grounds of their compatibility with the European Convention on Human Rights.[45] The appeal provisions for FMPs imposed against business and individuals by the Environment Agency and Natural England, for example, permit an appeal to be brought on the three mandatory grounds, and 'for any other reason'.[46]

Double jeopardy

5.53 If a regulator imposes an FMP against a business, that business cannot later be prosecuted for the original offence. This rule against double jeopardy is applicable in three separate scenarios, and in respect of each it is impermissible to commence criminal proceedings against the business or individual concerned:

(i) at any time before the expiration of the period for payment of the discharge payment: s. 41(a)(i);

(ii) at any time following the payment of a discharge payment: s. 41(a)(ii); and

(iii) at any time following the imposition of an FMP: s. 41(b).

5.54 Ordinarily, there is no procedural bar to having concurrent criminal and civil liability for an alleged wrongdoing; the fact that there is express provision preventing double jeopardy lends itself to the suggestion that the sanctions possess criminal characteristics.[47]

Failing to pay

5.55 In order to ensure that the sanctioning scheme remains credible to its stakeholders, it is vital that regulators take swift and decisive action when an FMP remains unpaid, firstly through enforcement and then through the collection of the penalty.[48]

5.56 The BERR, *Regulatory Enforcement and Sanctions Act 2008: Guidance to the Act* suggests that there should be 'an efficient and streamlined procedure for recovering monetary penalties'.[49] This is provided for in s. 52, which states that: '[A]n order under this Part which confers power on a regulator to require a person to pay a fixed monetary penalty … may include provision for enforcement of the penalty.'

5.57 The minister may, at his discretion, include provision in the order for the enforcement of FMPs and any interest arising, either by way of a civil debt through the civil courts,[50] or via the more streamlined process of recovery by treating the penalty as if it were payable under a court order.[51]

---

[45] See further paras 4.09–4.22.

[46] Environmental Civil Sanctions (England) Order 2010, SI 1157/2010, Sch. 1, para. 8(2)(a) and see Chapter 7.

[47] For more about the true nature of the sanctions see para. 4.09.

[48] The following-up of enforcement actions is one of the recommended Seven Characteristics of a sanctions regime: Richard Macrory, *Regulatory Justice: Making Sanctions Effective*, p. 10.

[49] Para. 40, p. 33.

[50] RESA, s. 52(2)(a).

[51] Ibid., s. 52(2)(b).

The procedure for recovering any unpaid monies will differ depending on whether or not **5.58** there has been an appeal to the First-tier tribunal. Both routes to the recovery of monies are set out below.

Procedure following an appeal

Under the Tribunals, Courts and Enforcement Act 2007, if the First-tier Tribunal finds in **5.59** the regulator's favour at an appeal, the unpaid sum will be recoverable as if it were payable under an order of a county court or the High Court in England and Wales.[52] Similar provisions apply in Scotland[53] and Northern Ireland.[54]

As the BERR, *Regulatory Enforcement and Sanctions Act 2008: Guidance to the Act* explains, **5.60** in practice this means that the regulator will skip the initial stages of registering a claim for the unpaid sum in court and will be able to proceed direct to enforcement.[55]

Procedure where there is no appeal

Where the business chooses not to appeal against the imposition of the FMP and does not **5.61** pay the penalty, the unpaid amount must be pursued in the ordinary way through the civil courts. Alternatively, the minister making the order may also make provision for any unpaid sums to be recoverable as if 'on the order of' a county court or the High Court, i.e. via the streamlined process.[56]

If the streamlined process is adopted, the regulator must follow the applicable procedure **5.62** rules[57] and in doing so it must apply for an order to the court for the district where the person against whom the award was made resides or carries on business, unless the court otherwise orders. Applications for an order can be dealt with by a court officer without a hearing. Once the order has been made, the regulator may proceed to enforcement action. There will be a fee for the application although the regulator can reclaim this from the defaulter in the event of a successful enforcement.[58]

Enforcement tools

A full discussion of the enforcement tools available to regulators in the event of a defaulting **5.63** business is outside the scope of this text. In summary, once a court order has been obtained, a regulator will have a number of enforcement options available to it. These include:

(i) warrant of execution—allowing a bailiff to seize goods or money to the value of the amount recovered;

(ii) charging order—an order of the court placing a charge on the defaulting business's property; and

(iii) third party debt order—to stop, for example, the business taking money out of its bank account.

---

[52] Tribunals Courts and Enforcement Act 2007, s. 27(1).
[53] Ibid., s. 27(2).
[54] Ibid., s. 27(3).
[55] At p. 34, para. 40.
[56] RESA, s. 52(2)(b).
[57] Rule 70.5 of the Civil Procedure Rules 1998.
[58] BERR, *Regulatory Enforcement and Sanctions Act 2008: Guidance to the Act*, p. 34, para. 40.

5.64 A fee will be payable by the regulator should it utilize any of these enforcement tools, although this can be reclaimed from the defaulter in the event of a successful enforcement action.

D. Discretionary requirements

Introduction

5.65 The power of a minister to award discretionary requirements to a regulator in respect of a relevant offence is found in s. 42(1): '[T]he provision which may be made under this section is provision to confer on a regulator the power by notice to impose one or more discretionary requirements on a person in relation to a relevant offence.'[59]

5.66 'Discretionary requirements' are a package of sanctions that are intended to be used for mid to high levels instances of non-compliance. They are intended to be constructive in their nature, aimed at remedying the consequences of any offence and promoting good working relationships between regulators and businesses. As the BERR, *Regulatory Enforcement and Sanctions Act 2008: Guidance to the Act* points out, this is an end that is not often served by a traditional prosecution.[60]

5.67 If the regulator is awarded all three discretionary requirements (variable monetary penalty, compliance requirement and restoration requirement), they may use them in isolation or in combination. Such an arrangement offers the regulator a flexible suite of remedies, particularly suitable for addressing complex cases of non-compliance where there are a number of areas that require resolution.

5.68 There are three types of requirement that may be awarded:

(i) variable monetary penalties (VMP)—requiring the payment of a financial sum of an amount determined by the regulator: s. 42(3)(a);

(ii) a compliance requirement—a requirement to take steps specified by the regulator within a stated period, designed to secure that that offence does not continue or reoccur: s. 42(3)(b); and

(iii) a restoration requirement—a requirement to take such steps as specified by the regulator within a specified time period so as to restore the position to what it would have been if the offence had not been committed: s. 42(2)(c).

Types of discretionary requirement

Variable monetary penalty

5.69 Unlike the FMP, the level of which must be set by the minister in the order, this penalty is variable so that the regulator can determine the appropriate level on a case-by-case basis. This inherent flexibility will allow regulators to take into account both the circumstances of the breach and of the non-compliant business. For example, the penalty may be set at such a level so as to remove any financial gain from the commission of the offence, to reflect the gravity of the failure or a history of non-compliance.[61]

---

[59] See paras 4.58–4.80 for the definition of 'regulator' and 'relevant offence'. By virtue of s. 36(2), the term 'minister' also includes 'Welsh minister'.

[60] P. 37, para. 44.

[61] BERR, *Regulatory Enforcement and Sanctions Act 2008: Guidance to the Act*, p. 35, para. 44.

The only limit to the level of the VMP is that in respect of summary only offences, the level **5.70** of the VMP must not exceed the statutory maximum amount of the fine that could have been imposed were the matter to have been dealt with by the criminal courts.[62] Subject to any maximum level set out in the relevant order, there is no such cap when the offence in question is triable either way or on indictment, which in effect means that businesses could be required to pay VMPs running into five, or even six, figure sums.[63]

Compliance requirement

Compliance requirements are intended to be used in situations where a business needs to **5.71** take steps to bring itself back into compliance, for example by making good an unsafe piece of equipment, changing a process or providing training.[64]

Restoration requirement

Restoration requirements are (unsurprisingly) intended to be restorative in nature and can **5.72** be used to ensure that a business deals with the consequences of the potential offence. This might involve, for example, cleaning up an area contaminated as a result of a particular failing, or in other instances, reimbursing customers' money.[65]

Determining the level of a variable monetary penalty

It will be for the regulator to set the level of the VMP in each case, a decision that must be **5.73** made against published criteria. Given that one of the explicit aims of the VMP is to remove the financial gain from regulatory non-compliance,[66] it is expected that these penalties will be significant. Macrory considered that the removal of financial benefit or gain from regulatory non-compliance ought to be one of the key principles of any sanctions regime.[67]

The determination of the level of a VMP is likely to involve a calculation beginning with an **5.74** estimation of the financial benefit from non-compliance and including an 'uplift' to reflect the deterrent aspect inherent in the penalty. The costs of investigation can also be included in this calculation. The penalty guidance must set out any calculations that will be applied in determining the level of the penalty, including any starting points, multipliers and examples that show how the calculation will be reached.

The BERR Regulatory *Enforcement and Sanctions Act 2008: Guidance to the Act*[68] suggests **5.75** that when a regulator is determining the level of a VMP, the following aggravating and mitigating factors may be relevant:

Aggravating factors

(i) the seriousness of the regulatory non-compliance, e.g. the harm to human health or the environment, duration of the non-compliance etc.;

---

[62] RESA, s. 42(6).
[63] See for example the levels set and draft methodology for calculation now published by the Environment Agency and considered in Chapter 7.
[64] BERR, *Regulatory Enforcement and Sanctions Act 2008: Guidance to the Act*, p. 35, para. 44.
[65] Ibid., p. 35, para. 44.
[66] See Richard Macrory, *Regulatory Justice: Making Sanctions Effective*, p. 47, para. 3.37.
[67] Ibid., p. 10.
[68] At p. 38.

(ii) a history of non-compliance by the business;

(iii) financial gain made by the business as a result of the non-compliance with regulations;

(iv) the conduct of the business after the non-compliance has been discovered; and

(v) previous actions taken by the regulator or other regulators to help the business into compliance.

Mitigating factors

(i) a previously good compliance record;

(ii) actions taken to eliminate or reduce the risk of damage resulting from regulatory non-compliance;

(iii) voluntary reporting of regulatory non-compliance;

(iv) actions taken to repair the harm done by regulatory non-compliance; and

(v) cooperation with the regulator in responding to the non-compliance.

5.76 The Guidance stresses that these lists are not exhaustive and that each decision will depend on the regulatory area and the circumstances of the individual case. These factors, adapted to suit the nature of the particular regulator and area of enforcement, may be included in the published enforcement policy.[69]

5.77 Regulators may wish to include a provision in the order conferring or extending their powers to obtain information from those under investigation, for example, to obtain information relevant to the setting of a VMP.[70]

5.78 One of the key decisions for regulators will be which individual within the organization has the responsibility for setting the level of the VMP. Whilst field staff and inspectors may be able to provide useful recommendations as to the appropriate level of penalty, for reasons previously outlined these decisions should be taken independently and, given the sums involved, probably by senior officials.[71] Some regulators use financial investigators to make such decisions.[72]

Imposing a discretionary requirement where there is a primary authority contract

5.79 If a local authority regulator has entered into a primary authority contract with another local authority, they will require the permission of that authority before they can impose a discretionary requirement.[73] Once they have informed the primary authority of their intention to issue the sanction, they must then wait five days before they may act,[74] unless such a delay would be inappropriate for either of the reasons set out in para. 3.129 above.[75]

5.80 Chapter 3 of this text provides a full discussion of the issues arising where there is a primary authority contract in existence.

---

[69] See further paras 6.51–6.62 for more about the requirement to publish an enforcement policy.
[70] RESA, s. 55(3)(b).
[71] See Richard Macrory, *Regulatory Justice: Making Sanctions Effective*, p. 50, paras 3.43 and 3.44.
[72] The Security Industry Authority, for example.
[73] RESA, s. 28(1)–(5).
[74] Ibid., s. 28(9)(a).
[75] The Co-ordination of Regulatory Enforcement (Enforcement Action) Order 2009, SI 665/2009, para. 3.

Power to impose

Before a discretionary requirement may be imposed against a business or regulated individ- **5.81**
ual, the regulator must be satisfied beyond reasonable doubt that the person has committed
the relevant offence.[76]

'Beyond reasonable doubt'

Guilt is therefore a jurisdictional fact that needs to be established before the notice setting **5.82**
out the regulator's intention to impose the sanction may be served.

The same standard of proof that is required to be met before an FMP may be imposed **5.83**
must also be met before a regulatory authority imposes a discretionary requirement against
a business. For a detailed consideration of the application of the criminal standard of proof
in this context see para. 5.19.

Procedure for issuing discretionary requirements

Introduction

Once a regulator has been awarded the power to impose discretionary requirements and has **5.84**
determined to the requisite standard of proof that the relevant offence has been committed,
it must then follow the procedure set down in s. 43(2) for the imposition of the sanction.
The procedure is the same as it is for the imposition of an FMP in every respect save for one;
instead of the possibility of discharging its liability through discharge payments, a business
can instead offer an undertaking as to action to be taken[77] in order to mitigate (as well as
potentially discharge) its liability.

It is a requirement that the procedural steps set out in s. 43(2) are provided for in the **5.85**
order made by the minister. The minimum procedural requirements for the imposition of
a discretionary requirement that must appear in the order are as follows:

 (i) provision requiring the regulator to serve a notice of what is proposed (a 'notice of
     intent') which complies with subs. (3): s. 43(2)(a);
 (ii) provision for the business to make written representations and objections to the regula-
     tor about the proposed imposition of the discretionary requirement: s. 43(2)(b);
 (iii) provision permitting the business the opportunity to offer an undertaking as to action,
     for the regulator to accept or reject it and for the regulator to take it into account when
     making the decision whether to impose a discretionary requirement: s. 43(5);
 (iv) provision requiring the regulator to decide whether to impose the discretionary require-
     ment (with or without modifications) after the period for making representations has
     elapsed: s. 43(2)(c);
 (v) provision permitting the regulator to decide not to impose the VMP because the busi-
     ness has a defence to the offence or for any other reason that the minister may provide
     for in the order: s. 43(4)(a)–(b);
 (vi) where the regulator decides to impose the discretionary requirement, a provision requir-
     ing service of a final notice, which complies with subs. (6): s. 43(2)(d); and

---

[76] RESA, s. 42(2).
[77] Ibid., s. 43(5).

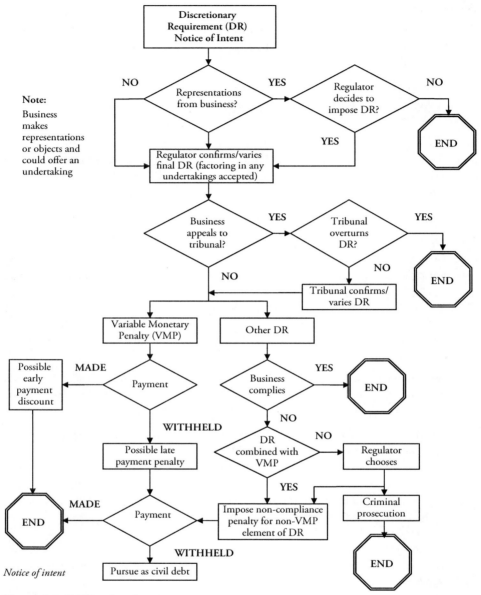

Figure 5.2 Issuing discretionary requirements

(vii) provision permitting the business to appeal the imposition of the discretionary requirement, securing the results in s. 43(7): s. 40(2)(e).

5.86 Figure 5.2 summarizes the process for imposition, enforcement and appeal of discretionary
requirements.[78]

---

[78] Reproduced from the BERR, *Regulatory Enforcement and Sanctions Act 2008: Guidance to the Act*, p. 36.

Notice of intent

An order awarding a regulator the power to impose a discretionary requirement on a person **5.87** must include a provision requiring the regulator to serve a notice of intent.[79]

The notice of intent gives the business notification that the regulator proposes to impose the **5.88** penalty and affords it the opportunity of making representations or objections to the proposed imposition of the penalty. In the case of discretionary requirements, it also permits a business the chance to offer to make an undertaking as to action, in order to attempt to mitigate (and potentially discharge) its liability to the sanction.[80]

The notice of intent must comply with the provisions of s. 43(3), which stipulates that **5.89** certain minimum information must be included within it:

(i) the grounds for proposing to impose the discretionary requirement: s. 43(3)(a);
(ii) the right of the business to make representations and objections against the proposed penalty: s. 43(3)(b);
(iii) the circumstances in which the regulator is not allowed to impose the discretionary requirement: s. 43(3)(c); and
(iv) the period of time within which the business may make representations and objections, which may not exceed twenty-eight days beginning with the day on which the notice of intent was received, or any other shorter period that may be provided for in the order: s. 43(3)(d).

The order awarding the power to impose a discretionary requirement must also make provi- **5.90** sion prohibiting the issuing of a notice of intent to impose a discretionary requirement where an FMP has already been imposed in respect of the same act or omission or the person has discharged their liability to an FMP in respect of the same act or omission.[81]

As with FMPs, the service of the notice of intent will often be the first indication that a busi- **5.91** ness will have that it has been adjudged to have committed an offence and is liable to a penalty. For this reason, it is important that regulators provide as much information as possible about the evidence upon which they have based this decision. This is considered in full in the context of the issuing of the notice of intent in respect of FMPs (para. 5.37) as well as in Chapter 6, in the context of publishing an investigation policy.

Representations and objections

Section 43(2)(b) provides that any order made under Part 3 must make provision for a busi- **5.92** ness to be able to make representations and/or objections to the regulator in relation to the proposed imposition of the discretionary requirement. This information must also be included in the notice of intent.[82] Any representations must be made in writing. The period of time within which the business may make representations and objections may not exceed twenty-eight days beginning with the day on which the notice of intent was received, or any shorter period that the minister may provide for in the order.

---

[79] RESA, s. 43(2)(a).
[80] Ibid., s. 43(5).
[81] Ibid., s. 51(1)(b).
[82] Ibid., s. 43(3)(b).

The regulator's decision

5.93   By virtue of s. 43(2)(c)(ii), any order made under Part 3 must include a provision securing the following result:

> [A]fter the end of the period for making such representations and objections, the regulator must decide whether to—
>> (i)   impose the discretionary requirement, with or without modifications, or
>> (ii) impose any other discretionary requirement which the regulator has power to impose under section 42.

5.94   The decision about whether or not to impose the discretionary requirement (with or without modifications) must take place no sooner than twenty-eight days after the date of receipt of the notice of intent by the business. During this twenty-eight-day period, a business may also raise any defences to the proposed sanction. Section 43(4)(a) requires that the notice of intent must include a provision stipulating that the regulator, when considering any representations or objections, must also consider whether or not to impose the discretionary requirement were it to be satisfied that the business 'would not, by reason of any defence … be liable to be convicted of the relevant offence'.

5.95   A minister may, by virtue of s. 43(4)(b), include in the order further provisions granting the regulator the power to not impose a discretionary requirement in situations other than where there is a statutory defence available to the business, for example 'by creating new defences to the offence'.[83]

5.96   Having already determined beyond reasonable doubt that the offence has been committed, the effect of s. 43(4)(b) is to permit the regulator the ability to make a redetermination as to liability, taking into account any defences raised. In many cases, particularly where a defence is raised or the charge is contested for any other reason, this determination of liability would be best made by an independently appointed panel and after the hearing of oral evidence and argument. This issue is discussed further in the context of the imposition of FMPs at para. 5.47.

Undertaking as to action

5.97   Any order made under this section must contain a provision requiring the regulator, in making the decision as to whether or not to impose the discretionary requirement,[84] to consider accepting any undertaking as to action offered by the business.

5.98   Undertakings as to action are the discretionary requirement equivalent of a discharge payment,[85] permitting the business the opportunity of seeking to mitigate its liability prior to the civil sanction being imposed against it. Section 43(5) provides that the order must make provisions for:

> (a) [T]he person on whom the notice of intent is served to be able to offer an undertaking as to action to be taken by that person (including the payment of a sum of money) to benefit any person affected by the offence,
> (b) the regulator to be able to accept or reject such an undertaking, and
> (c) the regulator to take any undertaking so accepted into account in its decision.

---

[83] *Regulatory Enforcement and Sanctions Act 2008: Explanatory Notes*, p. 22, para. 116.
[84] RESA, s. 43(2)(c).
[85] Discharge payments for fixed monetary penalties are discussed at para. 5.38.

The purpose of an undertaking as to action is to provide the business with the opportunity **5.99** to make recompense to third parties that have been affected by the offence, including through the payment of compensation, perhaps resulting in a reduction of the level of a VMP payable. It is up to the regulator to decide whether to accept the offer and how to take it into account when making its decision as to sanction. It may choose to consult those affected by the actions (or inaction) of the business.

It is conceivable that whilst the primary purpose of these undertakings is to enable a **5.100** business to advance mitigation, regulators may come to use them to enable businesses to discharge their liability entirely, by accepting them as a direct alternative to imposing the discretionary requirement. Such an approach would not be inconsistent with the terms of s. 43(5)(c).

Undertakings as to action may be accepted in conjunction with compliance or restoration **5.101** requirements.

Final notice

At the end of the period for making representations and objections, and having decided to **5.102** impose the discretionary requirement, the regulator must issue a notice imposing the penalty, known as the final notice. According to s. 43(6), the final notice must, as a minimum, contain information as to the following:

(i) the grounds for imposing the discretionary requirement;
(ii) where the discretionary requirement is a VMP, provision as to how the payment should be made, the period within which it must be made, and if they exist, any early payment discounts or late payment penalties;
(iii) the rights of appeal; and
(iv) the consequences of failing to pay the penalty.

Service of the final notice is a formality; it not only sets out important information about **5.103** enforcement but triggers the start of the time limit for any appeal.

Appeal

An order granting the power to impose a discretionary requirement must contain a provision **5.104** entitling the person against whom it is imposed to appeal that decision: s. 43(2)(e). The order must also contain the permissible grounds of appeal. Section 45(4) sets out the minimum grounds for an appeal that must be included in the order. Those are as follows:

(i) that the decision was based on an error of fact;
(ii) that the decision was wrong in law;
(iii) that the decision was unfair or unreasonable;
(iv) in the case of a non-monetary discretionary requirement, that the nature of the requirement is unreasonable; and
(v) that the decision was unreasonable for any other reason.

A minister, in conferring the powers under this section, may make provision for appeals **5.105** on other grounds. Given that the business concerned may not have even been afforded the opportunity of seeing the evidence before a determination as to liability is made, let alone of challenging the evidence against it at a hearing, the question of whether to provide for an appeal 'as of right' has far-reaching implications. This is discussed further in para. 5.52.

Double jeopardy

5.106   Where a discretionary requirement is imposed or an undertaking as to action is accepted by the regulator, s. 44(2) provides that the person may not at any time be convicted of the relevant offence in respect of which either of these disposals has been deployed. This stands with one major exception, which is that non-compliance with a non-monetary discretionary requirement may mean that the original offence can be prosecuted in the criminal courts if the regulator so wishes. The explanation given by BERR[86] for this is that because non-monetary discretionary requirements are less punitive in nature than VMPs, the same issues of double jeopardy 'do not arise'.[87]

5.107   Provision may also be made in the order extending the ordinary time limits for criminal prosecution in cases where a regulator is seeking to pursue a criminal prosecution against a business that has either previously failed to comply with a non-monetary discretionary requirement imposed,[88] or previously failed to comply with an agreed undertaking as to action (without the imposition of a VMP).[89]

5.108   The minister making the order would not be able to extend these time limits retrospectively as any such action would be in contravention of Art. 7 of the ECHR,[90] not to mention well-established principles of common law.

Non-compliance penalty

5.109   An order awarding the power to impose discretionary requirements may also make provision for the regulator to impose a financial penalty upon the business in the event of non-compliance with a non-monetary requirement, or an undertaking as to action. Such a provision is known as a non-compliance penalty. Failure to comply with a VMP may be dealt with by seeking to recover the costs through the civil debt procedures or as if payable under a court order.[91]

5.110   Section 45(1) provides that:

> Provision under section 42 may include provision for a person to pay a monetary penalty (a 'non-compliance penalty') to a regulator if the person fails to comply with —
>> (a)   a non-monetary discretionary requirement imposed on the person, or
>> (b)   an undertaking referred to in section 43(5) which is accepted from the person.

Serving notice

5.111   Any order granting a regulator the power to impose a non-compliance penalty must make provision for the manner of its service on the non-compliant business or individual. Section 45(3)(a) provides that the non-compliance penalty may only be imposed by notice served by the regulator.

---

[86]   Now the Department for Business Innovation and Skills (BIS).
[87]   BERR, *Regulatory Enforcement and Sanctions Act 2008: Guidance to the Act*, p. 39.
[88]   RESA, s. 44(4).
[89]   Ibid., s. 44(3).
[90]   Art. 7 provides that: 'No one shall be held guilty of any criminal offence on account of any act or omission which did not constitute a criminal offence under national or international law at the time when it was committed ...'
[91]   As to recovery of any unpaid monies under a VMP see para. 5.63.

Apart from setting out the grounds of appeal against the notice, there is no further require-   **5.112**
ment in RESA as to the form or content of the notice. As a matter of good practice however,
the notice ought usually to contain information as to the grounds for imposing the non-
compliance penalty (e.g. date, place and nature of non-compliance), the sum payable, how
payment must be made, the period of time for payment, the consequences of non-payment,
and circumstances (if any) in which the regulator may reduce the amount of the penalty.

Appeal against the notice

The permitted grounds of appeal against the notice imposing the non-compliance penalty   **5.113**
must be specified in the order and set out in the notice served on the business. The permissible grounds of appeal include, but are not limited to, the following:[92]

 (i) that the decision to serve the notice was based on an error of fact;
 (ii) that the decision was wrong in law; and
 (iii) that the decision was unfair or unreasonable for any reason (including, in a case where
    the amount of the non-compliance penalty was determined by the regulator, that the
    amount is unreasonable).

Setting the level of the non-compliance penalty

In making provision in the order for the imposition of a non-compliance penalty, the   **5.114**
minister may additionally make further provision as to the level of the penalty payable.[93]
The order may:

 (i) specify the amount of the non-compliance penalty;
 (ii) provide for the amount to be calculated by reference to prescribed criteria;
 (iii) provide for the amount to be determined by the regulator; or
 (iv) provide for the amount to be determined in any other way.

E. Stop notices

Introduction

In making an order under Part 3, s. 46(1) enables a minister to confer on a regulator the   **5.115**
power to impose a stop notice against a business in order to prevent or stop the commission
of a relevant offence:[94] 'The provision which may be made under this section is provision
conferring on a regulator the power to serve a stop notice on a person.'

Stop notices can either be used to prevent future conduct occurring or to prohibit current   **5.116**
activity, where such activity is causing, or presents a significant risk of causing, serious harm.
Stop notices may be used in cases where, for example, a business is carrying out a dangerous
manufacturing process, misusing a particular piece of equipment or selling an unsafe
product.

Once issued, they prohibit a business or person from carrying on any activity that is causing   **5.117**
harm or presents a significant risk of causing serious harm, until they have taken the steps
specified in the order. According to the BERR, *Regulatory Enforcement and Sanctions Act*

---

[92] RESA, s. 45(4).
[93] Ibid., s. 45(2).
[94] See paras 4.58–4.80 for more on the definition of 'regulator' and 'relevant offence'.

2008: Guidance to the Act, the objective in both cases is to prohibit the business from carrying out the activity until the steps necessary to secure compliance with the law have been taken and, by that means, to encourage the business back into compliance.[95] These are serious sanctions intended for serious breaches; non-compliance with a stop notice is a criminal offence.[96]

5.118 Some regulators already use stop notices but their form varies;[97] Macrory wanted to ensure that all regulators had access to statutory notices of this nature in order to ensure consistency.[98]

Imposing a stop notice where there is a primary authority contract

5.119 If a local authority regulator has entered into a primary authority contract with another local authority, it will require the permission of that authority before it can issue a stop notice.[99] Once it has informed the primary authority of its intention to issue the notice, it must then wait five days before it may act,[100] unless such a delay would be inappropriate for any of the reasons set out in para. 3.129 above.[101]

5.120 In cases where the public are placed at risk by virtue of an ongoing activity of a business, or are likely to be put at such risk in the future, regulators are likely to be able to rely upon the 'urgent' exception, in which case they may proceed to issue the stop notice without having previously notified the primary authority of their intention to do so. Chapter 3 of this text provides a full discussion of the issues arising where there is a primary authority contract in existence.

Power to impose

5.121 Any order granting a regulator the power to impose a stop notice must make provision for the circumstances in which it may be imposed. Regulators may seek to impose stop notices in two scenarios: as an injunctive measure, where the activity is already being carried on; or as a preventative measure, where the activity is likely to be carried on in the near future.

Where the activity is being carried on

5.122 A stop notice may be served on a business if it is carrying on an activity that the regulator reasonably believes is causing, or presents a significant risk of causing, serious harm, and the activity involves, or is likely to involve, the commission of a relevant offence.

5.123 Any order made under this part may make provision for the imposition of stop notices only in the following circumstances:[102]

(i) where the person is carrying on the activity;

---

[95] P. 40, para. 51.
[96] RESA, s. 49.
[97] For example, Trading Standards have access to 'stop now' notices and the Health and Safety Executive to prohibition notices.
[98] See Richard Macrory, *Regulatory Justice: Making Sanctions Effective* (November 2006), p. 61, box 4.3.
[99] RESA, s. 28(1)–(5).
[100] Ibid., s. 28(9)(a).
[101] The Co-ordination of Regulatory Enforcement (Enforcement Action) Order 2009, SI 665/2009, para. 3.
[102] RESA, s. 46(4) and (6).

(ii) the regulator reasonably believes that the activity as carried on by that person is causing, or presents a significant risk of causing, serious harm to human health, the environment (including the health of animals and plants) and the financial interest of consumers; and

(iii) the regulator reasonably believes that the activity as carried on by that person involves or is likely to involve the commission of a relevant offence by that person.

The term relevant offence is defined in s. 38 and has a different meaning depending on whether the regulator is a Sch. 5 regulator or an authority that has an enforcement function in relation to one of the enactments in Schs 6 or 7. For a detailed analysis of this term, see paras. 4.66–4.70. **5.124**

Where the activity is 'likely to be carried on'

An order under this part may provide for the imposition of a stop notice where a business is not currently in contravention of the law, but is nevertheless adjudged by the regulator to be likely to be so in the future. Any order under Part 3 must additionally include the criteria for the imposition of a stop notice in these circumstances. Section 46(5) provides that a stop notice may only be imposed in these circumstances where a regulator reasonably believes that: **5.125**

(i) the person is likely to carry on the activity;

(ii) the activity as likely to be carried on by that person will cause, or will present a significant risk of causing, serious harm to human health, the environment (including the health of animals and plants) and the financial interest of consumers; and

(iii) the activity as likely to be carried on by that person will involve or will be likely to involve the commission of a relevant offence by that person.

Definition of 'reasonable belief'

Before a stop notice can be imposed in either scenario set out above (where the activity is being carried on, or where it is likely to be carried on), the regulator must be satisfied that it 'reasonably believes' that the prerequisites for the imposition of the order exist: that serious harm is or will be caused, and that a relevant offence is or will be committed. The additional feature present in cases where the business is not said to actually be carrying on the activity at present, but is likely to do so in the future, is that the regulator in those cases will also need to have a reasonably held belief that the person is likely to carry out the activity. **5.126**

As with the imposition of FMPs and discretionary requirements, it will be for the regulator (or more precisely, an official within the regulatory authority) to satisfy itself that the standard of proof has been met, there being no requirement in RESA that this decision needs to be taken by an independent authority or tribunal.[103] This decision is taken in the first instance before the business or individual has an opportunity to respond to the charge against them and without them having been afforded the opportunity to make representations about their liability. **5.127**

Strikingly, whilst the *failure to comply* with a stop notice is a criminal offence, a regulator *does not have* to be satisfied to the criminal standard of proof of any of these matters before it **5.128**

---

[103] See para. 4.109 for an analysis of the compatibility of the civil sanctions with the provisions of Art. 6 of the European Convention on Human Rights.

imposes the notice. This can be contrasted with the position for FMPs and discretionary requirements, where the criminal standard of proof *does* apply.

5.129   Reasonable belief is not defined in RESA nor is any guidance given to regulators as to how they ought to go about making this decision. The courts have been called on, on a number of occasions, to consider the question of what constitutes a reasonable belief. In *Hussain v Sarkar*,[104] the Court of Appeal held that 'reasonable belief is more than mere suspicion'. According to Lord Denning in *Taylor v Alisdair*[105] a person holds a reasonable belief if he 'honestly believes on reasonable grounds … [and that it is] not necessary to prove that he is in fact incapable or incompetent'. In employment law, the test of reasonable belief requires the decision maker to be satisfied of the fact or belief of misconduct, have reasonable grounds to sustain that belief and have carried out as much investigation as is reasonable in the circumstances.[106]

5.130   Whilst a belief can still be reasonably held even if it ultimately proves to be incorrect, given the injunctive nature of the remedy and that the ultimate sanction for a breach of a stop notice is criminal prosecution, regulators should be particularly vigilant to ensure that sufficient investigation is carried out to enable them to establish a firm foundation for their decisions. The availability of compensation[107] in prescribed cases will also, no doubt, serve as an additional incentive for caution prior to service. Regulators seeking to impose stop notices will not be required to obtain conclusive proof that the activity is being carried on, or that it will cause or presents a significant risk of causing serious harm, but they ought to ensure they have a sound evidential basis for so believing.

5.131   Decisions made by regulators imposing stop notices should be based on objectively observable evidence, and made preferably by reference to the published enforcement policy.[108] For reasons previously given, it will be highly desirable for the ultimate decision maker to be quite distinct from the investigator, in order that the decision is not compromised.[109] As with FMPs and stop notices, regulators would be wise to ensure that the individual making this important decision is sufficiently experienced and trained to undertake such an important task.

'Significant risk of serious harm'

5.132   The effect of a stop notice can be draconian, requiring a business to cease carrying out certain processes or perhaps stop trading altogether. According to the BERR, *Regulatory Enforcement and Sanctions Act 2008: Guidance to the Act*, it is for this reason that the test of significant risk of serious harm is deliberately stringent, to ensure that only the most serious cases are captured.[110]

5.133   In considering whether something amounts to a significant risk, the courts have held that the term 'significant' means more than a mere possibility of occurrence and could be taken to mean 'noteworthy, of considerable amount or importance'.[111] Whether something can be

---

[104] [2010] EWCA Civ 301.
[105] [1978] ICR 445.
[106] *British Home Stores Ltd v Burchell* [1980] ICR 303.
[107] See para. 5.146 below.
[108] For a further discussion about enforcement policies, see paras 6.51–6.62.
[109] See paras 6.33–6.38 for a further discussion on the manner of the investigation.
[110] Para. 53, p. 41.
[111] *R v Lang* [2006] 1 WLR 2509.

said to be significant has also been held to mean something more than what would just be needed to prevent it from being brushed aside as *de minimis*.[112]

The fact that a business or person has not previously committed any harm should not auto-   **5.134**
matically lead to the conclusion that harm will not occur in the future. The test of significant harm is forward looking, requiring the regulator to determine whether the activity will cause, or will present a significant risk of causing, serious harm in the future. The decision will be made by reference not only to past conduct, but also through an assessment of future risk. The fact that no harm has actually been caused by a person to date is, again, not necessarily determinative of the risk they may pose in the future. In the context of assessing the future risk of offending by a defendant, the criminal courts have held that it does 'not automatically follow from the absence of actual harm caused by the offender to date that the risk that he would cause serious harm in the future was negligible'.[113]

Procedure for issuing

The procedure for the imposition of stop notices is governed by ss 47–49 RESA and any   **5.135**
order made under s. 46 must secure the results contained therein. Section 47(2) stipulates the minimum procedural requirements pertaining to the serving of a stop notice that must appear in any order:

  (i) the contents of the stop notice must comply with s. 47(3);
  (ii) provision must be made for the person against whom the notice is imposed to appeal against it;
  (iii) provision must be made about the issuing of a completion certificate: upon the regulator's own initiative, if they are satisfied that the person has taken the steps specified in the notice, or pursuant to an application by the person upon whom the notice is served (in both cases the notice must then cease to have effect);
  (iv) provision as to the time in which the regulator must make the decision as to whether to issue a completion certificate pursuant to an application, which must be no later than fourteen days after the application; and
  (v) provision permitting the person against whom the notice is served to appeal against the decision not to issue a completion certificate.

The order awarding the power to impose a stop notice must also make provision prohibiting   **5.136**
the issuing of that notice where an FMP has already been imposed in respect of the same act or omission, or the person has discharged their liability to an FMP in respect of the same act or omission.[114]

Figure 5.3 shows the process by which stop notices may be imposed, challenged or satisfied   **5.137**
and ultimately enforced where necessary.[115]

The procedure for the imposition of a stop notice is quite different to that which is required   **5.138**
for FMPs and discretionary requirements. Stop notices are intended to provide a quick and effective mechanism for stopping activities carried on by businesses that are dangerous, and

---

[112] *Lambeth LBC v Grewal* (1985) 82 Cr App R 301.
[113] *R v Johnson* [2006] EWCA Crim 2486.
[114] RESA, s. 51(2)(b).
[115] Reproduced from the BERR, *Regulatory Enforcement and Sanctions Act 2008: Guidance to the Act*, p. 41.

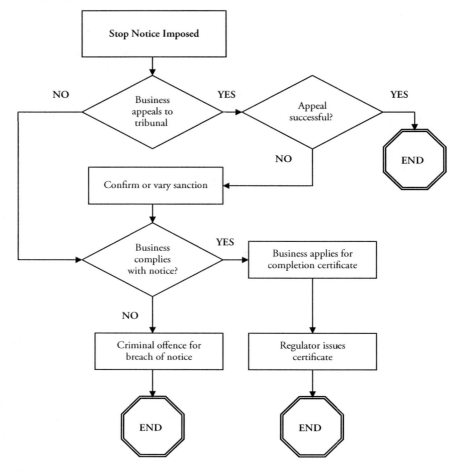

Figure 5.3 Issuing stop notices

from which the public require immediate protection. For that reason, the process for apply-ing these sanctions is truncated. The regulator does not need to serve a notice of intent, nor is there a provision permitting the business to make any representations or objections to the regulator before the sanction is imposed. A regulator seeking to impose a stop notice need only satisfy itself that the requirements of s. 46(4) or (5) have been met[116] (and thus guilt established) before it can then go on to impose the notice. It will then be for the business or individual against whom the notice has been imposed to either appeal against the imposition of the notice, or seek to comply with its terms and apply for a certificate of completion to neutralize its effect.

---

[116] Namely that an activity that is causing or is likely to cause significant serious harm is being carried on or is likely to be carried on, and that that activity involves or is likely to involve the commission of a relevant offence.

Contents of a stop notice

Any order under this section awarding the power to impose a stop notice must make provision for the information that must be contained in such a notice. Section 47(3) provides that the following minimum information must be included:

   (i) the grounds for serving the notice;
   (ii) rights of appeal; and
   (iii) the consequences of non-compliance with the notice.

5.139

The notice should also specify any steps that the business must take to enable it to move back into compliance. Any such steps must be aimed at removing or reducing the harm or risk of harm referred to in s. 46(4)(b) or (5)(b) and identified by the regulator in the notice.

5.140

A stop notice will remain in place until the person has taken the steps specified in the notice. If the business does not comply with any such requirements, the notice will remain extant.

5.141

Completion certificate

Once a stop notice has been served upon a business or individual, they can either appeal that decision or, as soon as they consider that they have moved back into compliance (or indeed if they consider they are compliant already), they may apply for a completion certificate.

5.142

A regulator must issue a completion certificate of its own initiative where it is satisfied that the person has taken the steps specified in the notice.[117]

5.143

The person on whom the notice is served may at any time apply for a completion certificate and the regulator must make a decision as to whether to issue such a certificate within fourteen days of any such application, or any shorter period that the minister may provide in the order.[118] In circumstances where the notice prohibits a business from carrying out its activities, this represents a significant delay to businesses before they are lawfully permitted to operate again and could have serious financial and reputational consequences.

5.144

Upon issue of a completion certificate, the stop notice ceases to have effect.[119]

5.145

Compensation

Orders giving regulators the power to serve stop notices must provide for regulators, on application, to compensate businesses where they have suffered loss because of either the service of a stop notice, or the refusal of the regulator to issue a completion certificate.

5.146

The power to award compensation, provided for in s. 48, provides a significant safeguard for businesses against the misuse of stop notices by regulators. Whilst no amount of financial compensation is able to repair any damage likely to be caused to the reputation of a business wrongly served with such a notice, the provision will nonetheless be welcomed by businesses. Given the serious nature and potentially devastating effect that this sanction may have on businesses, this provision represents an important protection against ill-considered applications to impose stop notices.

5.147

---

[117] RESA, s. 47(2)(c).
[118] Ibid., s. 47(2)(e) and (f).
[119] Ibid., s. 47(2)(c) and (d).

5.148 Compensation will not be available to all applicants in all cases. The order must provide that it only be available in prescribed cases and in relation to prescribed descriptions of loss.[120] Both of these criteria will be provided for in the order by the minister, who will determine the specific grounds under which compensation may be awarded. The Environmental Civil Sanctions (England) Order 2010,[121] which awards the Environment Agency and Natural England the power to impose, inter alia, stop notices, provides that a business may be compensated for any loss resulting from the service of a stop notice or a refusal to issue a completion certificate where:

    (i) a stop notice is subsequently withdrawn or amended by the regulator because the decision to serve it was unreasonable or any step specified in the notice was unreasonable;

    (ii) the operator successfully appeals against the stop notice and the First-tier Tribunal finds that the service of the notice was unreasonable; or

    (iii) the operator successfully appeals against the refusal of a completion certificate and the Tribunal finds that the refusal was unreasonable.

5.149 According to the BERR, *Regulatory Enforcement and Sanctions Act 2008: Guidance to the Act*:[122]

> Compensation might be appropriate where a business wins an appeal against imposition of a stop notice and where the regulator is considered to have acted unreasonably or in serious default. Compensation will not be appropriate in all cases, for example, it may not be appropriate if an appeal was upheld on a technicality.

5.150 Businesses must be provided with the right to appeal against decisions by regulators not to award compensation and against the amount of compensation awarded.[123]

Appeal

5.151 Any order under Part 3 granting a regulator the power to impose stop notices must make provision for a business so affected to appeal against:

    (i) the imposition of the stop notice: s. 47(2)(b);

    (ii) the refusal of the regulator to issue a completion certificate: s. 47(2)(g); and

    (iii) the refusal of the regulator to award compensation or as to the level of compensation awarded: s. 48(3)(a) and (b).

5.152 The order must set out the permissible grounds of any appeal, which by virtue of s. 47(4) must include the following:

    (i) that the regulator's decision to serve the stop notice was based on an error of fact;

    (ii) that the regulator's decision to serve the stop notice was wrong in law;

    (iii) that a requirement imposed by the notice was unreasonable;

    (iv) that the business has not committed the relevant offence and would not have committed it had the stop notice not been served; and

    (v) that the business would not, by reason of a defence, have been liable to be convicted of the relevant offence had the notice not been served.

---

[120] RESA, s. 48(2).

[121] SI 1157/2010. The position concerning Natural England and the Environment Agency is considered in further detail in Chapter 7.

[122] Para. 56.

[123] RESA, s. 48(3).

Provision may also be made by the minister in any conferring order for appeals on other **5.153** grounds. For the reasons set out in paras 5.47–5.96, it is of particular importance that regulators consider seeking for appeals against stop notices to be 'as of right'. Businesses that have been caused to cease trading, for example, need to have access to an effective mechanism for a fair determination of liability, where they are able to advance their defence or explanation to the charge and test the evidence against them. The consequences of failing to comply with a stop notice are serious and, for that reason, it may well be thought that the procedural protections afforded to those charged with criminal offences ought to apply and, in particular, that business be afforded the right to have their case heard by an unbiased tribunal before which, as far as reasonably practicable, the rules of natural justice and the provisions of Art. 6 HRA will be observed.[124]

Refusal to issue a completion certificate

A business on which a stop notice is served and which applies for a certificate of completion **5.154** may also appeal the decision of the regulator to deny it that certificate. Provision for such an appeal must be made in the order setting out the grounds under which such an appeal may be brought. These must include, but are not limited to, the grounds stipulated in s. 47(5), namely that:

   (i) the decision was based on an error of fact;
   (ii) the decision was wrong in law; and
  (iii) the decision was unfair or unreasonable.

Surprisingly perhaps, no provision is made in RESA dealing with what happens to the stop **5.155** notice when there is an appeal. It is expected that the minister's order will deal with whether the stop notice is suspended on appeal or not. The decision as to whether to include such a provision will have a huge impact on businesses and regulators alike; this issue is discussed in more detail in paras 8.150–8.152.

The refusal of the regulator to award compensation or as to the level of compensation awarded

As well as providing the right for a business to apply for compensation should a stop notice **5.156** cause any loss, the order must provide for the business to be able to appeal against the refusal of the regulator to award compensation or the level of compensation awarded.

Failure to comply

Regulators serving stop notices should take proactive steps to follow them up promptly, **5.157** especially in cases where there is no appeal and no application for a completion certificate has been made by the business concerned. Notices that are left to languish have the ability to severely undermine their use as an effective sanction tool, especially in cases where the public has been placed directly at risk by the illegal activity concerned. Effective monitoring also allows businesses to evaluate outcomes more effectively, which in turn enables better risk assessment in the future.[125]

---

[124] *Ridge v Baldwin* [1963] 2 All ER 66.
[125] Macrory saw the following-up of enforcement action as an essential component of a sanctions regime: see Richard Macrory, *Regulatory Justice: Making Sanctions Effective*, p. 10.

5.158 A business that does not comply with the stop notice served on it, may be guilty of a criminal offence and liable:

(i) on summary conviction, to a fine not exceeding £20,000, or imprisonment for term not exceeding:
  (a) six months in England[126] or Northern Ireland;[127] or
  (b) twelve months in Scotland;[128]
or both; or
(ii) on conviction on indictment, to imprisonment for a term not exceeding two years, or a fine, or both.

F. Enforcement undertakings

Introduction

5.159 Section 50 permits a minister by way of an order under Part 3, to grant the award of enforcement undertakings to regulators who may apply them in cases where they have reasonable grounds to suspect that a business has committed a relevant offence.[129]

5.160 Enforcement undertakings are undertakings 'to take such action as may be specified in the undertaking within such period as may be so specified'.[130] They are a method of dealing with regulatory non-compliance in a constructive and consensual manner by way of an agreement between the regulator and the business as to the steps that must be taken to secure compliance.

5.161 Unlike the other civil sanctions under this Part, it will be for a business to propose to give an undertaking to the regulator, and for the regulator to decide whether or not to accept that undertaking. Regulators are not obliged to accept enforcement undertakings in any particular case. The nature of these sanctions means that the business takes ownership of the regulatory solution presented; offering appropriate and proportionate conditions to remedy the underlying breach and being held to account for its non-compliance.

5.162 Enforcement undertakings are a legal novelty in the UK,[131] as the BERR *Regulatory Enforcement and Sanctions Act 2008: Guidance to the Act* explains:[132]

> The Macrory report noted that current sanctions regimes do not allow for creative ways of addressing regulatory non-compliance. There have been cases where businesses have recognised that they have fallen into non-compliance and proposed innovative and restorative ways of returning to compliance. Until now, there has been no legislative basis to facilitate or encourage this kind of creative measure.

---

[126] This term will be increased to twelve months' imprisonment for offences committed after s. 154(1) of the Criminal Justice Act 2003 comes into force.
[127] RESA, s. 49(2)(b).
[128] Ibid., s. 49(1)(a).
[129] See paras 4.58–4.80 for an analysis of the terms 'regulator' and 'relevant offence'.
[130] RESA, s. 50(2).
[131] They are used in both Australia and the US. See for further detail, Richard Macrory, *Regulatory Justice: Making Sanctions Effective,* p. 69.
[132] P. 43, para. 59.

Power to impose

A regulator awarded access to enforcement undertakings must only deploy them in accordance with the terms of s. 50(1)(a), that is to say where the regulator has reasonable grounds to suspect that the person has committed a relevant offence. **5.163**

'Reasonable grounds to suspect'

The only statutory precondition to the acceptance of an enforcement undertaking by a regulator is that it must have reasonable grounds to suspect that a relevant offence has been committed by the business. The threshold of 'reasonable grounds' is not further particularized in RESA, nor elaborated on in the BERR, *Regulatory Enforcement and Sanctions Act 2008: Guidance to the Act.* **5.164**

In the criminal context, police officers deploying their statutory powers of stop and search may do so only if they have reasonable grounds to suspect that an offence has been, or may be, committed. That suspicion is to be judged objectively and must be based on relevant facts, information and intelligence;[133] it can never be supported on the basis of personal factors of the suspect alone without reliable supporting intelligence or information, and cannot be based on generalizations or stereotypical images of certain groups. Even so, it has been held that 'the threshold for the existence of reasonable grounds for suspicion is low'.[134] **5.165**

The European Court of Human Rights, in the case of *Fox, Campbell and Hartley v United Kingdom*[135] have held that 'having a "reasonable suspicion" presupposes the existence of facts or information which would satisfy an objective observer that the person concerned may have committed the offence'. Lord Hope in *O'Hara v Chief Constable of the Royal Ulster Constabulary*[136] stated that 'the question whether it provided reasonable grounds for suspicion depends on the source of his information and its context, seen in the light of the whole surrounding circumstances'. **5.166**

A regulator will not need to be able to show that a relevant offence has actually been committed, nor will it need to carry out an investigation before it can be said to have reasonable grounds for suspicion: **5.167**

> Suspicion in its ordinary meaning is a state of conjecture or surmise where proof is lacking: 'I suspect but I cannot prove'. Suspicion arises at or near the starting point of an investigation, of which the obtaining of prima facie proof is the end … There is another distinction between reasonable suspicion and prima facie proof. Prima facie proof consists of admissible evidence. Suspicion can take account of matters that could not be put in evidence at all.[137]

It is likely that in the majority of cases, the business will have come to the regulator with an admission of one form or another and as such, little more by way of investigation will need to be carried out before the requisite threshold is met for the imposition of the sanction. **5.168**

---

[133] Code A (Codes of Practice, Police and Criminal Evidence Act 1984).
[134] *Comr of the Police of the Metropolis v Mohamed Raissi* [2008] EWCA Civ 1237.
[135] (1990) 13 EHRR 157 at para. 32.
[136] [1997] AC 286, at 298C-E.
[137] *Shaaban bin Hussein v Chong Fook Kam* [1970] AC 942, at 949B; [1970] 2 WLR 441; [1969] 3 All ER 1626.

'Relevant offence'

5.169 The term 'relevant offence' is defined in s. 38 and has a different meaning depending on whether the regulator is a Sch. 5 regulator or an authority that has an enforcement function in relation to one of the enactments in Sch. 6 or 7. A full analysis of this term appears in paras 4.68–4.80.

Process for making an enforcement undertaking

Introduction

5.170 In common with the other civil sanctions under this Part, the procedure to be adopted when making an enforcement undertaking is largely left to the minister to determine in the order. Unlike the other sanctions, the process for making an enforcement undertaking is far less circumscribed by the terms of RESA, and much of the procedure dealing with the operation of this sanction is optional rather than mandatory. The only procedural requirement that must be provided for in the order is a provision preventing double jeopardy.

5.171 Figure 5.4 sets out the procedure for the making of an enforcement undertaking.[138]

Action specified in the enforcement undertaking

5.172 In practice, enforcement undertakings are likely to be applied to conduct brought to the attention of the regulator by the business, rather than to misconduct identified by the regulator. Either way, a discussion is likely to take place between the regulator and the business as to what the terms of the agreement will be in any particular case. Whilst the specific terms of any undertaking will vary from case to case, the underlying aims of those terms must meet the ends specified in s. 50(3) and be preventative, restorative or retributive in nature.

5.173 According to s. 50(3), the action that a business can offer to undertake must be:

(i) action to secure that the offence does not continue or recur;
(ii) action to secure that the position is, so far as possible, restored to what it would have been if the offence had not been committed;
(iii) action (including the payment of a sum of money) to benefit any person affected by the offence, or
(iv) action of a prescribed description.

5.174 The terms of the undertaking could provide for compensation to be paid, or reimbursement or other redress to be made to an affected party. Actions may also include requirements that an offender undertake a service to the community, such as funding or implementing a compliance education programme, and may also include a restorative element.[139]

Double jeopardy

5.175 An order awarding enforcement undertakings to regulators must secure the consequences in s. 50(4), prohibiting a business that has complied with an undertaking to later be prosecuted for the same conduct or having one of the other administrative sanctions[140] imposed on it. Protection against double jeopardy is only afforded to a business that complies with the

---

[138] Reproduced from the BERR, *Regulatory Enforcement and Sanctions Act 2008: Guidance to the Act*, p. 44.
[139] Richard Macrory, *Regulatory Justice: Making Sanctions Effective*, p. 66, para. 4.27.
[140] FMP or discretionary requirement.

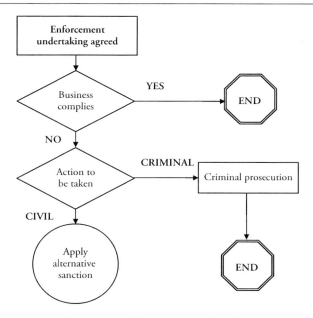

Figure 5.4 Issuing enforcement undertakings

enforcement undertaking and would not apply where it had failed to comply with some or all of its terms.

Provision may also be made in the order extending the ordinary time limits for criminal **5.176** prosecution in cases where a regulator is seeking to pursue a criminal prosecution against a business that has breached the terms of an undertaking in whole or in part.[141]

The minister making the order would not be able to extend these time limits retrospectively **5.177** in contravention of Art. 7 of the ECHR.[142]

Other procedural provisions

Many of the recommendations advanced by Macrory[143] about the content of enforcement **5.178** undertakings have found their way into s. 50(5), which provides that the order may also include detail:

(i)   as to the procedure for entering into an undertaking;
(ii) as to the terms of an undertaking;
(iii) as to publication of an undertaking by a regulator;
(iv) as to variation of an undertaking;
(v)   as to circumstances in which a person may be regarded as having complied with an undertaking;
(vi) as to monitoring by a regulator of compliance with an undertaking;

---

[141] RESA, s. 50(5)(k).
[142] Art. 7 provides that: 'No one shall be held guilty of any criminal offence on account of any act or omission which did not constitute a criminal offence under national or international law at the time when it was committed ...'
[143] See, for example, Richard Macrory, *Regulatory Justice: Making Sanctions Effective*, p. 67.

(vii) as to certification by a regulator that an undertaking has been complied with;

(viii) as to provision for appeals against refusal to give such certification;

(ix) in a case where a person has given inaccurate, misleading or incomplete information in relation to the undertaking, as to provision for that person to be regarded as not having complied with it; and

(x) in a case where a person has complied partly but not fully with an undertaking, as to provision for that part compliance to be taken into account in the imposition of any criminal or other sanction on the person.

5.179 It will be for the minister to determine which, if any, of these procedural requirements should be provided for in the order.

Appeal

5.180 There is no requirement in RESA that the order make provision for a business to be able to appeal against the making of an enforcement undertaking, largely because such undertakings come about through the mutual agreement of the business and the regulator.

5.181 Where the order provides that the business may apply for a certificate that the undertaking has been complied with, it must also provide for the business to be able to appeal against a refusal to grant such a certificate.[144] In those circumstances, the order should also stipulate the grounds on which such an appeal may be brought and in doing so, may usefully have regard to the permissible grounds for an appeal against a refusal of a regulator to issue a certificate of completion after the issuing of a stop notice:[145] error of fact, wrong in law, unfair or unreasonable and any other ground as the minister may provide for in the order.

Failure to comply

5.182 Where an enforcement undertaking has been agreed, it is of critical importance that the regulator follows it up. It is recognized that this will place an increased burden on regulators to monitor businesses; however, the integrity of this sanction depends upon regulators being seen to take decisive action when an undertaking is not complied with. Where there is a breach of an undertaking, or any part of it, a regulator may decide to bring criminal proceedings against the business for the original offence or impose one of the other civil sanctions to which it has access.

G. Costs and monies

Costs

5.183 An order awarding the civil sanctions may contain a provision enabling a regulator to recover the costs (by notice) from a person on whom a discretionary requirement or stop notice is imposed.[146] No costs may be recovered in respect of the imposition of an FMP or an enforcement undertaking, which may ultimately prove to be a disincentive to regulators to pursue these particular sanctions.

---

[144] RESA, s. 50(5)(h).
[145] Ibid., s. 47(5).
[146] Ibid., s. 53(1) and (2).

What costs can be recovered?

In respect of discretionary requirements, the order may provide for the recovery of 'costs incurred by the regulator in relation to the imposition of the discretionary requirement up to the time of its imposition'.[147] **5.184**

For stop notices, the costs that may be recovered by the regulator are those 'costs incurred by the regulator in relation to the service of the notice up to the time of service'.[148] **5.185**

In respect of both of these sanctions, the nature of the costs that may be recovered includes:[149] **5.186**

(i) investigation costs;
(ii) administration costs; and
(iii) costs of obtaining expert advice (including legal advice).

This list is not exhaustive, leaving open the possibility that the minister may include other recoverable costs in the order. **5.187**

The order may also make provision for the recovery of costs where the regulator has to take enforcement action against a business or individual that has defaulted on a monetary penalty (FMP, VMP or non-compliance penalty).[150] Section 53(5) provides that where a financial penalty is imposed, the order may additionally provide for the following costs to be recovered: **5.188**

(i) interest or other financial penalty for late payment, the level of which must not exceed that of the penalty: s. 52(1)(b); and
(ii) for enforcement of the penalty:[151] s. 52(1)(c).

Where the order includes a provision permitting the recovery of costs against defaulting businesses, the minister may also make provision for the manner in which these costs may be recovered, either by the regulator as a civil debt, or on the order of a court, as if payable under a court order.[152] **5.189**

Procedure for seeking costs

In a case where a regulator wishes to recover any costs incurred by it this must be done 'by notice'.[153] An order awarding a regulator the power to recover costs must provide for the notice to secure the following results:[154] **5.190**

(i) that the notice specifies the amount required to be paid;
(ii) that the regulator may be required to provide a detailed breakdown of that amount;
(iii) that the person required to pay costs is not liable to pay any costs shown by the person to have been unnecessarily incurred; and

---

[147] Ibid., s. 53(1).
[148] Ibid., s. 53(2).
[149] Ibid., s. 53(3).
[150] Ibid., s. 45(1).
[151] Ibid., s. 53(5).
[152] Ibid., s. 52(2)(a) and (b).
[153] Ibid., s. 53(1) and (2).
[154] Ibid., s. 53(4).

(iv) that the person required to pay costs may appeal against the decision of the regulator to impose the requirement to pay costs and the decision of the regulator as to the amount of those costs.

5.191 Whilst there is no provision in RESA as to the manner or timing of the service of any such notice, it would be sensible for it to be served at the same time as the final notice imposing the sanction, unless that is not practicable. It would be good practice for a regulator to provide a detailed breakdown of costs incurred at this stage as a matter of course, rather than simply on request.

5.192 RESA does not stipulate the mechanism by which the cost assessment will be carried out, although it would be sensible to include this information in the enforcement policy. Generally, those costs that may be recovered are those reasonably incurred as a result of any non-compliance, and if a person can demonstrate that any costs sought have been unnecessarily incurred they will not be required to pay such costs.[155]

Appeal of a notice to pay costs

5.193 The person served with a notice requiring them to pay costs may appeal against the decision of the regulator to impose the requirement to pay costs and/or the amount of the costs sought. The Procedural Rules of the First-tier Tribunal[156] deal with the method and timing of any such appeal and are considered in Chapter 8.

5.194 The costs recoverable under this section are those actually incurred in investigating non-compliance and as such regulators will be able to retain such monies and will not need to pay them into the consolidated fund.

Monies

5.195 This short section is concerned with the provisions that may be included in the order dealing with the payment of monies related to the civil sanctions.

Payment of penalties into consolidated fund

5.196 Section 69(1) provides that any monies relating to the following must be paid into the consolidated fund for the respective country, and may not be retained by the regulator:

(i)   from FMPs, VMPs or non-compliance penalties;
(ii) any interest or other financial penalties for late payment of a penalty mentioned in (i) above; or
(iii) any sum paid in discharge of liability to FMPs.

5.197 Industry accepted this section was a very welcome addition to RESA, quietening earlier criticism that the monies generated from the civil sanctions would simply be siphoned directly back to the regulator, thereby incentivizing enforcement. It should, for the same reason, be welcomed by those responsible for enforcement, who would otherwise have been obliged to rebut suggestions in individual cases that their motivation was other than to secure proper regulatory compliance. Simply, regulation should not be a source of income for regulators

---

[155] Ibid., s. 53(4)(c).
[156] The Tribunal Procedure (First-tier Tribunal) (General Regulatory Chamber) Rules 2009, rule 10.

and neither would it be helpful for there be any perverse financial incentives that might in any way influence a regulator's choice of sanction.

Other provisions

Any order awarding the power to impose financial penalties may also include a provision for the following: **5.198**

  (i) discounts for early payments: s. 52(1)(a);
 (ii) for late payment to be recoverable, on the order of a court, as if payable under a court order: s. 52(2)(b); and
(iii) for enforcement of the penalty:[157] s. 52(1)(c).

---

[157] Either through the civil courts or through the more streamlined process of recovery by treating the penalty as if it were payable under a court order: s. 52(2)(a)–(b).

6

IMPLEMENTATION OF THE SANCTIONS

A. Introduction

A regulator gaining access to the suite of civil sanctions will need to undertake a carefully **6.01** planned process of implementation. Procedures will need to be reset so that the sanctions are used properly and in line with the guidance to RESA and the Hampton principles.[1] A considerable amount of time will need to be devoted to the retraining of staff; inspectors for example will need to be trained in order to be able to apply the sanctions and to ensure that their use is consistent. Regulators will also have to be careful to avoid any unforeseen perverse incentives for the issuing of certain sanctions. It would be prudent, for example, for

---

[1] RESA, s. 5(2).

staff appraisal criteria to be reviewed within the regulating body in the light of the new powers available.[2]

6.02 In addition to the somewhat limited procedural protections afforded to businesses and individuals against whom the sanctions might be imposed,[3] RESA provides five further safeguards aimed at achieving consistency in the deployment of the sanctions, and preventing misuse by regulators:

(i) the requirement to publish guidance about the use of the civil sanctions (penalty guidance): s. 63;

(ii) the requirement to publish guidance about the enforcement of relevant offences (enforcement policy): s. 64;

(iii) the requirement to publish enforcement outcomes: s. 65;

(iv) review by the minister of the operation of the order awarding the sanctions: s. 67; and

(v) suspension of the power to impose the civil sanctions by the minister: s. 68.

6.03 This chapter considers these operational safeguards, as well as addressing the questions of how regulators should decide when the sanctions should be deployed, and how they should be used alongside their existing enforcement tools. Finally, in Part F of this chapter (and in Chapter 7, in respect of the Environment Agency and Natural England), businesses and stakeholders are able to gain an insight into the approach that the Sch. 5 regulators have taken, and propose to take in the future, with respect to the civil sanctions.

B. Penalty guidance

Introduction

6.04 Many regulators[4] will already be familiar with the process of issuing guidance to help those who are regulated navigate their way through the maze of rules and regulations relating to enforcement. Regulators exercising enforcement functions must ensure that they operate transparently. Guidance that is widely published, regularly updated and consistently followed, helps to achieve this aim and ensures that regulators remain accountable and maintain legitimacy in the eyes of their stakeholders.

6.05 The existence of properly drafted and consistently followed guidance will afford protection to business and to regulators alike, against arbitrary and ad hoc decision making on the one hand, and challenge and possible litigation on the other.

6.06 It is obligatory for regulators to issue guidance as to their use of the sanctions (penalty guidance)[5] and to have regard to that guidance when exercising their functions.[6] The penalty

---

[2] The avoidance of perverse incentives is the sixth and final Penalty Principle espoused by Richard Macrory in his report *Regulatory Justice: Making Sanctions Effective*, p. 10.

[3] The right to make representations, to appeal and (in the case of FMPs and discretionary requirements) not to have the sanction imposed at all unless the regulator can be satisfied beyond reasonable doubt that the relevant offence has been committed.

[4] Research carried out by Macrory for his report found that only seventeen out of the fifty-six regulators studied had published an enforcement policy: Richard Macrory, *Regulatory Justice: Making Sanctions Effective*, p. 32, para. 2.12.

[5] RESA, s. 63(1) and (2)(a).

[6] Ibid., s. 63(2)(e).

guidance must contain information about the civil sanctions and how they will be used by the regulator. This guidance deals with decisions taken after a business is found to have been non-compliant, and not with how that decision itself is reached (this would be covered by any investigation policy prepared).[7]

For businesses and individuals, this guidance will be an invaluable tool by which they will be **6.07** able to determine whether they are being treated fairly, and may ultimately act as a basis for legal challenge should the guidance not be followed consistently by the regulator. Any regulator that repeatedly fails to follow the penalty guidance could have their power to impose the civil sanctions suspended by the minister.[8] See part E.

Who should prepare the guidance?

RESA is silent on the issue of who should prepare the penalty guidance; the responsibility is **6.08** likely to vary depending on the regulatory regime involved. The BERR *Regulatory Enforcement and Sanctions Act 2008: Guidance to the Act* suggests that where a regulation is enforced by national regulators and local authorities, national regulators will take the lead in producing penalty guidance in consultation with the relevant government department, local authorities and the Local Better Regulation Office. Where regulations are primarily enforced by local regulators such as environmental health, planning or trading standards, there are no clear national regulators to take the lead in producing penalty guidance.[9] In such cases, the Local Better Regulation Office, in consultation with the relevant government department, can take the lead in providing support to local authorities in producing penalty guidance.[10]

Whilst many regulators will be familiar with the preparation of guidance documents already, **6.09** regulators would do well to look at the sensible and practical suggestions provided in the *Code of Practice on Guidance on Regulation*[11] when preparing the penalty guidance. Whilst this is strictly only applicable to government departments and their agencies when new legislation is passed, the eight 'golden rules of good guidance',[12] including ease of use and access, act as a helpful checklist to regulators when drafting their own penalty guidance.

Consultation

The duty on a regulator to consult may arise at two stages: first, when it issues penalty **6.10** guidance and later when it comes to revise such guidance. Prior to issuing any guidance under this part, regulators must consult such persons as 'the provision may specify'.[13] The order may specify specific groups of interested parties that must be consulted, or, as is the case with the Environmental Civil Sanctions (England) Order 2010, a generic provision requiring consultation with 'such persons as … appropriate' may be provided for.[14]

---

[7] As to which see below, part C.
[8] RESA, s. 68.
[9] P. 47.
[10] RESA, s. 6. For more about the general functions of the LBRO, see Chapter 2.
[11] Published October 2009. A copy can be found on the Department for Business Innovation and Skills (BIS) website: <http://www.bis gov.uk>.
[12] (1) Based on a good understanding of users (2) Designed with input from users and their representative bodies (3) Organized around the user's way of working (4) Easy for the intended users to understand (5) Designed to provide users with confidence in how to comply with the law (6) Issued in good time (7) Easy to access and (8) Reviewed and improved.
[13] RESA, s. 63(2)(d).
[14] Para. 13.

6.11 When revising guidance, s. 63(2)(d) places a further duty on regulators to consult with those specified in the order. The guidance must be revised where appropriate after this consultation process.[15]

Contents of the guidance

6.12 In respect of all the sanctions, bar enforcement undertakings, RESA requires that certain minimum 'relevant information' must be included in the penalty guidance.[16] Relevant information is defined in a different way in relation to each of the civil sanctions.

6.13 In relation to fixed monetary penalties (FMPs), 'relevant information' is defined in s. 63(3) as being information as to:

(i) the circumstances in which the penalty is likely to be imposed;
(ii) the circumstances in which it may not be imposed;
(iii) the amount of the penalty;
(iv) how liability for the penalty may be discharged and the effect of discharge;
(v) the right to make representations and objections; and
(vi) rights of appeal.

6.14 In the case of discretionary requirements, 'relevant information' is defined in s. 63(4) as being information as to:

(i) the circumstances in which the requirement is likely to be imposed;
(ii) the circumstances in which it may not be imposed;
(iii) in the case of a variable monetary penalty (VMP), the matters likely to be taken into account by the regulator in determining the amount of the penalty (including, where relevant, any discounts for voluntary reporting of non-compliance); and
(iv) rights to make representations and objections; and
(v) rights of appeal.

6.15 Where a regulator has been awarded the power to impose a VMP, the penalty guidance ought to provide for the identity of the person who will determine the level of the penalty. A model adopted by some regulators in respect of financial penalties is to have an independent financial investigator, who fixes the level of the penalty.[17]

6.16 In relation to stop notices, 'relevant information' is defined in s. 63(5) as being information as to:

(i) the circumstances in which the regulator is likely to serve the notice;
(ii) the circumstances in which it may not be imposed; and
(iii) rights of appeal.

6.17 There is no specific requirement in RESA detailing the information that must be included in the penalty guidance in respect of enforcement undertakings.

---

[15] RESA, s. 63(2)(c).
[16] Ibid., s. 63(2)(b).
[17] For example, the Security Industry Authority.

Revising the guidance

Guidance about the use of penalties will need to evolve over time to reflect the experiences **6.18**
of the regulator in its enforcement activities. Section 63(2)(d) requires regulators to revise
the guidance as appropriate. No further detail is given as to how frequently this exercise
should be undertaken; regulators might consider including such information in the
guidance itself.

Status of the guidance

Section 63(2)(e) provides that the regulator must 'have regard' to the guidance or revised **6.19**
guidance when exercising its functions. This is not a requirement to follow the guidance in
all circumstances, but a mandatory requirement to consider it, deviating only in appropriate
circumstances. In any such case it would be prudent for the regulator to document briefly
both the consideration and the ground upon which any decision was taken to deviate.

Where a regulator repeatedly fails (without good reason) to act in accordance with any **6.20**
guidance it publishes under this section, the minister may suspend the regulator's power to
use the civil sanctions. This is considered further in part E below.

C. Investigation policy

Introduction

RESA makes no provision about the procedures that must be followed when regulators are **6.21**
investigating the possible commission of offences, or determining liability. The mandatory
penalty guidance and enforcement policies both relate to considerations relevant *after* the
decision to impose a (civil) sanction has been reached, and thus after a determination of
culpability.

This is a vast area in relation to which the legislature will have no input whatsoever; regulators **6.22**
are able to determine the mechanisms by which cases are investigated and liability determined, without recourse to any statutory provisions. Fundamental decisions, such as who
should conduct the investigation, what methods may properly be deployed, what evidence
will be provided to the non-compliant business, how it will be presented and who will make
the decision on guilt or innocence, are all left to individual regulators to make provision for,
with seemingly limitless discretion.

Whilst regulators will have to decide how they propose to investigate and 'try' offences to **6.23**
which the civil sanctions may be attached, RESA places no obligation on regulators to prepare or publish a policy setting these processes out. Although many regulators will be accus-
tomed to conducting investigations, few will have experience of determining liability and
imposing sanctions against non-compliant businesses.

There is a common interest amongst regulators and those regulated in ensuring that the civil **6.24**
sanctions are deployed in a fair and consistent manner. Absent a comprehensive investigation
policy that is consistently applied, the potential for inconsistent decision making is enhanced,
as is the likelihood of legal challenge to the regime and any decisions emanating from it.

It is for these reasons that regulators should turn their minds to designing and implementing **6.25**
a written policy, aimed at directing the way that investigations are conducted and allegations

made out to the applicable standard of proof. From a practical perspective (for example, due to budgetary or personnel considerations) it would be sensible to commence this exercise at the earliest possible stage of policy development.

Content of the policy

6.26 There is no 'one size fits all' approach to the manner in which investigations are conducted and liability determined. Accordingly each regulator, whether by virtue of its remit, size or case-load, will need to tailor these suggestions to meet its own ends and in the light of past experience. Whilst each policy will differ according to the nature of the regulator and the regulated activity, what follows are some general suggestions as to the minimum consider-ations that ought to be addressed:

The decision to investigate

6.27 Not all matters coming to the attention of a regulator will fall within its remit and require investigation with a view to the imposition of a civil sanction. In deciding whether informa-tion brought to its attention merits further consideration by the regulator as a potential complaint, the policy needs to stipulate the minimum criteria applicable to the acceptance of a complaint.

6.28 The litmus test of whether a matter merits further consideration by the regulator might be where the conduct complained of *could* amount to a relevant offence for which the civil sanc-tions are available. In these circumstances, the regulator will need to be able to identify the alleged non-compliant business and know broadly the dates, times and locations of any alleged wrongdoing. The criteria may also helpfully cover matters such as the stance taken in relation to anonymous complaints and conduct occurring some time in the past.

6.29 Through the consistent application of the criteria, the regulator will be required to consider whether the information it has received about a supposedly non-compliant business or individual is sufficient to warrant further investigation, or whether the matter falls outwith its remit.

6.30 Regulators may also wish to consider including a 'public interest' test in this initial screening phase.[18] Even where the information provided in a particular case is sufficient to warrant further investigation, there may be compelling public interest reasons for the matter not to be pursued. If the matter warrants further consideration by the regulator, careful considera-tion should be given to whether the enforcement objectives can be met through a less burdensome approach, for example through the provision of advice and/or guidance. Advice and guidance remains at the heart of a well-graduated system of enforcement.

6.31 Finally, provision should be made for account to be taken of any investigations and/or sanc-tions imposed by other regulators relating to the same matter. It is good practice for regula-tors to have memoranda of understanding with other regulators where this kind of coordination is necessary.

6.32 The decision to terminate a complaint at this early stage should only be made by reference to these written criteria and not on an ad hoc basis. The criteria need to be applied by suitably

---

[18] See e.g. the Code for Crown Prosecutors (22 February 2010), a copy of which can be found at <http://www.cps.gov.uk/>.

trained staff and decisions susceptible to oversight by senior management, preferably through a system of random reviews.

The investigation

The policy should deal clearly and comprehensively with the methods and procedures that will be used by the regulator at the information-gathering stage. **6.33**

The methods of investigation that may be deployed should, as far as possible, be detailed in the policy. **6.34**

In circumstances where there has been prior police involvement, it is likely that much of the investigation into suspected non-compliance will already have been carried out. Where this is the case, and given the power of a regulator to obtain disclosure from the police, Crown Prosecution Service etc.,[19] much of the required evidence will be provided to the regulator by that enforcement authority, necessitating little, if any, further investigation. **6.35**

In all other cases, regulators need to decide how they will go about investigating suspected wrongdoing. Do they propose for example to invite the business to attend an investigatory interview and, if so, in what circumstances; will they deploy covert surveillance;[20] will signed statements be taken from witnesses or simply a précis of their evidence? All investigation avenues and techniques should be considered by the regulator and an appropriate level of information as to such matters provided in the policy. **6.36**

The employment level/category of the individual or group of individuals who will be conducting the investigation will also need to be clearly identified in the policy. **6.37**

Finally, where the regulator has been awarded powers to enter premises and/or request information from the regulated person,[21] these powers should be set out in the policy alongside examples of when and how the regulator may seek to deploy them. **6.38**

Evidential considerations

Once all the evidence has been gathered, a charge needs to be prepared, specifying the allegation against the business or individual. The charge needs to be sufficiently particularized to enable the regulated person to know unequivocally the case against them and should include, wherever possible, the date, time and detail as to the manner and nature of the transgression alleged. No particular form of words need be used, although it would be good practice to follow the wording of the statute creating the criminal offence to which the sanction is to be attached. **6.39**

The charge should be served on the suspect, and the evidence supporting the offence provided alongside it. Best practice would be for the evidence to be provided in the form of statements, rather than in summary form. **6.40**

Regulators will need to consider what provision, if any, they choose to include in respect of 'unused material', that is to say material in their possession which does not necessarily support their case and upon which they do not propose to rely, but which may support the case of the **6.41**

---

[19] RESA, s. 70.
[20] See further para. 5.23 for a discussion about the applicability of the Regulation of Investigatory Powers Act 2000.
[21] RESA, s. 55(3).

regulated business or undermine its own. Will this be served as a matter of course, or will it be reviewed once it is known what the business has to say about the suspected offence?

Decision as to liability

6.42   Once the investigator has gathered all the evidence, served it upon the business or individual concerned, and the time for the provision of representations or objections has elapsed (and no discharge payment has been accepted), the regulator will need to move to determine liability.

6.43   Whilst the provisions of RESA do not require there to be a hearing at which the business is entitled to make oral representations, regulators are not precluded from considering liability in this way. In certain cases, for example where a business disputes an allegation (and pleads a defence) and thus may appeal an adverse decision in any event, it may be more cost effective for the regulator to have a full determination at this stage.

6.44   Whether the determination of liability process allows for the hearing of oral arguments or not, the precise details about the way in which the decision will be made should be set out in any policy. The ultimate arbiter should be clearly identified and distinct from any person involved in the investigation process. Other matters that may be detailed include procedural and evidential considerations, such as setting out the nature of the evidence to which the decision maker will have regard, any guidance that will be used in applying the standard of proof and how the decision maker will treat hearsay evidence. It will also be helpful if the policy recites any relevant legislative provision and even, in certain areas, significant case law.

6.45   In common with the penalty guidance and enforcement policy, it would be good practice for any investigation policy prepared to be published on the regulator's website. An additional benefit of adopting such an approach is that such material will also provide the regulator's own staff with a clear and unambiguous set of guidelines for any process to be followed.

6.46   The decision whether the matter should proceed and a notice of intent issued, should be subjected to independent review by a senior member of staff disassociated with the investigation and determination processes.

Selecting the appropriate sanction

6.47   A key decision for any regulator will be what level of decision maker should be involved in selecting the appropriate sanction. It is important that the decision maker has sufficient experience, training and authority to make such decisions. The policy should identify the employment level/category of the individual or group of individuals.

D. Enforcement

Overview

6.48   Macrory placed the issuing of enforcement guidance at the heart of his vision of a model enforcement system, citing it as the first characteristic of a fair and effective sanctions regime,[22] the following up of enforcement action being another of the key characteristics of such a regime.[23]

---

[22]   Richard Macrory, *Regulatory Justice: Making Sanctions Effective*, p. 10.
[23]   Ibid.

It is essential to the credibility of any enforcement regime that any sanctions imposed are moni- **6.49** tored, followed up and enforced where necessary. Effective enforcement of the civil sanctions will require regulators to measure outcomes beyond simply reporting the number of sanctions imposed; follow up needs to be systematically approached. This may be achieved through follow up of businesses on a risk-adjusted basis, including the use of randomized follow up.

Full consideration of the enforcement provisions relating to each of the four sanctions can be **6.50** found alongside the discussions about their operation in Chapter 5. This part is concerned with the statutory requirements on a regulator to issue an enforcement policy and to publish enforcement outcomes.

Enforcement policy

Introduction

Regulators acquiring access to the suite of civil sanctions must prepare and publish an **6.51** enforcement policy, detailing the approach that will be taken by the regulator in respect of the commission of relevant offences by the regulated person. In contrast to the penalty guid- ance, this guidance is focused on how particular offences are enforced by the regulator, and should set out what the public and the regulated community can expect when a regulatory breach has been identified.

In broad terms, the guidance should explain when a particular enforcement course is likely **6.52** to be adopted in preference to another, for example when prosecutions are likely to be pur- sued in preference to one or more of the civil sanctions.

The 'Six Principles' Macrory recommended should be central to any sanctions regime are **6.53** set out in Chapter 1. [24]

The publication of an enforcement policy introduces transparency into the activities of the **6.54** enforcement body, resulting in more consistent decision making and protection for stake- holders against the misuse of regulators' powers.

Consultation

Before preparing and publishing an enforcement policy, regulators must consult such per- **6.55** sons as they consider appropriate.[25] After the consultation process, the regulator may revise the guidance as appropriate. Paragraph 4.106 looks in more detail at the manner and form of consultations in general.

Contents

It will be for the regulator to determine the contents of the policy, subject to the requirement **6.56** to include guidance as to the following:

(i) the sanctions (including criminal sanctions) to which a person who commits the offence may be liable;
(ii) the action which the regulator may take to enforce the offence, whether by virtue of this Part or otherwise; and
(iii) the circumstances in which the regulator is likely to take any such action.[26]

---

[24] See para. 1.34 and Macrory, *Regulatory Justice: Making Sanctions Effective*, p. 10.
[25] RESA, s. 64(4).
[26] Ibid., s. 64(2).

6.57 In respect of (iii) above, the *Regulatory Enforcement and Sanctions Act 2008: Explanatory Notes* suggest that the policy might include a statement that criminal prosecution may be more likely where the person has a history of regulatory non-compliance.[27] Another relevant factor may be where there has been deliberate or wilful non-compliance, perhaps over a lengthy period of time.

6.58 Other matters which may be addressed in the guidance might include the circumstances in which no punitive action may be taken, the range of enforcement penalties that are available, the criteria for deciding which option to pursue, the scheme for imposing FMPs, the mechanism for calculating VMPs, details about the complaints and appeal processes, circumstances in which a stop notice might be imposed and the scheme for entering into enforcement undertakings.

6.59 Where the order awarding the civil sanctions makes provision for cost recovery by the regulator, pursuant to s. 53,[28] provision must also be made in the order awarding the civil sanctions, requiring the regulator to publish guidance about how it will exercise the power conferred by this provision.[29] This guidance could conveniently be included in the enforcement policy. Part G of Chapter 5 looks in more detail at the question of costs.

Review

6.60 Section 64(3) provides that the regulator may 'from time to time revise the guidance published under this section and publish the revised guidance'. It would be sensible if the guidance provided a period and/or circumstances upon which it would be reviewed.

Publication

6.61 It is the responsibility of the regulator to prepare and publish the enforcement policy.[30] No provision is made in RESA as to the manner or frequency of such publication; best practice would be to ensure that it was available in hard copy as well as being published on the regulator's website.

Status of the guidance

6.62 Where a regulator repeatedly fails to act (without good cause) in accordance with any guidance it publishes under this section, the minister may suspend the regulator's power to use the civil sanctions. This is considered further in part E below.

Publication of enforcement action

6.63 Section 65 requires regulators to publish the details of any enforcement action taken by them against businesses or individuals, and the order conferring the power to impose civil sanctions must include such a provision. Not all enforcement action need be published however, as will be seen below.

Decisions that must be publicized

6.64 Regulators must publish reports specifying the cases in which any one of the civil sanctions under Part 3 has been imposed. Reports should include cases where a business or individual

---

[27] Para. 167.
[28] See paras 5.183–5.194.
[29] RESA, s. 53(6).
[30] Ibid., s. 64(1).

has discharged their liability to an FMP via payment of a discharge penalty[31] and where an undertaking as to action is accepted in respect of a discretionary requirement.[32]

Decisions that need not be publicized

There are two scenarios provided for in RESA whereby decisions of a regulator need not be publicized: **6.65**

(i) where the civil sanction has been overturned on appeal: s. 65(3); and
(ii) where the relevant authority considers that it would be inappropriate to do so: s. 65(4).[33]

The circumstances in which it may be considered *inappropriate* for a regulator to publicize   **6.66** enforcement action that it has undertaken are not detailed in RESA, leaving it to the regulator to exercise its judgement on a case-by-case basis. The *Regulatory Enforcement and Sanctions Act 2008: Explanatory Notes*[34] suggest that a regulator may consider it inappropriate for a particular case to be publicized for data protection reasons.

The requirement to publicize any enforcement action taken is specifically concerned with   **6.67** the sanctions provided for in Part 3 and does not restrict a regulator's other publicity options, such as issuing press releases, which may be suitable where a high profile or serious case has been resolved by way of one of the civil sanctions, or where the matter was of particular local concern.

In seeking to comply with the terms of this section, the regulator may choose to append   **6.68** to its annual report a list of the cases it has taken in the year or maintain a database on its website of sanctioning decisions it has taken.[35] Indeed many other regulators (for example the GMC and the Health Professions Council) choose to publicize their enforcement action in this way.

Frequency of publication

Section 65(2) simply provides that the regulator must publish reports 'from time to time'. In   **6.69** any event, such publicity will be much less than would result from an appearance in the criminal courts and as such is likely to be welcomed by businesses.

E. Ministerial oversight

Introduction

The relevant minister, having already awarded the sanctioning powers under Part 3, then   **6.70** has the responsibility to oversee ('review') and ultimately, remove ('suspend') those powers, in accordance with the terms of ss 67 and 68 of RESA. These are important safeguards built into RESA with the aim of preventing serious and persistent misuse of the powers by regulators.

---

[31] Ibid., s. 40(2).
[32] Ibid., s. 43(5).
[33] Section 71 defines 'relevant authority' as a minister of the Crown or Welsh minister.
[34] Para. 169.
[35] BERR *Regulatory Enforcement and Sanctions Act 2008: Guidance to the Act*, p. 48, para. 71.

Review of the sanctions

6.71 By virtue of s. 67, there is a duty placed on the minister making an order under Part 3 to conduct a post-implementation review of that order. This review must take place as soon as practicable after the end of a period of three years after the order was made.[36]

6.72 RESA does not lay down in specific terms precisely what the minister must consider when reviewing the operation of the order. Section 67(3) provides only that the review must consider whether the provision has implemented its objectives 'efficiently and effectively'. In conducting the review, the minister must consult such persons as he considers appropriate.[37]

6.73 The minister must publish the results of the review[38] and lay a copy of the review before Parliament, or the National Assembly for Wales, as appropriate.[39]

By the regulator

6.74 Regulators may wish to conduct *internal* reviews of the efficacy of the civil sanctions, in order to provide stakeholders with information as to their operation. Such reviews may address questions such as whether the sanctions have achieved their objectives, the cost of their having been used, and any improvements that could be made to the regime. Such reviews are also likely to prove to be helpful to the minister in the exercise of his statutory function of review.

Suspension of the sanctions

Introduction

6.75 Where a minister is satisfied that the regulator is repeatedly misusing the powers conferred on it under this Part in certain prescribed ways, he may suspend that regulator's power to impose the sanctions.

6.76 Section 68 enables the minister making the order conferring the civil sanctions on a regulator to be able to direct the regulator not to issue any further notices imposing one of the civil sanctions, or to accept any further enforcement undertakings.

6.77 A s. 68 direction is a serious step intended as a safeguard against persistent misuse of the civil sanctions by the regulator. RESA incorporates three important safeguards in an attempt to ensure that such directions are issued in a fair, open and consistent manner: consultation, laying a copy of the direction before Parliament, and publicity of the direction.

Grounds for suspension

6.78 The grounds for suspension of the sanctions are threefold. The powers may be suspended where a minister is satisfied that the regulator has failed on more than one occasion:

(i) to comply with any duty imposed on it under or by virtue of this Part in relation to that offence;

(ii) to act in accordance with the guidance it has published in relation to that offence (in particular, the guidance published under ss 63 and 64[40]); or

---

[36] RESA, s. 67(2).
[37] Ibid., s. 67(4).
[38] Ibid., s. 67(5).
[39] Ibid., s. 67(6).
[40] Penalty guidance (see part B) and enforcement policy (see part D).

(iii) to act in accordance with the principles referred to in s. 5(2)[41] (the Principles of Good Regulation) or with other principles of best practice in relation to the enforcement of that offence.[42]

6.79 The minister may revoke the original direction if he is satisfied that the regulator has taken appropriate steps to remedy the identified failures.[43]

Safeguards

6.80 Suspension of the sanctioning powers is a serious step, taken only after careful consideration by the minister and subject to two further safeguards: consultation and laying a copy of the direction before Parliament.

6.81 In respect of the former, before giving a direction to revoke the regulator's power to impose civil sanctions, the minister must consult both the regulator and any such other persons as the authority considers appropriate.[44]

Publication

6.82 Where the minister gives a direction under this section, 'the regulator must publish the direction in such manner as the relevant authority thinks fit and take such other steps as the regulator thinks fit or the relevant authority may require to bring the direction to the attention of other persons likely to be affected by it'.[45] In all likelihood, this would be through an announcement on the regulator's website.

F. The civil sanctions in practice: Schedule 5 regulators

Introduction

6.83 RESA contains only a broad framework for the award and imposition of the civil sanctions; the necessary detail of their operation will be provided for in the secondary legislation awarding the sanctions to the regulator. Inevitably, in the translation and amplification of these enabling provisions, inconsistency will be introduced into the manner in which the sanctions operate. So, for example, the available grounds of appeal in respect of a decision to impose the same sanction against the same non-compliant business[46] may vary from one regulator to another, as may the requirement on a business to pay the costs incurred by the regulator in the imposition of the sanction. Further, given the virtually unfettered discretion regulators will have as to how they will make decisions on liability prior to imposing the sanctions, non-compliant businesses could find that they have very different 'rights' when it comes to the transgression of offences enforced by different regulators.[47]

---

[41] Those principles are that regulatory activities should be carried out in a way that is transparent, accountable, proportionate, consistent and targeted only at cases in which action is needed.

[42] RESA, s. 68(2).

[43] Ibid., s. 68(3).

[44] Ibid., s. 68(4).

[45] Ibid., s. 68(6).

[46] Albeit for different offences.

[47] For example, a regulator may at its discretion provide for service on the business of the evidence upon which it relies, permit the hearing of oral submissions, or provide for an internal review of the decision to impose the sanction.

6.84 In April 2010, the first order under Part 3 of RESA came into force, granting the Environment Agency and Natural England the power to impose civil sanctions.[48] The approach that these bodies have taken, not only as regards the provisions of the order, but also in the detail of the proposed penalty guidance and enforcement policy, is certainly informative and likely to become the blueprint for use by other regulators seeking the award of the civil sanctions. For those affected by the reach of those regulators awarded the powers in the future, watching how they frame their penalty guidance and enforcement policy will be particularly instructive. These two environmental regulators are given separate and detailed consideration in Chapter 7.

6.85 This part considers the approach that the class of regulatory authorities provided for in Sch. 5 (designated regulators) are taking with respect to the acquisition and implementation of the civil sanctions under Part 3.[49] At the time of writing, many designated regulators have yet to reach a settled position on whether they would be seeking the award of the civil sanctions.

British Hallmarking Council

6.86 The British Hallmarking Council is a small organization and, accordingly, has decided that at present it does not have the resources to apply for the civil sanctions or, indeed, to initiate any enforcement activity independently. The Council proposes to continue to work with trading standards and the police, and encourage them to enforce the Hallmarking Act 1973.

Charity Commission for England and Wales

6.87 The Charity Commission for England and Wales is a statutory body created pursuant to the Charities Act 1993. It performs its functions independently of the Crown or other government department. Any institution that is a charity within the statutory definition[50] is subject to the jurisdiction of the Charity Commission.

6.88 The Commission has several statutory objectives, functions and duties relating to the administration of charitable organizations. The most relevant in the context of enforcement are:

(i) the 'compliance objective', which is designed to promote compliance by charity trustees with their legal obligations in managing the administration of their charities;[51] and

(ii) the function of identifying and investigating apparent misconduct or mismanagement in the administration of charities and taking remedial or protective action in connection with that.[52]

6.89 In performing its functions, the Commission must have regard to the Principles of Good Regulation (proportionate, transparent, consistent and targeted only at cases where action is required).[53]

---

[48] The Environmental Civil Sanctions (England) Order 2010, SI 115/2010.
[49] Details of the approach taken by the multitude of local authorities and other regulators (whether by Schs 6 or 7) that have access to these sanctions can be found by accessing the bodies' websites directly.
[50] Charities Act 1993, s. 96(1) and (2).
[51] Ibid., s. 1B(3)(3).
[52] Ibid., s. 1C(2), para. 3.
[53] Ibid., s. 1D(2), para. 4.

Offences and enforcement

The Commission has the power to make wide-ranging orders in relation to its regulatory **6.90** function. For example, it can institute inquiries with regard to charities or a particular charity or class of charities, make orders calling for the disclosure of information or requiring a default to be made good, and take any other action that the Commission considers to be expedient in the interests of the charity. Any breach of such an order may be dealt with either on the application of the Commission to the High Court, or as the breach of an order to the High Court. Persistent non-compliance with the Commission's orders may result in criminal sanction.[54]

The Commission has a variety of other powers that enable it to act for the protection of chari- **6.91** ties through inquiry, audit, calling for documents, seizure of documents and by making specific orders consequent upon its investigations.[55]

Application of the civil sanctions

The Charity Commission has considered making use of the civil sanctions regime under **6.92** RESA. However, at the present time it has decided not to apply for the additional enforcement powers under Part 3. The Commission's view is that it already has a number of administrative sanctions available to it in the Charities Act 1993, which it can use to tackle maladministration and mismanagement within charities, and therefore has little need at present for further powers.

Coal Authority

The Coal Authority (the Authority) came into being pursuant to the Coal Industry Act 1994 **6.93** (the 1994 Act), when the coal industry was privatized. The regulatory role of the Authority is fairly limited and where there is the need for enforcement, ss 31–34 of the 1994 Act provide appropriate powers. These powers have only been used on a limited number of occasions in the past.

The 1994 Act did not give the Authority a direct role in relation to the regulation of the **6.94** privatized part of the coal industry in matters such as health and safety, the environment or the national requirement for coal supplies. Accordingly, the Authority considers that RESA is unlikely to be of significant use to it.

Competition Commission

The Competition Commission has carefully considered this Act but has not felt it necessary **6.95** to take up the RESA powers to date.

Countryside Council for England and Wales

The Countryside Council for Wales (CCW) describes itself as 'the Government's statutory **6.96** advisor on sustaining natural beauty, wildlife and the opportunity for outdoor enjoyment in Wales and its inshore waters'.

The Assembly government held a joint consultation with DEFRA on the proposed civil **6.97** sanctions and the draft order and regulations which closed on 14 October 2009.

---

[54] Ibid., s. 87(2).
[55] Ibid., ss 8, 9, 18, 18A, 19A, 19B, 31A and 69.

6.98 On 2 December 2009 the Minister for Environment, Sustainability and Housing announced that she had been asked to consider delaying the conferral of civil sanctioning powers on the Countryside Council for Wales (CCW) until such time as a compliance review had been undertaken to enable her to determine whether CCW would act in accordance with the regulatory principles set out in the Regulatory Enforcement and Sanctions Act 2008.

Environment Agency

6.99 See Chapter 7 for detailed consideration of this regulator.

Financial Services Authority

6.100 The Financial Services Authority (FSA) has decided not to apply for the civil sanction powers under Part 3 of RESA, at least for the foreseeable future. Having considered carefully the potential uses of the powers, including in the context of unauthorized financial services, the FSA has concluded that the additional powers would not make a material difference to the effectiveness of its enforcement action. Specifically, the FSA does not consider that the new powers would deliver better outcomes than the existing enforcement avenues available to it, namely, criminal prosecution, orders from the High Court, and insolvency proceedings.

6.101 The FSA reports that in reaching this decision, one of the factors that it considered in particular was the need to be satisfied to the criminal standard of proof before a financial penalty could be imposed under RESA.

Food Standards Agency

6.102 The Food Standards Act 1999 established the Food Standards Agency as an independent government department, and in 2010 the Meat Hygiene Service became part of the Food Standards Agency. The Agency's primary aim is to protect the health of the public, and the interests of consumers, in relation to food. Its published objectives include the development of effective policies relating to food safety and other interests of consumers in relation to food and making decisions and taking action proportionate to the risk 'and with due regard to costs and benefits'. These objectives apply to all aspects of the food chain, from primary producers to final consumers.

Offences and enforcement

6.103 Food law enforcement is primarily the responsibility of environmental health officers (EHOs) and trading standards officers (TSOs) working within local authorities throughout the UK. The Food Standards Agency is an enforcement authority in its own right. It is also responsible for providing support and advice to local authorities and the auditing of enforcement activity concerning food safety.

6.104 Where responsibility for food law enforcement does not rest with local authorities, it is undertaken by central government or its enforcement agencies.

6.105 The Food Standards Agency in England, Scotland and Wales[56] is the enforcement authority in respect of all premises in the UK producing meat for sale for human consumption.

---

[56] The Food Standards Agency acts through the Department of Agriculture and Rural Development (DARD) Veterinary Service in Northern Ireland.

Approximately 1,700 premises are licensed for this purpose. They include slaughterhouses, cutting plants and cold stores. The licensing and operation of such premises (which includes enforcement by way of investigations and prosecutions) is also the responsibility of the Agency, which also enforces the EU wine regulations.[57]

Application of the civil sanctions

In June 2008 the Food Standards Agency reviewed its regulatory functions and in particular, considered the implications of the soon to be enacted Regulatory Enforcement and Sanctions Bill.[58] Analysing the opportunities presented by the new legislation, the Agency said that it saw 'particular value in the use of the alternative sanctions regime in relation to meat hygiene'.[59] **6.106**

In preparing for a Hampton review, the Food Standards Agency has identified certain weaknesses, including a need for staff to 'understand business better', the creation of an effective and business-focused mechanism for providing advice to business, the provision of greater strategic direction, in terms of the priorities for food law regulation, to local authorities and encouraging enforcement officers to focus on the highest risk issues. **6.107**

Despite these early indications, there are no signs of any immediate intention on the part of the Agency to seek to implement the provisions of RESA on its own behalf. **6.108**

Football Licensing Authority

The Football Licensing Authority (FLA) is an independent public body set up under the Football Spectators Act 1989, with the primary aim of ensuring the safety of spectators at professional football grounds. It only has direct enforcement responsibility for enforcing the (very minimal) conditions of its licence, leaving it to the local authority to undertake all general enforcement on its behalf, under its oversight. In those circumstances, it does not consider the provisions in Part 3 of RESA to be applicable to it. **6.109**

Forestry Commission

The Forestry Commission (Great Britain) advises the UK government.[60] The principal enforcement objectives of the Forestry Commission are to prevent: **6.110**

 (i) the illegal felling of trees;
 (ii) the import or export of timber, timber products and timber packaging in breach of plant health regulations;
(iii) environmental damage caused by forestry operations; and
(iv) the marketing in seed, cuttings or planting stock in contravention of the forest reproductive material regulations.

In 2009, the Commission reviewed the administrative burden associated with the regulations relevant to the areas of legislation for which it was responsible. The total administrative **6.111**

---

[57] These businesses will include wholesalers and warehouses, as well as the vineyards themselves.
[58] *Better Regulation Update: Administrative Burden Reduction; Hampton; a World Class Regulator.* A copy is available on the Food Standards Agency website: <http://www.food.gov.uk>.
[59] *Better Regulation Update: Administrative Burden Reduction; Hampton; a World Class Regulator*, para. 21. FSA 08/06/05, 11 June 2008.
[60] Which includes the devolved administrations in Scotland and Wales.

costs[61] of regulation for the financial year ending December 2010 were estimated at nearly £1.5 m.

Application of the civil sanctions

6.112   The Commission's *Enforcement Policy Statement* follows the Regulators' Compliance Code and the seven Hampton Principles of good regulation. The findings of a review carried out by a review team[62] in September 2009[63] concluded that the Commission may wish to consider whether its current mix of delivery methods and approaches is sufficient to achieve its desired outcomes.

6.113   The review of the Commission's enforcement policy is ongoing. In the meantime, it is understood that the Forestry Commission has no intention in the short term to seek to apply for the civil sanctions in Part 3 of RESA.

Gambling Commission

6.114   In view of its wide-ranging powers in relation to licensed operators, in particular under the Gambling Act 2005, the Gambling Commission has not to date actively pursued obtaining additional powers of enforcement under RESA. The Commission has, however, recognized that in relation to unlicensed operators there is a case for considering whether the additional sanctioning powers under Part 3 of RESA would assist it in meeting its aims and objectives.

Gangmasters Licensing Authority

6.115   The Gangmasters Licensing Authority (GLA) is the government agency that is tasked with regulating those who supply labour or use workers to provide services in agriculture, forestry, horticulture, shellfish gathering and food processing and packaging. The GLA operates a licensing scheme for those acting as 'gangmasters'.[64]

6.116   The GLA was established under the provisions of the Gangmasters (Licensing) Act 2004 (the 2004 Act). The impetus behind the government establishing the GLA was to bring an end to worker exploitation in the relevant sectors by introducing a licensing system and taking action against those that continued to operate outside of the legal parameters.

6.117   The GLA defines its mission as being to 'safeguard the welfare and interests of workers whilst ensuring Labour Providers operate within the law'.[65] The ways in which it aims to achieve this mission include:

(i)   taking enforcement action against those who operate illegally or who for other reasons are judged unfit to hold a licence; and

(ii) supporting enforcement of the law, by or in conjunction with the enforcement authorities of other government departments, and others as appropriate, through shared information and joint working.

---

[61]   Defined as 'the [recurring] costs of administrative activities that businesses are required to conduct in order to comply with the information obligations that are imposed through central government regulation'.

[62]   Which included a representative from the Better Regulation Executive.

[63]   Published in January 2010. A copy of the HIR is available on the BIS website: <http://www.bis.gov.uk>.

[64]   As to the meaning of 'gangmaster' see the Gangmasters (Licensing) Act 2004, s. 4.

[65]   See the GLA's *Mission Statement*, available on the GLA website: <http://www.gla.gov.uk>.

Offences and enforcement

The 2004 Act includes a number of criminal offences. Under the Act it is illegal to operate **6.118** as a gangmaster without a licence,[66] or use an unlicensed gangmaster.[67] The maximum penalty for operating without a licence is ten years' imprisonment and a fine.[68] The maximum penalty for using an unlicensed gangmaster is six months' imprisonment and a fine.[69]

It is also an offence to hold false documents with the intention of causing a third party to **6.119** believe that the person in possession of the documentation or another person is a licensed gangmaster,[70] as well as to obstruct a GLA officer in the course of his duties or fail without reasonable cause to comply with a requirement made of him by a GLA officer.[71]

The GLA enforces these criminal offences on behalf of the Department for Environment, **6.120** Food and Rural Affairs (DEFRA) in England, and the Department of Agriculture and Development in Northern Ireland.

The GLA has published and operates in accordance with an *Enforcement Code of Practice* **6.121** and a *Compliance Code of Practice.*[72] The GLA identifies in its *Enforcement Code of Practice* that '[t]he enforcement powers are not intended to place additional burdens on business, but to safeguard the welfare and interests of workers whilst ensuring labour providers operate within the law'. The GLA also publishes enforcement policy statements.[73]

Current enforcement practice

One of the key components of the 2004 Act was to require labour providers in the relevant **6.122** industries to obtain a valid licence. Once a licence has been obtained, the GLA then carries out targeted, intelligence-based compliance checks. These checks are prioritized according to the principles established by the Home Office National Intelligence Model. The checks provide the GLA with an effective method of checking that licensed labour providers remain compliant with the licensing standards.

Application of the civil sanctions

In its most recent enforcement policy statement, the GLA forewarned: **6.123**

> Other sanctions may become available under new civil and criminal legislation, allowing for the use of administrative financial penalties or a caution coupled with a reparative or restorative penalty. When such sanctions become available the GLA will consider their inclusion in its enforcement approach to ensure that offences continue to be dealt with in a proportionate manner.[74]

The GLA has clearly given consideration to the possibility of using civil sanctions as part of **6.124** its wider enforcement toolkit. However, as at May 2010, whilst the GLA has commenced

---

[66] Gangmasters (Licensing) Act 2004, s. 12(1).
[67] Ibid., s. 13(1).
[68] Ibid., s. 12(4).
[69] Ibid., s. 13(4).
[70] Ibid., s. 12(2).
[71] Ibid., s. 18(1).
[72] Gangmasters Licensing Authority, *Enforcement Code of Practice* (November 2006); Gangmasters Licensing Authority, *Compliance Code of Practice* (July 2006).
[73] Gangmasters Licensing Authority, *Enforcement Policy Statement* (V2.0, February 2008), pp 1–2.
[74] Gangmasters Licensing Authority, *Enforcement Policy Statement*, p. 1.

discussions with DEFRA, it has not yet sought ministerial approval for its use of civil sanctions.

6.125 The GLA consider that in due course the use of civil sanctions may assist them in more effectively enforcing their licensing regime. They note that there are clear similarities between their existing power to issue a 'revocation with immediate effect' notice to licensed operators in breach of licensing standards, and the 'stop notice' provided for under RESA. They consider that the existing power in that respect is probably better suited to their current enforcement needs. By contrast, the GLA consider that the use of FMPs or VMPs would be of considerable use to them. In broad terms, these civil sanctions could be used by the GLA to fine operators who are licensed and operating lawfully, but who had in the past operated illegally prior to legitimizing their position. It is envisaged that if the variable monetary penalty route was adopted the quantum of the fine could be ascertained by a matrix that calculated several key factors, such as the period of time of unlawful operation, the number of workers employed unlawfully, and the lost revenue to the GLA from missed licence and inspection fees. It is envisaged that these powers would allow the GLA to remove the financial benefit that has been gained by businesses that deliberately sought to gain a commercial advantage through non-compliance with their regulatory obligations.

Health and Safety Executive

6.126 The Health and Safety Executive (HSE) is the non-departmental public body sponsored by the Department for Work and Pensions. The HSE is responsible for assisting, advising and encouraging the promotion of health and safety in the workplace as well as regulating and enforcing relevant health and safety legislation in England and Wales and Scotland.

6.127 The Health and Safety Commission (HSC) was formed on 1 January 1975 under the provisions of the Health and Safety at Work etc. Act 1974[75] (the 1974 Act), subsuming a number of regulatory and scientific organizations existing at that time.

6.128 The HSE has given consideration to the possibility of using civil sanctions as part of its enforcement toolkit, most recently in September 2009. The HSE continues to monitor the situation and the experience of other regulators, but so far has remained of the view that its current enforcement toolkit is effective and sufficiently flexible, incorporating a range of options to include informal action (advice or guidance), issuing an improvement notice[76] (saying what needs to be done and specifying a timeframe for action of at least twenty-one days), issuing a prohibition notice[77] (taking effect immediately or after a specified time period) or proceeding to a criminal prosecution.[78] The HSE considers that prosecution is and remains an essential enforcement tool and that it is proportionate, bearing in mind the harm to human health that results, or can result, from health and safety regulatory infringements.

Hearing Aid Council

6.129 Section 123 of the Health and Social Care Act 2008 provided for the repeal of the Hearing Aid Council Act 1968, and for the abolition of the Hearing Aid Council, whose enforcement

---

[75] S. 10.
[76] 1974 Act, s. 21.
[77] 1974 Act, s. 22.
[78] 1974 Act, s. 33.

functions were duly transferred to the Health Professions Council (HPC) on 1 April 2010.[79] The provisions of Part 3 do not extend to the enforcement functions of the HPC.

Historic Buildings and Monuments Commission for England (English Heritage)

The Historic Buildings and Monuments Commission for England (English Heritage) was established by the National Heritage Act 1983 (the 1983 Act). English Heritage is the government's statutory advisor on the historic environment. **6.130**

The 1983 Act defines English Heritage's key statutory duties. The two most relevant in the context of enforcement are its duties: **6.131**

(i) to secure the preservation of England's ancient monuments and historic buildings situated in England;[80] and

(ii) to promote the preservation and enhancement of the character and appearance of England's conservation areas.[81]

English Heritage describes these functions as 'heritage protection', which includes the protection of heritage through the controls contained within the planning system.[82] **6.132**

Offences and enforcement

The 1983 Act empowers English Heritage to initiate, in its own name, prosecutions for offences under Part 1 of the Ancient Monuments and Archaeological Areas Act 1979, the Planning (Listed Buildings and Conservation Areas) Act 1990, and proceedings for injunctive relief to restrain contraventions under the same Acts. Further enforcement powers are specifically provided for in the Planning (Listed Buildings and Conservation Areas) Act 1990. **6.133**

English Heritage's direct involvement in the enforcement of breaches is, however, limited under these Acts. Primary responsibility for the enforcement of heritage protection is conferred upon the local authority planning authorities. Aside from the general powers to prosecute and seek injunctive relief provided by the 1983 Act, the enforcement powers of English Heritage are largely limited to the London area.[83] **6.134**

Under s. 38, English Heritage is empowered to issue a 'listed building enforcement notice' if it 'appears' that works have been, or are, being executed to a listed building without, or in contravention of a condition of, listed building consent, *and* the body considers the issue of the notice to be 'expedient … having regard to the effect of the works on the character of the building as one of special architectural or historic interest'. This may be contrasted with the position under RESA, where a notice can only be issued where the regulator 'is satisfied beyond reasonable doubt that the person has committed a relevant offence'. The RESA sanction clearly functions as an alternative to prosecution (for which the described standard of proof is appropriate), not a precursor to it.[84] **6.135**

---

[79] The Health Professions (Hearing Aid Dispensers) Order 2010, SI 233/2010.

[80] 1983 Act, s. 33(1)(a).

[81] 1983 Act, s. 33(1)(b).

[82] See the website:< http://www.english-heritage.org.uk>.

[83] See, e.g. Planning (Listed Buildings and Conservation Areas) Act 1990, ss 45 and 54.

[84] Although note that in respect of the imposition of non-monetary discretionary requirements such as restoration notices, provided that a variable monetary penalty has not also been imposed, the regulator is not

6.136 The other enforcement powers available to English Heritage, such as the power to enter land and take steps to ensure compliance with a listed building enforcement notice,[85] are quite different in nature to those contained in Part 3 of RESA.

Enforcement powers in the Draft Heritage Protection Bill

6.137 In 2007, following consultation on the Government's White Paper, *Heritage Protection for the 21st Century*, a draft Heritage Protection Bill was produced. Clause 129 of the Bill empowers local planning authorities to issue a 'heritage asset enforcement notice' in very similar circumstances to those set out in s. 38 of the Planning (Listed Buildings and Conservation Areas) Act 1990, as above.

Application of the civil sanctions

6.138 At the time of writing, whilst English Heritage have not publicly declared any intention to take advantage of the civil sanctions available to it under Part 3 of RESA, material in the public domain (an article on their website, summarizing the powers potentially available to it under Part 3) suggests that they are at least alive to the possibility of acquiring them in the future.

6.139 It is understood that English Heritage is alive to the possibility of using the sanctions available under RESA although the process of consultation between that body and the relevant minister has not yet commenced. Instead English Heritage are adopting a 'wait and see approach', observing how the sanctions operate in practice following their roll-out by other designated regulators, such as the Environment Agency and Natural England.

Tenant Services Authority (formerly Housing Corporation)

6.140 The Housing and Regeneration Act 2008 (the 2008 Act) established the Office for Tenants and Social Landlords. This replaces the Housing Corporation as the new regulator for social housing.[86] The regulator is commonly referred to as the Tenant Services Authority or TSA. The 2008 Act introduced new regulatory powers that took effect for all social housing providers from 1 April 2010. A common set of standards now applies to all providers including local authorities, housing associations and other forms of provider.

Offences and enforcement

6.141 The 2008 Act introduces a graduated suite of intervention and enforcement powers. The major change under the 2008 Act is that councils that own socially rented homes are now included on the TSA's register and hence are subject to the same regulation as all other social landlords.

6.142 The TSA is tasked with monitoring providers' compliance with regulatory requirements and will exercise its enforcement powers where it suspects or has evidence of a failure against one or more of its standards, or where a provider has mismanaged[87] its affairs.[88]

---

precluded from later prosecuting that person if they fail to comply with the non-monetary discretionary requirement: RESA 2008, s. 44.

[85] Planning (Listed Buildings and Conservation Areas) Act 1990, s. 42, London boroughs only.
[86] Housing and Regeneration Act 2008, s. 81.
[87] 'Mismanaged' in relation to the affairs of a provider is defined in s. 275 of the 2008 Act.
[88] See *The regulatory framework for social housing in England from April 2010*, ch. 6.

The TSA has a range of new enforcement powers that apply to all registered social landlords, **6.143** including the power to issue an enforcement notice, direct a tender of management or direct a transfer of management. It also has powers that can be used for providers who are not local authorities including penalty fines,[89] compensation awards,[90] appointments of new management,[91] direction of a transfer of land,[92] making and executing an amalgamation of an industrial and provident society,[93] the power to remove an officer in circumstances such as bankruptcy,[94] and appointment of new officers.[95]

In addition to those enforcement powers, the TSA has specific powers in relation to local **6.144** authorities to appoint advisors to a local authority and to censure a local authority officer or agent during or following an inquiry.[96] The TSA may use its powers singly or in combination as appropriate and in accordance with the *Regulators' Compliance Code*.[97] Before taking enforcement action the TSA must consider the desirability of a provider being free to choose how to provide services, whether the failure is serious, whether the failure is a recurrent or isolated incident and the speed with which the failure needs to be addressed.[98]

The application of the civil sanctions

The TSA's position at the date of writing is that it has not yet concluded its internal discus- **6.145** sions about the appropriateness of the use of civil sanctions under RESA in tandem with, or as an alternative to, its powers under the Housing and Regeneration Act. The civil sanctions do not add much to the TSA's extensive suite of new powers. Given that the TSA has only recently published its approach to the use of its new enforcement powers under the 2008 Act, it seems unlikely it will apply to make use of the additional civil sanctions available, at least in the short term.

Human Fertilisation and Embryology Authority

In July 1982 the Warnock Committee (the Committee) was set up 'to examine the social, **6.146** ethical and legal implications of recent and potential developments in the field of human assisted reproduction'.[99] In July 1984, the Committee presented to Parliament the *Report of the Committee of Inquiry into Human Fertilisation Embryology* (the *Warnock Report*). The *Warnock Report* made sixty-four recommendations and also proposed the establishment of a regulatory authority, independent of government, health authorities or research institutions, 'to regulate and monitor practice in relation to those sensitive areas which raise fundamental ethical questions'.[100]

---

[89] Housing and Regeneration Act 2008, ss 226–235.
[90] Ibid., ss 236–245.
[91] Ibid., ss 251–252.
[92] Ibid., ss 253–254.
[93] Ibid., s. 255.
[94] Ibid., ss 266–268.
[95] Ibid., s. 269.
[96] Ibid., ss 252A, 269A and 269B.
[97] Issued under s. 22 of the Legislative and Regulatory Reform Act 2006. See Chapter 4.
[98] Ss 219–225.
[99] *Report of the Committee of Inquiry into Human Fertilisation Embryology*, preamble by (the then) Dame Mary Warnock DBE.
[100] The Warnock Report, para. 13.3.

6.147 The recommendations in the *Warnock Report* led in due course to The Human Fertilisation and Embryology Act 1990, which made provision for the establishment of a body corporate called the Human Fertilisation and Embryology Authority (the HFEA). The HFEA is an executive non-departmental public body, sponsored by the Department of Health.

Offences and enforcement

6.148 Under the 1990 Act as amended, certain activities can only be carried out under the authority of a licence awarded by the HFEA (or a third party agreement).[101]

6.149 The HFEA can issue four types of licence: for providing treatment services,[102] for non-medical fertility services,[103] for storage of gametes, embryos and human admixed embryos,[104] and for research.[105]

6.150 Every licence issued by the HFEA will be subject to mandatory conditions[106] that relate to issues such as 'record keeping, traceability, obtaining of relevant consents in writing, provision of information and counselling to patients and donors, time limits for storage of gametes and embryos, the provision of information and documentation to the HFEA, under HFEA's right of access to, and inspection of, centres'.[107]

6.151 To operate without a licence or provide false information for the purposes of obtaining a licence is an offence, punishable by conviction on indictment by imprisonment for up to two years (summary conviction up to six months) or with a fine or both.[108]

6.152 In addition to activities that require a licence, the 1990 Act as amended also prohibits outright a number of other activities.

6.153 Failing to observe these prohibitions is an offence, liable on conviction on indictment to imprisonment for up to ten years, or a fine, or both.[109]

6.154 As of October 2009, the HFEA has had a specific statutory duty to promote compliance with the requirements of the 1990 Act as amended, and the HFEA's own Code of Practice.[110] The HFEA's approach to compliance is set out in the Code of Practice and the *Compliance and Enforcement Policy*.[111] *The Compliance and Enforcement Policy* records that the HFEA is committed to the Regulators' Compliance Code.[112]

---

[101] According to s. 2A(1) of the 1990 Act as amended, a third party agreement is an agreement in writing between a person who holds a licence and another person which is made in accordance with any licence conditions imposed by the Authority for the purpose of securing compliance with the requirements of Art. 24 of the first Directive (relations between tissue establishments and third parties) and under which the other person procures, tests or processes gametes or embryos (or both), on behalf of the holder of the licence, or supplies to the holder of the licence any goods or services (including distribution services) which may affect the quality or safety of gametes or embryos.

[102] Human Fertilisation and Embryology Act 1990, s. 11(1)(a) and Sch. 2, para. 1(1).

[103] Ibid., s. 11(1)(aa) and Sch. 2, para. 1A.

[104] Ibid., s. 11(1)(b) and Sch. 2, para. 2.

[105] Ibid., s. 11(1)(c) and Sch. 2, para. 3.

[106] 1990 Act as amended, ss 12–18.

[107] Summary taken from the HFEA publication, *About the Human Fertilisation and Embryology Authority* (October 2009), para. 1.17. A copy is available on the HFEA website: <http://www.hfea.gov.uk>.

[108] Human Fertilisation and Embryology Act 1990, s. 41.

[109] Ibid.

[110] Ibid., s. 25. Version 8 of the Code of Practice is available on the HFEA website.

[111] Published 1 October 2009. A copy is available on the HFEA website.

[112] See further para. 4.35.

The purpose of sanctions is threefold: to promote compliance with the 1990 Act as amended **6.155** and the Code of Practice; to protect users or those otherwise affected by services licensed by the HFEA; and to maintain public confidence in the conduct of licensed activities.[113]

The HFEA utilizes a range of enforcement tools that are categorized as informal and formal. **6.156** Formal enforcement action powers have been delegated by the HFEA to the Licence and Research Licence Committees (the Committees).

The HFEA does not have any power to prosecute. Further, the 1990 Act as amended, pro- **6.157** vides that no proceedings for an offence can be instituted against non-compliant organiza-tions without the consent of the Director of Public Prosecutions.[114] Any recommendation to refer a matter to the police or obtain a warrant to search premises must first be notified to the chief executive.

As at December 2008, action to revoke a licence has been initiated by the HFEA on ten occa- **6.158** sions, of which only two were as a result of a criminal breach. Of the ten occasions when action was initiated, a licence has only been revoked once, in relation to a non-criminal offence.[115]

Application of the civil sanctions

At its authority meeting on 17 December 2008, the HFEA Committee agreed to apply **6.159** for three of the powers available under RESA as a means of broadening its enforcement capabilities, these being discretionary requirements, stop notices and enforcement under-takings.[116] It was recognized by the HFEA that it had not developed consistent practices of enforcement and that it was overly lenient in its approach to transgressions due largely to its inability to apply proportionate sanctions. Whilst informal action often lacks the necessary weight, direct action in respect of a licence,[117] or referral to the police, are often unnecessarily draconian. The RESA powers will give the Licence Committee increased flexibility to deliver better targeted and more consistent regulation.

Discretionary requirements

Discretionary requirements fall somewhere between informal action and the suspension **6.160** or revocation of licences on the spectrum of sanctions. It is envisaged that access to these sanctions will encourage the Licensing Committee to intervene in non-compliant action earlier, 'preventing the escalation of offences to those warranting more serious action, such as suspension or revocation of a licence'.[118]

Stop notices

The use of stop notices will provide greater flexibility in securing the cessation of non- **6.161** compliant behaviour; where for example a breach occurs in one portion of a business, rather than shutting the entire clinic that activity alone can be halted. It is anticipated that stop notices could be used 'where an action was not directly jeopardising physical patient

---

[113] *Human Fertilisation and Embryology Authority Indicative Sanctions Guidance For Licence Committees* (1 October 2009). A copy is available on the HFEA website.
[114] 1990 Act as amended, s. 42.
[115] HFEA Authority Paper 477, Agenda Item 14, para. 5.4. A copy is available on the HFEA website.
[116] Ibid., Agenda Item 2, para. 15.
[117] Variation, revocation or suspension.
[118] HFEA Authority Paper 477, Agenda Item 14, para. 6.3.3.

safety or clinical safety'[119] or where an organization does not have a licence for just one particular area of its activities. In these situations, 'a stop notice would carry more weight than simply ordering these businesses to stop because failure to comply would result in another criminal offence'.[120]

Enforcement undertakings

6.162 Enforcement undertakings will complement the existing 'incident alert' system, whereby any adverse incidents or near misses in relation to treatment involving a third party must be reported to the HFEA within twenty-four hours of discovery.

6.163 The HFEA underwent a Hampton Implementation Review (HIR) in April 2009. The findings of the HIR, which were published in December that year, were broadly favourable, singling out for praise the design of regulations, advice and guidance in the Code of Practice, data requirements and transparency and inspections. The Department for Business Enterprise and Regulatory Reform (now BIS) noted that the:

> process of applying sanctions can be long winded. By law, licensing decisions must be made by the 'Licence Committee' and, unlike other regulators, HFEA's inspectors are unable to take immediate action themselves when they identify a serious breach. . . The HFEA does not utilise the full range of its sanctions, in part because its existing sanctioning options appear to the Review Team not to be flexible enough to handle different levels of non-compliance.[121]

6.164 The deficiencies identified in the HIR chimed with those shortcomings already identified by the HFEA itself. Many of the weaknesses of the current regime identified in the HIR will be remedied by the acquisition of the civil sanctions.

Next steps

6.165 The HFEA recognizes that resource implications will be a key drawback in any application for the civil sanctions. Some organizational restructuring and development of a communications strategy will be required to allow publication of details of all enforcement action and to disseminate information and guidance on how the new sanctions will be enforced. The HFEA also recognizes that the requirement that any action undertaken to use powers granted by RESA will require 'proof beyond reasonable doubt' will necessitate further training for the HFEA inspection team and an internal review system. Nonetheless, the HFEA is ready to prepare itself to utilize the sanctions once the Home Office has carried out the necessary public consultation and developed the necessary secondary legislation. It is anticipated that the earliest this will occur is 2011–12.

6.166 In July 2010, the newly elected Coalition government announced that the HFEA is likely to be dissolved. Whatever form the body that takes over the HFEA's licensing and enforcement functions takes, lessons can certainly be learnt from the HIR about the need for a wider sanctioning toolkit to effectively enforce the licensing regime in this area.

---

[119] Ibid., para. 6.4.6.
[120] Ibid.
[121] Better Regulation Executive, *Human Fertilisation and Embryology Authority: A Hampton Implementation Review Report* URN:09/1542 (December 2009). Available at <http://www.bis.gov.uk/files/file53852.pdf> (last accessed 29 November 2010).

Human Tissue Authority

The Human Tissue Authority (HTA) is an executive non-departmental body sponsored by **6.167** the Department of Health, established on 1 April 2005 under the Human Tissue Act 2004. The HTA regulates and licenses premises that engage in the removal, storage, use or disposal of human tissue in England, Wales and Northern Ireland.

When the application of civil sanctions was last considered in January 2010,[122] the HTA **6.168** concluded that there was little or no merit in applying for powers under RESA, particularly bearing in mind the favourable Report on the HTA in July 2009, following the Hampton Implementation Review. In reaching this decision, the HTA also took into account the burden of proof required to take civil action under RESA, namely the criminal standard. The associated costs and resources required for the implementation of systems, processes and training were felt to be unjustifiable where the new powers were likely to be used only very rarely.

Information Commissioner's Office

The Information Commissioner's Office is the UK's independent authority set up to uphold **6.169** information rights in the public interest, promoting openness by public bodies and data privacy for individuals.

The Information Commissioner's Office was created under the Data Protection Act 1984. **6.170** Following the coming into force of the Data Protection Act 1998 in 2000, the Data Protection Registrar became the Data Protection Commissioner. In 2001, the office was given responsibility for the Freedom of Information Act 2000, and changed its name to the Information Commissioner's Office.

The Information Commissioner's Office has functions under the Data Protection Act 1998 **6.171** and the Freedom of Information Act 2000. In relation to data protection work, it considers its functions to be principally regulatory in nature, whereas in respect of the Freedom of Information work its principal function is considered to be to 'investigate and adjudicate on complaints from individuals'.[123]

Offences and enforcement

The Information Commissioner has a full panoply of powers at its disposal. The powers vary **6.172** depending upon the legislation upon which the Information Commissioner is fulfilling its regulatory function. Under the Freedom of Information Act, the Information Commissioner is able to use the following types of regulatory action: assessment,[124] enforcement notices,[125] information notices,[126] and decision notices.[127] Non-formal regulatory action includes issuing practice recommendations setting out the steps necessary to ensure conformity with the Codes, negotiation, monitoring, requiring undertakings, and reporting to Parliament.

---

[122] Minutes of the forty-first meeting of the Human Tissue Authority, 26 January 2010, item 10. A copy is available on the HTA website: <http://www.hta.gov.uk>.

[123] *A Code of Practice for Regulators–A Consultation, Response of the Information Commissioner* (Cabinet Office, August 2007) and Better Regulation Executive; *Consultation on the Draft Regulatory Enforcement and Sanctions Bill, Response of the Information Commissioner* (August 2007).

[124] Freedom of Information Act, s. 47(3).

[125] Ibid., s. 52.

[126] Ibid., s. 51.

[127] Ibid., s. 50.

In addition to the power to prosecute for criminal breaches of the Data Protection Act, the Information Commissioner may issue enforcement notices,[128] impose monetary penalty notices,[129] s. 159 orders,[130] make applications for injunctions[131] and enforcement orders,[132] and conduct audits both consensually[133] and compulsorily.[134] There is a published policy outlining the circumstances in which these powers are likely to be used, and the factors that will be considered by the Information Commissioner in making any determination as to the appropriate sanction for each breach. The stated aim of the Information Commissioner is to ensure that the action taken is purposeful, targeted and proportionate; consistent with the Principles of Good Regulation.

6.173 The Criminal Justice and Immigration Act 2008 introduced new provisions into the Data Protection Act 1998, allowing for the imposition of VMPs[135] and assessment notices for breaches of the data protection principles (not usually a criminal offence). This new power permits the imposition of penalties, similar in nature to those in Part 3 of RESA, for regulatory breaches falling outwith RESA's ambit. Extensive guidance[136] has been issued in relation to the use of the VMPs, which has been laid before Parliament and approved. A VMP of up to £500,000[137] can be imposed for a breach of the data protection principles. A VMP can be imposed if a data controller has seriously contravened the data protection principles, and the contravention was of a kind likely to cause substantial damage or distress. Additionally, the contravention must have been deliberate or the data controller must have known or ought to have known that there was a risk that a contravention would occur and failed to take reasonable steps to prevent it.

Application of civil sanctions

6.174 The offences within the Data Protection Act 1998 and the Freedom of Information Act 2000 to which the new sanctions under RESA would apply are limited. This was recognized by the Information Commissioner at the time of the Consultation on the Regulatory Enforcement and Sanctions Bill (the Bill), and whilst the Information Commissioner did not seek to be excluded from the list of Sch. 5 regulators within RESA, it did state that it did 'not think that the additional sanctioning powers other than the proposed power to impose fixed monetary penalties, provide us with any more effective regulatory tools than we currently have available to us, whether on a statutory or non-statutory basis'.[138] It has not yet requested the powers under RESA, nor indicated any intention to do so.

---

[128] Data Protection Act 1998, s. 40, and the Privacy and Electronic Communications (EC Directive) Regulations 2003, SI 2426/2003, reg. 31.

[129] Ibid., ss 55A–55E.

[130] Consumer Credit Act 1974, s. 159.

[131] Unfair Terms in Consumer Contract Regulations 1999, SI 2083/1999, reg. 12.

[132] Enterprise Act 2002, s. 213.

[133] Data Protection Act 1998, s. 51(7).

[134] Ibid., s. 41A.

[135] Ibid., s. 55A.

[136] Information Commissioner's guidance about the issue of monetary penalties prepared and issued under s. 55C(1) of the Data Protection Act 1998 (12 January 2010).

[137] Data Protection (Monetary Penalties) (Maximum Penalty and Notices) Regulations 2010, SI 31/2010, reg. 2.

[138] Cabinet Office and Better Regulation Executive, *Consultation on the Draft Regulatory Enforcement and Sanctions Bill, Response of the Information Commissioner*, p. 5.

Local fisheries committees

The Sea Fisheries Committees (SFCs) have, since their establishment in 1888,[139] been the statutory body charged with the management of inshore fisheries in England and Wales.[140] The passing of the Marine and Coastal Access Act 2009 (MCAA) has, however, heralded a new era in the management of our inshore fisheries, with SFCs and the Sea Fisheries Regulation Act 1966, under which they operate, being abolished.[141]

6.175

The MCAA provides for their replacement in England by Inshore Fisheries and Conservation Authorities (IFCAs), whereas in Wales, responsibility for fisheries management is being devolved to the Welsh ministers.[142] The provisions in relation to Wales are already in force,[143] and it is understood that the provisions relating to IFCAs will come into force in April 2011.[144]

6.176

There are no known plans to replace the reference to SFCs in Sch. 5 to RESA with a reference to IFCAs; accordingly, once IFCAs replace the SFCs, the potential for the civil sanctions contained in Part 3 of RESA itself to be utilized in the context of fisheries regulation will be lost.

6.177

It was thought that, given that the responsibility for certain fisheries management lies not with the SFCs (or any of their successor bodies) but with the Environment Agency (EA),[145] the civil sanctions contained in RESA might have continued to have some application in the context of fisheries regulation if used by the EA in its capacity as a designated regulator under Sch. 5. However, since the coming into force of the Environmental Civil Sanctions (England) Order 2010 (the 2010 Order), it is clear that this will not be the case: by virtue of art. 4 of the 2010 Order, the civil sanctions can only be used in respect of the offences contained in Sch. 5 of the 2010 Order, none of which relate to fisheries regulation.

6.178

Interim use of civil sanctions (SFCs)

In view of the limited remaining lifespan of the SFCs and the lengthy process for obtaining the civil sanctions under RESA there have been only limited opportunities for the SFCs to seek the award of the Part 3 powers, and it now seems unlikely that this will ever be achieved.

6.179

Offences and enforcement (IFCAs)

Whilst IFCAs will not have the power to use the civil sanctions contained in RESA, there are certain civil sanctions contained in the MCAA that mirror, or at least are inspired by,

6.180

---

[139] Under the Sea Fisheries Regulation Act 1888, s. 1.

[140] Fisheries management in Scotland, Northern Ireland, Guernsey, Jersey and the Isle of Man is separate from that in England and Wales. This chapter refers exclusively to fisheries management in England and Wales.

[141] Marine and Coastal Access Act 2009, s. 187.

[142] Ibid., s. 189.

[143] S. 187 came into force in relation to Wales on 1 April 2010; s. 189 came into force in relation to Wales on 12 November 2009.

[144] P. Winterbottom, 'Management of English and Welsh Inshore Waters and the Marine and Coastal Access Bill' (2008) 19 WL 145, 148.

[145] See the Agency's duties under the Environment Act 1995, s. 6, read with the Marine and Coastal Access Act, s. 153.

those contained in RESA, and which it is understood that the IFCAs or their officers will be empowered to use, for example the power to impose FMPs under s. 142 of the MCAA,[146] and the power to issue penalty notices under s. 294 of the MCAA.[147]

6.181 The civil sanctions in MCAA bear more than a passing resemblance to the procedural requirements for the imposition of the sanctions provided for in RESA.[148]

6.182 The situation is, however, not yet quite the same in respect of the power to issue penalty notices under s. 294. Section 294(3) defines a penalty notice as 'a notice offering the opportunity, by payment of a specified sum of money, to discharge any liability to be convicted of the offence to which the notice relates'. This is essentially the same as the definition of an FMP.[149] However, whereas the procedure in relation to FMPs issued under s. 142 is clearly defined in the MCAA,[150] s. 294 merely provides the framework for providing such procedures.[151] The result is that, until an order is made under the section granting the power to issue a penalty notice to an enforcement authority, and detailing the procedure for doing so, how closely such a scheme will reflect the provisions of RESA cannot be known.

Other civil sanctions in the MCAA

6.183 Whilst the only civil sanctions contained in the MCAA that reflect the civil sanctions contained in RESA, and which the IFCAs are likely to be empowered to use, are those detailed above, elsewhere in the MCAA, provision is made for the use of a much wider range of civil sanctions, mirroring those contained in RESA. These include:

   (i)   the issue of compliance notices;[152]
   (ii) the issue of remediation notices;[153]
   (iii) the issue of stop notices;[154]
   (iv) the imposition of VMPs;[155] and
   (v)   the imposition of FMPs.[156]

6.184 The use of these civil sanctions is, however, confined to the Secretary of State and counterparts in the devolved administrations, marine enforcement officers,[157] and a number of persons appointed either by the Secretary of State, the Department of Environment for Northern Ireland, or the Scottish ministers, in respect of marine licensing.[158]

6.185 It therefore appears that the effect of the passing of the MCAA has been to deprive the body responsible for the management of the inshore waters and fisheries in England of the

---

[146] That is, for breach of byelaws created under ss 129 or 132 of the MCAA.

[147] MCAA, s. 94 provides for the creation of an administrative penalty scheme for 'offences relating to sea fishing': s. 294(2).

[148] See further Sch. 10 to the MCAA for the specific provisions.

[149] See MCAA, ss 142(3) and 143(2)(b).

[150] See Chapter 5, part C.

[151] See MCAA, s. 294(4).

[152] Ibid., s. 90. These are similar in nature to compliance requirements, under RESA, s. 42(3)(b).

[153] Ibid., s. 91. These are similar in nature to restoration requirements, under RESA, s. 42(3)(c).

[154] Ibid., s. 102. These are similar in nature to stop notices, under RESA, s. 46.

[155] Ibid., s. 95.

[156] Ibid., s. 93.

[157] As defined ibid., s. 235.

[158] Ibid., ss 240–242.

potential use of the whole range of civil sanctions to which it would otherwise have had access under RESA.

Natural England

See Chapter 7 for a detailed consideration of this regulator.

6.186

Office of Communications (Ofcom)

To date, Ofcom has not sought to take advantage of the powers potentially available to it under RESA.

6.187

Office of Fair Trading

The Office of Fair Trading (OFT) is an independent non-ministerial government department that has a wide regulatory and criminal function.[159] Its stated mission is to 'make markets work for consumers'.[160] Whilst not primarily a regulator, it does exercise a regulatory function over consumer law enforcement,[161] credit licensing and anti-money laundering supervision. The OFT describes its work as supporting 'the development of competitive, efficient, innovative markets where standards of consumer care are high, consumers are empowered in making choices, business is not disproportionately burdened by government regulations and firms are encouraged to offer benefits to consumers beyond the protection afforded by law'.[162]

6.188

The OFT annually publishes a *Statement of Consumer Protection Enforcement Principles.*[163] The OFT is conscious of complying with the principles of the Hampton Review and Part 4 of RESA, and seeks to employ these when determining the appropriate action to take in respect of legal breaches. It has stated a commitment to adhering to the *Regulators' Compliance Code.*[164] Central to its *Enforcement Principles* is a staged escalation of available enforcement actions, ranging from education, guidance and advice, through to civil or criminal action at its highest point.[165]

6.189

At the time of writing, the OFT has not sought the powers under RESA. It is, however, along with the Department for Business, Innovation and Skills (BIS), consulting on a civil sanctions pilot. The pilot proposes 'to introduce the civil sanctions that mirror those set out in [RESA] into existing consumer protection legislation and to make them available to enforcers by way of amending regulations rather than by way of an Order under [RESA]'.[166] These are Regulations made under the European Communities Act 1972 to which RESA does not apply.[167]

6.190

---

[159] The OFT's enforcement duties and powers derive from a wide range of consumer and business related legislation, details of which can be found on the OFT website on the Enterprise Act, Part 8.

[160] Enterprise Act 2000, s. 8(1).

[161] Consumer Protection for Unfair Trading Regulations 2008, SI 1277/2008, General Product Safety Regulations 2005, SI 1277/2005.

[162] Simplification Plan, OFT 1067, para. 1.1.

[163] OFT 1221. The last edition was published in March 2010. A copy can be found on the OFT website at <http://www.oft.gov.uk>.

[164] Para. 3.21. For more about the status of the *Regulators' Compliance Code*, see para. 4.35.

[165] Para. 2.14.

[166] Para. 1.7, Civil Sanctions Pilot, *A Consultation on the Pilot Operation of Civil Sanction Powers for Consumer Law Enforcers* (March 2010).

[167] RESA, s. 4(3).

6.191 *The Civil Sanctions Pilot Consultation Paper* clearly indicates an intention to make the RESA sanctions available to all relevant consumer legislation.[168] The paper states that the roll-out of the powers to an area not covered by RESA 'will mean that in future, when the civil sanctions in the [RESA] are rolled out to all of the relevant consumer legislation there can be consistency across the application of the sanctions'. It is intended that the enforcers granted powers under the pilot will comply with the requirements in RESA. It is anticipated that the OFT will meet these requirements, although confirmation of this is awaited. The OFT's Hampton Implementation Review, the outcome of which was predominantly positive, took place in 2007.[169] Further assessment of this is to be determined with BIS following the outcome of the consultation process.

6.192 The OFT has stated its intention 'to take enforcement action only where there is no better route to securing compliance'.[170] It is committed to ensuring that decisions made about when to seek enforcement action, and the manner in which this is to be undertaken, are transparent and made only in accordance with clearly explained principles.

6.193 The availability of a wider sanctioning toolkit will make it easier for the OFT to be proportionate and to tailor its responses to regulatory breaches appropriately, ensuring consistency across the consumer field. Whilst the OFT continues to recognize the need for punitive sanctions and criminal prosecutions in appropriate circumstances, the wider range of sanctions would enable consumer breaches to be dealt with by way of compensation in appropriate cases, rather than relying upon individual consumers to seek civil remedies personally.

Office of Rail Regulation

6.194 The Office of Rail Regulation's (ORR) original intention in seeking to be named as a Sch. 5 Regulator under RESA was to preserve a degree of flexibility in relation to its enforcement powers in the future, whilst at the same time, in light of its enforcement functions in respect of the railway aspects of the Health and Safety etc. Act, continuing to align itself with the Health and Safety Executive. In addition to its criminal remedies, the organization already enjoys a significant range of civil sanctions including, for example, improvement notices and prohibition notices. For this reason it is understood that the ORR does not have any present intention to apply to the Secretary of State for additional powers under RESA, although that would not entirely rule out the possibility of such an application at some stage in the future, as the regime develops.

Pensions Regulator

6.195 The Pensions Regulator already enjoys, in addition to its criminal remedies, a significant range of civil sanctions under the Pensions Act 2004. For this reason it is understood that the authority does not have any present intention to apply to the Secretary of State for additional powers under RESA.

---

[168] *A Consultation on the Pilot Operation of Civil sanction powers for consumer law enforcers*, para. 1.9.

[169] In the report, *Effective inspection and enforcement: implementing the Hampton vision in the Office of Fair Trading* (March 2008). A copy can be found on the National Audit Office website: <http://www.nao.org.uk>.

[170] *Statement of consumer protection enforcement principles* (OFT1221) (March 2010), para. 2.3. A copy can be found on the OFT website <http://www.oft.gov.uk>.

Security Industry Authority

In March 1999, the government set out proposals for the statutory regulation of the private **6.196**
security industry.[171] The Private Security Industry Act 2001 (the 2001 Act) made provision
for the establishment of a new non-departmental public body, the Security Industry
Authority (SIA).

Under the provisions of the 2001 Act, the SIA was given responsibility for licensing indi- **6.197**
viduals working within designated sectors of the private security industry and the voluntary
approval of suppliers of such services.

Under this licensing regime, everyone working within designated sectors, which include **6.198**
those concerned with manned guarding, keyholding and the immobilizing, restricting
and removal of vehicles on private land (wheelclamping), private investigators, and security
consultants are required to have a licence issued by the SIA.

The 2001 Act provides a number of key offence provisions that are designed to ensure that **6.199**
those working within the designated sectors hold an appropriate licence and that the SIA has
sufficient powers to investigate suspected offences.

Offences and enforcement

The key offence provisions contained within the 2001 Act are: **6.200**

  (i) conduct prohibited without a licence;[172]
 (ii) employing unlicensed persons in licensable conduct;[173]
(iii) using unlicensed vehicle immobilizers;[174]
 (iv) contravening licence conditions;[175]
  (v) obstructing SIA officials or those with delegated authority;[176] and
 (vi) providing false information.[177]

The maximum penalty for operating without a licence is six months' imprisonment and a **6.201**
fine.[178] The maximum penalty for using an unlicensed operative is five years' imprisonment
and a fine.[179]

The SIA's current approach to enforcement is set out comprehensively in its Enforcement
Policy Code of Practice.[180]

Current enforcement practice

The 2001 Act did not afford the SIA an express power to prosecute. However, s. 1 provides **6.202**
the SIA with a number of functions and s. 1(3) provides that it is also empowered to do

---

[171] White Paper, *The Government's Proposals for Regulation of the Private Security Industry in England and Wales*, Cm. 4254.
[172] 2001 Act, s. 3.
[173] Ibid., s. 5.
[174] Ibid., s. 6.
[175] Ibid., s. 9.
[176] Ibid., s. 19.
[177] Ibid., s. 22.
[178] Ibid., s. 3(6).
[179] Ibid., s. 5(4).
[180] SIA, *Enforcement Policy Code of Practice* (23 December 2009). A copy is available on the SIA website.

'anything that is calculated to facilitate or incidental or conducive to, the carrying out of its functions'.

6.203 The Administrative Court has recently considered whether s. 1(3) can be interpreted to allow the SIA a power to prosecute. In the case of *R (on the application of Securiplan Plc & Ors) v SIA*,[181] the court held that the SIA *did* have a power to prosecute, because such prosecutions were calculated to facilitate, or were incidental or conducive to, the carrying out of the SIA's functions. Accordingly, the SIA uses prosecution as one of its enforcement tools. However, in accordance with the principles set out by the Crown Prosecution Service in the *Code for Crown Prosecutors*, the SIA will only commence prosecutions if there is sufficient evidence to provide a realistic prospect of conviction and a prosecution is in the public interest.

6.204 In addition to prosecution, the SIA currently utilizes a range of enforcement tools, including issuing written warnings and improvement notices as well as the revocation of licences. The SIA also publishes full details on its website of all prosecutions completed in the last twelve-month period.

6.205 The SIA considers that the enforcement tools currently available to it are broadly effective in ensuring compliance; it does recognize, however, that there are shortcomings with the current enforcement regime, which could be improved.

Application of the civil sanctions

6.206 The SIA is committed to the principles set out in the Legislative and Regulatory Reform Act 2006[182] and in the *Regulators' Compliance Code*. As part of its commitment to ensuring that compliance and enforcement action should deliver the intended regulatory outcomes, the SIA has recognized that civil sanctions would benefit its regulatory regime. The SIA underwent a Hampton Implementation Review (HIR) by the Department of Business, Enterprise and Regulatory Reform (now BIS) in February 2009. The outcome of that review was favourable. Summarizing the outcome of the review, the BERR reported that the SIA

> puts a high priority on regulating in line with the Hampton and Macrory Principles. This is reflected through all its key publications, and awareness of the spirit of the principles, notably the importance of working with businesses to secure compliance, runs throughout the organisation. However, the Review Team found that there were a number of areas, notably about integrating feedback from the industry and intelligence more fully into strategic planning, and working with the industry to develop a more effective approach to improving standards, that need some attention before the SIA can be regarded as fully Hampton compliant. We believe that the SIA is in a strong position to make these changes relatively easily.[183]

6.207 Since the HIR, the SIA has been working to address those areas identified for further improvement.

6.208 The SIA regards the main benefits of the use of civil sanctions as ensuring that, where businesses have saved costs through non-compliance, they do not gain an unfair advantage over those businesses that have been operating within the regime, and in achieving a more

---

[181] [2008] EWHC 1762 (Admin).
[182] The Principles of Good Regulation.
[183] SIA Hampton Implementation Review Report. A copy is available on the Department for Business Innovation and Skills website: <http://www.bis gov.uk>.

proportionate, consistent and cost-effective enforcement regime. It is envisaged that FMPs will be particularly useful in addressing low-level non-compliance, specifically for offending against ss 3[184] and 9[185] of the 2001 Act. VMPs and non-monetary discretionary requirements are considered to be more suitable for high-level non-compliance, particularly offending against s. 5[186] of the 2001 Act. The use of enforcement undertakings will be dependent on the willingness of the private security industry to participate with them. At present the SIA does not consider that stop notices will be of use to it.

The SIA identifies a number of drawbacks to the civil sanctions regime in Part 3 of RESA. **6.209** These include the initial outlay required to establish the internal structure required to administer the system, the requirement for the regulator to meet the criminal standard of proof before imposing certain sanctions, and the uncertainty surrounding 'best practice' within the internal appeal process and the potential for legal challenges against regulators for non-compliance with Art. 6 of the European Convention on Human Rights.

The SIA reports that despite its willingness to utilize the civil sanctions, the Home Office **6.210** has been unable to carry out the public consultation and develop the secondary legislation during 2009 and this is unlikely to happen in 2010. It is anticipated that the earliest this will now occur is in 2011–12.

Statistics Board

The Statistics Board was established on 1 April 2008 under the Statistics and Registration **6.211** Service Act 2007 (the 2007 Act). It is a Non-Ministerial Department, directly accountable to Parliament, and known publicly as the UK Statistics Authority. The executive office of the UK Statistics Authority is the Office of National Statistics (ONS).

The Statistics Board has a public enforcement function in relation to two relevant offences, **6.212** both of which relate to data collection.

The first offence is where an individual fails to complete a census return under the Census **6.213** Act 1920 and secondary legislation.[187] Provisions for the next Census, in 2011, are contained in the Census (England) Regulations 2010.[188] The Statistics Board's intention however is to retain criminal sanctions for breaches of these provisions and it is working with the Crown Prosecution Service to put in place procedures in time for the next Census.[189]

The second offence is where businesses fail to complete returns as required by s. 4 of the **6.214** Statistics of Trade Act 1947. In the vast majority of cases, businesses are brought into compliance by a combination of reminders, emails and personal telephone calls; criminal prosecution is a last resort. The view is taken that while the impact of individual failures to return business surveys is small, in combination they represent a significant risk to the quality of statistical data and the related national economic interest.

---

[184] Conduct prohibited without a licence.
[185] Contravening licence conditions.
[186] Employing unlicensed persons in licensable conduct.
[187] Census Act 1920, s. 8(1); the Act (as amended) provides that no person is liable to a penalty for refusing or neglecting to state any particulars in respect of religion (s. 8(1A)).
[188] Census (England) Regulations 2010, SI 532/2010, reg. 11.
[189] Source: Martin Stringfellow, ONS Legal Services team, 30 July 2010.

6.215 The Statistics Board have no plans to utilize the civil sanctions under RESA and consider that they 'gain a vast amount of data through the goodwill of the general public and do not see anything to be gained by being seen to take any measures beyond those we already use'.[190] Certainly, the combination of highly informal and strict prosecutorial approaches is perceived to work well.

6.216 The Statistics and Registration Service Act 2007 sets out a duty to comply with the Code of Practice for Statistics, but explicitly states that 'no action shall lie in relation to any ... failure' to do so.[191]

---

[190] Ibid.
[191] Statistics and Registration Service Act 2007, s. 13.

7

NATURAL ENGLAND AND THE ENVIRONMENT AGENCY

A. Introduction

On 6 April 2010, the Environment Agency and Natural England became the first two **7.01** Sch. 5 regulators to be awarded the civil sanctions under Part 3 of RESA.[1] The approach that they have taken in respect of the translation of the enabling provisions in RESA into secondary legislation should provide an invaluable point of reference to other authorities seeking the award of these sanctions in the future.

This chapter looks briefly at the two enforcement regimes as they were before the award of **7.02** the civil sanctions under Part 3, the procedural provisions in the secondary legislation for the imposition of the sanctions and finally, in parts D and E, at the statutory guidance to be issued by these two environmental regulators under ss 63–64 of RESA.

B. Offences and enforcement: the pre-RESA position

Introduction

It is informative to consider the regulatory and enforcement regimes as they stood before the **7.03** award of the civil sanctions in 2010, in order to contextualize these important new powers.

---

[1] RESA, s. 37.

Whereas, as has been shown, many regulators have either taken the view that their existing powers are sufficient to enable them to fulfil their statutory purpose (even where this involves a significant level of enforcement activity) and others, that their limited role in such matters would not justify the substantial investment required to secure the RESA powers, both Natural England and the Environment Agency have taken the view that, having considered their existing powers, such an initiative would be justified. It may be helpful for future applicants to consider the nature, extent and apparent deficiencies in those powers when considering whether a similar move on their part might be worthwhile for their own organization. An analysis of the financial implications of the decision once the new regime is established will also, no doubt, be instructive.

Environment Agency

7.04 The Environment Agency's (EA) stated purpose is 'to protect or enhance the environment, taken as a whole' so as to promote 'the objective of achieving sustainable development' as set out in s. 4 of the Environment Act 1995.

7.05 The functions of the EA are extensive and include pollution control, waste regulation, the management of water resources, flood and coastal risk-management, fisheries, conservation and navigation. The activities dealt with range from the regulation of simple recreational pursuits to the most complicated industrial processes.

7.06 The EA has enforcement responsibilities in a vast number of different areas.[2] The enforcement response to an offence will always be influenced by the consideration of published public interest factors.[3] This applies even though the importance of each factor will clearly vary with each offence and the individual circumstances of the case. Consideration of these public interest factors allows the Agency to concentrate resources in the areas where they are most required. By way of illustration, in 2008 the Agency completed some 726 prosecutions for a range of offences concerning, principally, illegal waste activity or producer responsibility (packaging) offences. The remainder were for water pollution and other miscellaneous offences such as breaching permit conditions. The average company fine was between £10,000 and £12,000 and total fines imposed were in excess of £3 m. Thirty per cent of that total annual fine was accounted for by just ten companies. A further 423 formal cautions were given and 315 varying types of enforcement notices served.

7.07 The EA's Enforcement & Prosecution Policy was first produced in 1998 and has been regularly revised and reissued since that time, the current policy being issued in August 2008. This sets out the EA's commitment to the Principles of Good Regulation by which all

---

[2] E.g. The Environmental Damage (Prevention and Remediation) Regulations 2009; The Environmental Permitting Regulations 2010, SI 675/2010; Environment Act 1995, ss 41 and 110 (obstruction of an EA officer and non-payment of subsistence fees); Water Resources Act 1991; waste offences under the Environmental Protection Act 1990; waste carrier/broker offences under the Control of Pollution (Amendment) Act 1989; Waste and Emissions Trading Act 2003; offences in relation to land quality, including breaches of remediation notices under Part IIA EPA 1990; offences in relation to water resources under the Water Resources Act 1991 etc.; fisheries legislation, including the Salmon and Freshwater Fisheries Act 1975; and certain offences under the Wildlife and Countryside Act 1981.

[3] (1) Environmental effect (categories of seriousness 1–3) (2) Nature of the offence (3) Financial implications (4) Impact on legitimate business activities (5) Deterrent effect (6) Intent (7) Previous history (8) Attitude of the offender (9) Personal circumstances (10) Foreseeability (11) Impact on EA resources.

enforcement action undertaken by the EA is governed.[4] The policy sets out the two tests that the EA applies when deciding whether or not to commence criminal prosecutions, namely the evidential sufficiency and public interest tests.

Natural England

Functions

Natural England was established in 2006 as the government's statutory adviser on the natural environment in England. Its role is comprised of two main elements: wildlife and landscapes, reflecting the two main constituent bodies that came together to create it (English Nature and the Countryside Agency).[5]   **7.08**

Natural England's statutory general purpose is set out in s. 2(1) of the Natural Environment and Rural Communities Act 2006 (the 2006 Act), and is to ensure that the natural environment is conserved, enhanced and managed for the benefit of present and future generations, thereby contributing to sustainable development.   **7.09**

Enforcement

Natural England has enforcement responsibilities in a number of different areas, including in relation to sites of special scientific interest (SSSI), heather and grass burning,[6] breaches of wildlife licences and notices issued by it,[7] pesticide poisoning to animals, damage caused by injurious weeds,[8] and environmental impact assessment relating to uncultivated land and semi-natural areas.[9] The powers fall into two main categories: wildlife management and licensing and protected areas. Natural England itself has identified that it has 382 different regulatory powers.[10] Natural England has the power to institute criminal proceedings under s. 12 of the 2006 Act.   **7.10**

The *Explanatory Memorandum to the 2010 Order*[11] notes that Natural England previously undertook five prosecutions per year and spent some £340,000 per year on enforcement action. The Hampton Implementation Review in 2009 found that Natural England had good levels of compliance with the Hampton criteria in many areas and had been making good steps to strengthen its regulatory performance.[12]   **7.11**

Sites of special scientific interest (SSSIs)

There are more than 4,000 SSSIs in England which cover some 7 per cent of the country's land area.[13] The majority of Natural England's enforcement work historically has been in relation to SSSIs. SSSIs are protected under Part II of the Wildlife and Countryside   **7.12**

---

[4] See further Chapter 1 for detail about the Principles of Good Regulation.
[5] Natural England also includes part of the former DEFRA Rural Development Service.
[6] See, for example, s. 20 of the Hill Farming Act 1946.
[7] See, for example, s. 8 of the Deer Act 1991 and s. 10 of the Protection of Badgers Act 1992.
[8] Under the Weeds Act 1959.
[9] Under the Environmental Impact Assessment (Agriculture) (England) (No. 2) Regulations 2006, SI 2522/2006.
[10] See BIS, *Natural England: A Hampton Implementation Review Report* (July 2009).
[11] *Explanatory Memorandum to The Environmental Civil Sanctions (England) Order 2010* and the Environmental Civil Sanctions (Miscellaneous Amendments) (England) Regulations 2010, SI 1159/2010. A copy is available on the Office of Public Sector Information website: <http://www.opsi.gov.uk>.
[12] BIS, *Natural England: A Hampton Implementation Review Report* (July 2009).
[13] See DBIS, *Natural England: A Hampton Implementation Review Report* (July 2009).

Act 1981. The offences arising in connection with SSSIs are set out in s. 28P of the 1981 Act. The main offences are as follows:

(i) Section 28P(1) provides that it is an offence to contravene s. 28E(1), which prevents an owner or occupier of any land included in an SSSI from carrying out, or causing or permitting to be carried out, on land within the SSSI, any operation specified in the SSSI notification issued under s. 28, without notice having been served on Natural England, and Natural England having given written consent, or the operation being in accordance with an agreement, a management scheme or a management notice.[14]

(ii) Section 28P(6) provides that it is an offence for any person, without reasonable excuse, intentionally or recklessly to:

(a) destroy or damage any of the flora, fauna or geological or physiographical features by reason of which the SSSI is of special interest; or

(b) disturb any such fauna, subject in both cases to the person knowing that what was affected was within an SSSI.

(iii) Under s. 28P(8) it is an offence to fail without reasonable excuse to comply with a requirement of a management notice issued under s. 28K.

(iv) Section 28P(2), (3) and (5A) provides that it is an offence for a public body or statutory undertaker[15] without reasonable excuse to fail to comply with certain aspects of the statutory scheme set out in ss 28H and 28I.

Approach to enforcement

7.13 The DEFRA guidance, *Civil sanctions for environmental offences*,[16] which includes the enforcement activities of Natural England, states that regulators will continue to apply the same kind of approach to assessing the seriousness of offences under the civil sanctions regime as has been previously applied under the wholly criminal regime.[17] It is relevant therefore to consider Natural England's existing policy on enforcement to help understand how it will operate the civil sanctions regime in the future. Natural England operates an external stakeholder group to help guide its enforcement work.

7.14 In order to provide a coherent approach to its enforcement role, in 2008 Natural England adopted a regulatory strategy and an enforcement strategy.[18] The regulatory strategy set out Natural England's role as a regulator. The enforcement strategy sets out the approach to be adopted in relation to enforcement. Under this strategy sits an enforcement policy, which sets out the principles to be applied by Natural England in taking enforcement action. Natural England said at the time of the adoption of these strategies that it would use its enforcement powers 'in a proportionate way, when required and when it is in the public interest to do so, to protect the natural environment of England'.[19]

7.15 Natural England's regulatory strategy (June 2008) states that the agency's principal focus will be the protection and enhancement of the natural environment of England. The agency committed to the principles of the Regulators' Compliance Code, stating that its regulatory

---

[14] See the 1981 Act, s. 28E(3).

[15] A s. 28G authority, as defined in the 1981 Act, s. 28G(3).

[16] January 2010. A copy is available on the DEFRA website: <http://www.defra.gov.uk>.

[17] It is understood that Natural England will pursue broadly the same approach under the civil sanctions regime as it adopted under the wholly criminal regime.

[18] See *Natural England Board Paper*, NEB PU11 04 (June 2008).

[19] Ibid.

actions would be consistent, proportionate, transparent, targeted and accountable. Within this, risk assessment would be used to target enforcement action and what is described as a 'tiered approach' would be taken to enforcement incidents. The main guiding principle when considering enforcement action is to ensure better 'environmental outcomes'.

Natural England's enforcement strategy (June 2008) stated its commitment to undertaking enforcement activity in a clear, consistent, fair and proportionate manner. The agency's enforcement resources are arranged under a central Regulatory Services Team, to deal with significant and contentious casework, with enforcement personnel also based in each of Natural England's nine regional areas, to deal with more minor matters. **7.16**

The enforcement strategy also sets out Natural England's commitment to using a standard classification of incidents, in order to prioritize enforcement action.[20] The categorization is based primarily on the environmental impact caused or threatened by the incident. Aggravating and mitigating factors, and the public interest element, would be taken into account in both categorization of the incident, and the decision on what enforcement action is to be taken. **7.17**

Natural England's enforcement policy (March 2009) commits the agency not only to the protection of the natural environment, but also to its restoration. The policy states that Natural England will be robust in its enforcement responses, in order to send a clear message, and will act so as to: deter future non-compliance; so far as possible, eliminate any financial gain or benefit from non-compliance; and change the behaviour of offenders and others. **7.18**

The enforcement policy expands on the mechanisms through which the Principles of Good Regulation[21] will be applied in relation to enforcement action. **7.19**

Regarding criminal sanctions, Natural England's enforcement policy recognizes that a decision to prosecute is a serious step. The agency is committed to applying the Code for Crown Prosecutors and in considering both the evidential and the public interest tests before deciding to commence a prosecution. In relation to the public interest test, the enforcement policy lists the main factors bearing on the public interest, including, of course, the impact of the incident on the natural environment, which is the predominant factor in considering the likely enforcement response. This could include consideration of the scale of the impact, how rare the elements of the environment affected were, how severe the impact is, and the potential for the recovery of the environment affected. **7.20**

Finally in respect of criminal prosecutions, the policy commits Natural England to using alternatives to prosecution, where prosecution would not be the most appropriate or proportionate enforcement mechanism. Alternatives have previously included warnings and cautions. **7.21**

Natural England also provides internal guidance to its officers; this is not available publicly, rather it is contained in an operational process manual covering enforcement practice.[22] **7.22**

---

[20] Natural England uses four categories to classify incidents: technical, minor, medium and significant breaches. Prosecutions would usually result from the latter two categories.

[21] See further Chapter 1 for more about the Principles of Good Regulation.

[22] See, for example, the references in BIS, *Natural England: A Hampton Implementation Review Report* (July 2009), and the Natural England enforcement strategy.

The manual contains guidance on, inter alia, the collection of evidence, the assessment of incidents, preparation of case documentation, enforcement mechanisms and cost recovery.

7.23   Businesses should be alert to the fact that Natural England's non-financial scheme of delegation contains formal delegations of decision-making on enforcement matters; the appropriate checks should be made to ensure that any action taken is properly authorized by a person holding a properly delegated power to so act. Different steps require authorization by officers of differing seniority; the more serious the step, the more senior the officer required to authorize it.

C. The civil sanctions

Introduction

7.24   The Environmental Civil Sanctions (England) Order 2010 (the 2010 Order)[23] came into force on 6 April 2010. It permits the Environment Agency and Natural England to impose the Part 3 civil sanctions against non-compliant businesses and individuals in relation to certain specified relevant offences.

7.25   The 2010 Order makes detailed provision about the procedure for issuing fixed monetary penalties (FMPs),[24] variable monetary penalties (VMPs), compliance notices, restoration notices, third party undertakings,[25] stop notices,[26] and enforcement undertakings.[27] Detailed commentary on each of these sanctions is provided in Chapter 5. An account of the special provisions sanctioned in relation to these two agencies now follows.

7.26   The 2010 Order should be read alongside the Explanatory Memorandum[28] to the Environmental Civil Sanctions (England) Order 2010 and the Environmental Civil Sanctions (Miscellaneous Amendments) (England) Regulations 2010.

To which offences may the sanctions be attached?

Environment Agency

7.27   Schedule 5 of the 2010 Order sets out the offences for which particular civil sanctions may be imposed so far as the Environment Agency is concerned. The offences specified in the 2010 Order do not include breaches of the Environmental Permitting Regulations 2007.[29] It is not anticipated that civil sanctions will be introduced for offences under those

---

[23]   Made under RESA, Part 3. The Environmental Civil Sanctions (Wales) Order 2010, SI 1821/2010 and the draft Environmental Civil Sanctions (Miscellaneous Amendments) (Wales) Regulations 2010, SI 1820/2010, along with an explanatory memorandum and regulatory impact assessment would make use of the powers to introduce civil sanctions in Wales. The draft order, as published at the time of writing, is in substantially the same form as that relating to England, save that the powers of entry conferred by art. 15 in respect of the latter are omitted, as is the power to impose such sanctions in respect of the Destructive Imported Animals Act 1932, Pests Act 1954, Weeds Act 1959, Wildlife and Countryside Act 1981 (thirty-eight offences), Deer Act 1991 and the Protection of Badgers Act 1992.

[24]   The 2010 Order, Sch. 1.

[25]   Ibid., Sch. 2.

[26]   Ibid., Sch. 3.

[27]   Ibid., Sch. 4.

[28]   <http://www.legislation.gov.uk/uksi/2010/1157/pdfs/uksiem_20101157_en.pdf>.

[29]   Environmental Permitting (England and Wales) Regulations 2007, SI 3538/2007.

regulations until at least 2011. The current consultation paper distributed by DEFRA[30] proposes (as reflected in regulation 8 of the draft Environmental Permitting (England and Wales) (Amendment) Regulations 2011 (July 2010)) that the following additional sanctions should be made available in due course for the offences listed in regulation 38 of the EP Regulations 2010:

Offence	Fixed monetary penalty	Variable monetary penalty	Enforcement undertaking
reg. 38(1)(a) and (b)	yes	yes	yes
reg. 38(2)	yes	yes	yes
reg. 38(3)	no	yes	no
reg. 38(4)(a) and (d)	yes	yes	yes
reg. 38(4)(b) and (c)	no	yes	no
reg. 38(5)(a)	yes	yes	yes
reg. 38(5)(b)	no	yes	no

If approved, this will considerably extend the operations of the Agency in this area. Until that time the numbers and types of civil sanctions issued by the Agency are likely to be low. Provisions have been made for a formal review of the new regime following the period of initial implementation.

Natural England

For Natural England, Sch. 5 to the 2010 Order also sets out the offences in relation to which the civil sanctions apply. These include offences under the following statutes: s. 6 of the Destructive Imported Animals Act 1932; s. 4 of the Pests Act 1954; ss 2 and 4 of the Weeds Act 1959; the Wildlife and Countryside Act 1981;[31] s. 8 of the Deer Act 1991; and ss 3 and 10 of the Protection of Badgers Act 1992. [32]

7.28

Schedule 5 does not include the offences related to heather and grass burning under ss 20 and 34 of the Hill Farming Act 1946, despite them being listed in Annex 1 of the DEFRA guidance, *Civil sanctions for environmental offences* (January 2010) as offences covered by civil sanctions and their being included in the draft of the order published for consultation in July 2009. It is to be assumed that this is an oversight that will be remedied in due course by amendment to the legislation.[33] There were other offences that were included in the draft order that have not been included in the 2010 Order as made.[34]

7.29

The Environmental Civil Sanctions (Miscellaneous Amendments) (England) Regulations 2010 amend the Environmental Impact Assessment (Agriculture) (England) (No. 2) Regulations 2006, to enable civil sanctions to be imposed for offences under the

7.30

---

[30] DEFRA Consultation on draft Environmental Permitting (England and Wales) (Amendment) Regulations 2011 (July 2010).

[31] Under ss 1, 5–9, 11, 13, 14, 17, 19XB, 28P, 28S and 51.

[32] The statutes were originally listed in RESA, Sch. 6.

[33] Although the Hill Farming Act 1946 was not listed in RESA, Sch. 6.

[34] For example, under the Conservation of Seals Act 1970 and the Food and Environment Protection Act 1985.

2006 Regulations.[35] The July 2009 DEFRA consultation on the draft regulations included other offences for the civil sanctions regime that have not been included in the legislation as made, including in relation to European protected species.[36] These remaining offences are likely to be brought into the civil sanctions regime in due course.

Which sanctions are available?

Fixed monetary penalties

7.31   Schedule 1 of the 2010 Order makes detailed provision regarding the imposition of FMPs. For both regulators, these have been fixed at £100 for an individual and £300 for a body corporate.[37] It should be noted that there is no provision for cost recovery, which may make the sanction a slightly less attractive option for the regulator.

7.32   As discussed in Chapter 5, the procedure for the imposition of an FMP requires in the first instance the service of a notice of intent, which affords the recipient an opportunity to discharge their liability for the proposed penalty. Discharge payments have been set at a reduction of 50 per cent of the penalty, payable within 28 days.[38]

7.33   Certain elements of a notice of intent are mandatory, including the ground(s) for the proposal to impose the fixed monetary penalty and the amount payable. A recipient of a notice of intent has twenty-eight days from its receipt to make representations and objections in relation to the proposed imposition of the penalty. There is no express time period within which a final notice must be served following service of a notice of intent, nor an express requirement for any response to be given to those objections or representations.

7.34   If a person is served with a notice of intent and makes representations or objections, then that person has an opportunity to discharge the notice by paying 50 per cent of the penalty within twenty-eight days. For the recipient of a notice who does not make representations, the full amount has to be paid within fifty-six days, and in those circumstances there is no discount for early payment.[39] If the penalty is not paid within fifty-six days, the amount payable increases by 50 per cent.

7.35   As required by s. 41 of RESA, provision is made in the 2010 Order prohibiting the commencement of criminal proceedings in respect of the same act or omission, before a period of twenty-eight days from the date on which the notice of intent is received. If a person discharges liability for a penalty that person may not at any time be convicted of the offence in relation to that act or omission (see further para. 5.53).

Discretionary requirements

7.36   Schedule 2 of the 2010 Order makes provision for the imposition of discretionary requirements. For VMPs, the maximum penalty where such a requirement is imposed in relation to

---

[35] Under regs 22(1), 23, 24(1), 26(1) and 30(8).

[36] Under the Conservation (Natural Habitats &c) Regulations 1994, SI 2716/1994 (see now the Conservation of Habitats and Species Regulations 2010, SI 490/2010) and the Heather & Grass Burning (England) Regulations 2007, SI 2003/2007. See Annex 4 to the July 2009 DEFRA consultation document (list of offences to be covered by secondary legislation).

[37] 2001 Order, Sch. 1, para. 1(3).

[38] See further Chapter 5 for detail about the imposition of FMPs generally.

[39] 2010 Order, Sch. 1, para. 6.

an offence that is triable summarily and punishable by a fine is the maximum amount of that fine. In all other cases, the maximum has been set at £250,000.[40]

7.37 The procedure for the imposition of discretionary requirements is broadly similar to that prescribed for the imposition of FMPs, in as much as a final notice is required to follow the initial service of the notice of intent.

7.38 An offer of a 'third party undertaking' can be made by any person on whom a notice of intent is served. Such offers may be accepted or rejected by a regulator. The regulator has to take into account any third party undertaking that it accepts when deciding whether or not to serve a final notice and the amount of any VMP it imposes.

7.39 The matters that a regulator would have to take into account when deciding whether to accept a third party undertaking are not set out in the 2010 Order. It is anticipated that penalty guidance to be issued under s. 63 will set out the consultation exercise that will be carried out with third parties prior to any decision to refuse or accept an undertaking being reached.

7.40 The usual six-month time limit for commencing criminal proceedings for summary only offences is extended by virtue of art. 9(3) to any time up to six months from the date when the regulator notifies the recipient of a restoration or compliance notice, or a person who has given a third party undertaking that has been accepted, that such a person has failed to comply with the particular notice or undertaking.[41]

Stop notices

7.41 Schedule 3 enables stop notices to be served on a person in relation to an offence under Sch. 5, if the table (in Sch. 5) indicates that such a notice is available for that offence.

7.42 A stop notice is defined as a notice prohibiting a person from carrying on an activity specified in the notice until the person has taken the steps specified in the notice. A stop notice can only be imposed where the regulator reasonably believes that an activity as carried on (or likely to be carried on) by that person is causing, or presents a significant risk of causing, serious harm to human health or the environment.[42]

7.43 Where, after the service of a stop notice, the regulator is satisfied that the person has taken the steps specified in the notice, the regulator must issue a completion certificate.

7.44 An offence is committed where a recipient of a stop notice fails to comply with it within the specified time limit. The sentence for such an offence is a fine of up to £20,000 or six months' imprisonment (on summary conviction) or two years' imprisonment and an unlimited fine (following conviction on indictment).[43]

7.45 A regulator will be obliged to compensate the recipient of a stop notice for loss suffered as a result of the service of the stop notice or the refusal of a completion certificate, where the regulator either withdraws or amends the stop notice because the decision to serve it was unreasonable, or any step specified in it was unreasonable; or the recipient successfully appeals against a notice or the refusal of a completion certificate and the Tribunal makes a

[40] 2010 Order, Sch. 2, para. 1(5).
[41] Ibid., para. 9(3).
[42] Ibid., Sch. 3, paras 4 and 5.
[43] Ibid., para. 6.

finding that the service of the notice or the refusal of the certificate was unreasonable. A right of appeal lies against any decision not to award compensation.

Enforcement undertakings

7.46 Schedule 4 of the 2010 Order makes provision in relation to enforcement undertakings. A regulator may accept an enforcement undertaking in a case where the regulator has reasonable grounds to suspect that a person has committed a specified offence, but it is not under a duty to do so.

7.47 An enforcement undertaking must specify certain matters, including the action required to secure that the offence does not continue or recur, and the action required to secure that the position, so far as possible, is restored to what it would have been if the offence had not been committed. It may also include action requiring the payment of a sum of money to benefit any person affected by the offence in question, or that will secure equivalent benefit or improvement to the environment, where restoration of the harm arising from the offence is not possible.[44]

7.48 A regulator who is satisfied that an enforcement undertaking has been complied with must issue a certificate to that effect.[45] The person offering the undertaking may also apply for a certificate, the refusal of which can be appealed. Where a person provides inaccurate, misleading or incomplete information in relation to an enforcement undertaking, that person is regarded as not having complied with the undertaking, and in such circumstances a regulator may also revoke the certificate.[46]

7.49 If a person fails to comply with an enforcement undertaking, the regulator may either serve a VMP notice, a compliance notice or a restoration notice, or bring criminal proceedings. Partial compliance must be taken into account in the imposition of any subsequent criminal sanction.

Combination of penalties

7.50 In accordance with s. 51 of RESA, the 2010 Order expressly prevents the combination of FMPs with the imposition of other types of civil sanction. As explained in Chapter 5, art. 5 of the 2010 Order prevents a regulator from combining an FMP with a VMP or in circumstances where a compliance, restoration or stop notice has been, or will be, served on an individual relating to 'the same act or omission'. It should be emphasized that there is nothing to prevent the combining of *other types* of civil sanction in relation to the same act or omission, and indeed, as has been suggested in earlier chapters, the flexibility inherent in this aspect of the new regime is considered to be one of its potential strengths.

Non-compliance and enforcement

7.51 Part 3 of the 2010 Order makes provision for non-compliance and enforcement. Article 6 states that the regulator may recover any FMP, VMP or non-compliance penalty on the order of a court, as if payable under a court order.[47]

---

[44] 2010 Order, Sch. 4, para. 2.
[45] Ibid., para. 5.
[46] Ibid., para. 6.
[47] See paras 5.55–5.64.

Non-compliance penalty notices

Where a person has failed to comply with a compliance notice, a restoration notice or a **7.52** third party undertaking, the regulator may serve a notice imposing a monetary penalty, known as a non-compliance notice.[48] Such a penalty may be imposed regardless of whether a variable monetary penalty has already been imposed in respect of the same offence. The amount of the non-compliance penalty is to be determined by the regulator, but must be a percentage of the costs of fulfilling the remaining requirements of the notice or third party undertaking.

A non-compliance penalty notice must include specified information as to: **7.53**

(i) the grounds for the imposition of the penalty;
(ii) the amount and method of payment;
(iii) the period within which it has to be paid,
(iv) the right of appeal against the penalty;
(v) consequences of any failure to make the required payment; and
(vi) any circumstances in which the regulator may reduce the amount of the penalty.

Importantly, if the requirements of the original compliance notice, restoration notice **7.54** or third party undertaking are complied with before the payment deadline of the non-compliance penalty, the penalty is not payable.[49]

The grounds of appeal against the service of a non-compliance penalty notice are wide- **7.55** ranging and effectively provide for an appeal as of right.[50] An appeal may be brought on the following grounds:

(i) that the decision to serve it was based on an error of fact;
(ii) that the decision was wrong in law;
(iii) that the decision was unfair or unreasonable for any reason;
(iv) that the amount of the penalty was unreasonable; and
(v) any other reason.

Enforcement cost recovery notices

Regulators may recover the costs of imposing certain penalties. Where the regulator has **7.56** imposed a VMP notice, compliance requirement notice, restoration notice or stop notice, art. 8 permits the service by the regulator of an enforcement cost recovery notice. This notice requires the non-compliant business to pay the costs incurred by the regulator in relation to the imposition of that notice, up to the time of its imposition.[51]

Recoverable costs include investigation costs, administration costs and the costs of obtain- **7.57** ing expert advice (including legal advice), subject to the proviso of those costs not being unnecessarily incurred. A right of appeal lies against the decision to serve such a notice or against the extent of the costs claimed in that notice or 'for any other reason'.[52]

---

[48] 2010 Order, art. 7. The provision for the imposition of such powers is RESA, s. 45. See para. 5.110.
[49] 2010 Order, art. 5(5).
[50] See para. 5.113.
[51] The power to make provision regarding recovering costs recovery is set out in RESA, s. 53.
[52] The 2010 Order, art. 8(5). Further consideration of cost recovery generally is found in Chapter 5, part G.

Withdrawing or amending a notice

7.58   A regulator may at any time withdraw a VMP notice, a non-compliance penalty notice or an enforcement cost recovery notice, or reduce the amount specified in the notice.[53] Compliance, restoration or stop notices can be withdrawn, or the steps contained within them amended to reduce the amount of work necessary to comply with the notice.

Supplementary powers

7.59   The 2010 Order makes provision for the supplementary powers envisaged in s. 55(3) of RESA and intended to facilitate the use of the civil sanctions, namely requests for information and the power to enter premises.

Requests for information

7.60   Schedule 2, para. 1(6) of the 2010 Order provides that before serving a 'notice relating to a variable monetary penalty', the regulator may require the person to provide such information as is reasonable to establish the amount of any financial benefit arising as a result of the offence.[54] This provision will enable the regulators to require the provision of information that is needed to assess any financial benefit from non-compliance, in order to set the level of the penalty accordingly. Its use (which is likely to be widespread) will enable regulators better to fulfil one of the key Macrory 'Principles', namely to aim 'to eliminate any financial gain or benefit from non-compliance'.[55]

7.61   The wide drafting of the provision ('notice relating to a variable monetary penalty') appears to permit the request for information to be made either prior to the issuing of the notice of intent or after, but before the final notice is served. Given, however, that a notice of intent must specify the amount of the proposed penalty, it seems unlikely that requests for further information will in practice be made after the issue of the initial notice of intent. 'Notably, there is no sanction for the non-provision of information requested pursuant to this power,[56] although businesses refusing to comply with such a request may find that their lack of engagement is held against them.'[57] In those circumstances, any such failure would also, no doubt, feature in any *Friskies*[58] schedule served by the prosecutor.

Power to enter premises

7.62   Natural England has also been granted a power under art. 15 of the 2010 Order to enter premises, other than exclusively domestic premises, in order to monitor compliance with civil sanctions.[59]

---

[53] Ibid., art. 9.
[54] 2010 Order, Sch. 2, para. 1(6).
[55] See Chapter 1 for further discussion concerning these principles.
[56] Contrast for example the use of planning contravention notices under the Town and Country Planning Act regime and offences for failure to comply with such notices.
[57] *Explanatory Memorandum to The Environmental Civil Sanctions (England) Order 2010* and the Environmental Civil Sanctions (Miscellaneous Amendments) (England) Regulations 2010, SI 1159/2010, p. 3, para. 4.8.
[58] *R v Friskies Petcare UK Ltd* [2000] EWCA Crim 95, [2000] 2 Crim App Rep (S) 401, [2000] EWCA Crim 95.
[59] Pursuant to RESA, s. 55(3).

Appeal

Article 10 makes provision for appeals against the imposition of the sanctions to the First-tier **7.63**
Tribunal. All notices (other than stop notices) are suspended pending such appeals. This is
an important safeguard that has been afforded to businesses, and is not a mandatory requirement of RESA.[60] The appeals regime that has been created represents new territory for both
the EA and NE, and will no doubt require their respective legal teams to consider the evidential requirements arising, as well as the applicable burdens and standards of proof.

On an appeal, the Tribunal may, in relation to the imposition of a requirement or service of **7.64**
a notice, withdraw, confirm or vary the requirement or notice, or take such steps as the regulator could take in relation to the act or omission giving rise to the requirement or notice.
This could entail the imposition of an entirely different sanction to that against which the
appeal is brought. The Tribunal also has power to remit the decision whether to confirm the
requirement or notice, or any matter relating to that decision, to the regulator.

D. Environment Agency: penalty guidance and enforcement policy

Introduction

Articles 11–14 of the 2010 Order set out the requirements placed on the Environment **7.65**
Agency (and Natural England) to consult and publish guidance about their use of civil sanctions (penalty guidance)[61] and their approach to the enforcement of the relevant offences to
which they attach (enforcement policy).[62] The issuing of penalty guidance and an enforcement policy is a mandatory requirement for all those regulators awarded the civil sanctions
under Part 3. See further Chapter 6, parts B and D.

The EA has yet to publish its revised enforcement policy following its consultation, *Fairer* **7.66**
and Better Environmental Enforcement: Implementing the new civil sanctions, which closed
in May 2010. As part of that consultation, however, it envisaged a suite of three documents,
comprising a draft *Enforcement and Sanctions Policy*,[63] draft *Enforcement and Sanctions
Guidance* and a document entitled *Offence Response Options*, which will be published by the
EA. Once issued in their final form, these documents will set out the Agency's approach to
enforcement and application of the civil sanctions, as well as providing details as to how it
will apply its new civil sanctioning powers in practice. Each is now considered in turn.[64]

Penalty guidance

The draft *Enforcement and Sanctions Guidance* (draft guidance) sets out in more detail how **7.67**
the EA will determine what response it will take to incidents of regulatory non-compliance.
It establishes that the starting point for the EA to determine what response it should take will
be a consideration of what outcome it is trying to achieve.[65] For example, it provides that

---

[60] See further paras 8.150–8.152.
[61] RESA, s. 63.
[62] Ibid., s. 64.
[63] To be renamed an 'Enforcement & Sanction Statement', due to a desire to make it clear that government
alone makes policy, whilst regulating bodies devise processes and procedures to implement it.
[64] The schemes proposed by the EA draw significantly upon the DEFRA guidance considered below in the
context of Natural England, which has yet to publish its own draft proposals.
[65] Chapter 7.

when dealing with overt criminality, gross negligence or reckless behaviour, or where the seriousness of an offence requires that it be heard in a public forum, it will normally choose to prosecute.

7.68 It should be borne in mind throughout the following part that, at the time of writing, the guidance issued is in draft form only and may be subject to amendment after the completion of the consultation exercise.

Public interest factors

7.69 In determining which type of sanction to impose, the draft guidance makes it clear that the public interest will be taken into account in such a determination. In relation to such factors, the draft guidance states (as previously indicated) that offences that appear to have been committed deliberately, recklessly or as a result of gross negligence are more likely to result in prosecution. Conversely, where an offence was committed as a result of an accident or a genuine mistake, this is more likely to result in the use of advice and guidance, warning, or an available alternative civil sanction. The following other 'relevant factors' are set out in the draft guidance:

(i) Foreseeability: where the circumstances leading to the offence could reasonably have been foreseen, and no avoiding and/or preventative measures were taken, the response will normally give rise to a sanction beyond advice and guidance or the issuing of a warning.

(ii) Environmental effect: the EA would consider a prosecution, formal caution or a VMP in relation to a category 1 or 2 incident on the EA's common incident classification system.[66] Where EA staff are obstructed in the conduct of their duties or where the EA is provided with false or misleading information, the EA will normally prosecute.

(iii) Financial implications: the EA will take into account the financial implications of the offender's behaviour. Where legitimate business is undercut, or where profits are made or costs are avoided (such as costs saved by not obtaining a permit) this will normally lead to the imposition of a VMP or a prosecution.

(iv) Deterrent effect: both on the offender and others, will be taken into account. Prosecutions, because of their greater stigma if a conviction is secured, may be appropriate even for minor instances of non-compliance where they might contribute to a greater positive environmental or social impact. Conversely, where the use of a criminal sanction is considered to be likely to reduce future self-reporting of offences or non-compliance, the draft guidance states that civil sanctions may be more appropriate.

(v) Previous history: the degree of offending and/or non-compliance (including site-specific offending or generic failures by the offender) will be taken into account. The enforcement response is anticipated to escalate in normal circumstances, unless a different sanction is considered more likely to achieve the desired outcome. For example, the draft guidance states that a VMP combined with a restoration notice may achieve a better outcome for the environment (in terms of deterrence and behaviour change) than a criminal prosecution.

(vi) Attitude of the offender: where the offender is perceived to have a poor attitude towards the commission of the offence and/or is uncooperative with the investigation

---

[66] For further information on the Agency's incident classification system see: <http://www.environment-agency.gov.uk/business/regulation/>.

or remediation, this will normally lead to a prosecution or a VMP being considered by the EA. Conversely, where the offender provides the details of an offence to the EA voluntarily or through a self-reporting mechanism, this will be taken into account and influence the EA's choice of sanction.

(vii) Personal circumstances: the EA will 'consider' the personal circumstances of the offender.

The draft guidance concludes that   **7.70**

> [c]onsideration of these factors will normally indicate the appropriate sanction(s) likely to produce the desired outcome, in terms of lasting compliance with the law, redress for environmental harm and obtaining a good and lasting benefit for the environment, affected local communities and ensuring a level playing field for others.

Choice of sanction

Having set out the public interest factors that the EA will take into account in determining   **7.71**
the type of sanction, the draft guidance then provides examples that illustrate 'the sort of circumstances' in which sanctions under Part 3 of RESA 'might be used or accepted'.

Enforcement undertakings (EU) for example will only be accepted where the EA has suffi-   **7.72**
cient confidence that the terms of the EU will be delivered, and that they are more likely to be accepted when offered early. The EA expects that the terms of any EU will normally contain an element of restoration, as well as steps to ensure future compliance, such as long-term investment in environmental management systems. The draft guidance states that 'EUs should encourage legitimate business operators to make amends, come into compliance and prevent recurrence'. Again, as with an FMP, it should be noted that there is no provision for cost recovery, which may make the sanction a slightly less attractive option for the regulator.

Another example is provided in respect of FMPs. The EA considers that these will be most   **7.73**
suitable for offences with minor or no direct environmental impact, 'such as paperwork and administration offences'. They will be most appropriate where advice and draft guidance has failed to secure the necessary improvements. They can be issued for minor offences that need some kind of enforcement action but which, depending on the public interest factors, may not be serious enough to warrant a prosecution.

Variable monetary penalties

The EA is planning to set the level of the VMP in any individual case following a published   **7.74**
methodology. The EA anticipates that such sanctions will be applied, for example, in cases where there has been significant environmental damage but where other factors, such as the actions taken by the operator to clean up and prevent recurrence and the circumstances of the offence, mean that imposing a VMP may be appropriate. The draft guidance states that 'VMPs will also be used, where appropriate, to remove an identifiable financial gain or saving resulting from the non-compliance'. The EA may also choose to use VMPs where there is evidence of negligence and mismanagement. See below para. 7.79 for more about the methodology to be used in the calculation of a VMP.

Compliance notices

The draft guidance suggests that the EA will use these in cases 'where the offender has previ-   **7.75**
ously been in compliance with a requirement, such as regularly submitting returns, but is

currently not fulfilling their obligations'. The draft guidance states that a compliance notice should ensure that the offender takes action to stop the non-compliance, addresses the underlying causes and returns to compliance. They may be used where previous advice or guidance to encourage compliance has not been followed and a formal notice has become necessary.

Restoration notices

7.76 The draft guidance suggests that these notices could be used where damage has been caused to the environment and the action and work needed to address the damage can be identified and carried out by the offender. NE also consider that these sanctions could be used to secure the restoration of damaged habitats or protected species. The EA has stated that they may be used where restoration has not been undertaken voluntarily or it considers that a formal notice is otherwise necessary.

7.77 The draft guidance also sets out various 'methodologies' in relation to each type of civil sanction, which outline the processes involved for each of the civil sanctions available to the EA.[67]

Offence response options

7.78 The third and final document in the suite of policy and guidance documents that the EA proposes to publish to explain its approach to civil sanctions is entitled *Offence Response Options*. The current draft *Offence Response Options* replicates in tabular form the availability of the sanctions for each relevant offence, and includes a list of factors that should be taken into account when deciding which sanction should be applied.

VMP calculation methodology

7.79 Of considerable significance is the methodology that the EA has proposed to employ in assessing the sum of any VMP;[68] separate consideration is given to this below.

7.80 In preparing the methodology, the EA acknowledges that the government has issued guidance to regulators on how they must calculate VMPs; the EA's methodology follows that guidance. The three main components in the calculation of the amount of a VMP are:

(i) a financial benefit component: to remove the financial benefit from the offence in question, including avoided costs such as permit fees, operating savings arising from being non-compliant (e.g. equipment, staff, consultants etc.); and the financial benefit arising from operating at lower costs;

(ii) deterrent component: based on one of three starting points determined by the characteristics of the offence, which is then adjusted according to aggravating and mitigating factors; and

(iii) cost-deduction component: a reduction of the penalty having regard to the costs incurred by the offender.

Each of these components is now considered in turn.

---

[67] See above, para. 7.27.
[68] *Fairer and Better Environmental Enforcement: Implementing the new civil sanctions*, Annex 5.

Financial benefit component

It is likely that the application of the calculation methodology, and particularly the reason- **7.81** ableness or otherwise of the financial benefit calculation, will be highly contentious. Representations at the notice of intent stage are likely to focus closely on the calculation of the financial benefit component of any VMP.

The EA acknowledges that financial benefit will not always be an identifiable feature of a **7.82** case, particularly in some water pollution cases where there may be strict liability for the offence, but very little obvious gain. It has noted, however, that even in these cases some avoidance might have been possible e.g. alarms not installed and maintained, inadequate bunding, or security measures not installed. It has stated that these failures will be investigated and 'any costs avoided will be considered as financial benefit'.[69]

The EA considers that the financial benefit component would include all avoided costs where **7.83** these can be identified and estimated. These costs, which it states may include fees, registrations, taxes (e.g. landfill, unless they are being recovered by the relevant authority), operating costs such as administration, staff, consultants and set-up costs, will be assessed and estimated. If disputed or if is otherwise necessary, the EA states it will seek evidence of them from the offender. It will also assess any relevant set-up costs based on either current set-up costs, or costs at the time of the offending, whichever are higher. This is in order to prevent any advantage from deferring operational costs until such time as technologies and operational practices are cheaper, or obtaining an advantage from interest on non-expended sums or tax differentials.

Other aspects of the financial benefit are anticipated to be included where their consider- **7.84** ation addresses any competitive advantage that offenders have gained as a direct result of the offending behaviour. Examples given include the return of money not invested in plant, equipment or training, or profit accrued as a result of the non-compliance. This may be the case where, for example, the operation is 'intrinsically and wholly linked to the offence', such as operating a waste management facility without obtaining a permit, and where the business could not have been set up and continued other than by committing the offence.

The EA states that wherever possible the calculation of financial gain should be evidence- **7.85** based. As previously discussed[70] offenders can be required by virtue of the powers under Sch. 2, para. 5 of the 2010 Order to provide the information necessary for the determination of a proportionate VMP, including financial information. If they fail to comply with this requirement, the EA will estimate the financial benefit based on evidence, or based on similar cases or industry practices.

Deterrent component

The deterrent component is to be calculated by the selection of a starting point, which can **7.86** be one of either of the following: the financial benefit; the cost of restoration required by a notice; or the statutory maximum of the offending.

The considerations relevant to the selection of the correct starting point are not altogether **7.87** clear. The EA proposes that 'to reflect the seriousness of the offence, the starting point

---

[69] Annex 5, para. 2.1.
[70] See further paras. 7.59–7.61.

for determining the deterrent component will be that which is the most significant in terms of characterizing the offence. This is likely to be the starting point with the highest value.'[71]

7.88 Having identified an appropriate starting point, aggravating and mitigating features are then taken into account. A maximum multiplier (which overall cannot exceed four times the starting point) can be applied to the deterrent component. Similarly, mitigating features will reduce the deterrent component. Application of mitigating features will normally allow up to an 80 per cent reduction of the deterrent element, but the regime can allow for 100 per cent reduction in exceptional circumstances.

7.89 In order to calculate the aggravating features multiplier, blameworthiness, history of previous offending, foreseeability and risk of environmental harm, and ignoring previous advice or warnings, are all to be considered against a sliding scale, in order to identify a multiplier (up to a maximum value of four). The deterrent component is then multiplied by the aggravating multiplier before mitigating factors and deductions are considered.

7.90 Mitigating factors are then considered, and assigned a percentage value that is then applied to the deterrent component in order to reduce the overall deterrent component. Preventative measures, self-reporting, immediate and voluntary restoration, attitude to the offence, personal circumstances and 'case-specific factors' are all assigned a maximum possible percentage value according to the draft methodology. These percentage reductions are then applied to the deterrent component.

Deductions

7.91 The third and final component in the calculation of a VMP, the deductions component, operates to reduce the overall penalty by such costs incurred by the offender, and are solely related to the offence. These costs will be based on evidence supplied by the offender where necessary. These costs include:

   (i) the costs of complying with a compliance notice;
   (ii) the costs to the offender of any restoration undertaken as a result of the serving of a restoration notice;
   (iii) any costs recovered by the EA from the offender using an enforcement cost recovery notice;
   (iv) a discretionary deduction to account for (and encourage) voluntary restoration and repayment; and
   (v) payments to compensate those affected as part of a third party undertaking, which can be taken into account on the basis of a £1 deduction per £2 spent, for up to one-third of the overall penalty. Deductions for a third party undertaking will be made before any other deductions are considered.

7.92 Where the total deductions equal or exceed the overall penalty, then a nominal VMP of £1 will be issued. In terms of maximum values, a VMP cannot exceed the statutory maximum for an offence that is summary in nature.

---

[71] Annex 5, para. 2.1.

Enforcement policy

The draft *Enforcement and Sanctions Policy*[72] sets out the general principles that the EA **7.93** intends to follow in relation to enforcement and sanctioning. It states expressly that when considering the appropriate course of action to ensure compliance, the EA aims to follow the Macrory Penalty Principles as set out in the *Regulators' Compliance Code*.[73] To ensure that senior management have close scrutiny of the use of these measures, internal procedures are being devised by the EA to ensure the necessary degree of involvement.

E. Natural England: penalty guidance and enforcement policy

Introduction

Natural England has committed to publishing guidance in relation to its civil sanction pow- **7.94** ers, and to consulting on the guidance before formal publication, in accordance with the statutory regime.[74] At the time of writing, no consultation has been launched by Natural England. It is understood that the consultation is proposed to be undertaken in early 2011.

Penalty guidance

DEFRA has published guidance entitled *Civil sanctions for environmental offences*[75] (January **7.95** 2010) about the use of the civil sanctions. The guidance applies to Natural England as well as to the Environment Agency. At the time of writing, it constitutes the only guidance about how the civil sanctions to which Natural England have access might operate. The guidance is non-statutory and sets out how the *government* expects the civil sanctions powers to be used in practice in this field.

Natural England's own policy and guidance will be developed to accord with the DEFRA **7.96** guidance. Amongst the principles that are said should be applied to civil sanctions for environmental offences are those to prevent harm from continuing or recurring, to ensure that damage is restored, to ensure that 'the polluter pays', and to remove any financial benefit from offending.[76]

The DEFRA guidance draws attention to the requirement for regulators to discuss the cir- **7.97** cumstances of an offence with those suspected of it, so that the circumstances can be taken into account when deciding on the best approach to respond to an incident, in all cases apart from those where immediate action is required.[77]

DEFRA recognizes that regulators have in the past been over-reliant on criminal prosecu- **7.98** tions and accordingly encourages the use of civil sanctions in place of prosecution where it is appropriate and proportionate to do so.

---

[72] To be renamed an 'Enforcement & Sanction Statement' from a desire to make it more evident that government alone makes environmental policy, whilst regulating bodies devise processes and procedures to implement it.

[73] See further paras 4.35–4.43.

[74] See 2010 Order, arts 11–13.

[75] A copy is available on the DEFRA website: <http://www.defra.gov.uk>.

[76] Para. 2.1.

[77] Para. 2.5.

7.99   The guidance deals with all aspects relating to the issuing of the civil sanctions; a number of the key features are considered below.

Compliance notices

7.100   The use of compliance notices is encouraged in order to address the causes of an offence, where the offence is continuing, or there is a risk that the offence might recur due to the continuation of a state of affairs. Compliance notices can for example require works to be undertaken, a change made to a process, or training of staff. In such circumstances it would be prudent for the regulator where possible to engage in discussions with the relevant business as to the precise wording of the notice, given the entitlement under art. 7 of the 2010 Order to impose a monetary penalty ('a non-compliance penalty') in respect of the same offence (irrespective of whether a VMP was also imposed in respect of that offence). The terms of the notice must therefore be clear and specific in terms of their requirements so that the imposition of any further penalty can, in the event of challenge, be properly justified.

Restoration notices

7.101   The use of restoration notices is encouraged where there has been harm to the environment, in order to remedy that harm. Restoration notices are used to ensure restoration of natural resources or the environment to the pre-existing position that would have persisted but for the offence. This could be by undertaking work on the affected site itself, or by improvements elsewhere. The guidance recognizes that in some cases the cost of restoration would be out of proportion to the benefit to be gained from restoration.

7.102   Examples of works that could be required by restoration notices include removal or treatment of contamination, reinstatement of natural resources such as plants and wildlife, and longer-term management of the affected site. The guidance stresses the importance of specifying clearly the actions required to be taken and the outcomes to be obtained.

Variable monetary penalties

7.103   VMPs are covered in the DEFRA guidance in some detail. The guidance illustrates how difficult it could be for regulators such as Natural England[78] to assess the amount of a VMP, and in particular the deterrent component, in a way that is fair and transparent. It is likely that regard will be paid to the methodology already published by the EA.

7.104   Whilst the 2010 Order caps the amount of a VMP for an either way offence at £250,000,[79] in setting the level of VMPs regulators are empowered to impose greater fines than those that may previously have been imposed in the criminal courts after a criminal prosecution. This is starkly demonstrated in the provided example of a calculation of a VMP for damage done to a site of special scientific interest, the resultant sum being far greater than would be expected for a fine for a similar offence imposed in a magistrates' court.[80] Only a small proportion of fines imposed by the criminal courts after successful prosecutions of offences for environmental damage have exceeded £250,000.

---

[78] The scheme set out in the methodology proposed by the EA and considered above draws significantly upon the DEFRA guidance.

[79] 2010 Order, Sch. 2, para. 1(5).

[80] See for example section 17.8 of Paul Stookes (ed.), *Costing the Earth: guidance for sentencers* (Magistrates Association, 2009). A copy is available at: <http://www.magistrates-association.org.uk>.

The ability to pay appears to be mentioned in the guidance as something of an afterthought, **7.105** whereas in the criminal setting, courts are obliged to take into account the financial circumstances of the offender.[81]

Enforcement undertakings

Enforcement undertakings are introduced by DEFRA as presenting opportunities for **7.106** streamlining enforcement action for environmental offences and, to this end, their use is encouraged. The guidance suggests that enforcement undertakings will only be acceptable in lieu of a formal civil sanction if they are sufficiently 'full and unreserved'. Such undertakings will not be acceptable in lieu of a proposed criminal prosecution. It is said that it should be demonstrated that the measures proposed in an enforcement undertaking fully restore the harm done.

From the perspective of a non-compliant business, given that the guidance seeks a full offer **7.107** of remedial action *and* compensation to affected parties, the only real advantage to be gained by a business in offering an enforcement undertaking would be to seek to avoid the issue of a VMP altogether (and the associated stigma that followed). The risk inherent in bringing non-compliant behaviour to the attention of the regulator is that, once done, unless the regulator considers that an enforcement undertaking has been wholly complied with, then a new civil sanction or criminal prosecution may be instituted.[82] Of course, prolonged and wilful failure to take such a step may equally, in the longer term, bring with it more serious consequences.

The guidance makes plain that the undertakings should not be negotiated, although it might **7.108** be appropriate for Natural England to seek clarification in relation to an undertaking that is offered by a non-compliant business.

Stop notices

Whilst stop notices are considered in the DEFRA guidance, they are introduced with cau- **7.109** tion, seemingly due to the considerations related to whether the overall public interest is served by their issue, particularly given the wider impact that these notices may have. The guidance also rightly draws attention to the provision permitting compensation to be paid where a stop notice is unreasonably imposed.

The impact assessment in the *Explanatory Memorandum to the 2010 Order*[83] states that it **7.110** could 'generally be assumed that regulators will only use stop notices where there are severe negative consequences of an operation and that the costs of stopping an installation will generally be justified by the benefits in terms of avoided negative consequences'.[84]

Choice of sanction

The *Explanatory Memorandum to the 2010 Order* states that prosecution should be **7.111** 'reserved for the worst offenders'.[85] The DEFRA guidance sets out the factors, which in the government's view, would tend to suggest that a criminal prosecution rather than a civil

---

[81] See Criminal Justice Act 2003, s. 164.
[82] Para. 4.3.
[83] *Explanatory Memorandum to The Environmental Civil Sanctions (England) Order 2010* and the Environmental Civil Sanctions (Miscellaneous Amendments) (England) Regulations 2010, SI 1159/2010.
[84] Para. 47.
[85] Para. 7.4.

sanction was more appropriate.[86] If one or more of the factors are present, this tends to suggest that a prosecution would be more appropriate.[87] It is only in the absence of any of the listed factors that a civil sanction can be expected.[88] However, the list of factors is so long, and the factors are so commonly occurring in situations where offences are committed, it is perhaps to be doubted that the guidance alone would result in many offences being steered away from the criminal prosecution route towards a civil sanction. For example, factors tending to suggest that a prosecution would be appropriate include where there has been a 'significant deviation' from a legal requirement, the offence was committed 'intentionally or with recklessness or negligence', or the incident was 'foreseeable'; few offences fall outside the ambit of this list of factors.

7.112   Furthermore, the risk of serious environmental harm is identified in the DEFRA guidance as a particular consideration that would normally tend to point towards prosecution rather than a civil sanction being appropriate.

7.113   The guidance highlights the fact that environmental offences are usually strict liability offences and that even though a person may be guilty of an offence, there is often limited culpability in the circumstances. The use of civil sanctions is positively encouraged in such circumstances and seen as being more fairly to recognize the situation.[89] Indeed, the guidance says that absent other aggravating factors, civil sanctions can be appropriate even in cases where substantial environmental damage has been caused.[90]

Appeals

7.114   Appeals to the First-tier Tribunal (General Regulatory Chamber)[91] can be made against the imposition of the civil sanctions as well as non-compliance penalties and enforcement cost recovery notices. Specific grounds of appeal are set out in the 2010 Order; notably the grounds of appeal are not finite and essentially, any reason may form a ground of appeal.[92]

7.115   In the impact assessment in the *Explanatory Memorandum to the 2010 Order*, Natural England predicted that of the eighty or so appealable sanctions to be issued each year, only four would be appealed to the First-tier Tribunal. Moreover, it predicted that of the thirty-six VMPs issued each year, only two would be appealed, or around 5 per cent. However, if VMPs are as high in comparison to fines on criminal convictions as the guidance suggests they might be, then an appeal rate of higher than 5 per cent is perhaps to be expected. The impact assessment recognizes that the appeal rates are 'relatively low' but says that this is because the regulators will be 'careful to avoid applying sanctions in a way that is unreasonable'.[93]

7.116   There is a further right of appeal to the Upper Tribunal on a point of law, subject to permission being granted by the First-tier Tribunal or the Upper Tribunal. The DEFRA guidance

---

[86]   Figure 2. Also referred to as 'Table B'.
[87]   Para. 3.13.
[88]   Para. 3.8.
[89]   Para. 3.12.
[90]   Para. 3.16.
[91]   See Chapter 8 for a full consideration of the appeals available.
[92]   See for example 2010 Order, Sch. 2, para. 8(2). These grounds of appeal under the 2010 Order are considerably wider than anticipated under RESA.
[93]   Annex 1, para. 8.

says that appeals against stop notices should be fast-tracked, as they are not suspended where an appeal is made unless the First-tier Tribunal so directs.

Enforcement policy

Natural England proposes to issue *functional guidance* intended to outline the available enforcement mechanisms and the decision-making process that Natural England will follow, as well as providing a broad indication of the likely enforcement action that will result for each relevant offence. At the time of writing, it is understood that the functional guidance has been drafted but has not yet been published, as it is intended to be revised to take account of the civil sanctions regime. Natural England's guidance under RESA, s. 64 will follow some considerable way down the line. **7.117**

Approach to the civil sanctions

In the absence of a published enforcement policy, those interested in the approach that Natural England will take with regard to the civil sanctions may be assisted by considering Natural England's stated approach to the new regime. **7.118**

Natural England welcomed being given the powers to impose the civil sanctions under Part 3, stating that the powers would enable it to tackle breaches of legislation in a more flexible manner than it had been able to in the past.[94] Natural England considered that civil sanctions would help fill a gap between mere warnings and full criminal prosecutions and that they would: '[e]nable regulators to match the strength of sanctions to the gravity of the offence, and [to] better reflect the fact that most breaches of environmental law are unintentional'. **7.119**

When responding to the Cabinet Office consultation on the draft Bill, Natural England provided a number of illustrations of how it might use its powers in practice. It indicated, for example, that it would seek to issue stop notices where work was being done that caused harm to an SSSI. A further example of how Natural England might deploy the civil sanctions was given by the Agency in its recent Hampton Implementation Review,[95] in which it was reported that Natural England would prefer to use a stop notice rather than a criminal prosecution against a property developer, as prosecution was sometimes an ineffective remedy, fines tending to be low when set against the profits potentially available to developers. **7.120**

The *Explanatory Memorandum to the 2010 Order*[96] included an impact assessment of how the Order would affect Natural England's work. It assumed that the cases which employ civil sanctions will generally be offences relating to SSSIs, which had previously been dealt with by way of cautions. The impact assessment predicted that some thirteen compliance notices would be issued each year, and thirty-six restoration notices with VMPs would be issued. It also predicted thirty-three FMPs each year. There was no corresponding prediction in the reduction of the number of criminal prosecutions. **7.121**

---

[94] Natural England press notice, dated 3 February 2010.
[95] BIS, *Natural England: A Hampton Implementation Review Report* (July 2009).
[96] *Explanatory Memorandum to the Environmental Civil Sanctions (England) Order 2010*, and the Environmental Civil Sanctions (Miscellaneous Amendments) (England) Regulations 2010, SI 1159/2010.

PART III

APPEAL AND JUDICIAL REVIEW

8

APPEAL AND JUDICIAL REVIEW

A. Introduction

Decisions taken by regulators to impose the civil sanctions under Part 3 of RESA are **8.01**
amenable to appeal, in the first instance to the First-tier Tribunal, and then onward, to the
Upper Tribunal on a point of law, and in certain prescribed circumstances, to the Court of
Appeal. Parts C–F of this chapter consider each stage of the appeal process, providing appellants and respondents with the information needed in order to navigate the new tribunal

system, as well as looking at the judicial review jurisdiction of the Upper Tribunal. Part G, on judicial review, applies as much to Parts 1 and 2 of RESA as it does to Part 3, setting out the position of the law in relation to the availability of relief by way of judicial review.[1] The compatibility of the Part 3 regime with the European Convention on Human Rights is given separate consideration in Chapter 4, part B.

B. Background to the RESA appeal regime

Tribunals Courts and Enforcement Act 2007

8.02 The Tribunals Courts and Enforcement Act 2007 (TCEA) provides the statutory framework for a far-reaching and significant restructuring of the tribunal system,[2] with two completely new tribunals, the First-tier Tribunal and the Upper Tribunal.

8.03 RESA provides that appeals against the imposition of the civil sanctions under Part 3, from non-compliant businesses and individuals, will be made, in the first instance, to the First-tier Tribunal.[3] In August 2010 the Tribunal Service established the specialist First-tier Tribunal (Environment) to handle appeals against the civil sanctions spearheaded by the DEFRA agencies[4] and a website for appeals to this tribunal.[5]

8.04 TCEA provides for onward appeal to the Upper Tribunal and ultimately, to the Court of Appeal.

The Leggatt Report

8.05 TCEA came about following a comprehensive review of the tribunal system in 2001 by Sir Andrew Leggatt, a former Lord Justice of Appeal.[6] The review had as its stated objective 'to recommend a [tribunal] system that [was] independent, coherent, professional, cost-effective and user-friendly. Together tribunals must form a system and provide a service fit for the users for whom they were intended.'[7]

8.06 A government White Paper in 2004,[8] which largely accepted Leggatt's recommendations, led ultimately to TCEA. According to the White Paper, the tribunal service was to:

> become a new type of organisation, not just a federation of existing tribunals. It will have a straightforward mission: to resolve disputes in the best way possible and to stimulate improved decision making so that disputes do not happen as a result of poor decision making.

---

[1] Law correct as of date of publication.

[2] The creation of a single Upper Tribunal and of a unified set of rules on appeal has been described as 'probably the most significant innovation in the tribunal system' (Carnwath LJ, Senior President of Tribunals, *Tribunals Transformed* (2010), para. 26).

[3] Or another tribunal created under an enactment: RESA, s. 54(1)(b).

[4] Environment Agency, Natural England and the Countryside Council for Wales.

[5] <http://www.tribunals.gov.uk/Environment/RulesLegislation.htm>. The website includes relevant decisions, forms and guidance, rules and legislation and links to related sources.

[6] *Tribunals for Users—One System, One Service* (August 2001). A copy is available on an archived page of the Ministry of Justice's website: http://www.tribunals-review.org.uk>.

[7] *Tribunals for Users—One System, One Service*, para. 1.

[8] *Transforming Public Services: Complaints, Redress and Tribunals.*

Macrory Review

Central to Professor Richard Macrory's vision of a new sanctions regime[9] was an appeal pro-   **8.07**
cess permitting businesses access to an effective and swift appeal route against administrative
penalties.[10] Macrory recommended that such appeals be heard by a new specialist independent tribunal and not by the criminal courts. In respect of the latter recommendation,
Macrory's vision has been fulfilled in the guise of the First-tier Tribunal, established under
TCEA, which is likely to hear all appeals brought against the civil sanctions.[11]

It is less easy at this stage to assess the extent to which the appeal regime under RESA and   **8.08**
TCEA is likely to be 'accessible', 'effective' and 'swift'. There is no provision in RESA requiring regulators to hold a hearing prior to the imposition of a civil sanction (although in many
cases this will be a prudent approach, as previously suggested), nor to hold a review of that
decision should the business be dissatisfied with the original assessment. If the order, or the
regulator's own guidance, goes no further than these minimum statutory requirements, the
only opportunity for a business wishing to challenge the administrative decision to impose
the penalty will be by way of an appeal to the First-tier Tribunal.

Appeals are generally expensive, time consuming and likely to require lawyers; in all proba-   **8.09**
bility it will be small businesses that will be hit the hardest by these provisions. Some small
and medium-size businesses may take the view that they have little option other than to
accept the penalty imposed against them, because the route to challenge is simply too costly
to contemplate. Appeals are more likely to come from larger companies which have the
funds to support potentially expensive litigation.

Internal review prior to an appeal

It was a recommendation of Macrory that there should be an internal review available to   **8.10**
businesses and individuals before they needed to have recourse to an external appeal.[12]
Regulators devising an appeal regime would be well advised to consider including such a step
in appropriate cases and ensure that any such process does not compromise or diminish to
any extent any existing right of appeal.

The remainder of this chapter comprehensively considers the various routes by which deci-   **8.11**
sions made under RESA can be challenged, both by way of the administrative tribunals
created under TCEA, and through the courts.

C. Overview of the RESA appeal provisions

RESA sets out the appeal requirements for which any order awarding the civil sanctions must   **8.12**
make provision, stipulating as a minimum which decisions must be made susceptible to an
appeal, and the minimum grounds of appeal that must be provided for.

---

[9] Considered in detail in Chapter 1.
[10] Richard Macrory, *Regulatory Justice: Making Sanctions Effective*, p. 53, para. 3.54.
[11] Appeals may also be heard by 'another tribunal created under an enactment': s. 54(1)(b).
[12] Macrory, *Regulatory Justice: Making Sanctions Effective*, p. 55, para. 3.62.

To where does appeal lie?

8.13   Section 54 of RESA provides that in the first instance all appeals will either be to the First-tier Tribunal[13] established under TCEA, or to any other statutory tribunal to be specified by the minister in the order.[14] According to the *Regulatory Enforcement and Sanctions Act 2008: Explanatory Notes,* this exception is to cater for tribunals that will not form part of the First-tier Tribunal (such as employment tribunals that currently hear some health and safety appeals) and as such may be an appropriate venue for hearing certain appeals under this part.[15]

8.14   TCEA provides that dissatisfied appellants can appeal further from the First-tier Tribunal to the Upper Tribunal[16] and then to the Court of Appeal on points of law.[17] Challenge by way of judicial review, both to the High Court and via the judicial review jurisdiction of the Upper Tribunal,[18] is also available in certain circumstances.[19]

Which decisions can be appealed?

8.15   In summary, any order made under Part 3 must provide for the following decisions taken by a regulator to be appealed (in so far as they are relevant):

(i)   the imposition of a fixed monetary penalty (FMP);[20]

(ii)   the imposition of a discretionary requirement;[21]

(iii)   the imposition of a stop notice;[22]

(iv)   the decision by the regulator not to issue a completion certificate to a business or individual who asserts they have complied with a stop notice;[23]

(v)   following the making of an enforcement undertaking, against the refusal of a regulator to certify that the undertaking has been complied with (subject to this being included by the minister in the order);[24] and

(vi)   the decision of a regulator to impose the requirement to pay costs and/or the amount of those costs.[25]

8.16   There is no requirement in RESA that the order make provision for a business to be able to appeal against the making of an enforcement undertaking, largely because such undertakings come about through the mutual agreement of the business and the regulator.

---

[13]   The General Regulatory Chamber of the First-tier Tribunal will hear the appeals.
[14]   RESA, s. 54(1)(b).
[15]   *Regulatory Enforcement and Sanctions Act 2008: Explanatory Notes,* para. 144.
[16]   TCEA, s. 11. Subject to being granted permission to appeal by one of the Tribunals.
[17]   Ibid., s. 13.
[18]   Ibid., s. 15.
[19]   See part H.
[20]   RESA, s. 40(2)(e).
[21]   Ibid., s. 43(2)(e).
[22]   Ibid., s. 47(2)(b).
[23]   Ibid., s. 47(2)(g).
[24]   Ibid., s. 50(5)(h).
[25]   Ibid., s. 53(4)(d).

D. Appeal to the First-tier Tribunal

Introduction

An order made under Part 3, awarding a regulator the civil sanctions, must also make provi-**8.17**
sion for a business or individual upon whom a sanction has been imposed, to be able to
appeal such a decision. Where the order provides for appeals against adverse decisions made
by regulators, those appeals will be, in the first instance, to the General Regulatory Chamber
of the First-tier Tribunal.[26]

The following discussion of the appeal process to the General Regulatory Chamber[27] of the **8.18**
First-tier Tribunal is based on an appeal from a decision of a regulator[28] to impose a RESA
Part 3 sanction.

Jurisdiction

The First-tier Tribunal has jurisdiction over a wide range of appeals formerly heard by other **8.19**
tribunals.[29] The Upper Tribunal may hear appeals from the General Regulatory Chamber of
the First-tier Tribunal against the imposition of the Part 3 sanctions, where the order so
provides.

The First-tier Tribunal is divided into six chambers[30] each of which has its own chamber **8.20**
president.

Grounds of appeal

The availability of an appeal and the permissible grounds of any such appeal will be provided **8.21**
for in the order and will vary from regulator to regulator, and from sanction to sanction. Any
order awarding the civil sanctions to regulators must provide for the following minimum
grounds of appeal:

Fixed monetary penalty
 (i) that the decision was based on an error of fact;
 (ii) that the decision was wrong in law;
 (iii) that the decision was unreasonable.[31]

Discretionary requirement
 (i) that the decision was based on an error of fact;
 (ii) that the decision was wrong in law;
 (iii) in the case of a variable monetary penalty (VMP), that the amount of the penalty is
     unreasonable;

---

[26] RESA, s. 54(1)(a). Or, another tribunal created under an enactment: s. 54(1)(b).
[27] See fn. 4 to para. 8.03 concerning the new First-tier (Environment) Tribunal which falls within the General Regulatory Chamber.
[28] See para. 4.58 for more on the definition of regulator.
[29] For a full list see the website of the Tribunal Service: <http://www.tribunals.gov.uk>.
[30] At the time of writing, a timetable for the establishment and remit of the seventh chamber, the Land Property and Housing Chamber, was yet to be decided.
[31] RESA, s. 40(6).

    (iv) in the case of a non-monetary discretionary requirement, that the nature of the requirement is unreasonable; and

    (v) that the decision was unreasonable for any other reason.[32]

Stop notice

    (i) that the decision was based on an error of fact;

    (ii) that the decision was wrong in law;

    (iii) that the decision was unreasonable;

    (iv) that any step specified in the notice is unreasonable;

    (v) that the person has not committed the relevant offence and would not have committed it had the stop notice not been served;

    (vi) that the person would not, by reason of any defence, have been liable to be convicted of the relevant offence had the stop notice not been served.[33]

8.22   There is no requirement in RESA that the order make provision for a business to seek to appeal against the making of an enforcement undertaking, largely because such undertakings come about through the mutual agreement of the business and the regulator.

Appeal as of right

8.23   Whilst most crucial decisions taken by a regulator will be susceptible to challenge by an aggrieved person, such appeals do not have to be provided for as of right.[34] Rather, RESA provides certain specific grounds of appeal that must be included in any order, and the minister retains a residual discretion to include others.

8.24   The government placed a good deal of emphasis on the independent appeal tribunal[35] as being a valuable safeguard available to businesses,[36] even though the terms of RESA attempt to limit the circumstances in which an appeal can be made. In order for the regime in its present form to achieve Convention compliance, regulators may wish to give careful consideration to seeking to provide for an appeal 'as of right', rather than on the more limited grounds that RESA envisages. A lack of conformity with the Convention at first instance may be capable of being rectified on appeal by a body that does conform to the Convention guarantees.[37]

8.25   The Environmental Civil Sanctions (England) Order 2010,[38] which awards the civil sanctioning powers to the Environment Agency and Natural England, permits appeals to be made on all of the required statutory grounds (under RESA, Part 3), as well for 'any other reason'.

---

[32] RESA, s. 43(7).

[33] Ibid., s. 47(4).

[34] An appeal as of right is an automatic appeal which the court or tribunal cannot refuse to hear.

[35] The First-tier tribunal, established by the TCEA.

[36] See for example Lord Bach's comments: Hansard, HL Deb., vol. 30, col. GC335 (January 2008).

[37] *Albert Le Compte v Belgium* (1983) 5 EHRR 533, para. 29; *Gautrin and Others v France* (1999) 28 EHRR 196. The courts have said that an appeal to a full court of jurisdiction 'does not purge a breach of the Convention. It prevents such a breach from occurring in the first place': *Tehrani v United Kingdom v Central Council for Nursing and Midwifery and Health Visiting* [2001] IRLR 2; [2001] Scot CS 19.

[38] SI 1157/2010. See also the the Environmental Civil Sanctions (Wales) Order 2010, SI 1821/2010, which makes similar provision.

Commencing an appeal

Notice of appeal

Appeals against the imposition of Part 3 sanctions to the First-tier Tribunal are to be made by **8.26** way of a notice of appeal, which must contain, *inter alia,* contact details of the appellant and his representative, the pleaded grounds of appeal and the relief ('result') sought.[39] The appellant is responsible for submitting at this stage any written decision that it has been provided with, or any statement of reasons for that decision that it can 'reasonably obtain'.[40]

All notices of appeal and accompanying documentation will be sent by the Tribunal to each **8.27** respondent.[41]

Time limit

The notice of appeal must be sent or delivered to the Tribunal so that it is received within **8.28** twenty-eight days of the date on which the regulator's decision was sent to the appellant.[42]

Appeals made outside this time may still be lodged, but must include a retrospective request **8.29** for an extension of time, along with any 'reason why the notice of appeal was not provided in time',[43] and may not be admitted unless the Tribunal agrees to extend the time allowed.[44] Extensions may be awarded by the Tribunal under its power in r. 5(3)(a) of the First-tier Tribunal Procedure Rules.

Responding to an appeal

Respondents are obliged to submit a response to the notice of appeal. The response must **8.30** include, as a minimum:

 (i) the name and address of the respondent;
 (ii) the name and address of the respondent's representative (if any);
 (iii) an address where documents for the respondent may be sent or delivered;
 (iv) any further information or documents required by a practice direction or direction;
 (v) whether the respondent would be content for the case to be dealt with without a hearing if the Tribunal considers it appropriate;[45]
 (vi) a statement as to whether the respondent opposes the appellant's case and, if so, any grounds for opposition 'which are not contained in another document provided with the response';[46] and
 (vii) where the respondent challenges a decision, a copy of any written record of that decision, and any statement of reasons for that decision, that the appellant did not provide with the notice of appeal and the respondent has or can reasonably obtain.[47]

---

[39] Tribunal Procedure (First-tier Tribunal) (General Regulatory Chamber) Rules 2009, SI 1976/2009, r. 22(2).
[40] Ibid.
[41] Ibid., r. 22(5).
[42] Ibid., r. 22(3).
[43] Ibid., r. 22(4)(a).
[44] Ibid., r. 22(4)(b).
[45] Ibid., r. 23(2).
[46] Ibid., r. 23(3).
[47] Ibid., r. 23(4).

8.31 The respondent is responsible for serving copies of the response and any accompanying documentation on all other parties, at the same time that the response is served on the Tribunal.[48]

Time limit

8.32 Rule 23(1) of the First-tier Tribunal Procedure Rules provides that the response must be sent or delivered to the Tribunal so that it is received within twenty-eight days of the date on which the respondent received notice of the appeal. The Tribunal may agree to the admission of late replies utilizing its power under r. 5(3)(a) to extend the time.

8.33 Responses submitted after this time must include a retrospective request for an extension of time under r. 5(3)(a) of the First-tier Tribunal Procedure Rules, and must include the 'reason why the response was not provided in time'.

Appellant's reply

8.34 Upon receipt of the respondent's response, the appellant may, but is not obliged to, submit a further statement or documentation by way of response.[49] The appellant is responsible for sending or delivering a copy of any reply and accompanying documents to the Tribunal.[50]

Time limit

8.35 Responses must be sent or delivered to the Tribunal within fourteen days of the date on which the respondent sent the response to the appellant.[51] Late replies must be accompanied by a 'request for extension of time and the reason why the reply was not provided in time'.[52] The Tribunal may agree to the admission of late replies utilizing its power under r. 5(3)(a) to extend the time.

The hearing

Nature of the hearing

8.36 Rule 32 of the First-tier Tribunal Procedure Rules provides that the Tribunal 'must hold a hearing before making a decision which disposes of the application'. This rule is subject to four important exceptions, where a hearing is not mandatory:

   (i) where each party consents to the matter being determined without a hearing;[53]

   (ii) where the Tribunal is satisfied that it can properly determine the issues without a hearing;[54]

   (iii) where the Tribunal agrees to strike out the appellant's case under r. 8;[55] or

   (iv) where the Tribunal has considered a preliminary issue, after the disposal of which no further issues remain to be determined.[56]

---

[48] Ibid., r. 23(7).
[49] Ibid., r. 24(1).
[50] Ibid., r. 24(5).
[51] Ibid., r. 24(2).
[52] Ibid., r. 24(3).
[53] Ibid., r. 32(1)(a).
[54] Ibid., r. 32(1)(b).
[55] Ibid., r. 33(1). See further para. 8.144 for more about the striking out procedure under r. 8.
[56] Ibid., r. 32(4).

There is a presumption that all hearings will be held in public, although r. 35(2) permits the **8.37** Tribunal to direct that all or some of the hearing may be held in private. Such decisions should be made only very rarely and where the interests of justice cannot otherwise be served. Reasons should be given for any such decisions made. The Tribunal is also empowered to exclude persons from the hearing in certain circumstances[57] and permitted to direct that witnesses are excluded until after they have given evidence.[58]

Each party is entitled to attend any hearing that is held and/or send written representations **8.38** to the Tribunal and each other party prior to the hearing.[59]

Proceeding in absence

The Tribunal is permitted to proceed to hear an appeal in the absence of a party if it: **8.39**

(i) is satisfied that the party has been notified of the hearing or that reasonable steps have been taken to notify the party of the hearing; and

(ii) considers that it is in the interests of justice to proceed with the hearing.[60]

Notice of the hearing

Notice of a hearing date and venue must be 'reasonable' and of no less than fourteen days **8.40** where the hearing is to consider disposal of the proceedings (unless parties agree a shorter period or in 'urgent or exceptional circumstances').[61]

Standard of proof

As discussed in previous chapters, the standard of proof will be stipulated in the order award- **8.41** ing the Part 3 powers to the regulator.

Decision making

Decisions must be announced orally at the hearing and, subject to the exceptions provided **8.42** in r. 14(10) as to prevention of disclosure or publication, must also be communicated in writing to each party as soon as practicable after the decision 'which finally disposes of all issues in the proceedings'.[62]

If the decision of the Tribunal is not unanimous, the decision of the majority is the decision **8.43** of the Tribunal. The presiding member has a casting vote if the votes are equally divided.[63] Where a matter is to be decided by two or more members of a Tribunal, the matter may, if the parties to the case agree, be decided in the absence of one or more (but not all) of the members chosen to decide the matter.[64]

Powers of the Tribunal

RESA does not provide a definitive list of the powers of the Tribunal on an appeal; instead, **8.44** s. 54(3)(b) enables the minister to make provision about the powers of any appellate body in

---

[57] Ibid., r. 35(4).
[58] Ibid., r. 35(5).
[59] Ibid., r. 32(4).
[60] Ibid., r. 36.
[61] Ibid., r. 34.
[62] Ibid., r. 38.
[63] First-tier Tribunal and Upper Tribunal (Composition of Tribunal) Order 2008, SI 2835/2008, art. 8.
[64] TCEA, Sch. 4, para. 15(6).

the order. Examples of the powers that may be included by the minister in the order are set out in s. 54(4), and provide that the Tribunal may be empowered to:

    (i) withdraw the requirement or notice;
    (ii) confirm the requirement or notice;
    (iii) take such steps as the regulator could take in relation to the act or omission giving rise to the requirement or notice;
    (iv) remit the decision whether to confirm the requirement or notice, or any matter relating to that decision, to the regulator; and
    (v) award costs.

8.45 The BERR *Regulatory Enforcement and Sanctions Act 2008: Guidance to the Act* suggests that detailed procedural rules governing how the Tribunal will use these powers may either be made under the establishing legislation of the Tribunal, or under powers in RESA.

8.46 The Tribunal Procedure Rules do not make detailed provision about the powers of the Tribunal on any appeal, providing only one substantive outcome in r. 37, namely a consent order. Instead, orders awarding the civil sanctioning powers will provide for the powers of the Tribunal on appeal. In respect of appeals from decisions to impose the civil sanction taken by the Environment Agency and Natural England, the First-tier Tribunal is empowered to do the following: suspend or vary a stop notice;[65] in relation to the imposition of a requirement or service of a notice, withdraw the requirement or notice;[66] confirm the requirement or notice;[67] vary the requirement or notice;[68] take such steps as the regulator could take in relation to the act or omission giving rise to the requirement or notice;[69] or remit the decision whether to confirm the requirement or notice, or any matter relating to that decision, to the regulator.[70]

Mistakes and omissions

8.47 Rule 40 of the First-tier Tribunal Procedure Rules empowers the First-tier Tribunal to be able to review its own decisions where there has been a clerical mistake, accidental slip or omission in a decision, direction or document produced by it.[71] This will obviate the need for an onward appeal in many cases, for example where there has been an obvious error in the record. Reviews may be carried out either of the Tribunal's own initiative, or following an application by any party who has a right of appeal in respect of the decision.[72] Such reviews may take place 'at any time'.

Powers on review

8.48 Tribunals exercising their review function may correct accidental errors in the decision or in a record of the decision,[73] amend the reasons given for the decision,[74] or set aside

---

[65] Environmental Civil Sanctions (England) Order 2010, SI 1157/2010, art. 10(5).
[66] Ibid., art. 10(6)(a).
[67] Ibid., art. 10(6)(b).
[68] Ibid., art. 10(6)(c).
[69] Ibid., art. 10(6)(d).
[70] Ibid., art. 10(6)(e).
[71] Tribunal Procedure (First-tier Tribunal) (General Regulatory Chamber) Rules 2009, SI 1976/2009, r. 40. Provision made pursuant to TCEA, s. 9(1).
[72] TCEA, s. 9(2).
[73] Ibid., s. 9(4)(a).
[74] Ibid., s. 9(4)(b).

the decision.[75] If a decision of the First-tier Tribunal is set aside under this provision, it must either redecide the matter concerned, or refer the matter to the Upper Tribunal.[76] If the matter is referred to the Upper Tribunal, it will then be responsible for redeciding the matter.[77]

8.49 No decision of the First-tier Tribunal may be reviewed more than once, and a decision of the Tribunal not to review a decision is not reviewable or appealable.[78] Further challenge of a decision beyond the single review may only be made by appeal on a point of law to the Upper Tribunal.

Composition of the First-tier Tribunal

8.50 Section 4 of TCEA makes provision for the composition of the First-tier Tribunal. The Tribunal comprises two categories of membership: judges and other members. The Senior President of Tribunals is in charge of assigning judges and other members of the First-tier Tribunal to a chamber.[79] A judge or other member may be assigned to different chambers at different times.[80] The Senior President of Tribunals is obliged to publish a document recording the assignment policy adopted by him.[81] The policy must be such as to secure, *inter alia,* that appropriate use is made of the knowledge and experience of the judges and other members of the Upper Tribunal.[82] Section 4 sets out in detail those who are judges and others who may sit as members of the First-tier Tribunal.[83]

Chamber President

8.51 For each chamber of the First-tier Tribunal, there is to be a person, or two persons, to preside over that chamber known as a chamber president.[84] Schedule 4 to TCEA deals with the appointment of chamber presidents[85] and Sch. 4 further deals with the appointment of deputy chamber presidents,[86] acting chamber presidents,[87] assignment of judges and other members of the First-tier (and Upper) Tribunal.[88]

---

[75] Ibid., s. 9(4)(c).
[76] Ibid., s. 9(5).
[77] Ibid., s. 9(6).
[78] Ibid., s. 9(11).
[79] Ibid., Sch. 4, para. 9(1)(a). The Senior President of Tribunals may assign a judge or other member of the First-tier Tribunal to a particular chamber of the First-tier Tribunal only with the concurrence of the chamber president of the chamber and the judge or other member: Sch. 4, para. 11(3). Note that under TCEA, s. 8(1), the Senior President of the Tribunals may delegate almost all of his functions to judges or other members of the First-tier or Upper Tribunal or to staff.
[80] TCEA, Sch. 4, para. 11(1)(b).
[81] Ibid., Sch. 4, para. 13(1).
[82] Para. 13(2)(a). By virtue of para. 13(4), the Senior President of Tribunals must keep the policy under review.
[83] See also Sch. 2 to TCEA for further provision in respect of judges and other members of the First-tier Tribunal, as well as terms of appointment, remuneration, allowances and expenses, training, and oaths and the Qualifications for Appointment of Members to The First-tier Tribunal and Upper Tribunal Order 2008, SI 2692/2008, art. 2.
[84] TCEA, s. 7(1), (2) and (4). Section 7(3) provides that a person may not at any particular time preside over more than one chamber of the First-tier Tribunal (but may at the same time preside over one chamber of the First-tier Tribunal and over one chamber of the Upper Tribunal).
[85] TCEA, Sch. 4, para. 1.
[86] Ibid., Sch. 4, para. 5.
[87] Ibid., Sch. 4, para. 6. Acting chamber presidents may be appointed if there is no one for the time being presiding over a chamber.
[88] Ibid., Sch. 4, Part 2.

8.52 The chamber president is required to make arrangements for the issuing of guidance on changes in the law and practice as they relate to the functions allocated to the chamber.[89]

Constitution of panels

8.53 Unlike in the Upper Tribunal where it is specified that the number of members who may hear a case may be one, two or three,[90] the number of members required to decide matters before the First-tier Tribunal must be determined by the Senior President of Tribunals. In making this determination, where the matter to be decided previously fell within the jurisdiction of another tribunal (before its functions were transferred to the First-tier Tribunal),[91] the Senior President must have regard to any provision[92] for determining the number of members of the former tribunal, and the 'need for members of tribunals to have particular expertise, skills or knowledge'.[93] The First-tier Tribunal (Environment) announced in August 2010 that it will be 'operated and governed under the existing specific General Regulatory Chamber Rules. Users will have their cases heard by judicial specialists trained to hear their specific appeals.'[94]

8.54 The principal judge of the environment jurisdiction in the First-tier Tribunal will be Professor John Angel, acting president of the General Regulatory Chamber and a deputy judge of the Administrative Appeals Chamber of the Upper Tribunal.

8.55 Where a matter is decided by two or more members of the Tribunal, the Senior President of the Tribunals must decide how many should be judges and how many other members there will be.[95] The Senior President of Tribunals must select one of the members (the presiding member) to chair the Tribunal.[96]

E. Appeal to the Upper Tribunal

Introduction

8.56 The main function of the Upper Tribunal is to decide appeals from decisions of the First-tier Tribunal; such appeals may only be brought on a point of law.

8.57 TCEA also makes provision for the Upper Tribunal to exercise a judicial review function where it has been designated to do so. That judicial review function may come to encompass regulatory matters in time, although on the present state of the case law scope for judicial review of the Upper Tribunal is very limited.

---

[89] Ibid., Sch. 4, para. 7.
[90] First-tier Tribunal and Upper Tribunal (Composition of Tribunal) Order 2008, SI 2835/2008, art. 3.
[91] By an order under TCEA, s. 30(1).
[92] Made by or under any enactment.
[93] First-tier Tribunal and Upper Tribunal (Composition of Tribunal) Order 2008, SI 2835/2008, art. 2.
[94] <http://www.tribunals.gov.uk>.
[95] First-tier Tribunal and Upper Tribunal (Composition of Tribunal) Order 2008, SI 2835/2008, art. 6. In The *Senior President of Tribunals' Annual Report: Tribunals Transformed* (February 2010), Sir Robert Carnwath explained that 'to date I have generally delegated to Chamber Presidents those functions that regulate the day to day running of the Chamber, for example, the function of choosing particular judges and members to decide cases. Outside of these formal delegations certain tribunal judges take the lead on particular issues on my behalf': p. 19, para. 24.
[96] First-tier Tribunal and Upper Tribunal (Composition of Tribunal) Order 2008, SI 2835/2008, art. 7.

Appeals to the Upper Tribunal are provided for in s. 11 of TCEA. An appeal is open to any party to a case[97] and lies in respect of any decision made by the First-tier Tribunal other than 'an excluded decision'.[98] An appeal may be brought only with permission[99] from the First-tier Tribunal, or the Upper Tribunal, on an application by the appealing party.[100] **8.58**

Grounds of appeal

In common with a large number of statutory regimes, s. 11(1) of TCEA provides that appeals to the Upper Tribunal lie only in respect of a point of law. **8.59**

Definition of 'point of law'

In *Nipa Begum v Tower Hamlets London Borough Council*,[101] the Court of Appeal had to decide whether s. 204 of the Housing Act 1996, which provided for an appeal to the county court 'on any point of law' arising from a decision of a housing authority relating to home-lessness, gave the county court a power akin to that of judicial review exercisable in the High Court. The court held that it did: a 'point of law' included not only matters of legal interpretation but also the full range of issues which would otherwise be the subject of an application to the High Court for judicial review.[102] A majority of the House of Lords expressly approved this approach in *Runa Begum v Tower Hamlets London Borough Council*.[103] **8.60**

This approach applies equally to the Upper Tribunal's jurisdiction to hear appeals on points of law under s. 11. It follows that appeals from the First-tier Tribunal on a point of law cannot include an appeal against findings of fact made by the First-tier Tribunal.[104] Further, a contention that the First-tier Tribunal had failed to give adequate weight to evidence or to a particular consideration would not be capable of giving rise to an error of law, as the weight to be attributed to such matters is a question for the decision maker.[105] Nor would it usually be appropriate for the Upper Tribunal to receive further evidence on primary facts in determining whether an error of law has occurred. In that exercise, the evidence would have to remain as it was before the First-tier Tribunal.[106] **8.61**

---

[97] TCEA, s. 11(2). This is subject to a power of the Lord Chancellor to make provision by order for a person to be treated as being, or to be treated as not being, a party to a case: s. 11(8).

[98] See further para. 8.86 for more about excluded decisions.

[99] TCEA, s. 11(3).

[100] Ibid., s. 11(4).

[101] [2000] 1 WLR 306.

[102] Per Auld LJ at 313.

[103] [2003] UKHL 5 [2003] 2 AC 430.

[104] Provided that the decision-maker does not err in how it reaches the decision, the substance of the decision is for them, not for the judicially reviewing tribunal, and it is the decision-maker's view or decision which must prevail: see *R v Secretary of State for The Home Department ex parte Khawaja* [1984] AC 74 per Lord Scarman at 100; *R v Hillingdon LBC, ex parte Puhlhofer* [1986] AC 484 per Lord Brightman at 518. It will often be necessary on appeal to distinguish between questions of 'fact' and 'law'. In *O'Kelly v Trusthouse Forte Plc* [1984] QB 90 CA at 122H-123A, Lord Donaldson MR explained (in the context of the Employment Appeal Tribunal) that 'while it may be convenient for some purposes to refer to questions of "pure" law as contrasted with "mixed" questions of fact and law, the fact is that the appeal tribunal has no jurisdiction to consider any question of mixed fact and law until it has purified or distilled the mixture and extracted a question of pure law'.

[105] *Tesco Stores Ltd v Secretary of State for The Environment* [1995] 1 WLR 759 per Lord Keith at 764G-H, per Lord Hoffmann at 780F-H and 784.

[106] See by analogy *Green v Minister of Housing and Local Government* [1963] 1 All ER 578 at 616. Under TCEA, s. 12(4)(b), the Upper Tribunal may make findings of fact when it has allowed an appeal and is making a redetermination of the matter.

8.62 Whilst this reflects the orthodox understanding of appeals on points of law, the Upper Tribunal may in time come to develop a role beyond the traditional limits of such appeals. Writing extra-judicially, the Senior President has suggested that 'even if the jurisdiction of the Upper Tribunal is limited to appeals on points of law, there is scope for it to develop a more extensive supervisory role, which may cross the traditional boundaries between law and fact as understood in the courts'.[107]

8.63 When considering whether the Upper Tribunal has jurisdiction to hear a particular appeal (whether it is indeed, 'on a point of law') practitioners may wish to consider the traditional grounds of challenge in judicial review proceedings as being analogous; full consideration of this is outside the scope of this work.

Application for permission to appeal

8.64 An applicant seeking to appeal the decision of the First-tier Tribunal to the Upper Tribunal must first obtain permission. Permission may either be granted by the First-tier Tribunal on an application under r. 42 of the First-tier Tribunal Procedure Rules or, where that application has been refused or has not been admitted, by the Upper Tribunal, under r. 21 of the Upper Tribunal Procedure Rules.

Application to the First-tier Tribunal

8.65 Rule 42(2) of the First-tier Tribunal Procedure Rules provides that the application for permission to appeal must be made in writing and be 'sent or delivered' to the Tribunal so that it arrives no later than twenty-eight days after the latest of the dates that the Tribunal sends to the applicant either:

   (i) written reasons for the decision;
  (ii) notification of amended reasons for, or correction of, the decision following a review; or
 (iii) notification that an application for the decision to be set aside has been unsuccessful.[108]

8.66 Applications made outside the appeal period may still be considered by the First-tier Tribunal, and should be accompanied by a retrospective request for an extension of time and the reason why the application has not been provided in time. On an application for an extension of time to appeal, the Tribunal may either extend the time allowed or it 'must not admit the application'.[109]

8.67 Although an application need not take a particular form, it must:

   (i) identify the decision of the Tribunal to which it relates;
  (ii) identify the alleged error of law in the decision; and
 (iii) state the result the party making the application is seeking.[110]

---

[107] R Carnwath, 'Tribunal Justice—a new start' [2009] PL 48 at 58.
[108] Subject to the Tribunal Procedure (First-tier Tribunal) (General Regulatory Chamber) Rules 2009, r. 42(3).
[109] Tribunal Procedure (First-tier Tribunal) (General Regulatory Chamber) Rules 2009, r. 42(4).
[110] Ibid., r. 42(5).

If the Tribunal, in considering an application to appeal, is satisfied that there is an error of **8.68** law in the decision,[111] it may refuse permission to appeal and decide instead to review the decision under r. 44.[112] See further paras 8.47–8.49 for more about the power to review decisions.

If the Tribunal decides not to review the decision, or reviews the decision and decides to **8.69** take no action in respect of it, it must proceed to consider whether to grant permission to appeal.[113] No time limit is provided for this exercise; r. 43(3) requires only that a record of the Tribunal's decision must be sent to the parties 'as soon as practicable'. Where permission is refused, the unsuccessful applicant may apply to the Upper Tribunal for permission.

Application to the Upper Tribunal

Rule 21 of the Upper Tribunal Procedure Rules provides the procedure for applying for **8.70** permission to appeal to the Upper Tribunal. Applications must be in writing, made within one month of the refusal of permission by the First-tier Tribunal being sent to the applicant[114] and include the information set out in r. 21(4) and (5). As with applications for permission to the First-tier Tribunal, applications out of time may be considered at the discretion of the Tribunal and require the applicant to make a retrospective request in the application for an extension of time, providing the reason why the application has not been made in time.[115] Where an application made out of time to the First-tier Tribunal was refused, it may be renewed to the Upper Tribunal, in which case r. 21(7) applies as to the content of that application.

Having considered the application for permission, the Tribunal must send a written notice **8.71** of its decision (to refuse or grant permission) to the appellant.[116]

Notice of appeal

Once permission is granted, subject to any direction by the Tribunal, the application **8.72** for permission stands as the notice of appeal, and the Tribunal must send a copy of the application to the respondents along with any documents provided with it.[117]

Response to the notice of appeal

Rule 24(1A) provides that the respondent may provide a response to the notice of appeal. **8.73** Responses must be in writing and be sent or delivered to the Tribunal no later than one month after the date on which the respondent was sent the notice of appeal. The Tribunal will send a copy of the response to all parties. The response must contain, as a minimum, the information provided in r. 24(3), namely:

(i) the name and address of the respondent;
(ii) the name and address of the representative (if any) of the respondent;
(iii) an address where documents for the respondent may be sent or delivered;
(iv) whether the respondent opposes the appeal;

---

[111] Ibid., r. 44(1).
[112] Ibid., r. 43(1).
[113] Ibid., r. 43(2).
[114] Tribunal Procedure (Upper Tribunal) Rules 2008, r. 21(3)(b).
[115] Ibid., r. 21(6).
[116] Ibid., r. 22(1).
[117] Ibid., r. 22(2)(b).

    (v) the grounds on which the respondent relies, including any grounds on which the respondent was unsuccessful in the proceedings that are the subject of the appeal, but intends to rely on in the appeal; and

    (vi) whether the respondent wants the case to be dealt with at a hearing.

8.74 Provision is made in r. 24(4) for service of a response out of time.

Appellant's reply

8.75 The appellant may, but need not, reply to the respondent's response within one month of the day that the appellant received a copy of the response.[118] Alternatively, the Tribunal may, with the consent of the parties, consider the appeal without obtaining any further response from the appellant.[119]

The hearing

Notice of the hearing

8.76 Notice of a hearing date and venue must be 'reasonable' and of no less than fourteen days where the hearing is to consider disposal of the proceedings (unless parties agree a shorter period or in 'urgent or exceptional circumstances').[120]

Nature of the hearing

8.77 The Tribunal will decide, having considered any views expressed by the parties, whether to hold a hearing to determine the case,[121] and provide 'reasonable' notice of it to all parties[122] (which must be of at least fourteen days,[123] or shorter period if the parties consent or in urgent or exceptional cases).[124] Where a hearing is held, each party is entitled to be present.[125]

8.78 Provision is made in the rules for proceeding in the absence of parties[126] and the holding of hearings in private.[127]

Powers on appeal

8.79 If in deciding an appeal the Upper Tribunal finds that the making of the decision concerned involved an error on a point of law,[128] and allows the appeal, various powers are available to it. It may set aside the decision,[129] remit the case to the First-tier Tribunal for its reconsideration,[130] or reconsider the matter itself.[131]

---

[118] Ibid., r. 25(2).
[119] Ibid., r. 22(2)(c).
[120] Tribunal Procedure (First-tier Tribunal) (General Regulatory Chamber) Rules 2009, r. 34.
[121] Tribunal Procedure (Upper Tribunal) Rules 2008, r. 34.
[122] Ibid., r. 36(1).
[123] Ibid., r. 36(2).
[124] Ibid., r. 36(2)(b).
[125] Ibid., r. 35.
[126] Ibid., r. 38.
[127] Ibid., r. 37.
[128] See above paras 8.60 et seq.
[129] TCEA, s. 12(2)(a).
[130] Ibid., s. 12(2)(b)(i).
[131] Ibid., s. 12(2)(b)(ii).

If it chooses to remit the case, the Upper Tribunal may also direct that the members of the **8.80** First-tier Tribunal who are chosen to reconsider the case are not to be the same as those who made the decision that has been set aside[132] and/or give procedural directions in connection with the reconsideration of the case by the First-tier Tribunal.[133]

If it chooses to reconsider the matter that was before the First-tier Tribunal, the Upper **8.81** Tribunal may make any decision that the First-tier Tribunal could make if the First-tier Tribunal were redetermining the matter,[134] and *may* make such findings of fact as it considers appropriate.[135]

Making findings of fact on a reconsideration

If the Upper Tribunal decides to reconsider the matter, having allowed an appeal, the Tribunal **8.82** need not be bound by any or all of the findings of fact made by the First-tier Tribunal. The Tribunal may either come to its own independent view of the facts on the basis of the evidence before the First-tier Tribunal, or receive further evidence and reconsider the factual findings made in light of that. Rule 15(2)(a)(ii) of the Tribunal Procedure (Upper Tribunal) Rules 2008 permits the Tribunal to admit fresh evidence not available to the previous decision maker. Fresh evidence may be adduced by a party to the proceedings, or on the Tribunal's own initiative.

Judicial review jurisdiction

Introduction

This section is concerned with the (limited and prescribed) circumstances in which the **8.83** Upper Tribunal may exercise what TCEA describes as a 'judicial review jurisdiction'.[136] It is not concerned with the possibility of challenging a decision of the Upper Tribunal by way of judicial review.[137]

Creation of judicial review jurisdiction

The Upper Tribunal's judicial review jurisdiction, in so far as it comes to exist at all in the **8.84** regulatory field, is wholly distinct from its jurisdiction to hear s. 11 appeals. No judicial review jurisdiction can come to exist in any field, however, unless (among other conditions)[138] provision is made for it in a direction given by the Lord Chief Justice with the agreement of the Lord Chancellor.[139] Where such provision is made, the clear statutory intention is for the Upper Tribunal to play a role as similar as possible to that being exercised by the Divisional Court before it.

---

[132] Ibid., s. 12(3)(a).
[133] Ibid., s. 12(3)(b).
[134] TCEA, s. 12(4)(a).
[135] Ibid., s. 12(4)(b).
[136] Ibid., s. 15.
[137] Part H.
[138] The additional preconditions for the availability of the jurisdiction are threefold: firstly, the application must not seek anything other than the relief described in TCEA, s. 15(1) (essentially paradigm 'judicial review' relief), or permission to bring the judicial review, or damages, or interest or costs (s. 18(4)); secondly, that the application does not call into question anything done by the Crown Court (s. 18(5)); and thirdly, that the judge presiding at the hearing of the application is of a seniority as set out in s. 18(8).
[139] Constitutional Reform Act 2005, s. 18(6), Sch. 2, Part 1.

Limits of jurisdiction

8.85 At the time of writing, the only classes of case in which the Upper Tribunal enjoys a judicial review jurisdiction are:

(i) any decision of the First-tier Tribunal on an appeal made in the exercise of a right conferred by s. 5(1) of the Criminal Injuries Compensation Act 1995 (appeals against decisions on reviews); and

(ii) any decision of the First-tier Tribunal made under Tribunal Procedure Rules or s. 9 of TCEA (r. 43(1) of the Upper Tribunal Procedure Rules)[140] where there is no right of appeal to the Upper Tribunal and that decision is not an excluded decision within paras (b), (c) or (f) of s. 11(5) of the TCEA.[141]

'Excluded decisions'

8.86 The following are 'excluded decisions' for these purposes and may not form the subject of judicial review proceedings to the Upper Tribunal:

(i) any decision of the First-tier Tribunal on an appeal under s. 28(4) or (6) of the Data Protection Act 1998 (appeals against national security certificate): TCEA, s. 11(5)(b);

(ii) any decision of the First-tier Tribunal on an appeal under s. 60(1) or (4) of the Freedom of Information Act 2000 (appeals against national security certificate): TCEA, s. 11(5)(c);

(iii) any decision of the First-tier Tribunal that is of a description specified in an order made by the Lord Chancellor: TCEA, s. 11(5)(f).

8.87 At the time of writing, no relevant orders had been made by the Lord Chancellor. It remains to be seen whether or not (and in respect of what decisions) the Upper Tribunal may come to enjoy a general judicial review jurisdiction in the regulatory field. As matters stand, it can only exercise that jurisdiction in the regulatory field in respect of those procedural or review decisions described in para. 8.85(ii) above.

Judicially reviewable decisions

8.88 Since the hearing of the first case before the Upper Tribunal in its present form, which unsurprisingly concerned a procedural issue,[142] there have been in excess of 500 reported decisions, although few relate to applications to the Upper Tribunal itself for judicial review.[143]

---

[140] TCEA, s. 9 is concerned with the First-tier Tribunal's power to review its own decisions. See further paras 8.47-8.49.

[141] LCJ Judge, Practice Direction (Upper Tribunal: Judicial Review Jurisdiction) [2009] 1 WLR 327 (29 October 2008). By para. 3, the direction does not have effect where an application seeks (whether or not alone) a declaration of incompatibility under s. 4 of the Human Rights Act 1998.

[142] *RS v Secretary of State for Defence* [2008] UKUT 1 (AAC).

[143] *EF v Secretary of State for Work and Pensions* [2009] UKUT 92 (AAC) concerned an application to the Upper Tribunal in Scotland for judicial review on the grounds that the Judge of the First-tier Tribunal had failed properly to exercise his discretion. The application was dismissed on grounds relating to jurisdiction peculiar to Scotland.

In *LM v SSWP*,[144] Upper Tribunal Judge Ward decided that the terms of the Lord Chief   **8.89**
Justice's Direction on Classes of Cases Specified under s. 18(6) of TCEA did not confer jurisdiction on the Upper Tribunal over such decisions prior to its formation:

> [T]he Upper Tribunal's judicial review jurisdiction does not in my view extend to the exercise
> or non-exercise of the power under regulation 57 of the 1999 regulations, which were the rules
> governing the practice and procedure to be followed not by the First-tier Tribunal, but by its
> predecessor.

Applications for permission to bring judicial review proceedings in the High Court will not   **8.90**
usually succeed if the applicant has available to him an appropriate remedy other than by
means of that application.[145] Similarly, in the Upper Tribunal, even if judicial review is available because the Lord Chief Justice has made provision for it, applicants could not, for
instance, use judicial review to challenge a decision that may be challenged by appeal to the
First-tier Tribunal instead.

Procedure

Introduction

A person seeking to bring judicial review proceedings before the Upper Tribunal under s. 16   **8.91**
of TCEA must follow the procedure in the Upper Tribunal Procedure Rules. Applicants
must first be granted permission by the Upper Tribunal to bring the proceedings, following
which the respondent has the opportunity to submit a response. The Tribunal may determine the application, with or without a hearing, and where the decision is in the applicant's
favour, grant the relief set out in s. 15(1).

Application for permission

An application for judicial review to the Upper Tribunal may only be made if permission   **8.92**
(or, in a case arising under the law of Northern Ireland, leave) to make the application has
been obtained from it.[146] Such applications are made under r. 28 of the Upper Tribunal
Procedure Rules.

The Upper Tribunal Procedure Rules provide that applications for permission must be made   **8.93**
'promptly' and in writing to the Upper Tribunal, no later than '3 months after the date of
the decision, action or omission to which the application relates'.[147] In respect of challenges
to decisions of the First-tier Tribunal, an application for permission may be made after
the three-month longstop, so long as it is made within one month of the date on which the
First-tier Tribunal sent the written reasons for the decision or notification that an application

---

[144] [2009] UKUT 30.

[145] See, for example, *R (on the application of Sivasubramaniam) v Wandsworth County Court* [2002] EWCA
Civ 1738 [2003] 1 WLR 475.

[146] TCEA, s. 16(2). In *R (JW through DW as litigation friend) v The Learning Trust* [2009] UKUT 197 (AAC)
where permission was granted to proceed with an application for judicial review, although the claim was ultimately dismissed, it was held that the Upper Tribunal in exercise of its judicial review jurisdiction has power to
order interim relief pending the decision of the First-tier Tribunal (*R (on the application of G) v London Borough of
Barnet* [2005] EWHC 1946 (Admin); [2006] ELR 4 considered) (para. 26). However, since the statutory structure in that case clearly envisaged that amendments to statements of special educational needs take effect forthwith
despite any appeal, the jurisdiction to order relief to the same effect in judicial review proceedings should be
exercised with considerable restraint and only where there are exceptional circumstances (paras 27– 29).

[147] Tribunal Procedure (Upper Tribunal) Rules 2008, r. 28(1) and (2).

for the decision to be set aside has been unsuccessful.[148] Applications made out of time may still be considered but will not be admitted unless the Upper Tribunal extends the time allowed. Late applications must contain a retrospective request for an extension of time, and state the reason why the application was not submitted in time.[149]

8.94 Applications must include the information set out in r. 28(4) and (5) and be accompanied by a copy of any written record of the decision in the applicant's possession or control, and copies of other relevant documents upon which the applicant intends to rely.[150] The Tribunal will send a copy of the application and accompanying documents to 'each person named in the application as a respondent or interested party'.[151]

Acknowledgment of service

8.95 Rule 29 of the Upper Tribunal Procedure Rules provides that:

> A person who is sent a copy of an application for permission under rule 28(8) (application for permission to bring judicial review proceedings) and wishes to take part in the proceedings must send or deliver to the Upper Tribunal an acknowledgment of service so that it is received no later than 21 days after the date on which the Upper Tribunal sent a copy of the application to that person.

8.96 Acknowledgment must be in writing and provide the information in r. 29(2), namely whether the person intends to oppose the application for permission, their grounds for any opposition or any other submission or information that the person considers may assist the Upper Tribunal, and the name and address of any other person not named in the application as a respondent or interested party whom the person providing the acknowledgment considers to be an interested party.

8.97 A person who fails to provide an acknowledgment of service will be precluded from participating in the proceedings if the application is successful.[152]

The decision on permission

8.98 The Upper Tribunal must send to the applicant, each respondent and any other person who provided an acknowledgment of service to the Upper Tribunal, and may send to any other person who may have an interest in the proceedings, written notice of its decision in relation to the application for permission. The Tribunal must additionally provide the reasons for any refusal of the application, or any limitations or conditions on permission.[153]

8.99 Section 16(3) of TCEA provides that the Tribunal may not grant permission (or leave) to make the application unless it considers that the applicant has a sufficient interest in the matter to which the application relates. This replicates the 'standing' requirement in s. 31(3) of the Senior Courts Act 1981 (the 1981 Act),[154] and similar considerations will apply.[155]

---

[148] Ibid., r. 28(3).
[149] Ibid., r. 28(6).
[150] Ibid., r. 28(7).
[151] Ibid., r. 28(8).
[152] Ibid., r. 29(3).
[153] Ibid., r. 30(1).
[154] The Senior Courts Act 1981 was previously called the Supreme Court Act 1981. Its name was changed by provision in the Constitutional Reform Act 2005.
[155] A detailed treatment of the question of 'standing' is beyond the scope of this work. A useful starting-point is the discussion in Woolf, Jowell and LeSueur, *De Smith's Judicial Review* (6th edn, London, 2007) at paras 2.016–2.018 and 2.024–2.041.

Similarly, the provisions in s. 16(4) and (5) of TCEA correspond to the provision relating **8.100** to delay in bringing judicial review proceedings, in s. 31(6) of the 1981 Act. They provide that where the Upper Tribunal considers that there has been undue delay in making the application, and that granting the relief sought on the application would be likely to cause substantial hardship to, or substantially prejudice the rights of, any person or would be detrimental to good administration, the Tribunal may refuse to grant permission (or leave) for the making of the application or refuse to grant any relief sought on the application.[156]

The Upper Tribunal should not give permission on any issue in a case that it regards as **8.101** unarguable.[157]

Rule 30(5) provides that an applicant who is refused permission (without a hearing) may ask **8.102** the Upper Tribunal to reconsider the application at a hearing.

Transfer of proceedings to the High Court

Where the Upper Tribunal receives applications under r. 28, but it does not have the function **8.103** of deciding the application, the Upper Tribunal must by order transfer the application to the High Court.[158] Where the application is transferred to the High Court in that way, the application is to be treated for all purposes as if it had been made to the High Court, and 'sought things corresponding to those sought from the tribunal'.[159] In those circumstances, any steps taken, permission (or leave) given, or orders made by the Tribunal in relation to the application are to be treated as taken, given or made by the High Court.[160]

Transfer of proceedings to the Upper Tribunal

Section 19(1) of TCEA provides that judicial review cases may be transferred from the **8.104** Divisional Court to the Upper Tribunal for the purpose of exercising the judicial review jurisdiction.[161] For the reasons explained in paras 8.83 onwards, this is currently of limited relevance in relation to the RESA civil sanctions regime. Any cases so transferred must be dealt with in accordance with r. 27 of the Upper Tribunal Procedure Rules.

Representations

Each party, and with the permission of the Upper Tribunal any other person, may: **8.105**

(i) submit evidence, except at the hearing of an application for permission;
(ii) make representations at any hearing that they are entitled to attend; and
(iii) make written representations in relation to a decision to be made without a hearing.[162]

---

[156] The case law on delay is beyond the scope of this work. See further Woolf et al., ibid., paras 18.051–18.053.

[157] See as a starting-point the classic statement of Lord Diplock in *R v Inland Revenue Commissioners, ex parte National Federation of Self-Employed and Small Businesses Ltd* [1982] AC 617, 644A.

[158] TCEA, s. 18(3).

[159] TCEA, s. 18(9)(a).

[160] Ibid., s. 18(9)(b).

[161] By ibid., s. 19(1), there is inserted a new s. 31A into the Supreme Court Act 1981, by which judicial review applications commenced in the High Court are to be transferred to the Upper Tribunal if four conditions as are set out there are met. For the position in respect of transfer from the Court of Session in Scotland see s. 20 of TCEA.

[162] Tribunal Procedure (Upper Tribunal) Rules 2008, r. 33.

The hearing

8.106   The applicant may not rely on any grounds, other than those grounds on which the applicant obtained permission for the judicial review proceedings, without the consent of the Upper Tribunal.[163]

8.107   The Tribunal will decide, having considered any views expressed by the parties, whether to hold a hearing to determine the case,[164] and provide 'reasonable' notice of it to all parties[165] (which must be of at least fourteen days,[166] or shorter period if the parties consent or in urgent or exceptional cases).[167] Where a hearing is held, each party is entitled to be present.[168]

8.108   Provision is made in the rules for proceeding in the absence of parties[169] and the holding of hearings in private.[170]

Orders available

8.109   Relief in judicial review always lies in the court's discretion. According to s. 15(1) of the TCEA, it is open to the Upper Tribunal to award any of five forms of relief (whether alone or in combination), as follows:

   (i)   a mandatory order (mandamus in Northern Ireland);
   (ii) a prohibiting order (prohibition in Northern Ireland);
   (iii) a quashing order (certiorari in Northern Ireland);
   (iv) a declaration;
   (v)   an injunction.[171]

8.110   In deciding whether to grant any of (i)–(iii) above, the Upper Tribunal must apply the same principles as the High Court would apply in a judicial review case.[172] In deciding whether to grant relief under (iv) and (v) above, the Upper Tribunal must apply the principles that the High Court would apply in deciding whether to grant that relief under s. 31(2) of the Supreme Court Act 1981 (cases arising in England and Wales) on an application for judicial review, and similarly apply relevant considerations in cases arising under the law of Northern Ireland.[173]

Quashing orders

8.111   TCEA makes supplementary provision in respect of quashing orders, providing that if such an order is made, the Upper Tribunal may additionally remit the matter concerned to the

---

[163]   Ibid., r. 32.
[164]   Ibid., r. 34.
[165]   Ibid., r. 36(1).
[166]   Ibid., r. 36(2).
[167]   Ibid., r. 36(2)(b).
[168]   Ibid., r. 35.
[169]   Ibid., r. 38.
[170]   Ibid., r. 37.
[171]   TCEA, s. 15(1). For the position in respect of cases transferred to the Upper Tribunal from the Court of Session in Scotland see s. 21 of the 2007 Act.
[172]   TCEA, s. 15(4). The long history and more recent use of mandatory, prohibiting and quashing orders is beyond the scope of this work. See generally Woolf et al., fn. 156 above, paras 15.014–15.043.
[173]   TCEA, s. 15(5).

court, tribunal or authority that made the decision, with a direction to reconsider the matter and reach a decision in accordance with its findings, or substitute its own decision for the decision in question.[174]

Having imposed a quashing order, and on reconsideration of the matter, the Upper Tribunal's power to substitute its own decision can only be exercised if: **8.112**

  (i) the decision in question was made by a court or tribunal (as opposed to, for instance, a regulator);

  (ii) the decision is quashed on the ground that there has been an error of law; and

  (iii) without the error, there would have been only one decision that the court or tribunal could have reached.[175]

The Upper Tribunal's powers of redetermination are thus more limited when it is exercising its judicial review jurisdiction, as opposed to when it is entertaining a s. 11 appeal. In substituting its own decision upon judicial review, for instance, it has no power to make fresh findings of fact.[176] **8.113**

Monetary remedies

In certain limited circumstances, monetary remedies may also be available to an applicant. Under TCEA s. 16(6), the Upper Tribunal may award damages, restitution or the recovery of a sum due (if the application includes a claim for such an award) arising from any matter to which the application relates. Before granting such relief to the applicant, the Tribunal must be satisfied that such an award would have been made by the High Court if the claim had been made in an action begun in the High Court by the applicant. An award under that provision may be enforced as if it were an award of the High Court.[177] **8.114**

Monetary remedies do not equate to a freestanding remedy of damages; as in the High Court, their purpose is to deal expeditiously with those cases in which an entitlement to damages, recovery of a debt or restitution arises in private law as a result of unlawful administrative action.[178] Thus an application for judicial review can never seek by way of relief a monetary remedy alone, only ever in combination with one of the remedies provided for in TCEA, s. 15(1). **8.115**

Enforcement

By s. 15(3) of TCEA relief granted by the Upper Tribunal under s. 15(1) has the same effect as the corresponding relief granted by the High Court on an application for judicial review, and is enforceable as if it were relief granted by the High Court on an application for judicial review. **8.116**

---

[174] Ibid., s. 17(1).
[175] Ibid., s. 17(2). Unless the Upper Tribunal otherwise directs, a decision substituted by it has effect as if it were a decision of the relevant court or tribunal (s. 17(3)).
[176] See the discussion above at paras 8.82 et seq.
[177] Ibid., s. 16(7).
[178] See for example, *R (Quark Fishing Ltd) v Secretary of State for Foreign and Commonwealth Affairs* [2005] UKHL 57 [2006] 1 AC 529 per Baroness Hale at para. [96]. An exception is a claim for 'just satisfaction' under the Human Rights Act 1998. See further generally Woolf et al., fn. 155 above, paras 19.025–19.105.

Composition of the Upper Tribunal

8.117 At the time of writing, there are four chambers of the Upper Tribunal. It is to the Administrative Appeals Chamber of the Upper Tribunal that appeals on points of law from the General Regulatory Chamber of the First-tier Tribunal will lie.[179]

8.118 Section 5 of TCEA makes provision for the composition of the Upper Tribunal. The Tribunal comprises two categories of membership: judges and other members.

8.119 Further provision is made in respect of judges and members of the Upper Tribunal in Sch. 3 to TCEA, dealing with matters such as terms of appointment,[180] remuneration, allowances and expenses,[181] training,[182] and oaths.[183]

Chamber president

8.120 Like the First-tier Tribunal, the Upper Tribunal is divided into a number of chambers. For each chamber of the Upper Tribunal, there is to be a person, or two persons, to preside over that chamber known as a chamber president.[184] Schedule 4 to TCEA makes provision for the appointment of deputy chamber presidents[185] and acting chamber presidents.[186]

8.121 The chamber president of a chamber of the Upper Tribunal must make arrangements for the issuing of guidance on changes in the law and practice as they relate to the functions allocated to the chamber.[187]

Senior President of Tribunals

8.122 The Senior President of Tribunals is in charge of assigning judges and other members of the Upper Tribunal to a chamber.[188] A judge or member may be assigned to different chambers at different times.[189] The Senior President is obliged to publish a document recording the assignment policy adopted by him.[190] The policy must be such as to secure, *inter alia,* that appropriate use is made of the knowledge and experience of the judges and other members of the Upper Tribunal.[191]

---

[179] *Senior President of Tribunals' Annual Report: Tribunals Transformed* (February 2010), pp 31–2 and 42–4.

[180] TCEA, Sch. 3, para. 4.

[181] Ibid., Sch. 3, para. 5.

[182] Ibid., Sch. 3, para. 9.

[183] Ibid., Sch. 3, para. 10.

[184] Ibid., s. 7 (1), (2) and (4). Section 7(3) provides that a person may not at any particular time preside over more than one chamber of the Upper Tribunal.

[185] Ibid., Sch. 4, para. 5.

[186] Ibid., Sch. 4, para. 6. Acting chamber presidents may be appointed if there is no one for the time being presiding over a chamber.

[187] Ibid., Sch. 4, para. 7.

[188] TCEA, Sch. 4, para. 9(1)(b). The Senior President may only assign a judge or member to a chamber with the concurrence of the chamber president and that judge or member: Sch. 4, para. 12(4). Note that under TCEA, s. 8(1), the Senior President may delegate almost all of his functions to judges or other members of the First-tier or Upper Tribunal or to staff.

[189] Ibid., Sch. 4, para. 12(2)(b).

[190] Ibid., Sch. 4, para. 13(1).

[191] Ibid., Sch. 4, para. 13(2)(a). By para. 13(4), the Senior President must keep the policy under review.

Constitution of panels

The number of members who may hear a case in the Upper Tribunal may be one, two or **8.123** three.[192] Where a matter falls to be considered by a single member, that member must be a judge unless the Senior President decides otherwise.[193] Where a matter is decided by two or more members of the Tribunal, the Senior President must decide how many should be judges and how many other members, or may delegate this function to chambers' presidents. Where a matter is to be decided by two or more members of a Tribunal, the matter may, if the parties to the case agree, be decided in the absence of one or more (but not all) of the members chosen to decide the matter.[194]

In all cases one of the members acts as presider. If the decision of the Tribunal is not unani- **8.124** mous, the decision of the majority is the decision of the Tribunal; and the presiding member has a casting vote if the votes are equally divided.[195]

F. General procedure: appeals to First-tier and Upper Tribunals

Introduction

Few detailed powers in respect of the conduct of appeals are bestowed on the Tribunals by **8.125** the primary legislation. TCEA, as an enabling act, provides only a framework for the estab- lishment of the Tribunals and their operation; the detail concerning the operation and deci- sion making of the Tribunals will be derived from the functions transferred to them from other tribunals and the relevant chamber's tribunal procedural rules.

This part looks at the general procedural provisions applicable to appeals and reviews to the **8.126** First-tier and Upper Tribunals. The specific provisions relating to the applying for and responding to appeals are dealt with in parts D and E.

Tribunal Procedure Rules

The procedural rules applicable in the First-tier and the Upper Tribunal are the Tribunal **8.127** Procedure Rules, created under s. 22 of TCEA, by the Tribunal Procedure Committee. In respect of the First-tier Tribunal, each chamber has its own set of rules; at the time of writing there were seven sets of procedural rules relating to the different chambers of the First-tier Tribunal.[196] For the Upper Tribunal, three sets of procedural rules exist.[197] For appeals against

---

[192] First-tier Tribunal and Upper Tribunal (Composition of Tribunal) Order 2008, SI 2835/2008, art. 3.
[193] Ibid., art. 4.
[194] TCEA, Sch. 4, para. 15(6).
[195] First-tier Tribunal and Upper Tribunal (Composition of Tribunal) Order 2008, SI 2835/2008, art. 8.
[196] Consolidated Asylum and Immigration (Procedure) Rules 2005 for First-tier Tribunal; Consolidated Asylum and Immigration (Fast-track Procedure) Rules 2005 for First-tier Tribunal; Tribunal Procedure (First-tier Tribunal) (Tax Chamber) Rules 2009, SI 273/2009 (as amended); Tribunal Procedure (First-tier Tribunal) (General Regulatory Chamber) Rules 2009, SI 1976/2009 (as amended); Tribunal Procedure (First–tier Tribunal) (Social Entitlement Chamber) Rules 2008, SI 2685/2008 (as amended); Tribunal Procedure (First–tier Tribunal) (Health, Education and Social Care Chamber) Rules 2008, SI 2699/2008 (as amended); and the Tribunal Procedure (First-tier Tribunal) (War Pensions and Armed Forces Compensation Chamber) Rules 2008, SI 2686/2008 (as amended).
[197] Tribunal Procedure (Upper Tribunal) Rules 2008, SI 2698/2008 (as amended); Lands Tribunal Rules 1996, SI 1022/1996; and the Upper Tribunal (Lands Chamber) Fees Order 2009, SI 1114/2009 (as amended).

the Part 3 sanctions to the First-tier Tribunal, the Tribunal Procedure (First-tier Tribunal) (General Regulatory Chamber) Rules 2008 (as amended)[198] apply (to be known in this chapter as the First-tier Tribunal Procedure Rules). For onward appeal to the Upper Tribunal, the Tribunal Procedure (Upper Tribunal) Rules 2008 (as amended)[199] apply (to be known in this chapter as the Upper Tribunal Procedure Rules and collectively to be known as the Procedural Rules).

The Tribunal Procedure Committee

8.128 When creating any procedure rules, the Tribunal Procedure Committee is constrained by the terms of TCEA, which requires that certain objectives must be met in the conduct of this exercise. These objectives are similar to the overriding objective in the Civil Procedure Rules. Section 22(4) provides that the power to make the tribunal procedure rules is to be exercised with a view to ensuring that: justice is done;[200] the tribunal system is accessible and fair;[201] proceedings before the First-tier Tribunal (or Upper Tribunal) are handled quickly and efficiently;[202] the rules are both simple and simply expressed;[203] and that the rules where appropriate confer on members of the First-tier Tribunal (or Upper Tribunal) responsibility for ensuring that proceedings before the Tribunal are handled quickly and efficiently.[204]

Overriding objective

8.129 The overriding objective of the Procedure Rules for both the First-tier Tribunal and the Upper Tribunal is to enable the respective Tribunals to deal with cases 'fairly and justly'.[205] This is said to include:

(i) dealing with the case in ways that are proportionate to the importance of the case, the complexity of the issues, the anticipated costs and the resources of the parties;

(ii) avoiding unnecessary formality and seeking flexibility in the proceedings;

(iii) ensuring, so far as practicable, that the parties are able to participate fully in the proceedings;

(iv) using any special expertise of the Upper Tribunal effectively; and

(v) avoiding delay, so far as compatible with proper consideration of the issues.[206]

8.130 The objective applies to both Tribunals when they are exercising their powers under their respective Procedural Rules, as well as when they are interpreting other rules and practice directions.[207] Parties are required to help the Tribunals to further the overriding objective and co-operate with the Tribunals generally.[208]

---

[198] SI 1976/2009 (as amended by SI 43/2010).

[199] SI 2698/2008 (as amended by SI 274/2009, SI 1975/2009, SI 43/2010, SI 44/2010 and SI 747/2010).

[200] TCEA, s. 22(4)(a).

[201] Ibid., s. 22(4)(b).

[202] Ibid., s. 22(4)(c).

[203] Ibid., s. 22(4)(d).

[204] Ibid., s. 22(4)(e).

[205] Tribunal Procedure (Upper Tribunal) Rules 2008 and the Tribunal Procedure (First-tier Tribunal) (General Regulatory Chamber) Rules 2009, r. 2(1).

[206] Tribunal Procedure (Upper Tribunal) Rules 2008 and the Tribunal Procedure (First-tier Tribunal) (General Regulatory Chamber) Rules 2009, r. 2(2).

[207] Ibid., r. 2(3).

[208] Ibid., r. 2(4).

Alternative dispute resolution and arbitration

In furtherance of the overriding objective, the Tribunals are required, where appropriate, to **8.131** bring to the attention of the parties the availability of any appropriate alternative procedure for the resolution of the dispute and, where the parties so wish, to facilitate the use of the procedure.[209]

Representatives

Parties may be represented (legally or otherwise), in which case the party (or the representa- **8.132** tive if a legal one and the appeal is in the Upper Tribunal) must notify the Tribunal and all other parties in writing of that fact, including details of the representative's name and address.[210] Where such notification has not been made, any party attending a hearing wishing to be represented must seek the Tribunal's permission to be so represented or assisted.[211]

Service of documents

Service of any document provided to the First-tier or Upper Tribunal under the Procedural **8.133** Rules, practice direction or Tribunal direction, must be:

  (i) sent by pre-paid post or delivered by hand to the address specified for the proceedings;
  (ii) sent by fax to the number specified for the proceedings; or
  (iii) sent or delivered by such other method as the Tribunal may permit or direct.[212]

The Procedural Rules permit parties to express a preference for service in a particular way[213] **8.134** and provide that any change of address must be notified in writing to the Tribunal.[214]

Rule 12 makes specific provision for the calculation of time in respect of acts required under **8.135** the Procedural Rules, in particular by providing that activities required to be done by or on a particular day must be done by 5 pm that day.

Case management powers

Where the TCEA or any other enactment is silent on the procedure that must be adopted, **8.136** the Tribunals may regulate their own procedure.[215]

General case management powers

The Tribunals have a general case management power and may issue directions 'in relation **8.137** to the conduct or disposal of proceedings at any time, including a direction amending, suspending or setting aside an earlier direction'.[216]

---

[209] Ibid., r. 3(1). Rule 3(2) provides that Part 1 of the Arbitration Act 1996 does not apply to proceedings before the tribunals.
[210] Tribunal Procedure (Upper Tribunal) Rules 2008 and Tribunal Procedure (First-tier Tribunal) (General Regulatory Chamber) Rules 2009, r. 11(1) and (2).
[211] Ibid., r. 5.
[212] Ibid., r. 15(2): requesting electronic service; or r. 15(3): refusing other communication (except pre-paid post or by hand).
[213] Tribunal Procedure (Upper Tribunal) Rules 2008 and Tribunal Procedure (First-tier Tribunal) (General Regulatory Chamber) Rules 2009, r. 13(1).
[214] Ibid., r. 13(5).
[215] Ibid., r. 5(1).
[216] Ibid., r. 5(2).

Specific case management powers

8.138 Tribunals are specifically empowered to:

(i) extend or shorten the time for complying with any rule, practice direction or direction;

(ii) consolidate or hear together two or more sets of proceedings or parts of proceedings raising common issues, or treat a case as a lead case;

(iii) permit or require a party to amend a document;

(iv) permit or require a party or another person to provide documents, information, evidence or submissions to the Tribunal or a party;

(v) deal with an issue in the proceedings as a preliminary issue;

(vi) hold a hearing to consider any matter, including a case management issue;

(vii) decide the form of any hearing;

(viii) adjourn or postpone a hearing;

(ix) require a party to produce a bundle for a hearing;

(x) stay (or, in Scotland, sist) proceedings;

(xi) transfer proceedings to another court or tribunal if that other court or tribunal has jurisdiction in relation to the proceedings and
(a) because of a change of circumstances since the proceedings were started, the Upper Tribunal no longer has jurisdiction in relation to the proceedings; or
(b) the Upper Tribunal considers that the other court or tribunal is a more appropriate forum for the determination of the case;

(xii) suspend the effect of its own decision pending an appeal or review of that decision (Upper Tribunal) or pending the determination by the First-tier Tribunal or the Upper Tribunal of an application for permission to appeal against, and any appeal or review of that decision;

(xiii) (the Upper Tribunal only) in an appeal, or an application for permission to appeal, against the decision of another tribunal, suspend the effect of that decision pending the determination of the application for permission to appeal, and any appeal; and

(xiv) (the Upper Tribunal only) require any other tribunal whose decision is the subject of proceedings before the Upper Tribunal to provide reasons for the decision, or other information.[217]

Directions

8.139 The First-tier Tribunal may give directions about the exchange of documents between parties that are relevant to the appeal, or relevant to particular issues, for the inspection of such documents,[218] and for the provision by parties of statements of agreed matters.[219]

8.140 Both Tribunals may give directions as to:

(i) issues on which they require evidence or submissions;

(ii) the nature of the evidence or submissions they require;

---

[217] Tribunal Procedure (Upper Tribunal) Rules 2008 and Tribunal Procedure (First-tier Tribunal) (General Regulatory Chamber) Rules 2009, r. 5(3).

[218] Tribunal Procedure (First-tier Tribunal) (General Regulatory Chamber) Rules 2009, r. 15(1)(a).

[219] Ibid., r. 15(1)(b).

(iii) whether the parties are permitted or required to provide expert evidence and, if so, whether the parties must jointly appoint a single expert to provide such evidence;

(iv) any limit on the number of witnesses whose evidence a party may put forward, whether in relation to a particular issue or generally;

(v) the manner in which any evidence or submissions are to be provided, which may include a direction for them to be given orally at a hearing or by written submissions or witness statement; and

(vi) the time at which any evidence or submissions are to be provided.

Applying for a direction

Any party seeking a direction may apply to the Tribunal under r. 6(1) of the Procedural Rules **8.141** seeking a direction about the conduct of the appeal. Applications must be made in writing by sending or delivering the application to the Tribunal.[220] Applications must include the reason for making the application and the Tribunal will (unless there is good reason not to so do) send a copy of it to every party and any person affected by the decision. Applications may also be made orally during the course of a hearing.[221] Rule 6(1) also empowers Tribunals to make directions of their own initiative. Rule 6(5) provides that if a party or any other person sent notice of the direction wishes to challenge that direction, they may do so by applying for another direction that amends, suspends or sets aside the first direction.

Failing to comply with rules, practice directions or Tribunal directions

Any irregularity resulting from a failure to comply with either the First-tier Tribunal **8.142** Procedure Rules or the Upper Tribunal Procedure Rules (and any other practice direction or Tribunal direction) will not 'of itself render void the proceedings or any step taken in the proceedings'.[222] The Tribunal may instead take any such action as it considers just in the circumstances, including:

(i) waiving the requirement;

(ii) requiring the failure to be remedied;

(iii) exercising its power under r. 8 (striking out a party's case)(see below);

(iv) restricting a party's participation in the proceedings (except in mental health cases in the Upper Tribunal); or

(v) in the case of the First-tier Tribunal, barring a party's participation in the proceedings;[223]

(vi) in the case of the First-tier Tribunal, refer the matter to the Upper Tribunal under art. 3 for it to exercise its powers under s. 25 of TCEA in respect of, *inter alia*, compelling the attendance of that person to give evidence or produce a document.

Respondents barred from taking part in the proceedings under r. 7(2)(e) of the First-tier **8.143** Tribunal Procedure Rules are permitted under r. 8(7) to apply for the lifting of that bar.

---

[220] Tribunal Procedure (Upper Tribunal) Rules 2008 and Tribunal Procedure (First-tier Tribunal) (General Regulatory Chamber) Rules 2009, r. 6(2)(a).

[221] Ibid., r. 6(2)(b).

[222] Ibid., r. 7.

[223] Tribunal Procedure (First-tier Tribunal) (General Regulatory Chamber) Rules 2009, r. 7(2)(e). There is no equivalent rule in the Tribunal Procedure (Upper Tribunal) Rules 2008.

Striking out a party's case

8.144 The Tribunals must strike out cases in certain circumstances, and may strike out cases in others. Where a case has been struck out, the appellant may apply in writing for it to be reinstated, subject to the time limits provided in the respective Procedural Rules.[224]

Mandatory power

8.145 Rule 8(1) provides that

> the proceedings, or the appropriate part of them, *will automatically* be struck out if the appellant or applicant has failed to comply with a direction that stated that failure by the appellant or applicant to comply with the direction would lead to the striking out of the proceedings or that part of them. (Emphasis added.)

The power to strike out must also be exercised where the Tribunal does not have jurisdiction in relation to the proceedings and does not use its power to transfer the proceedings to another court or Tribunal.[225]

Discretionary power

8.146 The Tribunal may strike out a party's case where:

(i) the appellant or applicant has failed to comply with a direction that stated that failure by the appellant or applicant to comply with the direction could lead to the striking out of the proceedings or part of them;

(ii) the appellant or applicant has failed to cooperate with the Tribunal to such an extent that the Tribunal cannot deal with the proceedings fairly and justly; or

(iii) in the case of the Upper Tribunal, in proceedings that are not an appeal from the decision of another tribunal or judicial review proceedings, the Upper Tribunal considers there is no reasonable prospect of the appellant's or the applicant's case, or part of it, succeeding;

(iv) in the case of the First-tier Tribunal, the Tribunal considers there is no reasonable prospect of the appellant's case, or part of it, succeeding.

Evidential considerations

8.147 The burden and standard of proof, where applicable, will be provided in the order awarding the regulator the civil sanctions. The Procedural Rules make general provision about the admissibility of evidence, providing in particular that Tribunals may admit evidence whether or not the evidence would be admissible in a civil trial in the UK or the evidence was available to a previous decision maker.[226]

8.148 Tribunals may, in their discretion, exclude evidence that would otherwise be admissible where:

(i) the evidence was not provided within the time allowed by a direction or a practice direction;

---

[224] Tribunal Procedure (Upper Tribunal) Rules 2008 and Tribunal Procedure (First-tier Tribunal) (General Regulatory Chamber) Rules 2009, r. 8(5).
[225] Ibid., r. 8(2).
[226] Tribunal Procedure (Upper Tribunal) Rules 2008 and the Tribunal Procedure (First-tier Tribunal) (General Regulatory Chamber) Rules 2009, r. 15(2)(a).

(ii) the evidence was otherwise provided in a manner that did not comply with a direction or a practice direction; or

(iii) it would otherwise be unfair to admit the evidence.[227]

Witness summonses

The Tribunals may, on application by the parties or of their own initiative, require by summons ('citation' in Scotland) any witness to attend as a witness or produce any documents in their possession or control which 'relate to an issue in the proceedings'.[228] Detailed provision is made in r. 16 of the Procedural Rules as to how parties should go about applying for summonses; the procedure is slightly different for applications before the First-tier Tribunal and the Upper Tribunal. **8.149**

Suspension of sanction or notice pending appeal

Requirements of RESA

The decision as to whether a sanction ceases to have effect once an appeal has been lodged, is one for the minister to take; it is not a requirement of RESA. Pursuant to s. 54(3)(a), the minister may include in the order 'provision suspending the requirement or notice pending determination of the appeal'. **8.150**

This section allows the minister to make provision for the suspensory effect of a fixed penalty or other requirement during any appeal. The *Regulatory Enforcement and Sanctions Act 2008: Explanatory Notes*[229] suggest two alternatives for the way in which this suspension may operate in respect of stop notices: **8.151**

(i) during an appeal, a person may apply for the effect of the stop notice to be suspended pending the result of the appeal. If this application is unsuccessful then the notice will remain in force during the appeal; or

(ii) should the person appeal, the effect of the stop notice may be automatically suspended until the result of the appeal is known.

Regulators seeking access to the Part 3 sanctions should carefully consider seeking the inclusion of such a provision in either of its forms. In respect of the imposition of the civil sanctions by the Environment Agency and Natural England, all notices (other than stop notices) are suspended pending appeal.[230] **8.152**

The Procedural Rules

Where an order awarding the Part 3 sanctions to a regulator provides in any terms for the Tribunal to stay or suspend a decision (the substantive decision) which is, or may be, the subject of an appeal to the Tribunal, pending such appeal, a person who wishes the Tribunal to decide whether the substantive decision should be stayed or suspended must make a written application to the Tribunal.[231] The Procedural Rules provide detail as to how and when such an application should be made, including the supplementary powers of the **8.153**

---

[227] Tribunal Procedure (Upper Tribunal) Rules 2008 and Tribunal Procedure (First-tier Tribunal) (General Regulatory Chamber) Rules 2009, r. 15(2)(b).
[228] Ibid., r. 16(1).
[229] *Regulatory Enforcement and Sanctions Act 2008: Explanatory Notes,* para. 145.
[230] The Environmental Civil Sanctions (England) Order 2010, SI 115/2010, art. 10(4).
[231] Tribunal Procedure (Upper Tribunal) Rules 2008, r. 20A(2) (inserted by SI 274/2009) and Tribunal Procedure (First-tier Tribunal) (General Regulatory Chamber) Rules 2009, r. 20(2).

Tribunal on any such application (giving directions and granting the suspension subject to conditions).

Withdrawal of case

8.154 Rule 17 of the Procedural Rules provides that parties may give notice to withdraw their case or any part of it at any time before a hearing to consider the disposal of the proceedings (or, if the Tribunal disposes of the proceedings without a hearing, before that disposal), in writing to the Tribunal or orally at a hearing. Notice of withdrawal will not take effect unless the Tribunal consents to the withdrawal (except in relation to an application for permission to appeal to the Upper Tribunal).

8.155 A party that has withdrawn its case may apply in writing to the Tribunal to have it reinstated, subject to the time limits set down in the order for making such an application.[232]

Costs

8.156 The TCEA makes very broad provision for the Tribunal's power to award costs. Section 9(1) provides as follows:

> The costs of and incidental to—
>
> (a) all proceedings in the First-tier Tribunal, and
> (b) all proceedings in the Upper Tribunal,
>
> shall be in the discretion of the Tribunal in which the proceedings take place.

8.157 That discretion is described as 'full' and permits the Tribunals discretion to determine by whom and to what extent the costs are to be paid,[233] subject to the Tribunal Procedure Rules.

The Tribunal Procedure Rules

8.158 Specific and detailed provision about the award of costs in both Tribunals is made in r. 10 of the Tribunal Procedure Rules. The power to award costs is limited in both arenas to wasted costs and costs incurred through unreasonable behaviour.[234] Costs are also recoverable in the Upper Tribunal in judicial review proceedings.[235]

Enforcement

RESA

8.159 Section 54(3)(c) of RESA provides that the minister may include in the order awarding the powers of civil sanction to regulators 'provision as to how any sum payable in pursuance of a decision of that Tribunal is to be recoverable'. This section empowers the minister to make provision for the mechanisms by which a regulator can recover any monies from a defaulting business that has appealed against a decision of the regulator (as provided for in the order).[236]

---

[232] Tribunal Procedure (Upper Tribunal) Rules 2008 and Tribunal Procedure (First-tier Tribunal) (General Regulatory Chamber) Rules 2009, r. 17(3).

[233] TCEA, s. 29(2).

[234] Tribunal Procedure (Upper Tribunal) Rules 2008, r. 10(3)(c) and (d) and Tribunal Procedure (First-tier Tribunal) (General Regulatory Chamber) Rules 2009, r. 10(1)(a) and (b).

[235] Tribunal Procedure (Upper Tribunal) Rules 2008, r. 10(3)(a).

[236] See para. 5.63 for a discussion of possible enforcement tools.

TCEA

The specific provisions on enforcement of Tribunal orders are contained in Part 1 of TCEA. **8.160**
They are to be distinguished from the more general provisions on enforcement by taking
control of goods and enforcement of judgments and orders, contained in Parts 2 and 3 of
TCEA. The latter provisions have not yet been implemented and every indication is that the
government will not implement them.

In relation to sums ordered to be paid by the First-tier or Upper Tribunals, TCEA provides **8.161**
that they will be recoverable as if they were payable under an order of the county court
or High Court.[237] This is subject to the Lord Chancellor's power to make certain orders
enforceable, either as county court or High Court orders only,[238] and to the possibility of the
Tribunal Procedure Rules limiting the application of this provision.[239] At the time of writing,
neither of these powers has been exercised in relation to awards in the General Regulatory
Chamber of the First-tier Tribunal or the Administrative Appeals Chamber of the Upper
Tribunal.

Awards of damages made in judicial review proceedings before the Tribunal may be enforced **8.162**
as if they were an order of the High Court.[240]

G. Appeal to the Court of Appeal

Any party to a decision made by the Upper Tribunal has a right of appeal to the relevant **8.163**
appellate court.[241] The relevant appellate court is that court which the Upper Tribunal specifies as the relevant appellate court, being one of either the Court of Appeal in England and
Wales, the Court of Session or the Court of Appeal in Northern Ireland.[242]

Limitations

There are a number of significant limitations to the right of appeal from the Upper Tribunal. **8.164**

'Excluded decisions'

First, certain decisions of the Upper Tribunal are excluded from the right of appeal;[243] **8.165**
these are known as 'excluded decisions'. The Lord Chancellor has the power to add to the list

---

[237] TCEA, s. 27(1).
[238] Ibid., s. 27(5).
[239] Ibid., s. 27(6).
[240] Ibid., s. 16(7).
[241] Ibid., s. 13(1) and (2).
[242] Ibid., s. 13(11)–(13).
[243] TCEA, s. 13(1). Section (8) provides that for the purposes of the right of appeal the following are
excluded decisions: (a) any decision of the Upper Tribunal on an appeal under s. 28(4) or (6) of the Data
Protection Act 1998 (appeals against national security certificate); (b) any decision of the Upper Tribunal on an
appeal under s. 60(1) or (4) of the Freedom of Information Act 2000 (appeals against national security certificate); (c) any decision of the Upper Tribunal on an application under s. 11(4)(b) (application for permission or
leave to appeal); (d) a decision of the Upper Tribunal under s. 10 (review of decision of Upper Tribunal) (i) to
review, or not to review, an earlier decision of the tribunal; (ii) to take no action, or not to take any particular
action, in the light of a review of an earlier decision of the tribunal; or (iii) to set aside an earlier decision of the
tribunal; (e) a decision of the Upper Tribunal that is set aside under s. 10 (including a decision set aside after
proceedings on an appeal under s. 13 have been begun); or (f) any decision of the Upper Tribunal that is of a
description specified in an order made by the Lord Chancellor.

of excluded decisions,[244] subject to the constraints set out in TCEA, s. 13(9).[245] The power to add to the list of excluded decisions can be used for one of two purposes only: in order to preserve existing appeal rights where those rights are, or include, something other than a right of appeal on a point of law; or to preserve, in cases where there is currently no appeal right, the existing position. At the time of writing the Lord Chancellor had not exercised his power to extend the categories of excluded decisions. A list of excluded decisions, so far as they are relevant to this field, is provided below in para. 8.175.

Permission to appeal

8.166 Second, the right of appeal may only be exercised with permission[246] given on an application by the party concerned to either the Upper Tribunal itself or, where the Upper Tribunal has refused permission, to the relevant appellate court.[247]

Important point of principle or some other compelling reason

8.167 Third, permission to appeal a decision of the Upper Tribunal in relation to an appeal on a point of law arising from a decision made by the First-tier Tribunal cannot be granted unless the Upper Tribunal or the relevant appellate court considers the proposed appeal would raise some important point of principle or practice or that there is some other compelling reason for the relevant appellate court to hear the appeal.[248]

Exclusion of parties

8.168 Finally, the Lord Chancellor has the power to make provision by an order for a person to be treated as being, or to be treated as not being, a party to a case for the purposes of the right to appeal.[249] Again, at the time of writing this power has not been exercised.

Powers on appeal

8.169 Where the appellate court determines that the Upper Tribunal has made an error of law,[250] it has a discretionary power to set aside the decision.[251] If the appellate court exercises that power it must either remit the case back to the Upper Tribunal (or, where the decision of the Upper Tribunal was on an appeal or reference from another tribunal or some other person, to that other tribunal or person, with direction for its reconsideration),[252] or the appellate court must remake the decision itself.[253]

Remit case

8.170 Where the decision is to remit the case back to the Upper Tribunal (or other tribunal or person), the appellate court may direct that the persons chosen to reconsider the case are not those who made the decision that gave rise to the appeal and it may also give procedural directions in connection with the reconsideration of the case. If, however, the decision was

---

[244] TCEA, s. 13(8)(f).
[245] Set out ibid., s. 13(9).
[246] Ibid., s. 13(3)(a).
[247] Ibid., s. 13(3)(b) and (4).
[248] See ibid., ss 11, 13(6) and (7) and art. 2 of the Appeals from The Upper Tribunal to The Court of Appeal Order 2008, SI 2834/2008.
[249] TCEA, s. 13(14).
[250] Ibid., s. 14(1).
[251] Ibid., s. 14(2)(a).
[252] Ibid., s. 14(2)(b)(i).
[253] Ibid., s. 14(2)(b)(ii).

made by the Upper Tribunal on an appeal or reference from another tribunal or some other person, the Upper Tribunal may (instead of reconsidering the case itself) remit the case to that other tribunal or person, with the directions given by the relevant appellate court for its reconsideration.[254] Furthermore, the Upper Tribunal may, in remitting the case back to the other tribunal or person, direct that the persons who are chosen to reconsider the case are not to be the same as those who made the decision in respect of which the appeal or reference to the Upper Tribunal was made and give procedural directions in connection with the reconsideration of the case by the other tribunal or person.[255]

Remake the decision

Where the appellate court determines to remake the decision, the appellate court may make any decision which the Upper Tribunal could make if the Upper Tribunal were remaking the decision or (as the case may be) that the other tribunal or person could make if that other tribunal or person were remaking the decision and may make such findings of fact as it considers appropriate. Consideration is given above to the ability of the Upper Tribunal to make its own findings of fact in relation to appeals from the First-tier Tribunal.[256] Those comments are relevant to the similar power enjoyed by the appellate courts. **8.171**

Procedure

Part 52 of the Civil Procedure Rules and Practice Direction 52 apply to appeals from the Upper Tribunal to the Court of Appeal. The appellant's notice must be filed within forty-two days of the date on which the Upper Tribunal's decision on permission to appeal to the Court of Appeal is given in the case of an appeal against a decision of the Administrative Appeals Chamber of the Upper Tribunal and, where the appellant wishes to appeal against a decision of any other chamber of the Upper Tribunal, the appellant's notice must be filed within twenty-eight days of the date on which the Upper Tribunal's decision on permission to appeal to the Court of Appeal is given. Practice Direction 52 lays down particular and detailed rules in relation to appeals from the Immigration Asylum Chamber of the Upper Tribunal, which are beyond the scope of this work.[257] **8.172**

H. Judicial review

Introduction

This part is concerned with the circumstances in which it may be possible to challenge decisions of the Upper Tribunal by way of judicial review. It is not concerned with the judicial review jurisdiction of the Upper Tribunal itself: that is the subject of paras 8.83–8.116. **8.173**

The decision in *Cart*

Whether or not (and if so in what circumstances) it may be possible to challenge decisions of the Upper Tribunal by way of judicial review is subject to litigation which, at the time of writing, is still ongoing. The current law, as applicable to England and Wales, is that resulting from the decision of the Court of Appeal in *R (on the application of Rex Cart) v The Upper* **8.174**

---

[254] Ibid., s. 14(5).
[255] Ibid., s. 14(6).
[256] See further para. 8.82.
[257] See PD52, 21.7 and 21.7B.

Tribunal ('*Cart*').[258] It may be, however, that *Cart* reaches the Supreme Court. Accordingly, the position set out below must be regarded as provisional and practitioners should check to see whether, at the time of reading, it has been superseded.

Excluded decisions

8.175 As explained in para. 8.163 above, an appeal from a decision of the Upper Tribunal will in most cases lie to the Court of Appeal. In such a case, a judicial review challenge would be unavailable. However, not all decisions of the Upper Tribunal are appealable in this way. Section 13(1) of TCEA precludes an appeal against a decision of the Upper Tribunal that is an 'excluded decision'. The excluded decisions relevant to the regulatory field are as follows:

(i) any decision of the Upper Tribunal on an application under TCEA, s. 11(4)(b) (application for permission or leave to appeal);[259]

(ii) a decision of the Upper Tribunal under TCEA, s. 10:

(a) to review, or not to review, an earlier decision of the Tribunal;

(b) to take no action, or not to take any particular action, in the light of a review of an earlier decision of the Tribunal, or

(c) to set aside an earlier decision of the Tribunal;[260]

(iii) a decision of the Upper Tribunal that is set aside under TCEA, s. 10 (including a decision set aside after proceedings on an appeal under TCEA, s. 13 have been begun);[261] or

(iv) any decision of the Upper Tribunal that is of a description specified in an order made by the Lord Chancellor.[262]

8.176 The issue in *Cart* was whether judicial review lies against the Upper Tribunal in respect of excluded decisions and specifically, on the facts, in respect of a decision of the Upper Tribunal on an application made to it for permission to appeal against a decision of the First-tier Tribunal (category (i) above).

8.177 Central to the case were two sections of the TCEA: s. 3(5), by which it is provided that 'the Upper Tribunal is to be a superior court of record'; and s. 25, which gives the Upper Tribunal in the discharge of its adjudicative functions 'the same powers, rights and privileges and authority as the High Court'. Founded principally on these provisions, it was argued that the Upper Tribunal was a body of equal power and standing to the High Court, placing it entirely beyond the latter's supervisory jurisdiction.[263] That argument was rejected. The Court of Appeal held that the Upper Tribunal was 'not an avatar of the High Court at all: far from standing in the High Court's shoes ... the shoes the Upper Tribunal stands in are those of the tribunals it has replaced'.[264]

---

[258] [2010] EWCA Civ 859 (on appeal from the Divisional Court [2009] EWHC 3052 [2009] STI 3167).

[259] TCEA, s. 13(8)(c).

[260] Ibid., s. 13(8)(d).

[261] Ibid., s. 13(8)(e).

[262] Ibid., s. 13(8)(f). According to s. 13(9), such a description may be specified only if: (a) in the case of a decision of that description, there is a right to appeal to a court from the decision and that right is, or includes, something other than a right (however expressed) to appeal on any point of law arising from the decision, or (b) decisions of that description are made in carrying out a function transferred under s. 30 and prior to the transfer of the function under s. 30(1) there was no right to appeal from decisions of that description.

[263] *Cart*, para. [11].

[264] Ibid., para. [19].

The court then went on to consider the available scope of judicial review of the Upper **8.178** Tribunal. It found that the complete reordering of administrative justice brought about by TCEA called for a reconsideration of the principles of law by which judicial review of the new Tribunals was to be governed.[265] In that context, certain factors were entitled to real weight:

> [t]he Tribunal system is designed to be so far as possible a self-sufficient structure, dealing internally with errors of law made at first instance and resorting to higher appellate authority only where a legal issue of difficulty or of principle requires it. By this means serious questions of law are channelled into the legal system without the need of post-*Anisminic*[266] judicial review.[267]

The Court of Appeal saw a 'true jurisprudential difference' between an error of law made in **8.179** the course of an adjudication that a tribunal was authorized to conduct, and the conducting of an adjudication without lawful authority. Errors of law *within* jurisdiction resided within the principle that a system of law, while it can guarantee to be fair, cannot guarantee to be infallible. However: '... [o]utright excess of jurisdiction by the [Upper Tribunal] UT and denial by it of fundamental justice, should they ever occur, are in a different class: they represent the doing by the UT of something that Parliament cannot possibly have authorised it to do.'[268]

Thus (to paraphrase the Court of Appeal's holding), if the Upper Tribunal embarks on deci- **8.180** sion making in a case that it has no statutory power to conduct, or if (even if it has such power) it nevertheless conducts itself in a way which is obviously procedurally irregular, it will be subject to judicial review. Absent such circumstances, however, and as the case law stands, the Upper Tribunal is beyond the supervisory jurisdiction of the High Court and its decisions may not be challenged through that route (though they may be on appeal if that is available).

That is not of course to say that, save in such circumstances, judicial review will have **8.181** no application in the new regulatory world created by RESA. Judicial review will still lie in respect of decisions by regulators and other public bodies that are not challengeable by way of appeal to the First-tier Tribunal (whether or not the Lord Chief Justice transfers jurisdiction for hearing such cases from the High Court to the Upper Tribunal in due course).[269] An example might be a challenge to a regulator's penalty guidance or enforcement policy that is claimed to be unlawful. The extent of the scope for such challenges remains to be seen.

The position in Scotland

It is important to note that *Cart* does not determine the position in Scotland. That is **8.182** subject to different litigation which, like *Cart*, is still ongoing. On 31 March 2010 the Outer

---

[265] Ibid., para. [29].
[266] Prior to the decision of the House of Lords in *Anisminic Ltd v Foreign Compensation Commission* [1969] 2 AC 147, an error of law needed to be 'jurisdictional' (or else on the face of the record) in order to be correctable by judicial review. Post-*Anisminic*, any error of law is correctable by way of judicial review; it need not be one going to jurisdiction. See the speech of Lord Reid in *Anisminic* at 174A–D.
[267] *Cart*, para. [30].
[268] Ibid., para. [367].
[269] That is, under the procedure for which provision is made in s. 18(6) of the 2007 Act (see above para. 8.89 et seq).

House gave judgment in *Eba*,[270] which raised the same issue as *Cart* in the Scottish context. With reasoning that differed from that of the Court of Appeal (and the Divisional Court) in *Cart*, Lord Glennie concluded that a decision of the Upper Tribunal in respect of which there lay no appeal could only be subject to review on pre-*Anisminic* grounds (i.e. excess of jurisdiction in the narrow sense) or because there has been a breakdown of fair procedure.[271] On appeal[272] the Inner House concluded that in Scotland the only civil courts that the Court of Session had regarded as not amenable to its supervisory jurisdiction were courts that were, in effect, manifestations of itself. As a consequence, it would not be right to exclude from judicial review on the ground of 'inappropriateness' a decision of the Upper Tribunal which, albeit having a wide and comprehensive jurisdiction in its specialist fields, was clearly not such a manifestation. The case would be remitted to the Lord Ordinary with a direction to proceed accordingly.

---

[270] Opinion of Lord Glennie in *The petition of Blajosse Charlotte Eba* [2010] CSOH 45.
[271] Ibid., para. [90].
[272] *Eba v Advocate General for Scotland* [2010] CSIH 78.

Appendices

APPENDIX 1

Regulatory Enforcement and Sanctions Act 2008

Schedule 3   Section 4(2)

Enactments Specified for the Purposes of Part 1

Accommodation Agencies Act 1953 (c 23), section 1

Administration of Justice Act 1970 (c 31), section 40

Agricultural Produce (Grading and Marking) Act 1928 (c 19)

Agriculture Act 1967 (c 22)

Agriculture Act 1970 (c 40)

Agriculture and Horticulture Act 1964 (c 28), Part 3

Agriculture (Miscellaneous Provisions) Act 1954 (c 39), section 9

Agriculture (Miscellaneous Provisions) Act 1968 (c 34)

Animal Boarding Establishments Act 1963 (c 43)

Animal Health Act 1981 (c 22)

Animal Health and Welfare Act 1984 (c 40)

Animal Welfare Act 2006 (c 45)

Anti-social Behaviour Act 2003 (c 38)

Breeding and Sale of Dogs (Welfare) Act 1999 (c 11)

Breeding of Dogs Act 1973 (c 60)

Breeding of Dogs Act 1991 (c 64)

Business Names Act 1985 (c 7)

Cancer Act 1939 (c 13), section 4

Caravan Sites and Control of Development Act 1960 (c 2)

Celluloid and Cinematograph Film Act 1922 (c 35)

Charities Act 1993 (c 10), sections 76 to 78

Charities Act 2006 (c 50), section 50

Children and Young Persons Act 1933 (c 12), Part 1

Children and Young Persons Act 1963 (c 37), Part 2

Children and Young Persons (Protection from Tobacco) Act 1991 (c 23)

Christmas Day (Trading) Act 2004 (c 26)

Cinemas Act 1985 (c 13)

Clean Air Act 1993 (c 11)

Clean Neighbourhoods and Environment Act 2005 (c 16), Parts 2, 6 and 7

Companies Act 1985 (c 6), Chapter 1 of Part 11 and section 693

Consumer Credit Act 1974 (c 39)

Consumer Protection Act 1987 (c 43)

Control of Pollution Act 1974 (c 40)

Control of Pollution (Amendment) Act 1989 (c 14)

Copyright, Designs and Patents Act 1988 (c 48), sections 107A and 198A

Countryside Act 1968 (c 41)

Courts and Legal Services Act 1990 (c 41), Parts 4 and 6

Criminal Justice and Police Act 2001 (c 16), Part 1

Criminal Justice and Public Order Act 1994 (c 33), Parts 5, 7 and 12

Crossbows Act 1987 (c 32)

Dangerous Dogs Act 1991 (c 65)

Dangerous Wild Animals Act 1976 (c 38)

Defective Premises Act 1972 (c 35)

Development of Tourism Act 1969 (c 51)

Disability Discrimination Act 1995 (c 50)

Dogs Act 1906 (c 32)

Education Reform Act 1988 (c 40), section 215

Employment Agencies Act 1973 (c 35)

Energy Act 1976 (c 76)

Enterprise Act 2002 (c 40), Part 8

Environment Act 1995 (c 25)

Environment and Safety Information Act 1988 (c 30)

Environmental Protection Act 1990 (c 43)

Estate Agents Act 1979 (c 38)

Explosives Act 1875 (c 17)

Explosives Act 1923 (c 17)

Explosives (Age of Purchase &c.) Act 1976 (c 26)

Factories Act 1961 (c 34)

Fair Trading Act 1973 (c 41)

Farm and Garden Chemicals Act 1967 (c 50)

Farriers (Registration) Act 1975 (c 35)

Fire and Rescue Services Act 2004 (c 21)

Fire Safety and Safety of Places of Sport Act 1987 (c 27)

Firearms Act 1968 (c 27)

Firearms Act 1982 (c 31)

Fireworks Act 2003 (c 22)

Food Act 1984 (c 30)

Food and Environment Protection Act 1985 (c 48), Parts 1 and 2

Food Safety Act 1990 (c 16), Parts 2 and 3

Food Standards Act 1999 (c 28)

Forgery and Counterfeiting Act 1981 (c 45)

Fraud Act 2006 (c 35)

Gambling Act 2005 (c 19)

Game Act 1831 (c 32)

Ground Game Act 1880 (c 47)

Guard Dogs Act 1975 (c 50)

Hallmarking Act 1973 (c 43)

Health Act 2006 (c 28), Part 1

Health and Safety at Work etc Act 1974 (c 37)

Highways Act 1980 (c 66)

House to House Collections Act 1939 (c 44)

Housing Act 1985 (c 68), Parts 8, 9 and 10

Housing Act 1996 (c 52), Part 8

Housing Act 2004 (c 34), Parts 2 to 5

Hypnotism Act 1952 (c 46)

Intoxicating Substances (Supply) Act 1985 (c 26)

Knives Act 1997 (c 21)

Legal Services Act 2007 (c 29), section 198

Licensing Act 2003 (c 17)

Litter Act 1983 (c 35)

Local Government Act 1972 (c 70), Parts 9 and 11

Local Government Act 1985 (c 51), Part 2

Local Government Act 1988 (c 9), Part 4

Local Government Act 2000 (c 22), Part 1

Local Government (Miscellaneous Provisions) Act 1976 (c 57)

Local Government (Miscellaneous Provisions) Act 1982 (c 30)

London Government Act 1963 (c 33)

London Local Authorities Act 1990 (c vii)

London Local Authorities Act 1991 (c xiii)

London Local Authorities Act 1994 (c xii)

London Local Authorities Act 1995 (c x)

London Local Authorities Act 1996 (c ix)

London Local Authorities Act 2000 (c vii)

London Local Authorities Act 2004 (c i)

London Local Authorities Act 2007 (c ii)

London Olympic Games and Paralympic Games Act 2006 (c 12)

Malicious Communications Act 1988 (c 27)

Medicines Act 1968 (c 67)

Mines and Quarries Act 1954 (c 70)

Mines and Quarries (Tips) Act 1969 (c 10)

Mock Auctions Act 1961 (c 47)

Motor Cycle Noise Act 1987 (c 34)

National Lottery etc Act 1993 (c 39), sections 12 and 13

Noise Act 1996 (c 37)

Noise and Statutory Nuisance Act 1993 (c 40)

Offices, Shops and Railway Premises Act 1963 (c 41)

Offshore Safety Act 1992 (c 15)

Olympic Symbol etc (Protection) Act 1995 (c 32)

Opticians Act 1989 (c 44)

Osteopaths Act 1993 (c 21)

Pedlars Act 1871 (c 96)

Performing Animals (Regulation) Act 1925 (c 38)

Pests Act 1954 (c 68)

Pet Animals Act 1951 (c 35)

Petroleum (Consolidation) Act 1928 (c 32)

Petroleum (Transfer of Licences) Act 1936 (c 27)

Plant Health Act 1967 (c 8)

Poisons Act 1972 (c 66)

Police, Factories, &c. (Miscellaneous Provisions) Act 1916 (c 31)

Pollution Prevention and Control Act 1999 (c 24)

Prevention of Damage by Pests Act 1949 (c 55)

Prices Act 1974 (c 24)

Private Hire Vehicles (London) Act 1998 (c 34)

Private Security Industry Act 2001 (c 12)

Property Misdescriptions Act 1991 (c 29)

Protection Against Cruel Tethering Act 1988 (c 31)

Protection from Harassment Act 1997 (c 40)

Protection of Animals Act 1911 (c 27)

Public Health Act 1936 (c 49)

Public Health Act 1961 (c 64)

Public Passenger Vehicles Act 1981 (c 14)

Refuse Disposal (Amenity) Act 1978 (c 3)

Regulatory Reform (Fire Safety) Order 2005 (SI 2005/1541)

Riding Establishments Act 1964 (c 70)

Riding Establishments Act 1970 (c 32)

Road Traffic Act 1988 (c 52), sections 15A, 17, 18, 41, 71, 81, 82 and 196

Road Traffic (Consequential Provisions) Act 1988 (c 54)

Road Traffic (Foreign Vehicles) Act 1972 (c 27)

Safety of Sports Grounds Act 1975 (c 52)

Sale of Goods Act 1979 (c 54)

Scotch Whisky Act 1988 (c 22)

Scrap Metal Dealers Act 1964 (c 69)

Sea Fisheries Regulation Act 1966 (c 38)

Serious Organised Crime and Police Act 2005 (c 15), Part 4

Slaughter of Poultry Act 1967 (c 24)

Slaughterhouses Act 1974 (c 3)

Sunday Trading Act 1994 (c 20)

Supply of Goods and Services Act 1982 (c 29)

Supply of Goods (Implied Terms) Act 1973 (c 13)

Theatres Act 1968 (c 54)

Theft Act 1968 (c 60)

Theft Act 1978 (c 31)

Timeshare Act 1992 (c 35)

Tobacco Advertising and Promotion Act 2002 (c 36)

Town Police Clauses Act 1847 (c 89)

Trade Descriptions Act 1968 (c 29)

Trade Marks Act 1994 (c 26), section 93

Trading Representations (Disabled Persons) Act 1958 (c 49)

Traffic Management Act 2004 (c 18)

Transport Act 1981 (c 56)

Unfair Contract Terms Act 1977 (c 50)

Unsolicited Goods and Services Act 1971 (c 30)

Vehicles (Crime) Act 2001 (c 3)

Veterinary Surgeons Act 1966 (c 36)

Video Recordings Act 1984 (c 39)

Violent Crime Reduction Act 2006 (c 38)

Water Industry Act 1991 (c 56), sections 77 to 85

Water Resources Act 1991 (c 57)

Weeds Act 1959 (c 54)

Weights and Measures &c. Act 1976 (c 77)

Weights and Measures Act 1985 (c 72)

Welfare of Animals at Slaughter Act 1991 (c 30)

Wildlife and Countryside Act 1981 (c 69)

Zoo Licensing Act 1981 (c 37)

SCHEDULE 4   Section 28(7)

ENFORCEMENT ACTION: REFERENCES TO LBRO

Reference by enforcing authority

1 (1) If the primary authority directs the enforcing authority as specified in section 28(2), the enforcing authority may with the consent of LBRO refer the proposed enforcement action to LBRO.

(2) On a reference under this paragraph—
   (a) if LBRO is satisfied as to the matters in sub-paragraph (3), it must confirm the direction;
   (b) in any other case, it must revoke the direction (and section 28(4)(b) shall accordingly cease to apply in relation to the direction).

(3) The matters referred to in sub-paragraph (2) are that—
   (a) the proposed enforcement action is inconsistent with advice or guidance previously given by the primary authority (generally or specifically),
   (b) the advice or guidance was correct, and
   (c) the advice or guidance was properly given by the primary authority.

(4) Where under sub-paragraph (2) LBRO confirms a direction of the primary authority, it may direct the enforcing authority to take some other enforcement action (and section 28(1) to (4) does not apply in relation to that action).

(5) The enforcing authority must comply with any direction under sub-paragraph (4).

Reference by regulated person

2 (1) If the primary authority does not direct the enforcing authority as specified in section 28(2), the regulated person may with the consent of LBRO refer the action to LBRO.

(2) On a reference under this paragraph—
    (a) if LBRO is satisfied as to the matters in sub-paragraph (3), it must direct the enforcing authority not to take the proposed enforcement action;
    (b) in any other case, it must consent to the action.

(3) The matters referred to in sub-paragraph (2) are that—
    (a) the proposed enforcement action is inconsistent with advice or guidance previously given by the primary authority (generally or specifically),
    (b) the advice or guidance was correct, and
    (c) the advice or guidance was properly given by the primary authority.

(4) The enforcing authority may not take the proposed enforcement action if it is directed as specified in sub-paragraph (2)(a).

(5) Where LBRO gives a direction under sub-paragraph (2)(a), it may direct the enforcing authority to take some other enforcement action (and section 28(1) to (4) does not apply in relation to that action).

(6) The enforcing authority must comply with any direction under sub-paragraph (5).

(7) LBRO may require a regulated person who makes a reference under this paragraph to pay such reasonable costs incurred by LBRO as a result of the reference as LBRO may specify.

Reference by primary authority

3 (1) The primary authority may with the consent of LBRO, instead of making a determination under section 28(2) in relation to a proposed enforcement action, refer the action to LBRO.

(2) On a reference under this paragraph—
    (a) if LBRO is satisfied as to the matters in sub-paragraph (3), it must direct the enforcing authority not to take the proposed enforcement action;
    (b) in any other case, it must consent to the action.

(3) The matters referred to in sub-paragraph (2) are that—
    (a) the proposed enforcement action is inconsistent with advice or guidance previously given by the primary authority (generally or specifically),
    (b) the advice or guidance was correct, and
    (c) the advice or guidance was properly given by the primary authority.

(4) The enforcing authority may not take the proposed enforcement action if it is directed as specified in sub-paragraph (2)(a).

(5) Where LBRO gives a direction under sub-paragraph (2)(a), it may direct the enforcing authority to take some other enforcement action (and section 28(1) to (4) does not apply in relation to that action).

(6) The enforcing authority must comply with any direction under sub-paragraph (5).

Effect of reference

4 The enforcing authority may not take the proposed enforcement action—
    (a) in any period during which the regulated person may make a reference under paragraph 2;
    (b) at any time after the making of a reference under this Schedule and before its determination.

Consultation

5 (1) Before making a determination for the purposes of this Schedule LBRO—
    (a) must consult any relevant regulator, where appropriate, and
    (b) may consult such other persons as it thinks fit.

(2) In sub-paragraph (1)(a) "relevant regulator" means a person (other than a local authority) with regulatory functions which relate to the matter to which the determination relates.

Procedure: general

6 (1) LBRO must determine any reference under this Schedule within the period of 28 days beginning with the day on which the reference is made.

(2) The Secretary of State may by order make further provision as to the procedure to be followed, for the purposes of this Schedule, by the primary authority, the enforcing authority, the regulated person and LBRO.

Guidance and directions

7 (1) LBRO may give guidance or directions to any one or more local authorities about any enforcement action referred to it.

(2) A local authority must have regard to any guidance, and comply with any direction, given to it under sub-paragraph (1).

(3) LBRO must publish any guidance or directions given under this paragraph in such manner as it considers appropriate.

Information

8 For the purposes of this Schedule LBRO may require the primary authority, the enforcing authority or the regulated person to provide it with such information as it may specify, being information which the authority may lawfully provide to LBRO.

SCHEDULE 5   Section 37(1)
DESIGNATED REGULATORS

British Hallmarking Council

Charity Commission for England and Wales

Coal Authority

Competition Commission

Countryside Council for Wales

Environment Agency

Financial Services Authority

Food Standards Agency

Football Licensing Authority

Forestry Commissioners

Gambling Commission

Gangmasters Licensing Authority

Health and Safety Executive

Hearing Aid Council

Historic Buildings and Monuments Commission for England ("English Heritage")

Housing Corporation

Human Fertilisation and Embryology Authority

Human Tissue Authority

Information Commissioner

Local fisheries committees

Natural England

Office of Communications
Office of Fair Trading
Office of Rail Regulation
Pensions Regulator
Security Industry Authority
Statistics Board

SCHEDULE 6   Section 37(2)

ENACTMENTS SPECIFIED FOR THE PURPOSES OF ORDERS UNDER PART 3

Accommodation Agencies Act 1953 (c 23), section 1

Administration of Justice Act 1970 (c 31), section 40

Agriculture Act 1947 (c 48), section 100

Agriculture Act 1967 (c 22), section 14(2)

Agriculture Act 1970 (c 40)

Agriculture and Horticulture Act 1964 (c 28), sections 14 and 15

Ancient Monuments and Archaeological Areas Act 1979 (c 46)

Animal Boarding Establishments Act 1963 (c 43), section 1(8)

Animal Health Act 1981 (c 22)

Animal Health and Welfare Act 1984 (c 40), section 10(6)

Animals (Scientific Procedures) Act 1986 (c 14)

Animal Welfare Act 2006 (c 45)

Anti-social Behaviour Act 2003 (c 38), sections 54 and 75

Aviation and Maritime Security Act 1990 (c 31), sections 15 and 48 and Part 3

Aviation Security Act 1982 (c 36), Part 2

Bees Act 1980 (c 12), section 1(7)

Breeding of Dogs Act 1973 (c 60)

Breeding of Dogs Act 1991 (c 64)

Building Act 1984 (c 55)

Cancer Act 1939 (c 13), section 4

Children and Young Persons Act 1933 (c 12), section 7(1)

Children and Young Persons Act 1963 (c 37), section 40

Children and Young Persons (Protection from Tobacco) Act 1991 (c 23)

Christmas Day (Trading) Act 2004 (c 26), sections 2 and 3

Chronically Sick and Disabled Persons Act 1970 (c 44), section 21

Clean Air Act 1993 (c 11)

Clean Neighbourhoods and Environment Act 2005 (c 16), sections 3 to 7 and Part 7

Coast Protection Act 1949 (c 74), sections 18(7) and 36

Commons Act 2006 (c 26), section 34(1)

Conservation of Seals Act 1970 (c 30)

Consumer Credit Act 1974 (c 39)

Consumer Protection Act 1987 (c 43), section 12

Control of Pollution Act 1974 (c 40), Part 3

Control of Pollution (Amendment) Act 1989 (c 14), sections 1, 5 and 7

Criminal Justice and Public Order Act 1994 (c 33), sections 77(3), 78(4), 166 and 167

Dangerous Dogs Act 1989 (c 30)

Dangerous Dogs Act 1991 (c 65)

Dangerous Vessels Act 1985 (c 22), section 5

Dangerous Wild Animals Act 1976 (c 38)

Deer Act 1991 (c 54)

Destructive Imported Animals Act 1932 (c 12), section 6

Disability Discrimination Act 1995 (c 50), Part 5

Diseases of Fish Act 1937 (c 33)

Diseases of Fish Act 1983 (c 30)

Education Reform Act 1988 (c 40), section 214

Employment Agencies Act 1973 (c 35), sections 5(2), 6(2), and 10(2)

Energy Act 1976 (c 76), section 18

Enterprise Act 2002 (c 40), section 227E

Environment Act 1995 (c 25), section 110

Environmental Protection Act 1990 (c 43), Parts 2, 2A and 3, and sections 118 and 150(5)

Estate Agents Act 1979 (c 38)

Explosives Act 1875 (c 17), sections 30 to 32, 43, 73 and 80

Fair Trading Act 1973 (c 41), sections 23, 30 and 120

Farriers (Registration) Act 1975 (c 35)

Fire Safety and Safety of Places of Sport Act 1987 (c 27)

Fireworks Act 2003 (c 22), section 11

Fisheries Act 1981 (c 29)

Fishery Limits Act 1976 (c 86)

Food and Environment Protection Act 1985 (c 48), Parts 1, 2 and 3

Food Safety Act 1990 (c 16), Parts 2 and 3

Food Standards Act 1999 (c 28)

Gambling Act 2005 (c 19)

Game Act 1831 (c 32), sections 3, 3A, and 24

Goods Vehicles (Licensing of Operators) Act 1995 (c 23)

Ground Game Act 1880 (c 47), section 6

Hallmarking Act 1973 (c 43), sections 1, 3, 5 to 7 and 11

Hares Preservation Act 1892 (c 8), section 2

Health and Safety at Work etc Act 1974 (c 37), section 33

Highways Act 1980 (c 66), Part 9

Horticultural Produce Act 1986 (c 20)

Import of Live Fish (England and Wales) Act 1980 (c 27), section 3

International Carriage of Perishable Foodstuffs Act 1976 (c 58), sections 6 to 11

Intoxicating Substances (Supply) Act 1985 (c 26), section 1

Knives Act 1997 (c 21)

Licensing Act 2003 (c 17)

Local Government (Miscellaneous Provisions) Act 1976 (c 57), Part 2

Local Government (Miscellaneous Provisions) Act 1982 (c 30), Part 8 and Schedules 3 and 4

London Local Authorities Act 1995 (c x), sections 24 and 25

London Local Authorities Act 2004 (c i), sections 22, 26 and 29

Medicines Act 1968 (c 67)

Merchant Shipping Act 1995 (c 21), Parts 1 to 5 and 9 to 12

Mines and Quarries (Tips) Act 1969 (c 10), Part 2

Motor Cycle Noise Act 1987 (c 34)

New Roads and Street Works Act 1991 (c 22), section 51

Noise Act 1996 (c 37)

Olympic Symbol etc (Protection) Act 1995 (c 32), section 8

Pedlars Act 1871 (c 96), sections 4, 12 and 14

Pests Act 1954 (c 68), sections 8, 9 and 12

Pet Animals Act 1951 (c 35)

Petroleum (Consolidation) Act 1928 (c 32), sections 1, 5 and 18

Pilotage Act 1987 (c 21)

Planning (Listed Buildings and Conservation Areas) Act 1990 (c 9)

Plant Varieties Act 1997 (c 66), sections 19, 31 and 32

Plant Varieties and Seeds Act 1964 (c 14), sections 16 and 25

Poisons Act 1972 (c 66)

Prevention of Damage by Pests Act 1949 (c 55), sections 3(4), 17 and 22(4)

Prices Act 1974 (c 24)

Property Misdescriptions Act 1991 (c 29)

Protection from Eviction Act 1977 (c 43), section 1

Protection of Badgers Act 1992 (c 51), sections 1 to 5 and 10

Protection of Wrecks Act 1973 (c 33)

Public Health Act 1936 (c 49), Part 2 and sections 269, 288 and 290

Public Health (Control of Disease) Act 1984 (c 22), sections 15 to 55

Public Passenger Vehicles Act 1981 (c 14), Part 2 and section 67

Radioactive Material (Road Transport) Act 1991 (c 27), sections 2 to 6

Railways Act 1993 (c 43), sections 119, 120 and 121

Railways and Transport Safety Act 2003 (c 20), sections 78 to 80

Refuse Disposal (Amenity) Act 1978 (c 3), sections 2(1) and 2B(2)

Rent Act 1977 (c 42), sections 77 and 81

Road Traffic Act 1988 (c 52)

Road Traffic (Driver Licensing and Information Systems) Act 1989 (c 22), sections 9 and 11

Road Traffic (Foreign Vehicles) Act 1972 (c 27), section 3

Road Traffic (New Drivers) Act 1995 (c 13), section 3

Road Traffic Offenders Act 1988 (c 53), sections 25, 62, 67, 90D and 91

Road Traffic Regulation Act 1984 (c 27), sections 5, 16, 47, 115 and 117

Safety of Sports Grounds Act 1975 (c 52), section 12(1) and (6)

Salmon Act 1986 (c 62), section 32(1)

Salmon and Freshwater Fisheries Act 1975 (c 51)

Scrap Metal Dealers Act 1964 (c 69), sections 1 and 5

Sea Fish (Conservation) Act 1967 (c 84)

Sea Fisheries Act 1968 (c 77)

Sea Fisheries Regulation Act 1966 (c 38)

Sea Fisheries (Shellfish) Act 1967 (c 83)

Solicitors Act 1974 (c 47), section 20

Sunday Trading Act 1994 (c 20)

Timeshare Act 1992 (c 35)

Trade Descriptions Act 1968 (c 29)

Transport Act 1968 (c 73), Part 6

Transport Act 1985 (c 67), sections 23, 30 and 101

Transport Act 2000 (c 38), section 148 and Part 3

Unsolicited Goods and Services Act 1971 (c 30), sections 2 and 3

Vehicles (Crime) Act 2001 (c 3)

Vehicle Excise and Registration Act 1994 (c 22), section 28A, Part 3 and section 59

Veterinary Surgeons Act 1966 (c 36)

Video Recordings Act 1984 (c 39), sections 9 to 14

Video Recordings Act 1993 (c 24)

Water Industry Act 1991 (c 56), sections 70(1), 86, 109, 111 and 118

Water Resources Act 1991 (c 57)

Weeds Act 1959 (c 54), section 2

Weights and Measures Act 1985 (c 72), Parts 2 to 7

Wildlife and Countryside Act 1981 (c 69), Parts 1 and 2

Zoo Licensing Act 1981 (c 37), section 19

SCHEDULE 7   Section 62

ENACTMENTS SPECIFIED FOR THE PURPOSES OF SECTION 62

Activity Centres (Young Persons' Safety) Act 1995 (c 15), section 2

Animal Health Act 1981 (c 22)

Animal Welfare Act 2006 (c 45), section 12

Aviation and Maritime Security Act 1990 (c 31), sections 36A, 41 and 42

Aviation Security Act 1982 (c 36), sections 20A, 21F and 21G

Channel Tunnel Act 1987 (c 53), section 11

Charities Act 1992 (c 41), sections 64 and 64A

Charities Act 2006 (c 50), section 63

Consumers, Estate Agents and Redress Act 2007 (c 17), section 59

Control of Pollution Act 1974 (c 40), section 17

Control of Pollution (Amendment) Act 1989 (c 14), section 2

Electricity Act 1989 (c 29), section 29

Environment Act 1995 (c 25), sections 87, 95 and 97

Environmental Protection Act 1990 (c 43), sections 140 and 156

Financial Services and Markets Act 2000 (c 8), section 168(4)(b)

Fisheries Act 1981 (c 29), section 30

Food Safety Act 1990 (c 16), Part 2

Food Standards Act 1999 (c 28), section 27

Gambling Act 2005 (c 19), sections 59(1) and 146

Gas Act 1986 (c 44), sections 18 and 47

Goods Vehicles (Licensing of Operators) Act 1995 (c 23), Schedule 1A

Hovercraft Act 1968 (c 59), section 1

Medicines Act 1968 (c 67), sections 91 and 95

Merchant Shipping Act 1995 (c 21)

Merchant Shipping (Oil Pollution, Preparedness, Response and Co-operation) Order 1997
  (SI 1997/2567), article 2

Motor Vehicles (International Circulation) Act 1952 (c 39), section 1

Pensions Act 1995 (c 26), section 116

Pensions Act 2004 (c 35), section 314

Petroleum Act 1998 (c 17), section 25

Plant Health Act 1967 (c 8), section 3

Pollution Prevention and Control Act 1999 (c 24), sections 2 and 3

Public Health (Control of Disease) Act 1984 (c 22), section 13

Public Passenger Vehicles Act 1981 (c 14), section 60

Railways Act 1993 (c 43), section 121A

Railways and Transport Safety Act 2003 (c 20), sections 9 and 11

Regulatory Reform Act 2001 (c 6), section 1

Road Traffic Act 1988 (c 52), sections 49, 61, 105 and 120 and Schedule 2A

Safety of Sports Grounds Act 1975 (c 52), section 6(2)

Salmon Act 1986 (c 62), section 31

Sea Fisheries Regulation Act 1966 (c 38), section 5

Vehicle Excise and Registration Act 1994 (c 22), sections 24 and 28 and Schedule 2A

Water Industry Act 1991 (c 56), section 69

Water Resources Act 1991 (c 57), section 92

Weights and Measures &c. Act 1976 (c 77), section 12

Weights and Measures Act 1985 (c 72), section 22

Local Better Regulation Office—Primary Authority Guidance
March 2009

This guidance is issued by LBRO under section 33 of the Regulatory Enforcement and Sanctions Act 2008 and should be read in conjunction with the Act and Orders under it.

Section 33(3) requires a local authority to have regard to any guidance given to it under this section.

In this guidance the following definitions are used: 'may' is used to mean actions that are discretionary in the light of the context and all of the circumstances; 'should' is used to mean actions that are compulsory as advised in this guidance and that therefore local authorities must have regard to; and 'must' is used to mean actions that are compulsory as set out in legislation.

FOREWORD

Effective support for business from local authority regulatory services depends on reliable, accessible advice. Where that advice is not consistent, business faces unnecessary costs. At the same time, the proper protection of consumers, workers and the environment also depends on good local regulation that meets the needs of local communities and provides appropriately targeted regulation of business. So, better and more consistent regulation drives prosperity and supports protection both for communities and compliant businesses – it can and should be a matter of 'win-win'.

The Primary Authority scheme is key to achieving better regulation at local level, promoting consistency across council boundaries, encouraging a new relationship between local authority regulators and giving businesses the confidence to invest and grow. It will drive efficient, effective and consistent regulation across the system for the benefit of all.

By liaising closely with businesses to gain a detailed understanding of their operations, primary authorities will be ideally placed to support compliance by providing specific advice on which businesses will be able to rely.

Primary authorities will also act as a resource for other local authorities as they work to deliver consistent, targeted and proportionate enforcement by providing valuable intelligence on businesses' operations through advice and the development of inspection plans.

Primary Authority is a new approach, and this guidance, along with experience of it in practice, will need to be reviewed to ensure that it is meeting the needs of both local authorities and businesses. We will undertake this review later this year and we welcome comments and suggestions.

Clive Grace
Chair
LBRO

Graham Russell
Chief Executive
LBRO

March 2009

EXECUTIVE SUMMARY

The Regulatory Enforcement and Sanctions Act 2008, and secondary legislation made under the Act, establishes Primary Authority as a statutory scheme for businesses trading across local authority boundaries.

The Primary Authority scheme offers local authorities the opportunity to develop a constructive partnership with a business that can deliver reliable advice and coordinated and consistent enforcement for the business. The scheme provides for new funding arrangements, allowing local authorities to consider recovering costs from partner businesses.

The Local Better Regulation Office (LBRO) has responsibility for administering this scheme and has set up a web-based IT system with a secure area to support it. This guidance for local authorities has been written to enable them to operate the scheme effectively.

Key elements of Primary Authority operate as follows.

- Primary Authority covers environmental health, licensing and trading standards legislation and applies to all local authorities that have responsibility for these functions. Due to the nature of reserved legislative authority in the devolved administrations, the application of the scheme in Scotland and in Northern Ireland is different from its application in England and Wales.

- A Primary Authority partnership with a particular business may originate in an approach from the business, or it may be proposed by a local authority and a business jointly, for example as a natural progression from an existing home or lead authority relationship.

- A written Primary Authority Agreement will be prepared by the local authority and the business and forms the basis for a request to LBRO to formally nominate and register the partnership.

- A primary authority has responsibility for providing the regulatory advice that the business requires in relation to specified areas of regulation, and the business will be able to rely on this advice.

- A primary authority may issue statutory advice to other local authorities and produce an inspection plan to which enforcing authorities must have regard.

- Where an enforcing authority has concerns about the compliance of a business that has a primary authority, it should discuss the issue with the primary authority at an early stage.

- If enforcement is envisaged there is a statutory requirement for enforcing authorities to notify the primary authority of the proposed enforcement action. However, exemptions allow certain enforcement action to proceed immediately, for example where action is needed urgently to prevent harm.

- Where actions of the business are potentially subject to enforcement action by an authority, the primary authority will advise on whether relevant advice has been given to the business and whether the proposed action is consistent with that advice.

- LBRO is empowered to make determinations in cases of disagreement as to whether proposed enforcement action is inconsistent with the advice given by the primary authority.

CHARACTERISTICS OF A PARTNERSHIP

Who can have a partnership?

1 The Primary Authority scheme is open to any business, charity or other organisation (referred to throughout this guidance as 'the business') that is regulated by two or more local authorities in respect of a relevant function (see glossary). Relevant functions are defined in the Regulatory Enforcement and Sanctions Act 2008 ('the Act')[1] and Orders made under it. Relevant functions cover matters that are commonly referred to as 'trading standards', 'environmental health' and 'licensing' legislation.

2 The following are examples of businesses that might want to have a partnership:
- a multi-site retailer with branches in a number of local authority areas;
- a food manufacturer whose goods are distributed for sale across a number of local authority areas;
- an internet retailer who sells goods or services over a wide area;
- a tour operator whose customers may be located in any area;
- an importer whose products are distributed nationally;
- a chain of gyms with outlets in a number of local authority areas;
- a charitable care home provider with premises in several local authority areas;
- a national chain of petrol filling stations; or
- a restaurant company that offers franchises across several local authority areas but retains central control of particular relevant functions.

What scope can a partnership have?

3 There are various elements to the scope of a partnership, as outlined in the following sections.

Regulatory scope

4 A local authority can form a partnership only in respect of those relevant functions for which it has regulatory responsibility. For example, a county council could become a primary authority for food standards matters but not food safety and hygiene matters.

5 LBRO has defined a number of categories which include all of the relevant functions within the scope of Primary Authority. LBRO recommends that, wherever possible, partnerships should cover one or more of the following complete categories of relevant function ('categories'):
- age-restricted sales
- agriculture
- animal establishments and companion animal welfare
- consumer credit
- environmental protection
- explosives licensing
- fair trading
- farm animal health
- food safety and hygiene
- food standards
- general licensing
- health and safety
- housing
- metrology
- petroleum licensing
- pollution control

---

[1] www.opsi.gov.uk/acts/acts2008/pdf/ukpga_20080013_en.pdf

- product safety
- road traffic.

These categories are listed in full in Annex 1, where further information is provided on the scope of each category.

6 A business can have a partnership for a single category or for multiple categories. This means that a business could have partnerships with different local authorities for different categories. For example, retailer 'A' may enter into a partnership with district council 'B' for health and safety, with county council 'C' for product safety and food standards, and with fire authority 'D' for petroleum and explosives licensing.

Geographical scope

7 The Primary Authority scheme applies differently in the different parts of the United Kingdom, as set out in the Act. The details of the scope of Primary Authority in relation to Scotland and Northern Ireland are defined in The Co-ordination of Regulatory Enforcement (Regulatory Functions in Scotland and Northern Ireland) Order 2009[2] and the geographical scope of each of the categories that can be covered by a partnership is detailed at Annex 1.

8 In England and Wales, Primary Authority is available for all the relevant functions exercised by local authorities.

9 In Scotland, a local authority can offer a partnership only for the relevant functions that remain the responsibility of the UK Government. In summary, these are principally included in the following categories:

- age-restricted sales (limited applicability)
- consumer credit
- explosives licensing
- fair trading
- health and safety (limited applicability)
- metrology
- product safety
- road traffic (limited applicability).

10 Relevant functions that have been devolved to the Scottish Government – for example, food standards and food hygiene – are outside the scope of Primary Authority.

11 In Northern Ireland, a local authority can offer a partnership only for the relevant functions that remain the responsibility of the UK Government where these are delivered by local authorities. These are principally included in the product safety category.

12 The way in which Primary Authority will operate for different functions in different areas is illustrated in the examples below.

Practical examples

A Scottish local authority can enter into a partnership in respect of health and safety that would apply across Scotland, England and Wales but would not extend to Northern Ireland.
A Scottish business trading across the UK that wanted a partnership for food hygiene would not be able to enter into a partnership with a Scottish local authority but could enter into a partnership with an English or Welsh local authority, but the partnership would extend only to England and Wales.
A manufacturer based in Wales could enter into a partnership covering product safety with a local authority in any part of the UK, and this partnership would be applicable across the whole of the UK.

---

[2] http://www.opsi.gov.uk/si/si2009/uksi_20090669_en_1

13 LBRO will respond to a request for advice from any local authority or business affected by issues concerning the geographical scope of Primary Authority on an individual basis.

14 LBRO will expect primary authorities to provide information and support, on request, to enforcing authorities in Scotland and Northern Ireland where they are voluntarily operating in line with Primary Authority despite being outside its geographical scope for particular functions. This will help to ensure that the business experiences consistent enforcement across the United Kingdom.

Company structures

15 A partnership may encompass more than one legal entity where the agreement is with a single legal entity that directs compliance on behalf of others. For example, a parent company with a number of subsidiaries based in different locations may choose to have one partnership covering all of its operations, or to have separate partnerships for the separate legal entities.

16 A partnership cannot cover more than one legal entity where these entities are not themselves related. For example, a trade association could not enter into a partnership that would encompass all of its member businesses. However, LBRO recognises that it will be necessary to ensure consistency across businesses within a sector, and that input from trade bodies will be important in achieving this.

17 A single legal entity can have only one partnership in respect of a particular category of relevant function.

What resources will be needed to operate an effective partnership?

18 In establishing a partnership, the partners will need to assess the likely resources necessary to deliver the advice and guidance requirements of the business. These will vary between partnerships. From the outset, both parties will need to have a clear understanding of the needs of the business for regulatory advice, the expectations of the business and the scope of the service being provided by the local authority. In establishing a partnership, the partners will also need to assess the likely resources necessary to deliver the requirements of other local authorities, in respect of:

- providing advice and guidance about how they should exercise their relevant functions in relation to the business;
- setting inspection plans, where appropriate; and
- advising on and responding to proposed enforcement actions.

19 In assessing the resources required, the partners should consider the amount of staff resource and the level of expertise needed, both in terms of knowledge of the relevant function and understanding of the business and its practices.

Practical examples

A large business with access to in-house regulatory advice may have little need for advice from the primary authority but might be likely to generate a relatively high number of enquiries and referrals from enforcing authorities.
A small business with no in-house expertise would be likely to require a higher level of advice and guidance but might be likely to generate a relatively low number of enquiries and referrals from enforcing authorities.
A new business, or one which had not previously had a close relationship with its local authority, might require a high level of advice in the early stages of the partnership that could be expected to diminish as the partnership matured.

How should the required resources be provided?

20 Having made an assessment of the resource requirements of the partnership, the local authority and the business will need to agree how costs will be met.

21 The local authority is entitled to charge the business for services supplied through the partnership. In deciding whether, and to what extent, to make a charge to the business, the local authority should consider all relevant matters, including:

- the local authority's policy in respect of supporting local economic prosperity;
- the existing resources provided to this business (both by the regulatory service and by other services of the local authority);
- any responsibility to provide free advice and guidance to the business under the Regulators' Compliance Code;[3]
- the requirement of the Regulators' Compliance Code, where applicable, that where advice and guidance go beyond basic advice and guidance, any charges should be reasonable; and
- when advice and guidance have been developed for use with more than one business, an individual business should pay no more than a reasonable proportion of the costs.

22 Where a local authority decides to charge for some or all of the services provided to a business, it can recover only the costs reasonably incurred in providing the service.

23 In calculating these costs, the local authority should have regard to the guidance issued by HM Treasury in *Managing Public Money*.[4]

What is the Primary Authority Agreement?

24 A partnership nomination must be supported by a written agreement ('the Primary Authority Agreement') between the local authority and the business. The agreement should include:

- the name of the legal entity or entities covered by the agreement;
- the category or categories of relevant function covered;
- the geographical scope of the partnership – this should coincide with all the areas of the UK where the relevant function is within scope;
- the limitations of liability;
- details of the resource requirements of the partnership and how these will be provided, including the basis for any charges that will be made;
- a statement about the status of information provided to and by the local authority and LBRO in respect of the Freedom of Information Act 2000, or the Freedom of Information (Scotland) Act 2002;
- arrangements for handling notifications of proposed enforcement action;
- arrangements for reviewing the agreement; and
- arrangements for terminating the agreement.

25 Partnerships are encouraged to use the template Primary Authority Agreement available from the LBRO website (www.lbro.org.uk), which addresses all these issues. This has been created and tested by the pilot partnerships in order to reduce costs for partnerships when setting up.

---

[3] www.berr.gov.uk/files/file45019.pdf
[4] www.hm-treasury.gov.uk/psr_mpm_index.htm

ESTABLISHING A PARTNERSHIP

How is a primary authority nominated?

26 Where a business and a local authority agree that they wish to establish a partnership, they should request LBRO to nominate the local authority as primary authority via the website at www.lbro.org. uk. The request should be accompanied by a Primary Authority Agreement endorsed by both parties, which will enable LBRO to assess the local authority's suitability for nomination. Where it is satisfied, LBRO will enter the partnership into its register, which is available on the LBRO website, and both parties will be notified. Where LBRO has concerns about the suitability of the proposed arrangements, it will seek to work with the parties to enable the suitability criteria to be met.

27 Where a business wishes to enter into a partnership but has not yet found a willing and suitable local authority, it can request LBRO to nominate a primary authority. LBRO will consult with any local authority that it considers might be suitable, in particular any local authority in whose area the business is administered or principally carried out.

28 Where a potential primary authority is identified by LBRO, the authority will then need to work with the business to develop an agreement.

How will LBRO assess suitability?

29 The suitability of a local authority will be assessed at the point at which a partnership is being considered. The criteria used by LBRO will be:

- the adequacy of the proposed arrangements for resourcing the partnership;
- the relevant expertise of the local authority;
- any proposed arrangements for preparing relevant local authority staff for the primary authority role; and
- the commitment of both parties to making the proposed arrangements operate effectively.

How can a partnership end?

30 The agreement should set out arrangements for either party to end the partnership by notifying LBRO. When a notification is received, LBRO will consider whether it is appropriate to consult with the parties before revoking its nomination of the partnership.

31 When LBRO is satisfied that it is appropriate to revoke its nomination, it will do so and will amend the register.

32 When a partnership is no longer operating effectively, then LBRO may review its nomination. Having consulted both parties, LBRO may decide to revoke its nomination, and in this circumstance both parties will be formally notified and the register amended.

PROVIDING EFFECTIVE ADVICE TO SUPPORT COMPLIANCE

How should Primary Authority Advice be provided to the business?

33 In entering a partnership, the local authority accepts responsibility for being the principal source of local authority regulatory advice and guidance to the business. 'Primary Authority Advice' is advice and guidance from the primary authority to the business that covers matters relating to compliance in the categories of relevant function defined in the agreement. Where a business has acted on advice given by the primary authority, it will be able to rely on that advice if challenged by another local authority.

34 Given the importance of Primary Authority Advice, the primary authority will need to consider, and agree with the business, the following:

- who can provide Primary Authority Advice;
- who can request and receive Primary Authority Advice;
- how Primary Authority Advice will be provided (it may be provided by different means, depending on the circumstances and as agreed by the partners – for example, by letter, in an email, during a meeting or by telephone);
- how and in what circumstances Primary Authority Advice will be recorded (the primary authority will always need to have regard to its responsibility to review advice at a future date, for example to ensure that it remains current or if the compliance of the business is challenged by another local authority);
- how both parties will be clear that Primary Authority Advice is being provided (the primary authority may have discussions with the business that do not constitute Primary Authority Advice, but both parties will need to be clear when this is happening and that these discussions cannot later be relied on as Primary Authority Advice); and
- what will happen if there are circumstances in which a business requests Primary Authority Advice on a matter on which the primary authority is unable to provide certainty.

Practical examples

A business contacts the primary authority late on a Friday afternoon with an urgent request for advice. The primary authority has a view and is able to provide appropriate advice during the telephone conversation that will constitute Primary Authority Advice. The business is entitled to rely on this advice, delivered during a telephone conversation, if its actions are subsequently challenged by another local authority.
The partners have previously agreed that all Primary Authority Advice provided during a telephone conversation will be recorded by both parties in a file note and that such file notes will be reviewed and agreed at the next meeting of the partners.
A store manager who is an employee of the business contacts the primary authority and asks for advice on an issue relating to the business's due diligence system for pricing checks. The primary authority discusses the matter with the store manager and gives an opinion.
The partners have previously agreed that Primary Authority Advice can be provided only to one of two named contacts at the head office of the business. The primary authority therefore makes it clear to the store manager that the opinion offered does not constitute Primary Authority Advice.

> Regular meetings are held between the primary authority and the business. At one such meeting, which is held at the business's premises, the officer of the primary authority is taken into the manufacturing area and is asked to give a view on the adequacy of guarding on a particular type of machine. The officer is able to confirm that the guarding is adequate, and this is recorded in the notes of the meeting.
>
> The partners have previously agreed that at the end of each meeting the notes of the meeting will be reviewed and the status of any advice provided will be confirmed. The officer confirms the advice relating to the guarding of the new machine as Primary Authority Advice, and the meeting notes are entered into the records of both parties.
>
> The business is able to rely on the Primary Authority Advice provided in relation to these machines.

35 Where an authority has provided advice and guidance to the business prior to being nominated as a primary authority by LBRO, it will need to consider with the business how, or whether, this earlier advice should be reviewed and issued as Primary Authority Advice.

36 There is no requirement for primary authorities to proactively publish the advice that they give to a business, although they would need to be able to produce this advice in response to a request for assistance from an enforcing authority. However, the LBRO website has a facility to enable partnerships, where both parties agree, to provide additional information to local authorities. Such information might include business documents that are commonly requested by enforcing authorities.

37 The primary authority should ensure that Primary Authority Advice:

- is capable of having effect in all areas where the business may seek to rely on it;
- is specific and tailored to the particular needs of the business, where appropriate;
- is considered and well researched;
- takes into account the relevant legislation and codes of practice;
- takes into account guidance from the Government, national regulators, LBRO and others, including, for example, the Local Authorities Coordinators of Regulatory Services (LACoRS) and professional bodies;
- takes into account industry practices and is consistent with advice being given to other businesses within the sector;
- takes into account advice and guidance given to the business by other primary authorities with responsibility for different relevant functions;
- takes into account advice and guidance given to the business by any national regulator with responsibility for the same relevant function;
- supports the business in identifying a method of achieving compliance;
- recognises the need not to impose unnecessary burdens on the business;
- is delivered in accordance with the Regulators' Compliance Code, where applicable;
- is provided in a form that enables the business to rely upon it; and
- is reviewed at appropriate intervals, and when circumstances change, to ensure that it remains current.

SUPPORTING LOCAL AUTHORITY REGULATION OF THE BUSINESS

What is the role of the primary authority in relation to other local authorities?

38 The primary authority has a role to play in:

- improving the targeting of local authority resources through the provision of inspection plans;
- improving the consistency of enforcement through the provision of Primary Authority Advice to local authorities;
- acting as a source of information on the business for local authorities that have identified compliance issues with the business; and
- responding to statutory notifications of proposed enforcement action from enforcing authorities.

What is an inspection plan?

39 An inspection plan is a document prepared by a primary authority to support other local authorities in targeting their local inspection resources in relation to the business.

40 Inspection plans may assist other authorities in assessing appropriate frequencies for their proactive interventions through their local risk assessment processes. For example, a primary authority could share details of a third party auditing scheme operated by the business, which may be relevant in the assessment of 'confidence in management' within a local risk assessment model.

41 Inspection plans will also allow primary authorities to assist other local authorities in the effective targeting of activity within proactive interventions. For example, areas of a business for which compliance has already been established nationally by the primary authority can be signposted, as well as areas where local inspection resource will have the greatest impact.

42 Examples of existing inspection plans to which LBRO has given consent are available on the LBRO website (www.lbro.org.uk) and may prove useful to partners in developing their own plans.

What are the requirements for an inspection plan?

43 An inspection plan:

- should include an expiry date, which may be revised by agreement with LBRO;
- should be reviewed by the primary authority at appropriate intervals or in response to information received from enforcing authorities;
- should define the scope of the relevant functions covered, and the geographical applicability of the plan;
- may provide information to assist local authorities in developing their risk-based and intelligence-led programmes of proactive interventions, including inspections, sampling and test purchasing (possibly including information on any existing systems for managing risk and recognised external accreditation);
- may inform local authorities of national inspection strategies coordinated by the primary authority in respect of the business and invite participation in those strategies;
- may recommend areas where local inspection activities might best be focused;
- may assist local authorities by identifying matters that are being dealt with nationally by the primary authority, for example where the primary authority has reviewed and given advice in respect of the business's health and safety policy; and
- should not address reactive interventions in response to a specific complaint or intelligence, or responses to specific local issues.

Practical examples

> A primary authority establishes that a business, a national petrol retailer, has a contract in place that sets out a national programme of third party checks of all of its petrol pumps on an annual basis. The retailer makes data from these checks available to its primary authority. The contract ensures that remedial action is taken in respect of all defective equipment within an appropriate timescale. The primary authority has arrangements in place to audit this process and to verify compliance via a small national sample of checks. The primary authority makes full details of this scheme available to local authorities through the LBRO website, and signposts in its inspection plan that enforcing authorities should take account of these checks in risk assessing the business.
>
> An enforcing authority should use the information in its risk assessment and on the basis of this may decide that it does not need to inspect the business in relation to that issue.
>
> An enforcing authority may check petrol pumps at the business in response to a complaint or incident, as this is outside the scope of the inspection plan.

> The primary authority for a national retailer identifies that vehicle movements represent the most significant risk for the business in terms of health and safety. The primary authority and the business develop a vehicle movement policy. This policy requires all stores to carry out an individual assessment of the local risks, and to put in place appropriate local management arrangements. The primary authority makes the national vehicle movement policy available via the LBRO website, and indicates in its inspection plan that local checking of implementation of the policy at store level is an area where local inspection resources can have greatest impact. The primary authority requests that local authorities provide feedback so that it can build up a national picture of the implementation of this national policy.
>
> An enforcing authority that has no planned inspections of the business will not need to take any action in this case. However, an enforcing authority that plans to inspect the business in relation to health and safety compliance should check local implementation of the vehicle movement policy and provide feedback to the primary authority via the secure LBRO website.

> A primary authority for a manufacturer of a meat product that is supplied nationally through independent takeaway outlets has a sampling programme at the manufacturer's premises in order to check compositional standards. The primary authority agrees with the manufacturer that the results of this sampling should be supplemented by a certain level of sampling at retail level.
>
> The primary authority invites participation, through an inspection plan, from a number of enforcing authorities that are willing to include this product in their sampling programme. The primary authority also indicates through its inspection plan that results will be available to authorities that do not participate and that they should therefore avoid other sampling of this product at retail level for compositional standards.

44 The primary authority must consult the business on the inspection plan, and LBRO recommends that this happens at an early stage so that the business can have input into its development.

45 Inspection plans should take into account guidance published by relevant national regulators, government departments and others. In particular, the plan should take account of the risk assessment methodologies of relevant national regulators. In addition, where a national regulator plays a significant role in relation to inspection of the business in respect of the relevant function, it should be consulted and offered the opportunity to be engaged in the development of the plan. For example, a large bakery firm that is both a producer and a retailer will be regulated in respect of health and safety by local authorities and the Health and Safety Executive (HSE). The primary authority should consult with the HSE in developing an inspection plan for the business.

46 Where an inspection plan exists for a business that is regulated in respect of the relevant function by both a national regulator and local authorities, the inspection plan will only apply to regulation undertaken by local authorities. However, inspection plans will be available to the national regulators through the secure LBRO website.

47 Where a business has more than one partnership, the primary authority that is considering making an inspection plan should consult with the other primary authorities for the business to ensure that their plans are compatible.

48 Inspection plans must be submitted to LBRO for its consent. LBRO will assess the proposed inspection plan and, if it finds that the plan has been prepared in accordance with this guidance and with the principles of better regulation, will consent to the inspection plan and will publish it on behalf of the primary authority through the secure LBRO website, where it will be available to all local authorities and relevant national regulators and government departments. If LBRO is not satisfied that the proposed inspection plan has been prepared in accordance with this guidance, it will work with the partners to address any issues.

How does a local authority meet its statutory duty in relation to inspection plans?

49 When an inspection plan has been published, a local authority must have regard to the plan when conducting its risk assessment of the business and its programmed activity at the business.

When is it appropriate to deviate from an inspection plan?

50 A local authority may deviate from an element of an inspection plan where it considers it appropriate to do so due to local circumstances. In these cases, the local authority should notify the primary authority, giving its reasons, via LBRO's secure website.

51 Notifications should normally be in advance. Where it is impractical to notify a deviation from an inspection plan in advance because of unforeseen circumstances, the local authority should notify the primary authority retrospectively, at the earliest practicable opportunity.

52 The primary authority is not required to respond to notifications of deviations from inspection plans made by other local authorities, although it may choose to do so. However, any notifications should be considered by the primary authority as part of its periodic review of the inspection plan.

How should the primary authority provide Primary Authority Advice to local authorities?

53 The primary authority has a function to give advice and guidance to other local authorities ('Primary Authority Advice to local authorities'). This advice may be given to one or more local authorities where they have responsibility for the relevant functions covered by the partnership, and must relate to the exercise of those functions in relation to the business. LBRO anticipates that Primary Authority Advice to local authorities will normally be issued to all local authorities.

54 Primary Authority Advice to local authorities:

- should be communicated through LBRO's secure website;
- should relate to a specific issue where the primary authority is actively addressing compliance on a national level with the business;
- should be time limited where it relates to improvement activity of the business;
- should not relate to the frequency or conduct of inspections, or the risk assessment of a business (which may be dealt with in an inspection plan);
- may relate to the precautions that a business is taking to achieve compliance, but should not relate to the local exercise of due diligence in following the nationally agreed precautions; and
- may be used as a basis for directing against enforcement action if the primary authority subsequently receives a notification of proposed enforcement action that would be inconsistent with the advice.

55 LBRO anticipates that Primary Authority Advice to local authorities will help to deliver consistent, proportionate and targeted regulatory activity in relation to the business. In particular, this advice may be used to help ensure a proportionate response to a specific compliance issue where a course of action has already been agreed between the primary authority and the business.

Practical examples

A minor error has occurred in the labelling of a batch of food product. The primary authority for the food manufacturer has considered the issue and has confirmed to the business that a product recall is not necessary. The defect has been remedied for all future batches. The primary authority may notify all local authorities of the specific details of the affected batch, explain the remedial action taken and advise that no further action is required.
The primary authority for a national supermarket agrees to an approach to administer all of its product recalls on a national basis. The primary authority should notify all enforcing authorities of the details of the scheme and how to refer matters to it. The primary authority should also advise all enforcing authorities not to require product recalls except via the national system operated by the primary authority.

NOTIFICATIONS AND DETERMINATION

How does Primary Authority support consistent enforcement?

56 The Primary Authority scheme has been designed to improve consistency of enforcement for those businesses that trade across local authority boundaries. In order to achieve this, notification of proposed enforcement action must be made to the primary authority, which is entitled, in certain circumstances, to direct the enforcing authority not to take the action. Where a compliance issue is identified that requires immediate action in order to prevent harm, and in other specific circumstances defined in the secondary legislation, the requirement to notify in advance of the action is waived, although retrospective notification is still required.

57 LBRO's administration of Primary Authority will encourage early dialogue between enforcing authorities and primary authorities with a view to agreeing an informed and consistent response to non-compliance. The full benefits of Primary Authority can best be realised if both the primary authority and the enforcing authority engage at an early stage over any proposed enforcement action rather than using statutory notifications as the beginning of that process.

58 For this reason an enforcing authority should discuss any possible non-compliance with the primary authority when considering enforcement action.

59 Where an enforcing authority is not considering enforcement action, it should still discuss the possible non-compliance with the primary authority when:

- the matter is likely to be a local example of wider non-compliance, for example a price promotion that is misleading, a labelling problem with a product that is widely sold or an unguarded machine that is known to be in use at other branches of the business;
- the enforcing authority has identified a contravention that requires an amendment to a national system or process, for example where pest control procedures used by the business are not proving effective; or
- the problem cannot be addressed purely through local action, for example where the local premises requires input from its head office, such as structural change to the premises that will incur costs.

What is the notification process?

60 The notification process arises where enforcement action is proposed against the business. It is not required where action is proposed against an individual employee of the business.

61 The Act requires an enforcing authority to notify the primary authority of proposed enforcement action prior to taking that action. Enforcement action is defined by The Coordination of Regulatory Enforcement (Enforcement Action) Order 2009[5], which also sets out exclusions to the requirement to notify in advance. These exclusions allow the enforcing authority to take action immediately under certain circumstances, particularly where the need for enforcement action is urgent, for example emergency prohibition notices and abatement notices for noise.

62 Investigative activities are not enforcement action for the purposes of Primary Authority and do not require formal notification to the primary authority. However, enforcing authorities will clearly benefit from a dialogue with the primary authority in relation to certain of these activities. Investigative activities include, for example:

- inspection of goods, records and documents;
- exercise of powers of entry into premises;
- seizure of goods, records and documents for evidential purposes;
- test purchasing of goods;
- sampling of goods;

---

[5] http://www.opsi.gov.uk/si/si2009/uksi_20090665_en_1

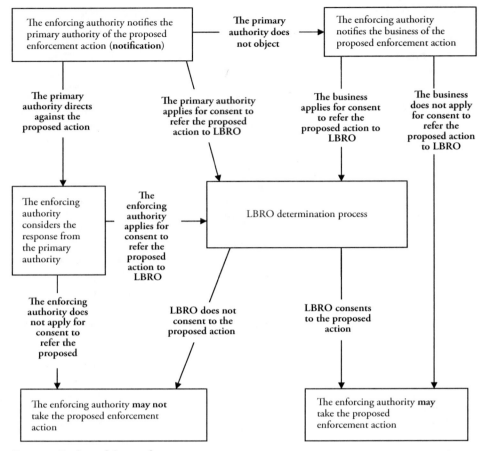

Figure 1 Outline of the notification process

- deployment of surveillance or covert human intelligence sources under Part 2 of the Regulation of Investigatory Powers Act 2000; and
- interviewing suspects under caution.

How long will the notification and determination process take?

63 Where a primary authority receives a notification of proposed enforcement action, it has five working days starting on and including the day after it is received, to respond to the enforcing authority or to ask LBRO for consent to refer the proposed action to LBRO for determination.

64 Where a business receives a notification of proposed enforcement action, it has 10 working days starting on and including the day after it is received, to ask LBRO for consent to refer the proposed action to LBRO for determination.

65 Where an enforcing authority is directed not to take its proposed action by a primary authority, it has 10 working days starting on and including the day after the primary authority so directs, to ask LBRO for consent to refer the proposed action to LBRO for determination.

66 The Co-ordination of Regulatory Enforcement (Procedure for References to LBRO) Order 2009 allows LBRO to accept applications after the deadline in exceptional circumstances.

67 Where LBRO consents to a referral from the primary authority, enforcing authority or business, it must make the determination within 28 days.

68 The Act defines working days as days other than a Saturday, Sunday, Christmas Day, Good Friday or certain bank holidays in England, Wales, Scotland and Northern Ireland. LBRO will include a clear indication of the relevant bank holidays on its website.

69 Where an enactment limits the period within which the enforcing authority may take enforcement action, any time during which the authority is prohibited from taking the action because of the requirements of Primary Authority must be disregarded in calculating this period.

How should an enforcing authority notify enforcement action?

70 Notification of proposed enforcement action by the enforcing authority should be made via LBRO's secure website by a person with authorisation to initiate the enforcement action proposed, or by a person who has been specifically authorised to make that notification. The notification should include the following details, which are provided for in the template notification on the secure LBRO website:

- full details of the contravention, including, where appropriate, the address of the relevant premises;
- full details of any affected products or services;
- details of the proposed enforcement action; and
- the reason for proposing the enforcement action.

71 Where the enforcing authority intends to propose proceedings relating to an Enterprise Act Enforcement Order that requires consultation with the Office of Fair Trading, the notification to the primary authority through the secure LBRO website will fulfil this requirement.

72 The enforcing authority cannot proceed with the proposed action within a period of five working days beginning on, and including, the day after notification to the primary authority is made.

73 Notification of enforcement action that has been taken and that did not require prior notification, such as emergency prohibition notices and abatement notices for noise, should be made via LBRO's secure website as soon as practicable after the action is taken.

What should the primary authority do when it receives a notification of proposed enforcement action?

74 The Act allows the primary authority five working days to respond to a notification, beginning on, and including, the day after a notification is received.

75 In responding to a notification, the primary authority is entitled to consider only whether the proposed enforcement action is inconsistent with any Primary Authority Advice to the business or any Primary Authority Advice to local authorities that it has previously given. Where no relevant advice has previously been given by the primary authority, it is not able to direct against the proposed enforcement action.

76 Responding to notifications about proposed enforcement action is a key factor in achieving an effective partnership. The primary authority will need to have robust internal arrangements in place for handling notifications of proposed enforcement action within the statutory timescale. In developing these arrangements, consideration should be given to:

- the appropriate person to receive notifications;
- the appropriate person to respond to notifications of different levels of enforcement action (for example, the primary authority may consider it appropriate for an inspecting officer to consider a proposed notice, whereas it may feel that a proposed prosecution ought to be considered at a more senior level); and
- the availability and form of information that will be needed to support any decision to direct an enforcing authority not to take a proposed enforcement action.

77 The primary authority should use the five working days to review its previous advice and guidance and to discuss the matter with relevant parties, which may include the enforcing authority, the business, LBRO and any relevant national regulator.

78 The primary authority should respond either to direct against the proposed action where it believes that the action is inconsistent with advice previously given, or to confirm that it will not be directing against the proposed action. Alternatively, the primary authority may apply to LBRO for consent to refer the matter to LBRO for determination within five working days of receiving the notification of proposed enforcement action from the enforcing authority.

79 Primary Authority is based on effective communication. Active and early responses should be provided by the primary authority to all notifications of proposed enforcement action.

80 The primary authority's response should be made to the person making the original notification within the relevant period and should be copied to LBRO. Where the primary authority directs the enforcing authority not to take the proposed action, the response should include:

- details of the advice previously given with which the proposed enforcement action would be inconsistent;
- details of how and when the advice was previously given; and
- the rationale for why the proposed enforcement action would be inconsistent with the advice previously given.

81 The Act does not allow a primary authority to revoke or revise its response to a notification once the five working days have elapsed.

What happens if the primary authority directs against the proposed action?

82 The enforcing authority cannot proceed with the proposed enforcement action if the primary authority directs against it. If the enforcing authority still feels that the proposed enforcement action is appropriate, then it may apply to LBRO for consent to refer the matter to LBRO for determination. This application must be made within 10 working days starting on, and including, the day after receipt of the primary authority's direction against the proposed enforcement action.

83 If the enforcing authority does not refer the matter to LBRO, or if LBRO does not consent to a referral, then the enforcing authority cannot take the proposed enforcement action.

What happens if the primary authority does not object to the proposed action or does not respond?

84 If the primary authority does not object to the proposed action or does not respond, the enforcing authority can proceed to notify the business of the proposed enforcement action. This notification should be in writing, by letter or by email, and should be addressed to the principal primary authority contact within the business, whose details are held by the primary authority. The notification should be copied to the primary authority.

85 The notification should:

- include full details of the contravention, including, where appropriate, the address of the relevant premises;
- include full details of any affected products or services;
- include details of the proposed enforcement action;
- confirm that the enforcing authority has notified the primary authority of the proposed action; and
- confirm that the primary authority did not object to the proposed enforcement action.

A template notification is available for enforcing authorities on the LBRO website.

86 On receiving notification of a proposed enforcement action, the business may, if it considers that the proposed action is inconsistent with Primary Authority Advice previously given, apply to LBRO within 10 working days starting on, and including, the day after it receives the notification, for consent to refer the matter to LBRO for determination.

87 The enforcing authority cannot proceed with the proposed action until the 10-day period has expired. Where LBRO advises the enforcing authority that it has received an application from the business for consent to make a reference, then the enforcing authority cannot proceed until LBRO either confirms that it has not given consent or confirms its determination.

What is LBRO's role in supporting decision making within Primary Authority?

88 LBRO will work actively with primary authorities, enforcing authorities and businesses with a view to reaching agreements without the use of the determination process.

89 The Act allows all three parties involved in a proposed enforcement action – the business, the primary authority and the enforcing authority – to apply for consent to refer proposed enforcement action to LBRO for determination. The application must be made within the defined period relevant to the party making the application.

How will the determination process work?

90 LBRO determination is a two-stage process. The local authority or business must first apply to LBRO for consent to make a referral. If LBRO gives consent, the application will enter the LBRO determination process.

91 LBRO will manage the referral, consent and determination process in line with its Determinations – Policy and Procedures document, available on the LBRO website.

92 A party can apply to withdraw its application for consent, or to withdraw the matter from the determination process, by notifying LBRO in writing.

GLOSSARY

Category of relevant functions	LBRO has grouped the legislation that is within the scope of Primary Authority into a number of broad categories on which partnerships may be based.
Determination	The process LBRO operates, having granted consent to an application from one of the parties, to determine whether the proposed enforcement action can proceed.
Enforcement action	Enforcement actions are those actions defined in The Co-ordination of Regulatory Enforcement (Enforcement Action) Order 2009[6]. They are actions that must be notified to the primary authority, either in advance or retrospectively.
Enforcing authority	All local authorities take on the role of enforcing authority in respect of relevant functions in their geographical area. This means that a primary authority for a business will also act as the enforcing authority within its own geographical area.
Inspection plan	A plan that a primary authority may elect to produce to assist other local authorities in discharging their relevant functions relating to proactive interactions with the partner business. All local authorities are required to have regard to these plans.
Local authority	A local authority is defined in the Regulatory Enforcement and Sanctions Act 2008 to include county, district and unitary councils (including London boroughs and metropolitan boroughs), port health authorities, and fire and rescue authorities.
Nomination	Nomination is the process through which a local authority is registered as a primary authority by LBRO.
National regulator	National regulators that have a role to play under Primary Authority include Animal Health, the Environment Agency, the Food Standards Agency, the Health and Safety Executive, the National Weights and Measures Laboratory, and the Office of Fair Trading.
Notification of enforcement action	The statutory notification required from an enforcing authority to a primary authority to notify of proposed enforcement action. In most circumstances this notification is required prior to taking the enforcement action. However, in certain circumstances it will be retrospective.
Primary authority	The primary authority is the local authority that has formed a partnership with the business and is registered on LBRO's website. Note that a business may have one primary authority for one category and another primary authority for another category.
Primary Authority Advice	Advice and guidance provided by the primary authority to the business under the provisions of the scheme.
Primary Authority Advice to local authorities	Advice and guidance provided by the primary authority to other local authorities with the same relevant function as to how they should exercise that function in relation to the business.

---

[6] http://www.opsi.gov.uk/si/si2009/uksi_20090665_en_1

Primary Authority Agreement	This is a written agreement produced by the partners prior to nomination of the partnership by LBRO that sets out how the partnership will operate. LBRO provides a template agreement for use by partners via its website.
Register of primary authority partnerships	This is a public register of all existing partnerships that have been registered by LBRO. The register is available on the LBRO website and includes details of the local authority, the business and the categories within the scope of the partnership (for example, 'health and safety' or 'fair trading').
Relevant function	The functions are defined in terms of legislation listed under Schedule 3 of the Regulatory Enforcement and Sanctions Act 2008 and certain legislation made under the European Communities Act 1972.
Relevant period	This refers to a defined period of time set out in the Regulatory Enforcement and Sanctions Act 2008 or the Co-ordination of Regulatory Enforcement (Procedure for References to LBRO) Order 2009[7].

---

[7] http://www.opsi.gov.uk/si/si2009/uksi_20090670_en_1

Annex 1: Categorisation of relevant enactments

Age-restricted sales

- Relevant enactments and secondary legislation that control the sale and supply of goods that have an age restriction associated with them
- Unitary[8] and county
- Some applicability in Scotland where matter is reserved
- Not within scope of Primary Authority for Northern Ireland

Agriculture

- Relevant enactments and secondary legislation concerning the manufacture, composition and labelling of animal feed and fertilisers, and food hygiene at primary producers
- Unitary and county
- Not within scope of Primary Authority for Scotland or Northern Ireland

Animal establishments and companion animal welfare

- Relevant enactments and secondary legislation concerning the licensing of animal establishments and the welfare of companion animals
- Unitary and district
- Not within scope of Primary Authority for Scotland or Northern Ireland

Consumer credit

- Relevant enactments and secondary legislation concerning the licensing and operation of consumer credit
- Unitary and county
- Applicable in Scotland
- Not within scope of Primary Authority for Northern Ireland

Environmental protection

- Relevant enactments and secondary legislation concerning environmental protection, including the control of noise, pollution (other than permitting), statutory nuisance, contaminated land, waste
- Unitary and district
- Not within scope of Primary Authority for Scotland or Northern Ireland

Explosives licensing

- Relevant enactments and secondary legislation concerning the licensing and storage of explosives
- Unitary, county and fire and rescue authorities
- Applicable in Scotland
- Not within scope of Primary Authority for Northern Ireland

Fair trading

- Relevant enactments and secondary legislation concerning business operations relating to business-to-consumer transactions, including pricing, description of goods and services, trading practices and intellectual property
- Unitary and county

---

[8] As defined in section 3 of the Regulatory Enforcement and Sanctions Act 2008.

- Applicable in Scotland
- Some applicability in Northern Ireland in relation to hallmarking

Farm animal health

- Relevant enactments and secondary legislation concerning the movement, importation and marking of farm animals and the control of animal disease
- Unitary and county
- Not within scope of Primary Authority for Scotland or Northern Ireland

Food safety and hygiene

- Relevant enactments and secondary legislation concerning the safety and hygiene of food, the controls under which food is manufactured, prepared and sold, and matters of pest control
- Unitary and district
- Not within scope of Primary Authority for Scotland or Northern Ireland

Food standards

- Relevant enactments and secondary legislation concerning the labelling and composition of food
- Unitary and county
- Not within scope of Primary Authority for Scotland or Northern Ireland

General licensing

- Relevant enactments and secondary legislation concerning the licensing of people, places and vehicles, including hackney carriage and private hire licensing, house-to-house collections, sex establishments, Sunday trading, charity collections, scrap metal dealers and pavement cafes, but not alcohol licensing or gambling[9]
- Unitary and district
- Not within scope of Primary Authority for Scotland or Northern Ireland

Health and safety

- Relevant enactments and secondary legislation concerning the health and safety of workers and visitors to local authority-regulated premises, but not fire safety (see footnote)
- Unitary and district
- Applicable in Scotland (Part 1 of the Health and Safety at Work Act 1974 only)
- Not within scope of Primary Authority for Northern Ireland

Housing

- Relevant enactments and secondary legislation concerning housing, provisions for area improvement, responsibilities of landlords, compulsory purchase, housing in multiple occupation and licensing of housing
- Unitary and district
- Not within scope of Primary Authority for Scotland or Northern Ireland

---

[9] The following legislative areas are within the scope of the Regulatory Enforcement and Sanctions Act 2008 but are excluded from the definition of enforcement under Primary Authority and are therefore outside the scope of the scheme:

- Alcohol licensing
- Fire safety
- Gambling licensing

Metrology

- Relevant enactments and secondary legislation concerning the control of weighing and measuring equipment and the sale of goods by quantity
- Unitary and county
- Applicable in Scotland
- Not within scope of Primary Authority for Northern Ireland

Petroleum licensing

- Relevant enactments and secondary legislation concerning the licensing and storage of petroleum
- Unitary, county and fire and rescue authorities
- Not within scope of Primary Authority for Scotland or Northern Ireland

Pollution control

- Relevant enactments and secondary legislation concerning the permitting of premises with respect to pollution control
- Unitary and district
- Not within scope of Primary Authority for Scotland or Northern Ireland

Product safety

- Relevant enactments and secondary legislation concerning the safety and labelling of products
- Unitary and county
- Applicable in Scotland and Northern Ireland

Road traffic

- Relevant enactments and secondary legislation concerning the control of overloaded and inappropriately loaded vehicles
- Unitary and county
- Some applicability in Scotland
- Not within scope of Primary Authority for Northern Ireland

APPENDIX 3

SI 2009 No. 669

REGULATORY REFORM

The Co-ordination of Regulatory Enforcement (Regulatory Functions in Scotland and Northern Ireland) Order 2009

Made	*5th March 2009*
Laid before Parliament	*16th March 2009*
Coming into force	*6th April 2009*

The Secretary of State makes the following Order in exercise of the powers conferred by section 24(1) of the Regulatory Enforcement and Sanctions Act 2008[1]

Citation, commencement and interpretation

1. This Order may be cited as the Co-ordination of Regulatory Enforcement (Regulatory Functions in Scotland and Northern Ireland) Order 2009 and comes into force on 6th April 2009.

Citation, commencement and interpretation

2. In this Order "the Act" means the Regulatory Enforcement and Sanctions Act 2008.

Regulatory functions

3.—(1) The following are specified in relation to a local authority in Scotland—

(a) any regulatory function exercised by that authority under a relevant enactment of imposing requirements, restrictions or conditions, or setting standards or giving guidance, in relation to any activity, and

(b) any regulatory function exercised by that authority which relates to the securing of compliance with, or the enforcement of, requirements, restrictions, conditions, standards or guidance which under or by virtue of a relevant enactment relate to any activity.

(2) In paragraph (1) "relevant enactment" means an enactment specified in Schedule 1 or an enactment made under such an enactment.

(3) In paragraph (1) "regulatory function" means, in relation to a relevant enactment specified in—

(a) Part 1 of Schedule 1, any function;

(b) Part 2 of Schedule 1, any function which relates to the protection of consumers;

(c) Part 3 of Schedule 1, any function which relates to the granting of licences or permits under those enactments;

(d) Part 4 of Schedule 1, any function which relates to product safety, compliance with standards, product labelling or weights and measures;

---

[1] 2008 c.13.

(e) Part 5 of Schedule 1, any function which relates to the regulation of business associations;

(f) Part 6 of Schedule 1, any function which relates to price indications;

(g) Part 7 of Schedule 1, any function which does not relate to the encouragement of and observance of equal opportunities requirements.

(4) Paragraph (1) shall not apply if or to the extent that a specified function relates to matters which are not reserved matters.

Regulatory functions

4.—(1) The following are specified in relation to a local authority in Northern Ireland—

(a) any regulatory function exercised by that authority under a relevant enactment of imposing requirements, restrictions or conditions, or setting standards or giving guidance, in relation to any activity, and

(b) any regulatory function exercised by that authority which relates to the securing of compliance with, or the enforcement of, requirements, restrictions, conditions, standards or guidance which under or by virtue of a relevant enactment relate to any activity.

(2) In paragraph (1) "relevant enactment" means—

(a) an enactment specified in Schedule 2 or an enactment made under such an enactment; and

(b) an enactment made under section 2(2) of the European Communities Act 1972[2] with respect to
  (i) the safety of consumers in relation to goods, or
  (ii) technical standards derived from European Community law, other than standards and requirements in relation to food, agricultural or horticultural produce, fish or fish products, seeds, animal feeding stuffs, fertilisers or pesticides).

(3) In paragraph (1) "regulatory function" means any function in relation to a relevant enactment set out in Schedule 2.

(4) Paragraph (1) shall not apply if or to the extent that a specified function relates to matters which are transferred matters.

---

[2] 1972 c.68.

Schedule 1

Part 1

Offices, Shops and Railway Premises Act 1963[3]

Firearms Act 1968[4]

Medicines Act 1968 (section 109)[5]

Unsolicited Goods and Services Act 1971[6]

Poisons Act 1972 (section 9)[7]

Health and Safety at Work, etc Act 1974[8]

Consumer Credit Act 1974[9]

Firearms Act 1982[10]

Video Recordings Act 1984[11]

Copyright, Designs and Patents Act 1988 (sections 107A and 198A)[12]

Timeshare Act 1992[13]

Trade Marks Act 1994[14]

Olympic Symbol etc (Protection) Act 1995[15]

Part 2

Explosives Act 1875[16]

Trade Descriptions Act 1968[17]

Development of Tourism Act 1969[18]

Supply of Goods (Implied Terms) Act 1973[19]

Fair Trading Act 1973[20]

Hallmarking Act 1973[21]

Prices Act 1974[22]

---

[3] 1963 c.41.
[4] 1968 c.27.
[5] 1968 c.67.
[6] 1971 c.30.
[7] 1972 c.66.
[8] 1974 c.37.
[9] 1974 c.39.
[10] 1982 c.31.
[11] 1984 c.39.
[12] 1988 c.48; sections 107A and 198A were inserted by the section 165(2) of the Criminal Justice and Public Order Act 1994.
[13] 1992 c.35.
[14] 1994 c.26.
[15] 1995 c.32.
[16] 1875 c.17.
[17] 1968 c.29.
[18] 1969 c.51.
[19] 1973 c.13.
[20] 1973 c.41.
[21] 1973 c.43.
[22] 1974 c.24.

Energy Act 1976[23]

Weights and Measures etc Act 1976[24]

Unfair Contract Terms Act 1977[25]

Estate Agents Act 1979[26]

Sale of Goods Act 1979[27]

Public Passenger Vehicles Act 1981[28]

Supply of Goods and Services Act 1982[29]

Motor Cycle Noise Act 1987[30]

Consumer Protection Act 1987[31]

Education Reform Act 1988[32]

Property Misdescriptions Act 1991[33]

Enterprise Act 2002, Part 8[34]

Fireworks Act 2003[35]

Crystal Glass (Descriptions) Regulations 1973[36]

Alcohol Tables Regulations 1979[37]

Package Travel, Package Holidays and Package Tours Regulations 1992[38]

Medicines (Advertising) Regulations 1994[39]

Unfair Terms in Consumer Contracts Regulations 1999[40]

Consumer Protection (Distance Selling) Regulations 2000[41]

Sale and Supply of Goods to Consumers Regulations 2002[42]

Consumer Protection from Unfair Trading Regulations 2008[43]

any enactment to which section 4(3) of the Act applies with respect to a matter specified in
    paragraph (d) of that subsection

---

[23] 1976 c.76.
[24] 1976 c.77.
[25] 1977 c.50.
[26] 1979 c.38.
[27] 1979 c.54.
[28] 1981 c.14.
[29] 1982 c.29.
[30] 1987 c.34.
[31] 1987 c.43: Part 4 which relates to enforcement of Parts 2 and 3 was amended by S.I. 2008/1277.
[32] 1988 c.40.
[33] 1991 c.29.
[34] 2002 c.40.
[35] 2003 c.22.
[36] S.I. 1972/1952.
[37] S.I. 1979/132.
[38] S.I. 1992/3288: Schedule 3 sets out enforcement provisions; paragraph 2 revoked by Article 3 of S.I. 2003/1376, and paragraphs 7 was revoked by Article 7 of, and Schedule 5 to, S.I. 2003/1400.
[39] S.I. 1994/1932, amended S.I. 1994/3144, S.I. 1999/267, S.I. 2002/236, S.I. 2003/2321, S.I. 2004/1480, S.I. 2005/2787, S.I. 2006/2407.
[40] S.I. 1999/2083; amended by the Enterprise Act 2002 c.40
[41] S.I. 2000/2334.
[42] S.I. 2002/3045; amended by inserted by S.I. 2008/1277, reg 30(1), Sch 2, Pt 2, para 97.
[43] S.I. 2008/1277.

PART 3

Cinemas Act 1985 (sections 1 to 3 and 5 to 16)[44]

Road Traffic Act 1988 (the whole Act except sections 39 to 40 and 157 to 159)[45]

Gambling Act 2005[46]

PART 4

Weights and Measures Act 1985[47]

Calibration of Tanks and Vessels (EEC Requirements) Regulations 1975[48]

Measuring Container Bottles (EEC Requirements) Regulations 1977[49]

Alcoholometers and Alcohol Hydrometers (EEC Requirements) Regulations 1977[50]

Aerosol Dispensers (EEC Requirements) Regulations 1977[51]

Taximeters (EEC Requirements) Regulations 1979[52]

Measuring Instruments (EEC Requirements) Regulations 1988[53]

Measuring Instruments (EEC Requirements) (Gas Volume Meters) Regulations 1988[54]

Simple Pressure Vessels (Safety) Regulations 1991[55]

Supply of Machinery (Safety) Regulations 1992[56]

Electrical Equipment (Safety) Regulations 1994[57]

Units of Measurement Regulations 1995[58]

Footwear (Indication of Composition) Labelling Regulations 1995[59]

Gas Appliances (Safety) Regulations 1995[60]

Toys (Safety) Regulations 1995[61]

Energy Information (Washing Machines) Regulations 1996[62]

Energy Information (Tumble Driers) Regulations 1996[63]

Energy Information (Combined Washer-driers) Regulations 1997[64]

Energy Information (Lamps) Regulations 1999[65]

---

[44] 1985 c.13; whole Act ceased to have effect in respect of England and Wales by the Licensing Act 2003, Schedule 6 paragraph 95.

[45] 1988 c.52.

[46] 2005 c.19.

[47] 1985 c.72; section 85 which relates to enforcement, amended by S.I. 2006/659.

[48] S.I. 1975/2125.

[49] S.I. 1977/932.

[50] S.I. 1977/1753.

[51] S.I. 1977/1140.

[52] S.I. 1977/1379.

[53] S.I. 1988/186.

[54] S.I. 1988/296.

[55] S.I. 1991/2749, amended by S.I. 2003/1400.

[56] S.I. 1992/3073, amended by S.I. 1994/2063, S.I. 2005/831.

[57] S.I. 1994/3260.

[58] S.I. 1988/1804.

[59] S.I 1995/2489.

[60] S.I. 1995/1629.

[61] S.I. 1995/204, amended by S.I. 2004/1769, S.I. 2005/1082.

[62] S.I. 1996/600, amended by S.I. 1997/803, S.I. 2001/3142, S.I. 2008/1277.

[63] S.I. 1996/601, amended by S.I. 2001/3142, S.I. 2003/1398, S.I. 2008/1277.

[64] S.I. 1997/1624, amended by S.I. 2001/3142, S.I. 2003/1398, S.I. 2008/1277.

[65] S.I. 1999/1517, amended by S.I. 2003/1398, S.I. 2008/1277.

Energy Information (Dishwashers) Regulations 1999[66]

Pressure Equipment Regulations 1999[67]

Non-automatic Weighing Instruments Regulations 2000[68]

Medical Devices Regulations 2002[69]

Personal Protective Equipment Regulations 2002[70]

Chemicals (Hazard Information and Packaging for Supply) Regulations 2002[71]

Energy Information (Household Electric Ovens) Regulations 2003[72]

Controls on Certain Azo Dyes and "Blue Colourant" Regulations 2003[73]

Creosote (Prohibition on Use and Marketing) (No 2) Regulations 2003[74]

Energy Information (Household Refrigerators and Freezers) Regulations 2004[75]

Biofuel (Labelling) Regulations 2004[76]

Recreational Craft Regulations 2004[77]

Medicines (Traditional Herbal Medicinal Products for human use) Regulations 2005[78]

Energy Information (Household Air Conditioners) (No 2) Regulations 2005[79]

General Product Safety Regulations 2005[80]

Weights and Measures (Packaged Goods) Regulations 2006[81]

Measuring Instruments (Automatic Discontinuous Totalisers) Regulations 2006[82]

Measuring Instruments (Automatic Rail-weighbridges) Regulations 2006[83]

Measuring Instruments (Automatic Catchweighers) Regulations 2006[84]

Measuring Instruments (Automatic Gravimetric Filling Instruments) Regulations 2006[85]

Measuring Instruments (Beltweighers) Regulations 2006[86]

Measuring Instruments (Capacity Serving Measures) Regulations 2006[87]

Measuring Instruments (Liquid Fuel and Lubricants) Regulations 2006[88]

---

[66] S.I. 1999/1679, amended by S.I. 2001/3142, S.I. 2003/1398, S.I. 2008/1277.

[67] S.I. 1999/2001, amended by S.I. 2002/1267, S.I. 2008/1597.

[68] S.I. 2000/3236, amended by S.I. 2008/738.

[69] S.I. 2002/618; relevant amending instruments are S.I. 2003/1697, S.I. 2005/2759, S.I. 2005/2909. S.I. 2007/400, S.I. 2008/2936.

[70] S.I. 2002/1144, amended by S.I. 2004/693.

[71] S.I. 2002/1689, amended by S.I. 2004.568, S.I. 2005/1732, S.I. 2005/2092, S.I. 2008/2337, S.I. 2008/2852; there are other amending instruments but none is relevant.

[72] S.I. 2003/751, amended by S.I. 2008/1277.

[73] S.I. 2003/3310, amended by S.I. 2004/2913.

[74] S.I. 2003/1511, amended by S.I. 2003/2650.

[75] S.I. 2004/1468, amended by SI 2008/1277.

[76] S.I. 2004/3349, amended by S.I. 2005/3355.

[77] S.I. 2004/1464, to which there are amendments which are not relevant for this Order.

[78] S.I. 2005/395, to which there are amendments which are not relevant for this Order.

[79] S.I.2005/1726.

[80] S.I 2005/1803, to which there are amendments which are not relevant for this Order.

[81] S.I. 2006/ 659.

[82] S.I. 2006/1255.

[83] S.I. 2006/1256, amended by S.I. 2006/2625.

[84] S.I. 2006/1257, amended by S.I. 2006/2625.

[85] S.I. 2006/1258.

[86] S.I. 2006/1259.

[87] S.I. 2006/1264.

[88] S.I. 2006/1266.

Measuring Instruments (Material Measures of Length) Regulations 2006[89]

Measuring Instruments (Cold-water Meters) Regulations 2006[90]

Measuring Instruments (Liquid Fuel Delivered from Road Tankers) Regulations 2006[91]

Electromagnetic Compatibility Regulations 2006[92]

Textile Products (Determination of Composition) Regulations 2008[93]

Cosmetic Products (Safety) Regulations 2008[94]

any enactment to which section 4(3) of the Act applies with respect to a matter specified in paragraph (h) of that subsection.

PART 5

Companies Act 1985[95], Part XI

Business Names Act 1985[96]

PART 6

Energy Act 1976[97]

PART 7

Disability Discrimination Act 1995[98]

SCHEDULE 2

PART 1

Consumer Protection Act 1987(Parts II and III)[99]

PART 2

Construction Products Regulations 1991[100]

Simple Pressure Vessels (Safety) Regulations 1991[101]

Supply of Machinery (Safety) Regulations 1992[102]

Electrical Equipment (Safety) Regulations 1994[103]

---

[89] S.I. 2006/ 1267.
[90] S.I. 2006/1268, amended by S.I. 2006/2625.
[91] S.I. 2006/1269.
[92] S.I. 2006/3418.
[93] S.I. 2008/15.
[94] S.I. 2008/1284, amended by S.I. 2008/2173, S.I. 2008/2566.
[95] 1985 c.6; Part XI has been amended by the Companies Act 1989 and the Companies Act 2006.
[96] 1985 c.7.
[97] 1976 c.76.
[98] 1995 c.50.
[99] 1987 c.43.
[100] S.I. 1991/1630, amended by S.I. 1994/3051.
[101] S.I. 1991/2749, amended by S.I. 1994/3098, S.I. 2003/1400.
[102] S.I. 1992/3073, amended by S.I. 1994/2063, S.I. 2005/831.
[103] S.I. 1994/3260.

Toys (Safety) Regulations 1995[104]

Gas Appliances (Safety) Regulations 1995[105]

Pressure Equipment Regulations 1999[106]

Medical Devices Regulations 2002[107]

Personal Protective Equipment Regulations 2002[108]

Recreational Craft Regulations 2004[109]

Medicines (Traditional Herbal Medicinal Products for Human Use) Regulations 2005[110]

General Product Safety Regulations 2005[111]

Cosmetic Products (Safety) Regulations 2008[112]

---

[104] S.I. 1995/204, amended by S.I. 2004/1769, S.I. 2005/1082.

[105] S.I. 1995/1629.

[106] S.I. 1999/2001, amended by S.I. 2002/1267, S.I. 2008/1597.

[107] S.I. 2002/618, relevant amending instruments are S.I. 2003/1697, S.I. 2005/2759, S.I. 2005/2909. S.I. 2007/400, S.I. 2008/2936.

[108] S.I. 2002/1144, amended by S.I. 2004/693.

[109] S.I. 2004/1464, to which there are amendments which are not relevant for this Order.

[110] S.I. 2005/2750, to which there are amendments which are not relevant for this Order.

[111] S.I. 2005/1803, to which there are amendments which are not relevant for this Order.

[112] S.I. 2008/1284.

Local Better Regulation Office, References to LBRO for Determination Policy and Procedure

1 EXECUTIVE SUMMARY

1.1 The Regulatory Enforcement and Sanctions Act 2008 (**the Act**) enables questions that arise in respect of enforcement action against businesses who have nominated a primary authority to be referred to the Local Better Regulation Office (**LBRO**).

1.2 LBRO may in particular consider questions that arise where a local authority (the **enforcing authority**) proposes to take enforcement action against a business (the **regulated person**) in circumstances where that business is claiming to have followed advice or guidance provided to it by its primary authority.

1.3 Applicants must first apply for consent to make a reference to LBRO. If consent is granted, LBRO will determine the reference within 28 days of the referral to LBRO (see the flowchart paragraph 2.1 below).

1.4 LBRO's powers to consider questions referred to it, and the reference process, are governed by the Act and the Co-ordination of Regulatory Enforcement (Procedure for References to LBRO) Order 2009 (**the Order**).

1.5 The actions by enforcing authorities that constitute 'enforcement action' are set out in the Co-ordination of Regulatory Enforcement (Enforcement Action) Order 2009.

1.6 LBRO will determine references by considering:
   a) whether the proposed enforcement action is inconsistent with advice or guidance given by the primary authority;
   b) whether the advice or guidance given was correct; and
   c) whether the advice was properly given by the primary authority.

1.7 Following consideration of these issues, LBRO will determine whether the enforcing authority may proceed with the proposed enforcement action.

1.8 If the advice or guidance was properly given by the primary authority, was correct, and is inconsistent with the proposed enforcement action, LBRO will determine that the enforcement action may not proceed. In all other cases it will determine that the enforcing authority may take the action proposed.

1.9 This document provides details of the circumstances in which questions may be referred to LBRO and how LBRO will deal with such references. It provides guidance as to the procedure and practice that LBRO intends to adopt in making determinations and it indicates the conduct that LBRO will expect of parties to the determination process.

1.10 This document is intended for all persons who may be parties to or have an interest in the determination process – especially for regulated persons, primary authorities and enforcing authorities. It is not a legally binding document, but is intended to be a source of information and assistance to those persons and their advisers. It is not a substitute for the statutory framework, but aims to summarise the effect of that framework as far as possible.

2 OVERVIEW OF THE REFERENCE PROCESS

2.1 The flowchart below shows the process for referring a question to LBRO:

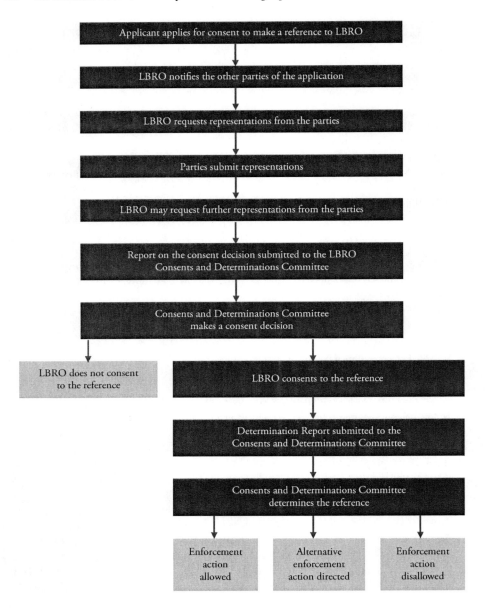

2.2 Referring a question to LBRO is a two stage process:
   a) Applicants must first apply for consent to make a reference;[1] and
   b) If consent is granted, the question raised will be automatically referred to LBRO, and LBRO will determine the reference within 28 days of such referral[2].

---

[1] Paragraphs 1(1), 2(1) and 3(1) of Schedule 4 to the Act.
[2] Paragraph 6 of Schedule 4 to the Act.

2.3   There will be three parties to each question referred to LBRO:
a)   the enforcing authority;
b)   the regulated person against which the enforcing authority wishes to take enforcement action; and
c)   the primary authority.

2.4   LBRO will communicate with and invite representations from all parties during the reference process. LBRO may also seek the views and representations of other regulators and of persons who are not parties but who may have an interest in the case or useful information to contribute.

2.5   A Consents and Determinations Committee (**the Committee**), which will normally consist of three members of LBRO's Board, will decide whether consent is granted, and will determine any reference made.

3   RESOLUTION OF QUESTIONS OUTSIDE OF THE FORMAL DETERMINATION PROCESS

3.1   LBRO encourages the parties to maintain contact with each other throughout the reference process, with a view to resolving questions before LBRO gives consent to a reference, or once a reference is made, before it is determined by LBRO.

3.2   In particular, an LBRO Account Manager will work actively with the parties to resolve the questions by arranging and facilitating negotiations between the parties.

3.3   If the parties do reach agreement before LBRO determines a reference, they should notify LBRO as soon as practicable that such agreement has been reached, and the applicant should request the withdrawal of the application.

4   APPLICATIONS FOR CONSENT TO A REFERENCE

How to apply to LBRO for consent to a reference

4.1   Applications for consent may only be made:
a)   by an enforcing authority which has been directed by a primary authority not to take enforcement action;[3]
b)   by a regulated person that has been informed by an enforcing authority that it proposes to take enforcement action, in circumstances where the primary authority has not directed that the enforcement action should not be taken;[4]
c)   by a primary authority which has been notified of proposed enforcement action by an enforcing authority, but has not directed the enforcing authority not to take the proposed action.[5]

4.2   Where an application for consent to a reference is made by a regulated person, LBRO may require that the regulated person pay reasonable costs incurred by LBRO in determining the reference (see paragraph 13 below).

4.3   The flow chart below shows the points in any proposed enforcement process at which the various parties may refer a question to LBRO.

4.4   LBRO would expect that in the majority of cases it will receive applications from either the regulated person (where the enforcement action has not been blocked) or the enforcing authority (where its action has been blocked).

---

[3] Paragraph 1, Schedule 4 to the Act.
[4] Paragraph 2, Schedule 4 to the Act.
[5] Paragraph 3 of Schedule 4 to the Act.

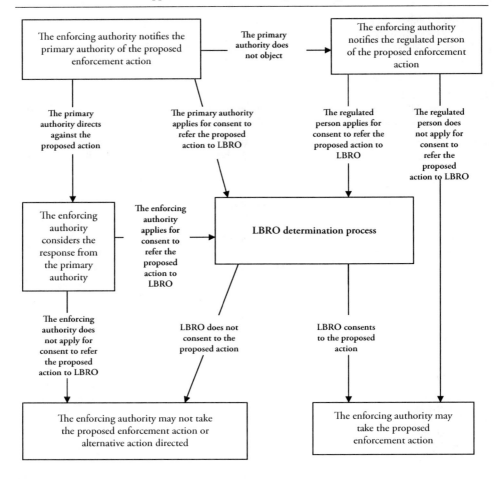

4.5   Where LBRO receives an application from a primary authority it will be because that authority has declined to make a definitive decision whether it should or should not direct that the enforcement action is not to take place. LBRO expects that a primary authority would only make a reference in default of this decision in exceptional circumstances, and that it would be able to provide good reasons why it was not appropriate for it to make the decision. These reasons will be relevant to whether or not LBRO grants consent to the application from a primary authority.

4.6   Applications must be submitted in writing to LBRO electronically to the following electronic address: pa@lbro.org.uk, or to any other address and by any other means (which may be electronic, postal or otherwise) as it may from time to time publish on its website.[6]

---

[6] Article 2, Order.

Timescales for applying for consent to a reference

4.7 Applications must be made as soon as reasonably practicable and in any event within the time periods set out below:

Applicant	Time period
Enforcing authority	10 working days beginning with and including the day after receipt of a direction from the primary authority (under section 28(2) of the Act) that the enforcement action should not be taken.[7]
Regulated person	10 working days beginning with and including the day after receipt of notification from the enforcing authority (under section 28(3) of the Act) of proposed enforcement action.[8]
Primary authority	5 working days beginning with and including the day after receipt of notification from the enforcing authority (under section 28(1) of the Act) of the proposed enforcement action.[9]

4.8 Applications received by LBRO after 5.00pm will be deemed to be received on the following working day.

4.9 LBRO may only extend the time period within which it will accept an application in exceptional circumstances.[10]

4.10 Parties seeking an extension of the time period for applications should normally be able to show that they have an effective process in place for dealing promptly with the relevant legal notices when they are received.

4.11 Parties seeking an extension of the time period for applications should contact LBRO before the expiry of the standard time period within which the relevant party could have made the application. LBRO will not usually consider applications for extensions of time made after the initial time period has expired.

4.12 LBRO will not normally consider applications for extending the time period for applications once the enforcement action in question has been commenced by the enforcing authority.

Information to be provided in the application for consent to a reference

4.13 Applications must contain the following information:

Information to be included in all applications	• the applicant's name;[11] • the applicant's business address and the name and contact details of an individual within the applicant's organisation who has responsibility for the application and reference;[12] • the names and business addresses of the other parties;[13] • a description of the proposed enforcement action.[14]

---

[7] Article 4, Order.
[8] Article 5, Order.
[9] Article 6, Order.
[10] Article 7, Order.
[11] Article 3(1)(a), Order.
[12] Article 3(1)(b), Order.
[13] Article 3(1)(c), Order
[14] Article 3(1)(d), Order.

Additional information to be included in applications from enforcing authorities	• a copy of any written notification sent to the primary authority under section 28(1) of the Act regarding the proposed enforcement action;[15] • a copy of any written direction by the primary authority under section 28(2) of the Act that the enforcing authority must not take the proposed enforcement action;[16] • a copy of the advice and guidance given by the primary authority (generally or specifically) to the enforcing authority under section 27(1) of the Act which is relevant to the proposed enforcement action;[17] • a statement as to why the enforcing authority considers that the proposed enforcement action is consistent with advice or guidance previously given by the primary authority (generally or specifically) under section 27(1) of the Act, why the advice or guidance given was not correct, or why the advice or guidance was not properly given.[18]
Additional information to be included in applications from regulated persons	• a copy of the advice and guidance received from the primary authority under section 27(1) of the Act;[19] • a copy of any document informing the regulated person, in accordance with section 28(3) of the Act, of the proposed enforcement action;[20] • a statement as to why the regulated person considers that the proposed enforcement action is inconsistent with the advice or guidance previously given by the primary authority (generally or specifically) under section 27(1) of the Act, why the advice or guidance given was correct, and why the advice or guidance was properly given.[21]
Additional information to be included in applications from primary authorities	• a copy of advice or guidance it has previously given (generally or specifically) under section 27(1) of the Act which is relevant to the proposed enforcement action;[22] • a copy of any written notification received under section 28(1) of the Act regarding the proposed enforcement action;[23] • a statement as to why the primary authority considers that the proposed enforcement action is inconsistent with advice or guidance previously given by the primary authority (generally or specifically) under section 27(1) of the Act, why the advice or guidance was correct, and why the advice or guidance was properly given.[24] • a statement of the primary authority's reasons for making the application.

4.14 LBRO expects applicants to provide all relevant information in as clear and succinct a form as possible and wherever possible using the templates available on LBRO's website at www.lbro.org.uk.

4.15 All applications should include a list of contents and pages should be numbered sequentially. Two paper copies should be provided to LBRO, on request, of any application or part of an application.

---

[15] Article 3(2)(a)(i), Order.
[16] Article 3(2)(a)(ii), Order.
[17] Article 3(2)(a)(iii), Order.
[18] Article 3(2)(a)(iv), Order.
[19] Article 3(2)(b)(i), Order.
[20] Article 3(2)(b)(ii), Order.
[21] Article 3(2)(b)(iii), Order.
[22] Article 3(2)(c)(i), Order.
[23] Article 3(2)(c)(ii), Order.
[24] Article 3(2)(c)(iii).

4.16 Failure to provide relevant information succinctly and to follow relevant guidance about the form and presentation of applications may delay the making of a consent decision by LBRO. Failure to provide information that is clear, complete and readily comprehensible may prejudice the case of the party providing it.

4.17 LBRO will check that all necessary information has been included in applications and will endeavour to alert applicants to any omissions as soon as reasonably practicable. Applicants should, however, note that it is their sole responsibility to make sure that applications are complete before the time period for making the application has expired, and that it may not be possible for LBRO to check applications within that time period. Consent may be refused for incomplete applications.

5 MULTIPLE AND RELATED APPLICATIONS

5.1 The making of an application by one party does not preclude another party from making an application in respect of the same question.

5.2 Regulated persons should note that an application by a primary authority does not automatically block enforcing authorities proceeding to take the relevant enforcement action. If, following an application for consent being made by a primary authority, a regulated person receives notice from the enforcing authority in accordance with section 28(3) that it continues to propose to take the relevant enforcement action, the regulated person may wish to consider making its own application for consent. Such an application will prevent the enforcing authority from progressing the proposed enforcement action until consent is declined or any resulting reference is determined.

5.3 If more than one application is received, LBRO will consider all applications but will not usually only grant consent to more than one. The question referred will be considered in the light of information provided by all of the parties, and LBRO will take into account the fact that more than one application was received if at any stage during the process it is asked to consent to the application or reference being withdrawn.

5.4 LBRO also envisages that it may receive related applications: these will most likely be applications arising from proposals for similar enforcement action by different enforcing authorities against the same regulated person with the same designated primary authority. Typically, for instance, this might occur if the same product has been supplied by a manufacturer within the areas of a number of enforcing authorities, and more than one of those authorities considers the product to breach a relevant regulation and therefore proposes to take action in relation to it.

5.5 Where related applications are received, LBRO will generally progress the first such application received and may delay making a consent decision in respect of related applications until after the first application has been determined. LBRO will inform the parties to any related applications as to why a consent decision is being delayed, and would expect to consider representations and other information provided in respect of related applications when determining the outcome of the first application.

6 REPRESENTATIONS FROM OTHER PARTIES

6.1 LBRO will notify the other parties in writing (electronically) on receipt of an application for consent.[25]

6.2 LBRO may, at the same time as notifying the other parties of receipt of an application, or at a later time if it deems it appropriate, request representations from the other parties.[26] LBRO expects that in most cases it will request representations before a consent decision is made.

6.3 Representations must be submitted in writing (electronically) to LBRO within the time period specified by LBRO in the request for representations.[27] LBRO intends to progress applications

---

[25] Article 8, Order.
[26] Article 9(1), Order.
[27] Article 9(2), Order.

quickly and generally expects that it will require representations to be submitted within 5 to 10 working days of a request for representations.

6.4   LBRO is likely to specify a longer time period for the submission of representations or delay requesting representations where the application received is incomplete or appears to relate to a question which would be inappropriate for LBRO to consider.

6.5   Representations should include the following information:[28]

Information to be included in representations from enforcing authorities	• the enforcing authority's business address and the name and contact details of an individual within the enforcing authority who has responsibility for responding to the application and reference; • a copy of any written notification sent to the primary authority under section 28(1) of the Act regarding the proposed enforcement action; • a copy of any written direction by the primary authority under section 28(2) of the Act that the enforcing authority must not take enforcement action; • a copy of the advice and guidance given by the primary authority (generally or specifically) to the enforcing authority under section 27(1) of the Act which is relevant to the proposed enforcement action; • a statement as to why the enforcing authority considers that the proposed enforcement action is consistent with advice or guidance previously given by the primary authority (generally or specifically) under section 27(1) of the Act, why the advice or guidance given was not correct, or why the advice or guidance was not properly given.
Information to be included in representations from regulated persons	• the regulated person's business address and the name and contact details of an individual within the regulated person's organisation who has responsibility for responding to the application and reference; • a copy of the advice and guidance received from the primary authority under section 27(1) of the Act; • a copy of any document informing the regulated person, in accordance with section 28(3) of the Act, of the proposed enforcement action; • a statement as to why the regulated person considers that the proposed enforcement action is inconsistent with the advice or guidance previously given by the primary authority (generally or specifically) under section 27(1) of the Act, why the advice or guidance given was correct, and why the advice or guidance was properly given.
Information to be included in representations from primary authorities	• the primary authority's business address and the name and contact details of an individual within the primary authority who has responsibility for responding to the application and reference; • a copy of advice or guidance it has previously given (generally or specifically) under section 27(1) of the Act which is relevant to the proposed enforcement action; • a copy of any written notification received under section 28(1) of the Act regarding the proposed enforcement action; • a statement as to why the primary authority considers that the proposed enforcement action is inconsistent with advice or guidance previously given by the primary authority (generally or specifically) under section 27(1) of the Act, why the advice or guidance was correct, and why the advice or guidance was properly given.

---

[28] Article 9(3), Order.

6.6   LBRO may specify that such further information as it reasonably believes appropriate should be included in representations.

6.7   Parties are expected to present relevant information clearly and succinctly in their representations. All representations should include a list of contents and pages should be numbered. Two paper copies should be provided to LBRO on request of any representations or part of any representations.

6.8   LBRO may request further information from the parties after representations have been submitted.[29] All such information should be submitted in writing, electronically if so directed by LBRO, promptly and within the time period set out in LBRO's request for the information.

6.9   Parties should be aware that LBRO can only make consent decisions and determinations on the basis of information presented to it. Failure to make timely, full, clear or adequate representations, or to provide information requested by LBRO within relevant time periods, may prejudice the determination process to the detriment of the party in default.

7   CONSENT DECISIONS

7.1   A report will be prepared on each application for the Committee. The report will consider the following and may include a recommendation as to whether consent should be granted:
       a)   whether the application is complete and properly made;
       b)   whether the subject of the application is an appropriate question for LBRO to determine;
       c)   whether multiple applications have been received in respect of the same question;
       d)   whether related applications have been received;
       e)   where the primary authority is the applicant, whether LBRO is satisfied that the primary authority has provided sufficient and appropriate reasons for making the application;
       f)   whether all of the information required for the determination process has been made available to LBRO.

7.2   Prior to preparing the report, LBRO may consult with relevant regulators and other third parties, take legal or other specialist advice, and request such further information as it thinks fit from the parties.

7.3   The report may be shared or any part of it, including the recommendation as to whether consent should be granted, with any or all of the parties, or the third parties mentioned in paragraph 7.2 above, prior to it being submitted to the Committee.

7.4   While it is expected that in most cases the Committee will follow the recommendation made in the report, it is not bound to do so and will exercise its own judgment based on the information before it.

7.5   Following receipt of the report the Committee may make a consent decision or defer making a consent decision pending the compilation of a fuller report or obtaining of more information.

7.6   The Committee will typically refuse consent if:
       a)   an application is incomplete or has otherwise been improperly made;
       b)   the subject of an application is not an appropriate question for LBRO to determine;
       c)   consent has already been given to another party relating to the same question;
       d)   consent has already been given to another applicant making a related application;
       e)   LBRO is not satisfied that the applicant has provided sufficient and appropriate reasons for making the application;
       f)   when the Committee considers the report, LBRO has not received the information it has requested from any party; and
       g)   the application is frivolous or vexatious.

---

[29] Paragraph 8, Schedule 4 to the Act.

7.7   Where consent has already been granted to a related application, the Committee will usually defer making a consent decision until the reference resulting from the related application has been determined.

7.8   LBRO will inform the applicant and the other parties in writing (electronically) of a consent decision as soon as reasonably practicable following the making of the decision.[30] If consent is refused, LBRO will provide all parties with a written statement of reasons for its decision.[31]

7.9   If LBRO consents to a reference, the reference is automatically deemed to be made on the day after the date on which the notice of consent is given to the parties.

7.10   Once made and communicated to the parties a consent decision is final and will not be reconsidered by LBRO.

8   REFERENCES

8.1   LBRO expects applicants to submit all information relevant to any reference with the application for consent to that reference. LBRO does not expect applicants to submit further information following the making of a reference (although LBRO may at any stage during the reference process request further information from any of the parties.[32])

8.2   References will be determined by LBRO within 28 days of the reference being made.[33]

8.3   A report will be prepared on each reference for the Committee. The report will be prepared following a consideration of the relevant information available and may include a recommendation as to how the reference should be determined. Relevant information will include:

a)   the application;

b)   representations from the parties;

c)   any other information received from the parties;

d)   any information received as a result of consultation with relevant regulators or other persons;

e)   any relevant guidance issued to the enforcing authority or the primary authority under section 6 of the Act;

f)   any relevant direction issued to the enforcing authority or the primary authority under section 7 of the Act;

g)   any relevant guidance and directions given to LBRO by the Secretary of State or the Welsh Ministers under sections 15 and 16 of the Act; and

h)   any previous determinations by LBRO in respect of similar references.

8.4   While the Committee will have regard to any recommendation contained in the report, it is not bound to follow it, but will exercise its own judgment based on the information before it.

8.5   Following receipt of the report the Committee may determine the question or may defer determination pending the compilation of a fuller report.

8.6   LBRO may if appropriate request that parties attend before the Committee and give oral representations and comments.

8.7   LBRO expects that it will rarely be appropriate to make such requests and that such requests will only be necessary where it is necessary for the purpose of determining factual matters or where the statutory timeframe within which references must be determined makes it particularly desirable for the Committee to meet the parties in person.

8.8   As LBRO can only consider the information presented to it, the failure of a party to attend on the Committee if requested to do so may prejudice the determination process to the detriment of that party.

---

[30] Article 10(2), Order.
[31] Article 10(3), Order.
[32] Paragraph 8, Schedule 4 to the Act.
[33] Paragraph 6(1), Schedule 4 to the Act.

8.9   References will be determined by the Committee as follows:

References by enforcing authorities	If LBRO is satisfied that: • the proposed enforcement action is inconsistent with advice or guidance given by the primary authority (generally or specifically); • the primary authority's advice or guidance was correct; and • the advice or guidance was properly given by the primary authority.	LBRO will confirm the direction of the primary authority preventing the enforcing authority from taking enforcement action.[34] LBRO may also direct the enforcing authority to take some other enforcement action.[35]
	If LBRO is not satisfied that: • the proposed enforcement action is inconsistent with advice or guidance given by the primary authority (generally or specifically); • the primary authority's advice or guidance was correct; and • the advice or guidance was properly given by the primary authority.	LBRO will revoke the primary authority's direction preventing the enforcing authority from taking enforcement action.[36]
References by regulated persons	If LBRO is satisfied that: • the proposed enforcement action is inconsistent with advice or guidance given by the primary authority (generally or specifically); • the primary's advice or guidance was correct; and • the advice or guidance was properly given by the primary authority.	LBRO will direct the enforcing authority not to take the enforcement action.[37] LBRO may also direct the enforcing authority to take some other enforcement action.[38]
	If LBRO is not satisfied that: • the proposed enforcement action is inconsistent with advice or guidance given by the primary authority (generally or specifically); • the primary authority's advice or guidance was correct; and • the advice or guidance was properly given by the primary authority.	LBRO will consent to the proposed enforcement action.[39]
References by primary authorities	If LBRO is satisfied that: • the proposed enforcement action is inconsistent with advice or guidance given by the primary authority (generally or specifically);	LBRO will direct the enforcing authority not to take the proposed enforcement action.[40]

---

[34] Paragraph 1(2)(a), Schedule 4 to the Act.
[35] Paragraph 1(4), Schedule 4 to the Act.
[36] Paragraph 1(2)(b), Schedule 4 to the Act.
[37] Paragraph 2(2)(a), Schedule 4 to the Act.
[38] Paragraph 2(5), Schedule 4 to the Act.
[39] Paragraph 2(2)(b), Schedule 4 to the Act.
[40] Paragraph 3(2)(a), Schedule 4 to the Act.

• the primary authority's advice or guidance was correct; and • the advice or guidance was properly given by the primary authority.	LBRO may also direct the enforcing authority to take some other enforcement action.[41]
If LBRO is not satisfied that: • the proposed enforcement action is inconsistent with advice or guidance given by the primary authority (generally or specifically); • the primary authority's advice or guidance was correct; and • the advice or guidance was properly given by the primary authority.	LBRO will consent to the proposed enforcement action.[42]

8.10 LBRO will normally direct an enforcing authority to take some other enforcement action only where LBRO considers that such enforcement action is necessary in the public interest.

8.11 In considering whether proposed enforcement action is inconsistent with advice or guidance given by the primary authority, LBRO will in particular consider:
   a) whether the regulated person has complied with the primary authority's advice or guidance; and
   b) the application of the advice or guidance to the enforcement activity.

8.12 In considering whether the advice or guidance given by the primary authority was correct, LBRO will in particular consider:
   a) whether the advice or guidance was legally correct, in that the advice or guidance was in accord with the correct interpretation of any relevant legislative provisions; and
   b) whether, with regard to other matters, the advice or guidance was within the range of advice or guidance that could reasonably have been given by the primary authority.

8.13 In considering whether the advice or guidance was properly given by the primary authority, LBRO will in particular consider:
   a) the primary authority's status as primary authority for the regulated person;
   b) the application of the Act to the enforcement activity; and
   c) whether the advice or guidance was effectively communicated to the regulated person.

8.14 As soon as reasonably practicable after determining a reference, LBRO will notify the parties in writing of its determination and make any relevant directions.[43] LBRO will provide the parties with a statement of its reasons for the determination as soon as reasonably practicable and in any event within 28 days of the determination being made.[44]

9 CONSULTATION WITH THIRD PARTIES

9.1 Before determining a reference, LBRO will consult with any relevant regulator.[45] Such consultation may take place before or after a consent decision is made and may involve the disclosure to the relevant regulator of any or all of the information provided to LBRO by the parties.

9.2 Before determining a reference, LBRO may consult such other persons as it thinks fit.[46] Such consultation may take place before or after the consent decision is made and may involve the

---

[41] Paragraph 3(5), Schedule 4 to the Act.
[42] Paragraph 3(2)(b), Schedule 4 to the Act.
[43] Article 13, Order.
[44] Article 14, Order.
[45] Paragraph 5(1)(a), Schedule 4 to the Act.
[46] Paragraph 5(1)(b), Schedule 4 to the Act.

disclosure to the other persons of any or all of the information provided to LBRO by the parties. Other persons with whom LBRO may consult include:

a) legal advisors;
b) technical experts; and
c) parties to related applications.

9.3   LBRO may but is not obliged to notify the parties before consulting with third parties.

10   WITHDRAWAL OF APPLICATIONS AND REFERENCES

10.1   Applicants may apply to LBRO in writing for the withdrawal of their application at any time before LBRO determines a reference. Applications may only be withdrawn by the applicant and may not be withdrawn without LBRO's consent.[47]

10.2   LBRO will consult with all parties before deciding whether to consent to the withdrawal of an application.[48] LBRO encourages resolution of questions by the parties outside of the formal reference process and is mindful that applications should not proceed in circumstances where none of the parties wishes them to do so. If no party expresses any objections, LBRO will generally consent to the withdrawal of an application or reference.

10.3   LBRO will normally only refuse consent for the withdrawal of a reference in the following circumstances:

a) where multiple applications were received and the withdrawal of the reference may prejudice other applicants;
b) where the time period for another party to make an application has expired and withdrawal of the current application or reference may prejudice the interests of that other party; and
c) where determination of the reference would be in the public interest.

11   SHARING OF INFORMATION

11.1   LBRO is not required to treat any information disclosed to it by any of the parties as confidential.[49] LBRO would generally expect to disclose the full content of an application and any representations and other information received from the parties to all parties.

11.2   LBRO may also disclose the full content of an application and any representations and other information received from the parties to any relevant regulator or such other persons that it consults during its consideration of the application.

11.3   No person may, without the consent of LBRO and the other parties, use any information disclosed to it in connection with an application for any purpose not directly connected to the application.[50]

12   PUBLICATION OF INFORMATION

12.1   LBRO will usually publish on the secure area of its website :

a) details of any applications received, including the names of the parties and the subject of the reference;
b) the outcome of consent decisions, including if appropriate LBRO's reasons for refusing to consent to a reference; and
c) reference determinations, including such information on the outcome as is appropriate and is not commercially sensitive.

---

[47] Articles 11(1) and 11(3), Order.
[48] Article 11(2) and 11(4), Order.
[49] Article 12(1), Order.
[50] Article 12(2), Order.

12.2 LBRO may also publish other relevant information, including guidance issued by a primary authority or details of proposed enforcement action.

12.3 LBRO will endeavour to ensure that the publication of information which is of genuine commercial sensitivity is not published, particularly where this has been highlighted by the parties.

13   COSTS

13.1 If a regulated person makes an application, LBRO may require the regulated person to pay such reasonable costs incurred by LBRO as a result of the reference as LBRO may specify.[51]

13.2 LBRO will usually require regulated persons who are applicants to pay costs resulting from references, but may choose in its discretion choose not to do so.

13.3 No costs will normally be payable where an application for a reference is withdrawn before a consent decision is taken or is declined at consent stage.

13.4 Whether the regulated person will be required to pay costs and the level of those costs may depend on factors including:
   a)   the outcome of the reference;
   b)   the conduct of all parties during the reference process;
   c)   the complexity of the reference;
   d)   any public interest implications of the reference;
   e)   any application made by the regulated person to withdraw the reference;
   f)   the circumstances of the regulated person; and
   g)   whether multiple or related applications have been considered by LBRO.

13.5 LBRO's costs will usually include its out-of-pocket expenses, such as the cost of external legal or technical advisers required for the purposes of assisting it, as well as an element of its own cost.

13.6 LBRO will aim to confirm to the regulated person that it is required to pay costs, and confirm the amount of those costs, within 28 days of determination of the reference.

---

[51] Paragraph 2(7), Schedule 4 to the Act.

SI 2009 No. 665

REGULATORY REFORM

The Co-ordination of Regulatory Enforcement (Enforcement Action) Order 2009

Made	*13th March 2009*
Laid before Parliament	*16th March 2009*
Coming into force	*6th April 2009*

The Secretary of State, in exercise of the powers conferred by sections 28(6) and 29(1) of the Regulatory Enforcement and Sanctions Act 2008[1], and with the consent of the Welsh Ministers makes the following Order:

Citation, Commencement and interpretation

1.—(1) This Order shall be known as the Co-ordination of Regulatory Enforcement (Enforcement Action) Order 2009 and shall come into force on 6th April 2009.

(2) In this Order "the Act" means the Regulatory Enforcement and Sanctions Act 2008.

Enforcement action

2.—(1) Subject to paragraph (2), each of the following actions is to be regarded as enforcement action for the purposes of Part 2 of the Act—

(a) the giving of any communication in writing which indicates that one or more of the actions referred to in subparagraphs (b) to (t) will be taken within, or at the end of, a period of time specified in the communication unless the regulated person acts (or ceases to act) in the manner specified in the communication;

(b) the service of a stop notice within the meaning of section 46(2) of the Act;

(c) the service of a prohibition notice under any of the following enactments—

   (i) section 22 of the Health and Safety at Work etc Act 1974[2],

   (ii) section 10 of the Safety of Sports Grounds Act 1975[3],

   (iii) regulation 15(3) of the Environmental Protection (Controls on Ozone-Depleting Substances) Regulations 2002[4],

   (iv) regulation 24(3) of the Fluorinated Greenhouse Gases Regulations 2008[5];

---

[1] 2008 c.13.
[2] 1974 c.37.
[3] 1975 c.52.
[4] S.I. 2002/528; regulation 15 was inserted by paragraph 5(1) of the Schedule to S.I. 2008/91.
[5] S.I. 2008/41.

(d)   the service of an abatement notice under section 80 of the Environmental Protection Act 1990[6];

(e)   the service of an emergency prohibition notice under any of the following enactments—

    (i)   section 12(1) of the Food Safety Act 1990[7],

    (ii)   regulation 22 of the Feed (Hygiene and Enforcement) (England) Regulations 2005[8],

    (iii)   regulation 22 of the Feed (Hygiene and Enforcement) (Wales) Regulations 2005[9],

    (iv)   regulation 8 of the Food Hygiene (England) Regulations 2006[10],

    (v)   regulation 8 of the Food Hygiene (Wales) Regulations 2006[11];

(f)   the imposition of an improvement notice under any of the following enactments—

    (i)   section 10 of the Animal Welfare Act 2006[12],

    (ii)   section 10 of the Food Safety Act 1990,

    (iii)   section 21 of the Health and Safety at Work etc Act 1974,

    (iv)   regulation 17 of the Feed (Hygiene and Enforcement) (England) Regulations 2005,

    (v)   regulation 17 of the Feed (Hygiene and Enforcement) (Wales) Regulations 2005,

    (vi)   regulation 6 of the Food Hygiene (England) Regulations 2006,

    (vii)   regulation 6 of the Food Hygiene (Wales) Regulations 2006;

(g)   the service of a remedial action notice or a detention notice under either of the following enactments—

    (i)   regulation 9 of the Food Hygiene (England) Regulations 2006,

    (ii)   regulation 9 of the Food Hygiene (Wales) Regulations 2006;

(h)   the service of a certificate under either of the following enactments—

    (i)   regulation 27 of the Food Hygiene (England) Regulations 2006,

    (ii)   regulation 27 of the Food Hygiene (Wales) Regulations 2006;

(i)   the service of a notice under section 4 of the Prevention of Damage by Pests Act 1949[13];

(j)   the service of a notice under section 60 of the Control of Pollution Act 1974[14];

(k)   the determination of an application under section 61 of the Control of Pollution Act 1974[15];

(l)   the imposition of a fixed monetary penalty or discretionary requirement within the meaning of section 39(3) or section 42(3) of the Act respectively;

(m)   the service of an enforcement notice under—

    (i)   regulation 15(1) of the Environmental Protection (Controls on Ozone-Depleting Substances) Regulations 2002,

    (ii)   regulation 36 of the Environmental Permitting (England and Wales) Regulations 2007[16],

---

[6]   1990 c. 43.

[7]   1990 c.16.

[8]   S.I. 2005/3280.

[9]   S.I 2005/3368.

[10]   S.1. 2006/14.

[11]   S.I. 2006/31.

[12]   2006 c.45.

[13]   1949 c.55; section 4 was amended by the Agriculture (Miscellaneous Provisions) Act 1972, section 26(3) and Schedule 6, and by section 17(2)(a) of the Interpretation Act 1978.

[14]   1974 c.40.

[15]   1974 c.40; section 61 was amended by section 133(2) of, and Schedule 7 to the Building Act 1984, section 120 of, and Schedule 24 to the Environment Act 1995, and by section 162 of and Schedule 15 paragraphs 15(1) and (3) to, the Environmental Protection Act 1990; and as regards Scotland it was amended by section 58 of, and Schedule 6 to, the Building (Scotland) Act 2003.

[16]   S.I. 2007/3538.

    (iii) regulation 24(1) of the Fluorinated Greenhouse Gases Regulations 2008;

(n) the service of a suspension notice under regulation 37 of the Environmental Permitting (England and Wales) Regulations 2007;

(o) the service of any of the following notices under the General Product Safety Regulations 2005[17]—

    (i) a suspension notice under regulation 11,

    (ii) a requirement to mark products under regulation 12,

    (iii) a requirement to warn consumers under regulation 13,

    (iv) a withdrawal notice under regulation 14,

    (v) a recall notice under regulation 15;

(p) the reference of any matter to a prosecuting authority other than a local authority with a view to the prosecuting authority considering the commencement of proceedings in relation to the matter;

(q) the commencement of proceedings in a court of law or tribunal created under an enactment;

(r) the imposition of any sanction (whether criminal or otherwise) in respect of any act or omission;

(s) the administering of a simple caution;

(t) the acceptance by the enforcing authority of any undertaking (under an enactment or otherwise) in respect of any act or omission.

(2) The following action is not to be regarded as enforcement action for the purposes of Part 2 of the Act:—

(a) action referred to in section 28(5) of the Act not specified in paragraph (1);

(b) action taken by an enforcing authority pursuant to or in connection with the exercise of functions under—

    (i) the Regulatory Reform (Fire Safety) Order 2005[18],

    (ii) the Licensing Act 2003[19], or

    (iii) the Gambling Act 2005[20].

Enforcement Action: Exclusions

3. Section 28(1) to (4) of the Act shall not apply in the following circumstances:

(a) where the enforcement action is required urgently, or in the opinion of the enforcing authority is required urgently, to avoid a significant risk of harm to human health or the environment (including the health of animals or plants) or the financial interests of consumers;

(b) where the enforcement action is the service of a notice referred to in Article 2(1)(d) or (e);

(c) where the application of section 28(1) to (4) of the Act would be, or in the opinion of the enforcing authority would be, wholly disproportionate.

Stephen Carter
Minister for Communications, Technology and Broadcasting
Department for Business, Enterprise and Regulatory Reform

13th March 2009

---

[17] S.I. 2005/1803.
[18] S.I.2005/1541.
[19] 2003 c.17.
[20] 2005 c.19.

EXPLANATORY NOTE

(This note is not part of the Order)

This Order specifies action which is and is not to be regarded as enforcement action for the purposes of Part 2 of the Regulatory Enforcement and Sanctions Act 2008. It also prescribes circumstances in which the enforcing authority does not have to notify the primary authority before it takes enforcement action, and cannot be directed not to take that action. In such circumstances, the enforcing authority must notify the primary authority of the enforcement action as soon as it reasonably can after taking the enforcement action.

Part 2 of the Regulatory Enforcement and Sanctions Act 2008 establishes a scheme for coordination of regulatory enforcement against a person (a "regulated person") where that person carries on an activity in the areas of two or more local authorities and each of those authorities has the same relevant function in relation to that activity. Under the scheme one authority can be appointed as "the primary authority" in relation to the regulated person. In such cases, other than in circumstances prescribed by Article 3 of this Order, the taking of enforcement action against the regulated person by any local authority other than the primary authority (an "enforcing authority") has to be notified to the primary authority, who may direct the enforcing authority not to take the action.

Article 2 describes what is, and what is not, to be regarded as enforcement action for the purposes of the primary authority scheme. Article 3 prescribes the circumstances in which the enforcing authority does not have to notify the primary authority before it takes enforcement action.

A full impact assessment of the effect that this instrument will have on the costs of business and the voluntary sector is available from the Department for Business, Enterprise and Regulatory Reform and is annexed to the Explanatory Memorandum which is available alongside the instrument on the OPSI website.

SI 2009 No. 670

REGULATORY REFORM

The Co-ordination of Regulatory Enforcement (Procedure for References to LBRO) Order 2009

Made	*5th March 2009*
Laid before Parliament	*16th March 2009*
Coming into force	*6th April 2009*

The Secretary of State makes the following Order in exercise of the power conferred by paragraph 6(2) of Schedule 4 to the Regulatory Enforcement and Sanctions Act 2008[1]:

Citation, commencement and interpretation

1.—(1) This Order may be cited as the Co-ordination of Regulatory Enforcement (Procedure for References to LBRO) Order 2009 and will come into force on 6th April 2009.

(2) In this Order—

"the Act" means the Regulatory Enforcement and Sanctions Act 2008;

"applicant" means the person applying or who has applied for consent to a reference;

"other parties" means, in relation to an application for consent to a reference or in relation to a reference, whichever of the enforcing authority, regulated person and primary authority is not the applicant in respect of that reference;

"reference" means reference of a proposed enforcement action to LBRO under Schedule 4 to the Act;

"working day" means a day other than—

(a) a Saturday or Sunday,

(b) Christmas Day or Good Friday, or

(c) a day which is a bank holiday under the Banking and Financial Dealings Act 1971[2] in—

   (i) the part of the United Kingdom where the primary authority is, or

   (ii) (if different) the part of the United Kingdom where the enforcing authority is.

Address for LBRO

2. Applications for consent to a reference and any representations made to LBRO in relation to a reference must be made in writing to the following electronic address: www.lbro.org.uk, or such other address (whether electronic or otherwise) as may from time to time be published by LBRO on its website.

---

[1] 2008 c.13.
[2] 1971 c.80.

Information to be included with an application to LBRO for consent to a reference

3.—(1) All applications to LBRO for consent to a reference must contain the following information—

(a) the applicant's name;

(b) the applicant's business address and the name and contact details of an individual within the applicant's organisation who has responsibility for the application and reference;

(c) the names and business addresses of the other parties; and

(d) a description of the proposed enforcement action.

(2) In addition, in each case, the following information must also be provided—

(a) where the enforcing authority is the applicant—

(i) a copy of any written notification sent to the primary authority under section 28(1) of the Act regarding the proposed enforcement action;

(ii) a copy of any written direction by the primary authority under section 28(2) of the Act that the enforcing authority must not take the enforcement action;

(iii) a copy of the advice and guidance given by the primary authority to the enforcing authority under section 27(1) of the Act which is relevant to the proposed enforcement action; and

(iv) a statement as to why the enforcing authority considers that—

(aa) the proposed enforcement action is consistent with advice or guidance previously given by the primary authority (generally or specifically) under section 27(1) of the Act,

(bb) the advice or guidance given was not correct, or

(cc) the advice or guidance was not properly given;

(b) where the regulated person is the applicant—

(i) a copy of the advice and guidance received from the primary authority under section 27(1) of the Act which is relevant to the proposed enforcement action;

(ii) a copy of any document informing the regulated person, in accordance with section 28(3) of the Act, of the proposed enforcement action; and

(iii) a statement as to why the regulated person considers that—

(aa) the proposed enforcement action is inconsistent with advice or guidance previously given by the primary authority (generally or specifically) under section 27(1) of the Act,

(bb) the advice or guidance given was correct, and

(cc) the advice or guidance was properly given;

(c) where the primary authority is the applicant—

(i) a copy of advice and guidance it has previously given under section 27(1) of the Act which is relevant to the proposed enforcement action;

(ii) a copy of any written notification received by it under section 28(1) of the Act regarding the proposed enforcement action; and

(iii) a statement as to why the primary authority considers that

(aa) the proposed enforcement action is inconsistent with advice or guidance previously given by the primary authority (generally or specifically) under section 27(1) of the Act,

(bb) the advice or guidance given was correct, and

(cc) the advice or guidance was properly given.

Time limits for making an application for consent to a reference

4. The enforcing authority must make an application for consent to a reference as soon as reasonably practicable, and in any event within the period of 10 working days beginning with the day after that on which the enforcing authority receives a direction from the primary authority under section 28(2) of the Act that the proposed enforcement action must not be taken.

Time limits for making an application for consent to a reference

5. The regulated person must make an application for consent to a reference as soon as reasonably practicable, and in any event within the period of 10 working days beginning with the day after that on which the regulated person is informed by the enforcing authority under section 28(3) of the Act of the enforcement action proposed to be taken.

Time limits for making an application for consent to a reference

6. The primary authority must make an application for consent to a reference as soon as reasonably practicable, and in any event within the period of 5 working days beginning with the day after that on which the primary authority is notified under section 28(1) of the Act that the enforcing authority proposes to take enforcement action against a regulated person.

Time limits for making an application for consent to a referenc

7. LBRO may, in exceptional circumstances, allow an application for consent to a reference to be made after the time limits set out in Articles 4, 5 and 6.

Time limits for making an application for consent to a reference

8. On receipt of an application for consent to a reference, LBRO must give notice of it to the other parties.

Representations

9.—(1) LBRO may request, before or after giving consent to a reference, that the other parties submit any written representations which they wish to make to LBRO in relation to that reference.

(2) Representations must be made within the time which LBRO shall specify in a request for representations.

(3) Representations from either of the other parties must include the information which that other party would have had to give under Article 3(2) if it had been the applicant.

Decision on application for consent to a reference

10.—(1) LBRO must decide whether to consent to a reference as soon as reasonably practicable after receiving an application for consent to that reference.

(2) LBRO must, as soon as reasonably practicable, inform the applicant and other parties in writing of its decision.

(3) If LBRO refuses consent to a reference, it must give a written statement of reasons for that decision at the same time as it informs the applicant and the other parties of the decision.

Withdrawal of application for consent or of reference

11.—(1) The applicant may apply to LBRO for consent to withdraw its application for consent to a reference by giving notice in writing to LBRO.

(2) LBRO shall not consent to the withdrawal of an application for consent to a reference without consulting the other parties.

(3) After LBRO has given consent to a reference, the applicant may apply to LBRO for consent to withdraw that reference by giving notice in writing to LBRO.

(4) LBRO shall not consent to the withdrawal of a reference after giving consent to it without consulting the other parties.

Confidentiality

12.—(1) LBRO shall not be required to treat information disclosed in connection with an application for consent to a reference or a reference as confidential.

(2) No person shall, without the consent of LBRO, the applicant and the other parties, use any information disclosed to it in connection with an application for consent to a reference or in connection with a reference for any purpose not directly connected to that application or reference.

Determination of a reference

13. As soon as reasonably practicable after determining a reference under paragraph 1, 2, or 3 of Schedule 4 to the Act, LBRO must notify the applicant and the other parties in writing of its determination.

Determination of a reference

14. LBRO must provide to the applicant and the other parties a written statement of reasons as soon as reasonably practicable after the determination has been made and in any event within 28 days of the determination being made.

Stephen Carter
Minister for Communications, Technology and Broadcasting,
Department for Business, Enterprise and Regulatory Reform

5th March 2009

EXPLANATORY NOTE

(This note is not part of the Order)

This Order makes provision for the procedure that will govern the reference of matters for determination by the LBRO in accordance with Schedule 4 to the Regulatory Enforcement and Sanctions Act 2008.

Part 2 of that Act establishes a scheme for co-ordination of regulatory enforcement against a person (a "regulated person") where that person carries on an activity in the area of two or more local authorities and each of those authorities has the same relevant function in relation to that activity. Under the scheme one authority can be appointed as "the primary authority" in relation to the regulated person. In such cases, the taking of enforcement action against the regulated person by any other local authority (an "enforcing authority") has to be notified to the primary authority, who may direct the enforcing authority not to take the action.

LBRO may determine a reference of a matter where there is dispute between the parties in relation to whether or not an enforcement action should or should not go ahead.

Article 2 of the Order gives the website address for LBRO and provides that applications for consent to a reference must be made in writing through that website. Article 3 sets out the information to be provided to LBRO by an applicant. Articles 4 to 7 set out time limits for making an application. Article 8 provides for notice of an application to be given to the other parties, i.e. whichever of the enforcing authority, regulated person and primary authority is not the applicant. Article 9 provides for the making of representations by the other parties to a reference. Article 10 provides for LBRO to take a decision as to whether to consent to a reference as soon as reasonably practicable, and also makes provision for LBRO to inform the parties of that decision.

Article 11 makes provision for the withdrawal of an application for consent to a reference or withdrawal of a reference once consent has been given by LBRO.

Article 12 makes provision in relation to confidentiality and use of information.

Articles 13 and 14 provide that LBRO must inform the parties of its determination in writing as soon as reasonably practicable, and provide written reasons for its determination.

A full impact assessment of the effect that this instrument will have on the costs of business and the voluntary sector is available from the Department for Business, Enterprise and Regulatory Reform, Bay 3134, 1 Victoria Street, London, SW1H 0ET, and is annexed to the Explanatory Memorandum which is available alongside the instrument on the OPSI website.

APPENDIX 7

Department for Business Enterprise and Regulatory Reform, Guidance on Creating New Regulatory Penalties and Offences

<u>Introduction</u>

1. This paper sets out guidelines on drafting new legislation to tackle regulatory non-compliance. It sets out:

    *   some general principles about when civil sanctions might be more appropriate than criminal offences;
    *   the new civil sanctions available to regulators under the Regulatory Enforcement and Sanctions (RES) Act 2008;
    *   guidance on formulating criminal offences, where that course of action is appropriate; and
    *   contact details for those in the Ministry of Justice and the Department for Business Enterprise and Regulatory Reform with whom proposals for new sanctions should be discussed at the earliest possible stage.

2. The guidelines represent agreed Government policy and following them will help you to get through the clearance process more smoothly. When seeking DA clearance for new proposals, you will have to justify any departure from the principles set out here.

<u>Background</u>

3. In the final report of his review of regulatory enforcement[1], Professor Macrory found that regulators were over-reliant on criminal prosecution as a means of enforcement and that this led to a compliance gap, where some regulators lack the appropriate enforcement tools to address regulatory non-compliance. Professor Macrory also found that criminal sanctions are often an insufficient deterrent to the truly criminal or rogue operators. He recommended introducing a set of administrative penalties that would allow regulators to impose proportionate, flexible and meaningful sanctions. Furthermore, he felt that the courts lacked the necessary tools to tackle non-compliance and recommended a range of improvements to criminal prosecution and sentencing.

4. He also recommended that the following principles should underpin any regulatory sanctioning regime:

    *   Aim to change the behaviour of the offender;
    *   Aim to eliminate any financial gain or benefit from non-compliance;
    *   Be responsive and consider what is appropriate for the particular offender and the regulatory issue;
    *   Be proportionate to the nature of the offence and the harm caused;
    *   Aim to restore the harm caused by the regulatory non-compliance, where appropriate; and
    *   Aim to deter future non-compliance.

5. The Macrory report's recommendations were accepted in full by the Government.

<u>Civil sanctions or criminal offences?</u>

6. In designing new enforcement regimes you will need to consider carefully whether the behaviour warrants the intervention of the criminal law at all, and what alternatives there

---

[1] Regulatory Justice: Making Sanctions Effective (Final Report) November 2006

may be to criminal offences. Professor Macrory envisaged that criminal prosecution should be reserved for the breaches of legislation which have serious consequences. You will need to decide when civil sanctions alone might be more appropriate.

7.   In creating any new civil or criminal sanctions, you should consider the following points:

- Nature and potential harm of the conduct to be targeted

    a.   What is the conduct that you are seeking to target? A particular event such as late filing of compulsory information? Or behaviour such as dishonesty, negligence, or repeated non-compliance?

    b.   What is the range of conduct that you are targeting? Can different kinds of conduct be identified and some of them addressed with more targeted sanctions? For example, can dishonest evasion of a regulatory obligation be separated from the wider non-compliance of failure to provide information to the regulator, where there may be no or little dishonest intent?

    c.   What are the consequences of the conduct you are targeting? Is there harm to particular victims or the environment? Does the conduct prejudice the integrity of the regulatory system?

- What are you seeking to do about that conduct?

    a.   Is the intention to punish, remedy, raise compliance standards, deter others or to stigmatize?

    b.   How does your proposed sanction fit in with your intention?

- Who are you targeting?

    a.   Is the person in breach likely to be an individual or company?

    b.   What sanction is that person likely to respond to?

    c.   Is it necessary to have sanctions for both individuals and companies and if so, can their respective conduct be differentiated?

- What existing sanctions might be available for that conduct?

    a.   Are there any existing criminal sanctions? Criminal courts now have much wider powers than those of fining and imprisonment and you might consider extending them to the conduct in question.

    b.   Are there any existing models of civil or administrative sanctions that you might adopt? Is the RES Act model appropriate? Do you want to follow fixed penalty notice models in, for example, the Road Traffic Act 1991 and the Environmental Protection Act 1990?

    c.   Is there a need to create new kinds of responses to the conduct you are seeking to target, such as publicity orders?

- Are there any constraints on your choice between criminal offences and civil sanctions?

    a.   Is there a need for consistency with existing regimes in similar regulatory areas? It may not always be appropriate to follow a precedent, but you need to take account of any precedents that exist.

    b.   Are you implementing an EU obligation? Does the obligation require 'dissuasive and proportionate' sanctions? (In appropriate circumstances this could mean the creation of criminal sanctions.) Be wary of 'gold plating' the directive. (When deciding whether to use primary or secondary legislation to import EC law, you should bear in mind that s. 2(2) of the European Communities Act 1972 is limited in respect of the length and severity of sanctions and penalties that can be created under it by Schedule 2, paragraph 1(d) to the Act.)

    c.   Is there a need for consistency with other regimes deriving from EU obligations?

> d. Are there any existing legislative powers you can use (for example, Order making powers or other secondary legislation making powers) or do you need to create new legislation?

- If you are consolidating existing offences, are they still necessary and proportionate?

> a. Is there any scope for fully decriminalising some of the conduct they cover?
> b. How often are the existing offences used?

8. If you wish to create new civil sanctions, please see section A below. If you wish to create a new offence, section B gives guidance on how offences should be formulated. If you propose to create parallel civil and criminal regimes, please see section C for further guidance.

A. Civil Sanctions – application to new regulatory regimes

9. The RES Act provides a set of civil sanctions which can be applied to existing relevant regulatory criminal offences by statutory order. The scope of the RES Act provisions is determined by Schedules 5-7 to the Act. There is no power in the Act to add to these. We would expect that new legislation creating regulators or offences that fall outside of the scope of Part 3 of the Act will make its own provision for civil sanctions, but should follow the Part 3 model, regardless of whether the penalties are alternatives to criminal prosecution. The benefits of following this model are that it has been thoroughly debated and scrutinised both by Parliament and through extensive public consultation. The RES Act model also provides robust safeguards which comply with ECHR obligations and following the model will ensure consistency for the regulated community.

10. Not all of the sanctions in the Part 3 model will be suitable for particular regulatory situations. You will be able to pick and choose the appropriate sanctions for your regime. We recognise that this model of civil sanctions will not be appropriate in all regulatory contexts; where there is a divergence, a clear justification should be considered. Such reasons could include the particular needs of the regulated bodies who will be subject to the sanctions. An explanation will be necessary for clearance purposes and increasingly Parliament will press this point.

11. The sanctions in the RES Act are as follows:

- Fixed monetary penalty (FMP) notices – under which a regulator will be able to impose a monetary penalty of a fixed amount, usually capped at £5,000. These are suitable for more minor instances of non-compliance, where for example there are simple facts to prove;

- Discretionary requirements – which will enable a regulator to impose one or more of the following:

   - a variable monetary (VMP) penalty whose amount will be determined by the regulator (although these are capped for summary only offences),
   - a requirement to take specified steps within a stated period to secure that an offence does not continue or happen again (a compliance notice), and
   - a requirement to take specified steps within a stated period to secure that the position is restored, so far as possible, to what it would have been if no offence had been committed (a restoration notice);

- Discretionary requirements are generally aimed at more complex cases of non-compliance.

- Stop notices – will prevent a business from carrying on an activity described in the notice until it has taken steps to come back into compliance. These are reserved for serious breaches, reflected in the high threshold before issue (there must be a 'significant risk' of 'serious harm' to human health, the environment or the financial interests of consumers); and

- Enforcement undertakings – will enable a business, which a regulator reasonably suspects of having committed an offence, to give an undertaking to a regulator to take one or more corrective actions set out in the undertaking. (These are a key element of the Macrory package of civil sanctions and will encourage a more collaborative approach to enforcement between the regulator and the business.)

12. An assessment process has been put in place to ensure that regulators are ready to receive the new civil sanctions powers in the RES Act. In particular, before making an order giving a regulator access to the new powers, the Act requires the Minister to be satisfied that a regulator will use the new powers in a way that is compliant with the principles of good regulation—transparent, accountable, proportionate, consistent and targeted only at cases where action is needed. Departments should apply the same criteria to regulators whenever new, non-RES Act civil sanctioning powers are to be conferred upon them.

Application

13. You will need to consider to whom the sanctions should apply. In particular, you will need to consider whether the new sanctions apply to individuals or companies (or other bodies corporate) or both. The primary focus of Part 3 of the RES Act is to tackle breaches of non-compliance by businesses, although it does allow some flexibility. (For example, the Act could allow the level of fixed monetary penalty to vary between an individual, such as a sole trader, and a larger business.)

Standard and Burden of proof

14. You will need to consider carefully what elements of the breach or non-compliance the regulator must prove, and to what standard, before imposing the sanction. For example, the standard of proof on the regulator could be balance of probabilities (the civil standard) or beyond reasonable doubt (the criminal standard). The RES Act requires the criminal standard for the imposition of Part 3 administrative sanctions as they are based on existing criminal offences. There may be some types of non-compliance which require lower standards of proof such as the reasonable opinion of the regulator. Whatever standard chosen, you must be prepared to explain and justify your choice. You will also need to consider on whom the burden of proof falls. These matters are likely to raise legal issues, particularly compatibility with ECHR obligations, on which you should consult your legal advisers.

Contesting a civil sanction—Appeals

15. The Government's preferred option is for appeals against new civil sanctions to be heard by the First-tier Tribunal, created by the Tribunals, Courts and Enforcement Act 2007. In creating appeal rights you will need to discuss your provisions with the Tribunals Service, part of the Ministry of Justice. Contact Glenn Dalton. Email: Glenn.Dalton@tribunals.gsi.gov.uk Tel: 0207 566 1295.

Enforcement of monetary penalties

16. If you are considering civil monetary penalties, consideration needs to be given about how unpaid penalties will be enforced. The wording of your legislation is important. If your legislation simply provides that such unpaid penalties are enforceable as a 'civil debt' then, for England and Wales, debt recovery proceedings must be commenced through the civil courts before any enforcement can take place. However, for England and Wales, legislation can give the courts power to order that a debt may be enforced as if it were payable under a court order. Legislation can also state directly that a penalty may be enforced as it if were a court order. In either of these cases enforcement may be made, subject to the provisions of Parts 70—74 of the Civil Procedure Rules 1998, directly through the courts without necessarily starting debt recovery proceedings. It may therefore be advisable to have one of these provisions in your legislation to make enforcement easier. The RES Act sets out a model for how unpaid penalties could be enforced through civil procedures and the Ministry of Justice Civil Enforcement Policy Team will be able to advise further on this and the proposed wording of any legislation. Enforcement of monetary penalties does not necessarily require punishment by a criminal offence. Contact Dr Sue Rayner Jacobs, Email Sue.RaynerJacobs@ justice.gsi.gov.uk Tel : 0203 334 6354

17. Any receipts from monetary penalties, late payment charges etc. should be paid into the Consolidated Fund. This reflects a key Macrory recommendation that there should be no financial incentives that could influence the sanctioning response.

B. Creating new regulatory criminal offences

18. As discussed above, the Macrory review suggested that the criminal law is used too readily in regulatory situations. Professor Macrory also recommended that the Government review the drafting and formulation of criminal offences relating to regulatory compliance, with a view to considering whether some offences should be decriminalised. If you are considering creating a regulatory offence, you need to consider carefully whether the behaviour warrants the intervention of the criminal law, and what alternatives there may be to criminal offences. If you are consolidating existing offences, you still need to consider whether the offences continue to be necessary and proportionate. Just because something has, historically, been a criminal offence is not justification in its own right. In particular, you will need to look at how often the existing offences are used.

Formulation of offences

19. A criminal offence is normally made up of two parts—the action and the state of mind of the person doing it. The main categories for the mental state are intention, recklessness or neglect. Some actions may be offences whatever your state of mind. You may need specific defences (such as 'due diligence') to make sure that, for example, if the action was inadvertent or unavoidable, it would not constitute an offence.

Burden of proof

20. The normal rule is that the prosecution has to prove all the elements of an offence. If you want to have any element in the offence which the accused will have to disprove, you will need to speak to your legal advisers at an early stage. Defences are normally for the accused to raise in their defence, and for them to prove.

Sanctions

21. If you are creating criminal offences you need to consider proportionate sanctions. Custodial penalties should be reserved for serious and violent offenders; such sanctions will be particularly inappropriate where the offenders are likely to be businesses. Fines need to be justifiable and proportionate. Where a business is involved, you may consider the existing statutory maximum fine available in the magistrates' courts (£5,000) to be an insufficient deterrent and that a much higher penalty, or exceptional summary maximum (ESM), is required. The criteria for an ESM are that the offence is serious enough to justify a penalty above the normal statutory maximum and the matters involved should be susceptible to fairly easy proof. The offence should also be lucrative, either because it will give rise to large profits or because it will result in significant savings. Also, it must be likely to be committed by companies or others with considerable resources. Under the ESM, a magistrates' court can issue a penalty of up to £50,000. All proposals for new penalties or changes to existing ones must be referred to the Ministry of Justice (Sentencing Policy and Penalties Unit), for consideration. Contact Chris Morris-Perry. Email: Chris.Morris-Perry@justice.gsi.gov.uk Tel: 0203 334 5039

Application

22. Again, you will need to consider to whom the offence needs to apply. You should consider whether the offence applies only to companies and organisations, only to individuals, or to both. Normally, an offence applies to both. Some offences, by their nature, may be wholly or mainly applicable to companies. In that case, you may need to consider whether the directors and other senior office holders in the company should also be liable for the offence, if the offence was committed with their consent or connivance or was allowed to happen as a result of their neglect.

C. Parallel Criminal and Civil Sanctioning Regimes

23.   It is possible to have regimes where the same misbehaviour can attract both a civil sanction and a criminal offence. Health and Safety offences are an example. The RES Act enables civil sanctions to be applied to conduct which otherwise attracts criminal liability. You may need to consider giving guidance to regulators and the public as to what factors might inform whether a civil sanction should be applied or criminal prosecution commenced.

Comparative safeguards

24.   Where you are proposing to create parallel criminal and civil sanctions for the same conduct, you will need to consider carefully the procedural safeguards available to the person accused under either regime. There may be human rights implications and fairness issues that require certain safeguards to be written into the sanctioning process. You may be called to explain the differences in the safeguards available under the criminal and civil sanctioning route in Parliament. You should discuss these issues with your legal advisers.

Double jeopardy

25.   Where parallel regimes are created, there is a risk of someone being punished twice for the same behaviour (also called double jeopardy). This could be contrary to domestic legal principles and European ones. If you are proposing to make the same behaviour both a criminal offence and a civil wrong, you need to think carefully about why this is necessary and discuss with your legal advisers at an early stage so as to minimise legal risk.

26.   You can have a civil regime which is accompanied by offences to protect the civil enforcement process. For example, there are offences of obstructing inspectors, failing to provide information or failing to comply with an enforcement notice, which supplement a civil sanctioning regime. These are usually acceptable from a double jeopardy perspective as they target different conduct.

D. Costs/regulatory impact of proposed sanctioning regime

27.   As well as considering the impact of your proposals on business, you will also need to think about the impact on the justice system: this means the courts, tribunals, legal aid, and correctional services such as prisons and probation. The starting point will be the number of likely prosecutions for the new offence, or number of new civil cases. You will only ever be able to estimate this. Costs can be given as within a range if necessary (for example between £50,000 and £70,000). But the estimate needs to be as accurate as possible. Numbers of prosecutions for similar offences, or for offences affecting the same sector, may be a guide.

28.   You must consult the Ministry of Justice over the costs of your proposals, both for the correctional services if relevant, and for costs associated with the trial process, whether civil or criminal, which include aspects such as court costs and legal aid. The Ministry of Justice is likely to ask that your Department meet the cost of any additional burden on the justice system, including the provision of extra judiciary, staff or tribunals or any additional training requirements for them. Contact Sue Rayner Jacobs. Email: Sue.RaynerJacobs@justice.gsi.gov.uk Tel: 0203 334 6354.

29.   The RES Act contains a power for regulators to recover certain costs (such as investigation costs) when imposing a discretionary requirement or stop notice. If you wish to replicate such a power you will need to discuss this with the Treasury.

E. Territorial extent

30.   This guidance, and particularly section B, relates to England and Wales only. However, where you are creating new sanctions, you will need to consider the effect of these in relation to reserved matters in Scotland and Northern Ireland. (See, for example, the powers in Part 3 of the RES Act, which can apply to Scotland and Northern Ireland in respect of reserved matters.)

F. Contact us

31. The MoJ has a responsibility for oversight of new offences and criminal penalties and must be consulted on any proposals in this area, as well as on costs (for contacts on costs see paragraphs 27-29 above). For new offences, contact Ben Shoben. Email: Ben.Shoben@justice.gsi.gov.uk Tel: 0203 334 5014. For penalties, contact Chris Morris-Perry. Email: Chris.Morris-Perry@justice. gsi.gov.uk Tel: 0203 334 5039.

32. BERR has a responsibility for better regulation generally and for new civil sanctioning regimes for regulatory non-compliance. Contact Dominic Smales. Email: dominic.smales@berr.gsi.gov.uk Tel: 0207 215 0295. If you are considering new regulatory offences please contact us at an early stage of policy development as this could save you time in the long run. You will already have considered and contacted the stakeholders who may have an interest in the legislation. But you may also need to consider whether other Government Departments have an interest and contact them at an early stage.

33. All proposed new powers of entry, search or seizure in England and Wales, whether civil or criminal, must be referred to the Home Office for consideration. The current guidance about such powers is available on the Home Office website at: http://police.homeoffice.gov.uk/publications/ operational-policing/GuidanceonPowersofEntry.pdf. For further information contact Neil Curtis, Policing Powers and Protection Unit, Home Office, 2 Marsham Street, London SW1P 4DF. Email: neil.curtis@homeoffice.gsi.gov.uk Tel: 0207 035 0881.

Date of issue: 26 January 2009

Date to be reviewed: 1 December 2010

INDEX